Snow White with the Red Hair

Sorata Akiduki

5

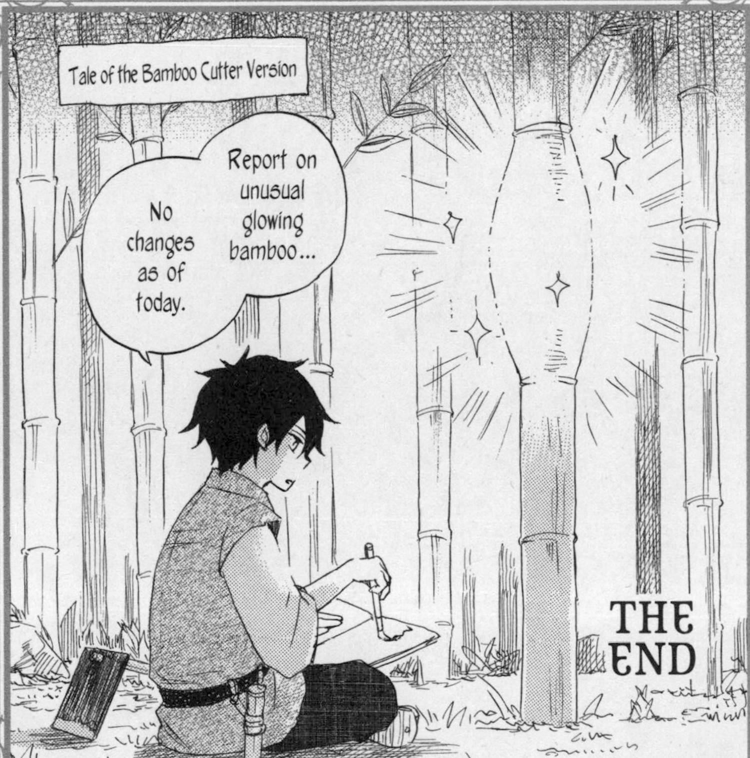
Tale of the Bamboo Cutter Version
Report on unusual glowing bamboo...
No changes as of today.
THE END

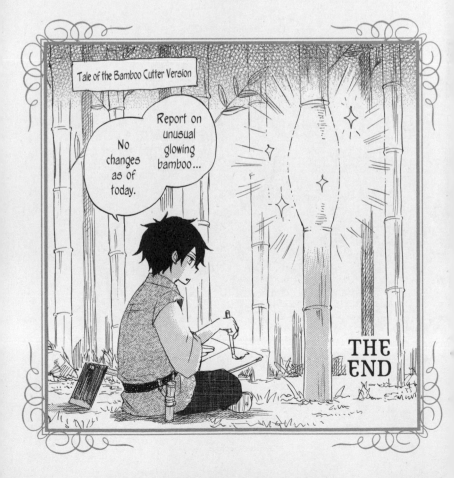

THE STORY

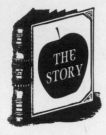

Shirayuki was born with beautiful hair as red as apples, but when her rare hair earns her unwanted attention from the notorious prince Raj, she's forced to flee her home. A young man named Zen helps her in the forest of the neighboring kingdom, Clarines, and it turns out he is that kingdom's second prince! Shirayuki decides to accompany Zen back to Wistal, the capital city of Clarines.

Shirayuki has met all manner of people since becoming a court herbalist, and her relationship with Zen continues to grow.

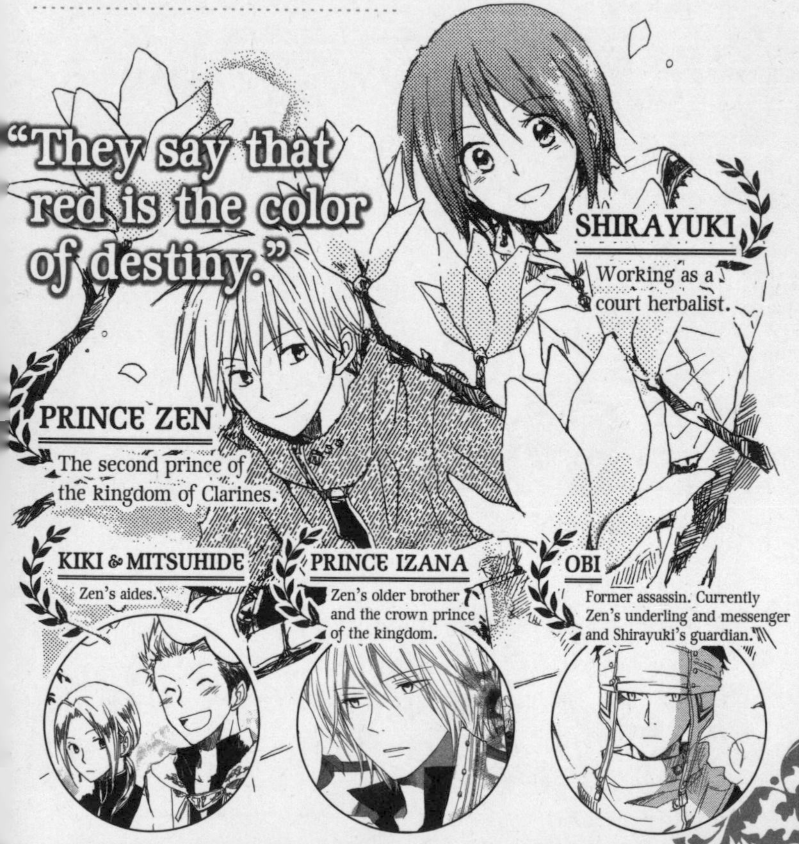

"They say that red is the color of destiny."
SHIRAYUKI
Working as a court herbalist.
PRINCE ZEN
The second prince of the kingdom of Clarines.
KIKI & MITSUHIDE
Zen's aides.
PRINCE IZANA
Zen's older brother and the crown prince of the kingdom.
OBI
Former assassin. Currently Zen's underling and messenger and Shirayuki's guardian.

The pair have already been through so much together, and now their true feelings have begun to shine through, prompting Zen to kiss Shirayuki...

In the woods near the palace, he declares to her, "I swear...to protect what we have," and she takes his hand in hers.

What awaits these two on the new path they now walk?!

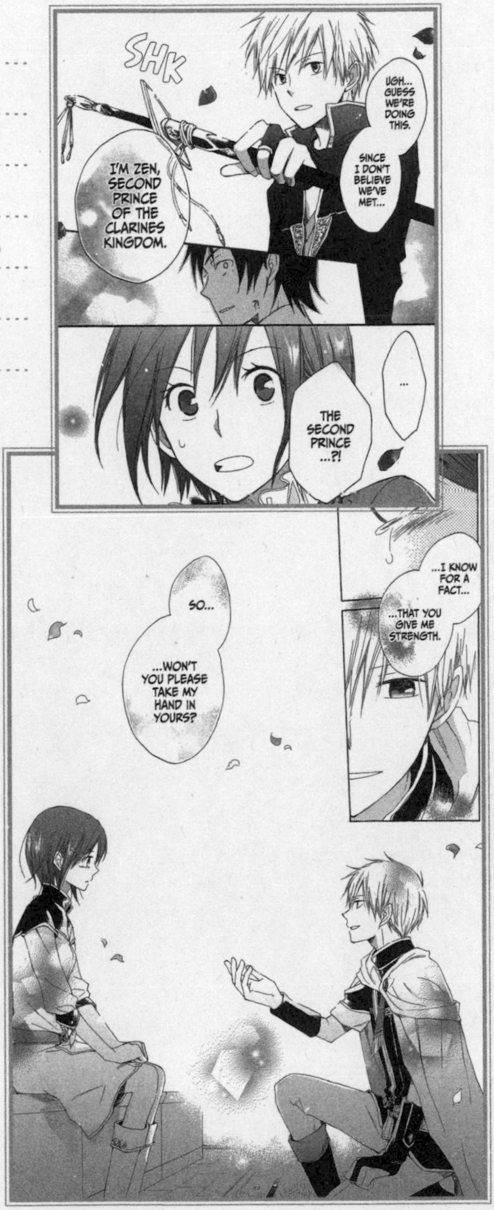

UGH... GUESS WE'RE DOING THIS.
SINCE I DON'T BELIEVE WE'VE MET...
SHK
I'M ZEN, SECOND PRINCE OF THE CLARINES KINGDOM.
...
THE SECOND PRINCE...?!
...I KNOW FOR A FACT...
...THAT YOU GIVE ME STRENGTH.
SO...
...WON'T YOU PLEASE TAKE MY HAND IN YOURS?

Snow White with the Red Hair

VOLUME 5
TABLE *of* CONTENTS

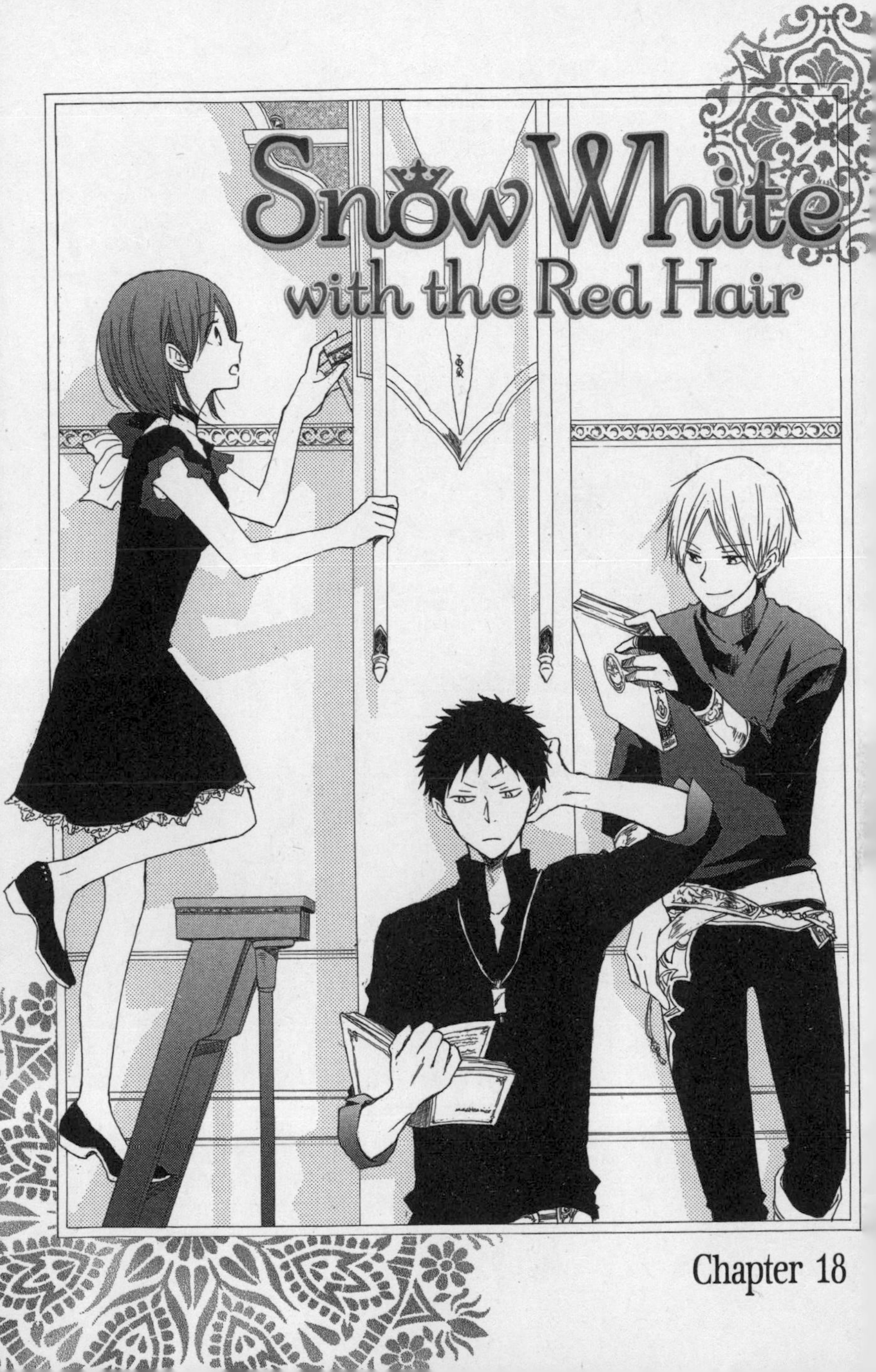
Snow White
with the Red Hair

Chapter 18

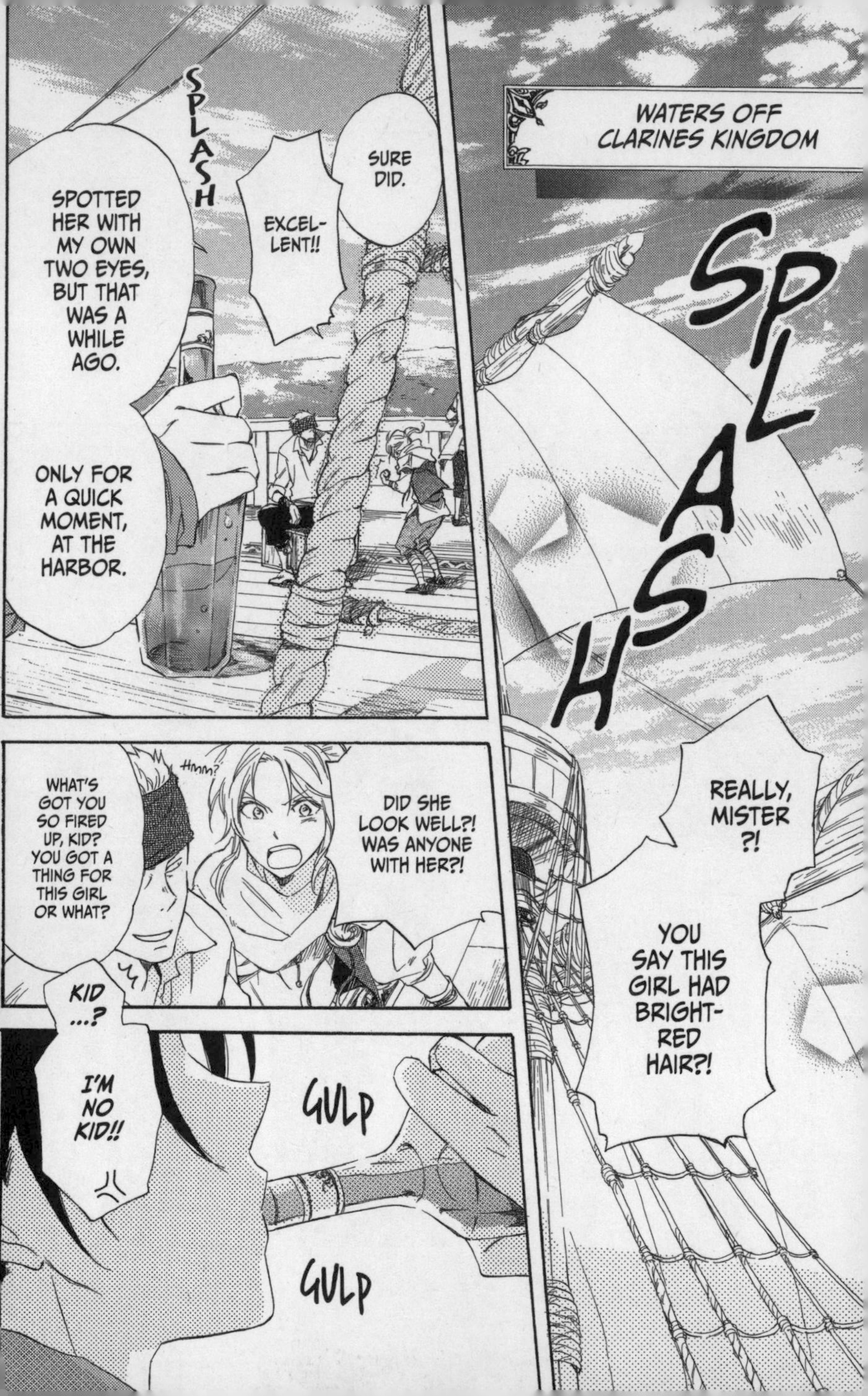
WATERS OFF CLARINES KINGDOM
SPLASH
REALLY, MISTER?!
YOU SAY THIS GIRL HAD BRIGHT-RED HAIR?!
SURE DID.
EXCEL-LENT!!
SPLASH
SPOTTED HER WITH MY OWN TWO EYES, BUT THAT WAS A WHILE AGO.
ONLY FOR A QUICK MOMENT, AT THE HARBOR.
DID SHE LOOK WELL?! WAS ANYONE WITH HER?!
Hmm?
WHAT'S GOT YOU SO FIRED UP, KID? YOU GOT A THING FOR THIS GIRL OR WHAT?
KID ...?
GULP
I'M NO KID!!
GULP

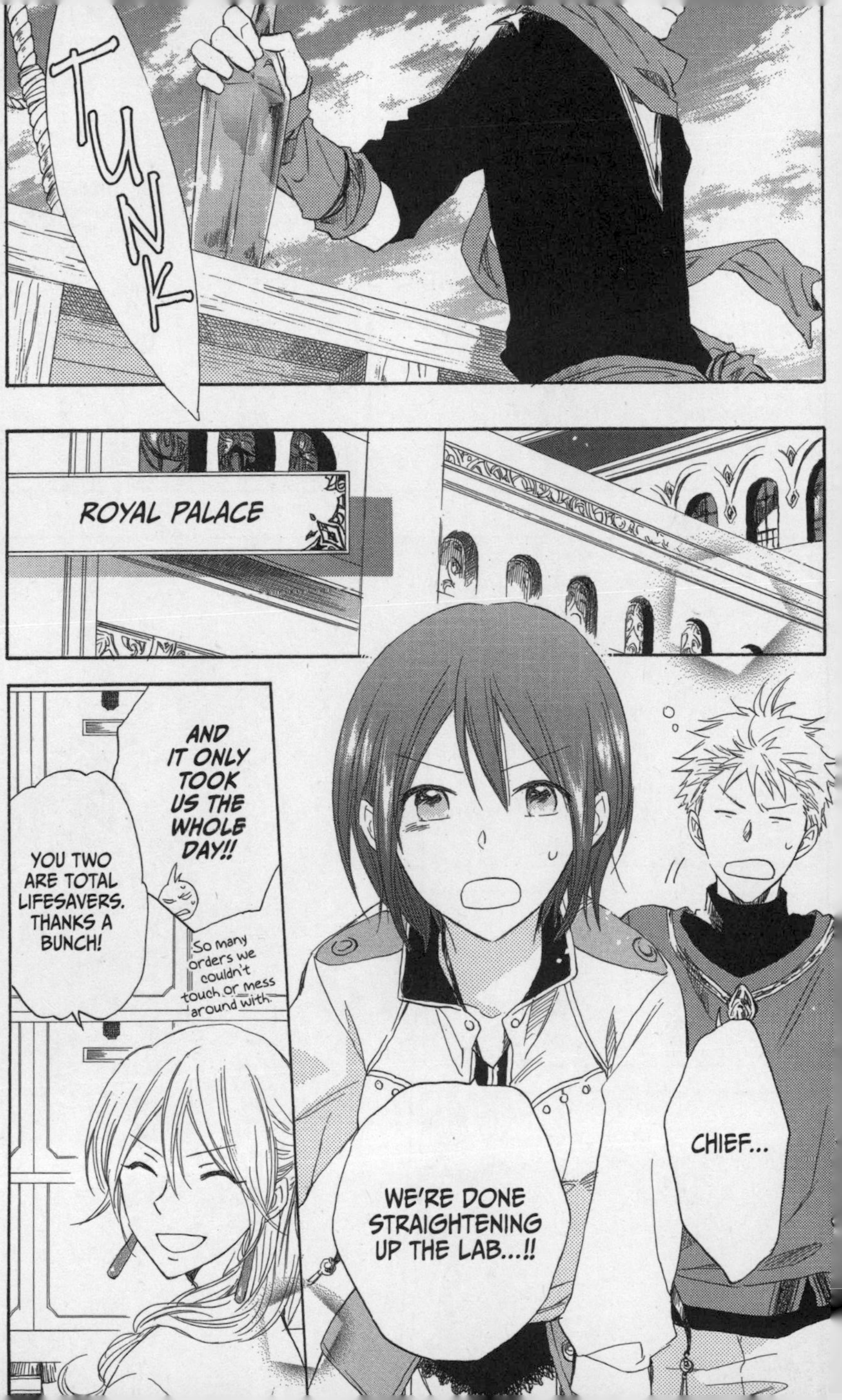
TUNK
ROYAL PALACE
CHIEF...
WE'RE DONE STRAIGHTENING UP THE LAB...!!
AND IT ONLY TOOK US THE WHOLE DAY!!
YOU TWO ARE TOTAL LIFESAVERS. THANKS A BUNCH!
So many orders we couldn't touch or mess around with.

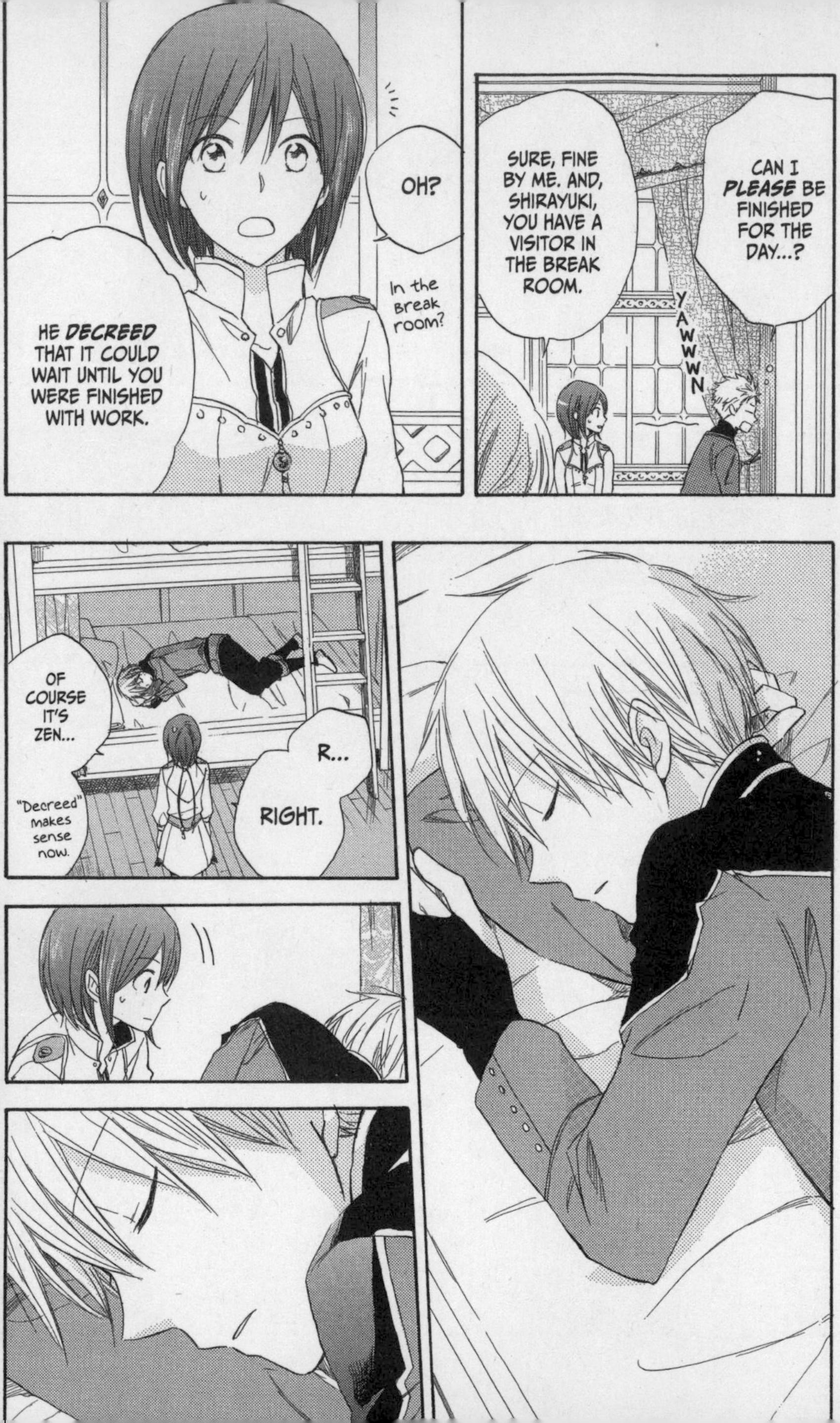
CAN I *PLEASE* BE FINISHED FOR THE DAY...?
SURE, FINE BY ME. AND, SHIRAYUKI, YOU HAVE A VISITOR IN THE BREAK ROOM.
YAWWWN
OH?
In the break room?
HE *DECREED* THAT IT COULD WAIT UNTIL YOU WERE FINISHED WITH WORK.
R...
RIGHT.
OF COURSE IT'S ZEN...
"Decreed" makes sense now.

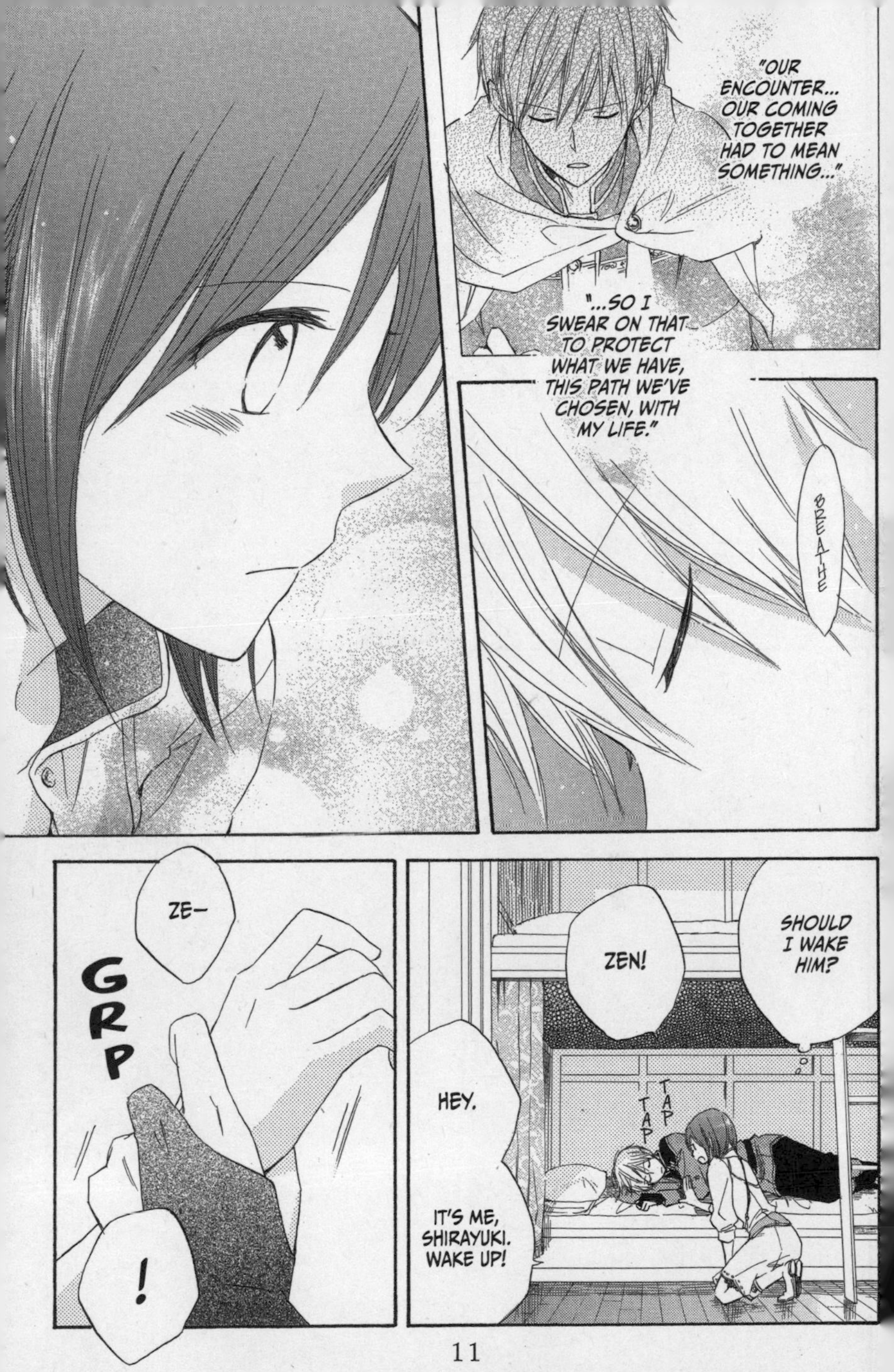
"OUR ENCOUNTER... OUR COMING TOGETHER HAD TO MEAN SOMETHING..."
"...SO I SWEAR ON THAT TO PROTECT WHAT WE HAVE, THIS PATH WE'VE CHOSEN, WITH MY LIFE."
BREATHE
SHOULD I WAKE HIM?
ZEN!
TAP TAP
HEY.
IT'S ME, SHIRAYUKI. WAKE UP!
ZE—
GRP
!

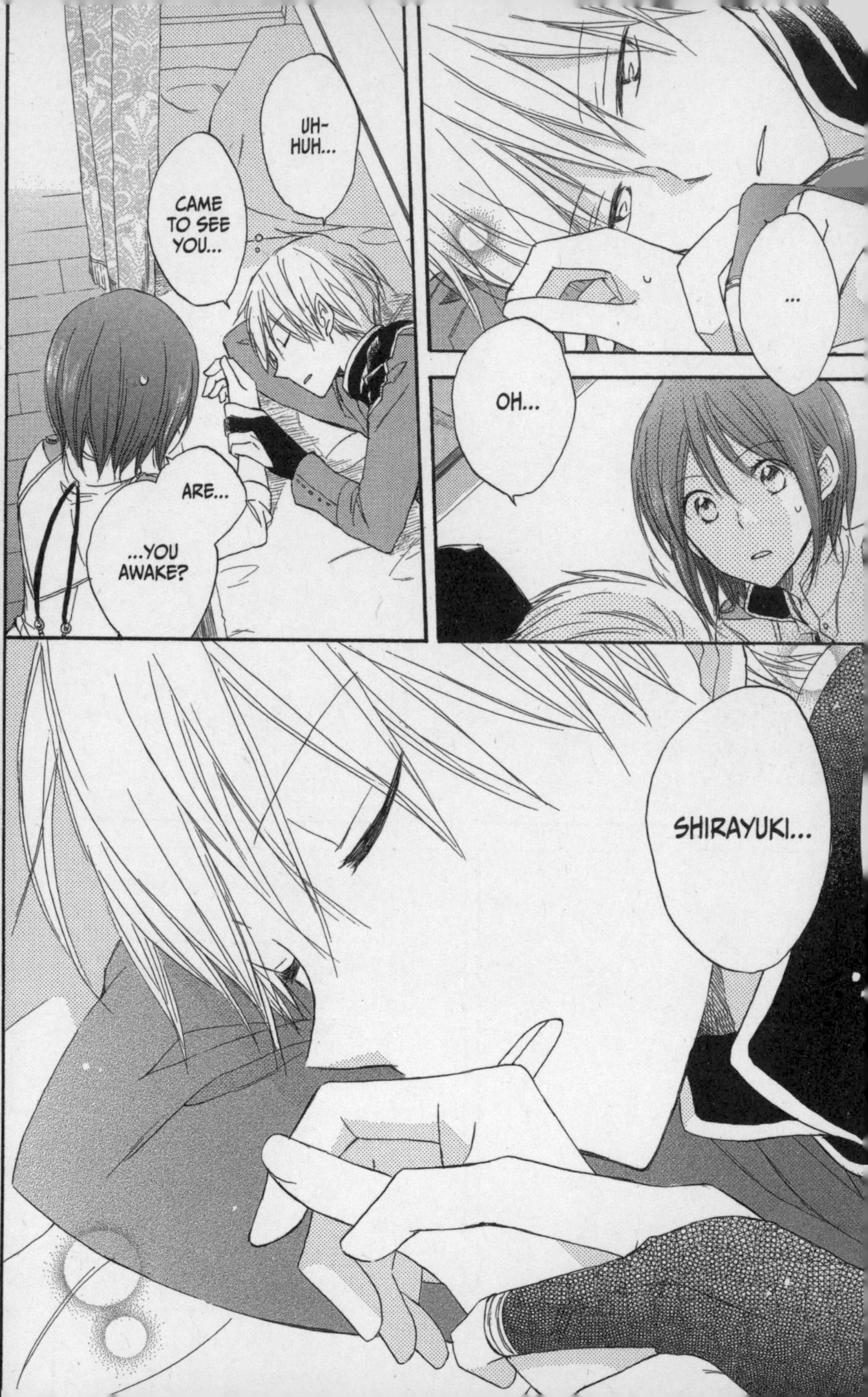
...
OH...
UH-HUH...
CAME TO SEE YOU...
ARE...
...YOU AWAKE?
SHIRAYUKI...

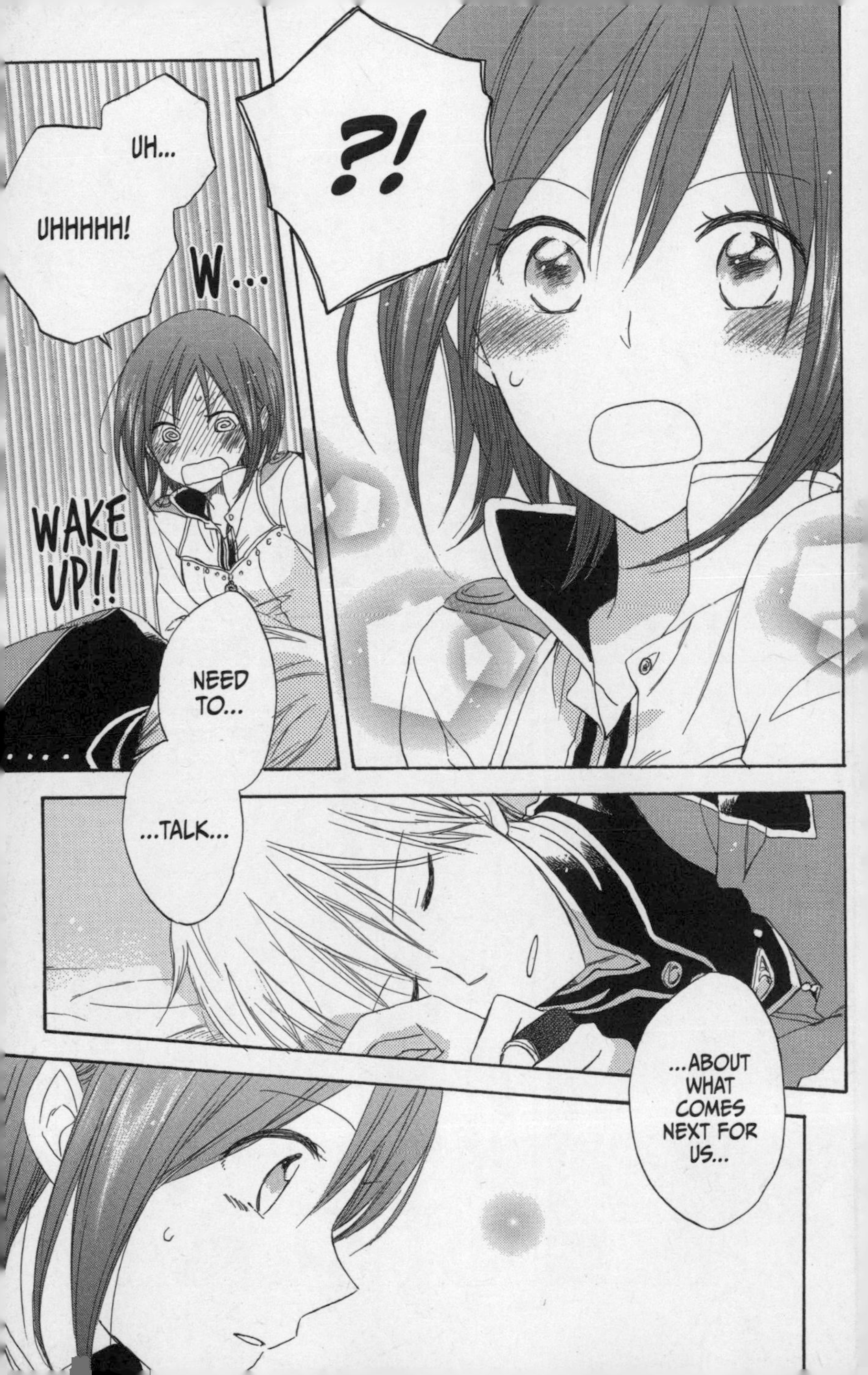
?!
UH...
UHHHHH!
W...
WAKE UP!!
NEED TO...
...TALK...
...ABOUT WHAT COMES NEXT FOR US...

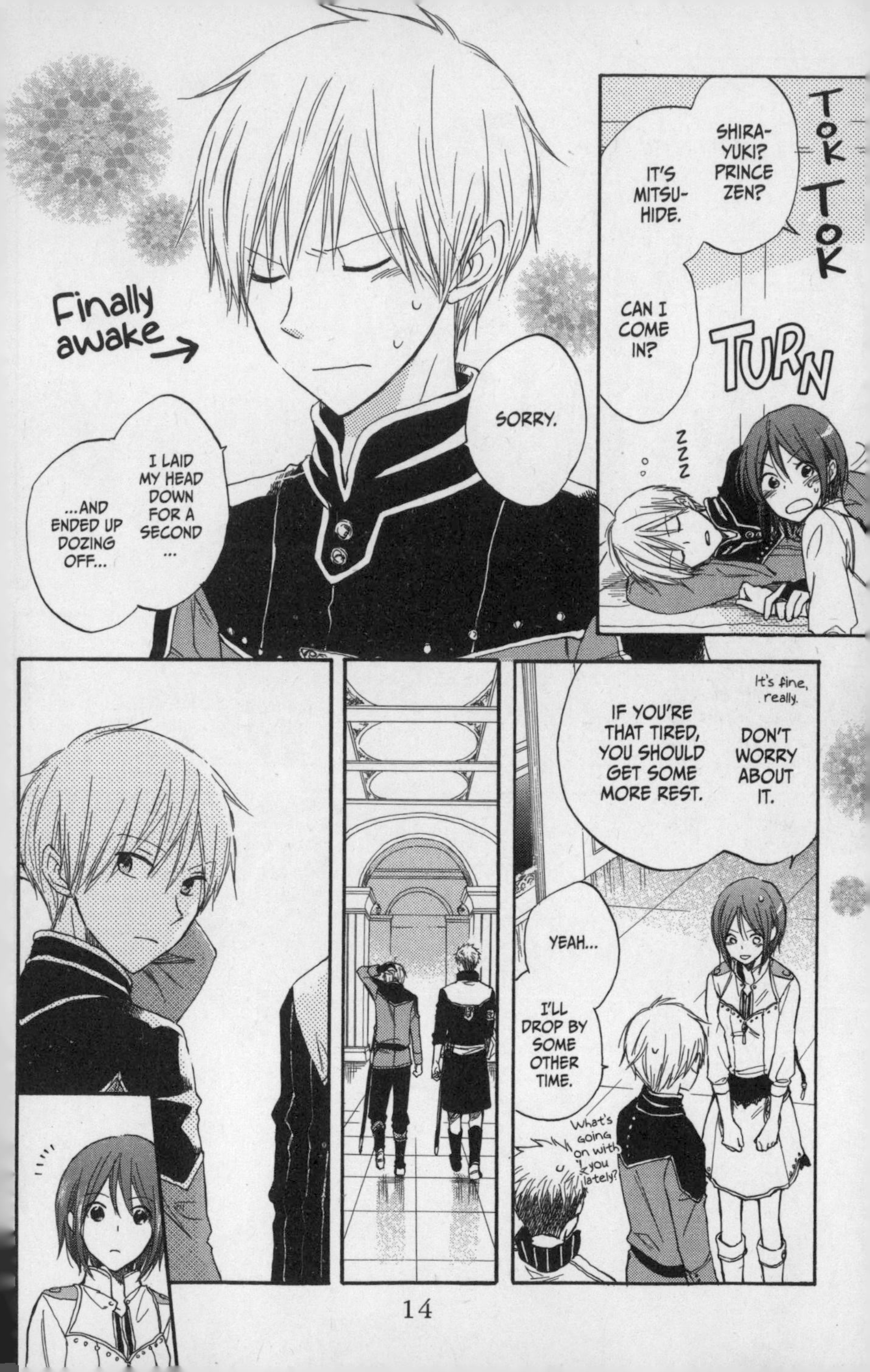
TOK TOK
SHIRA-YUKI? PRINCE ZEN?
IT'S MITSU-HIDE.
CAN I COME IN?
TURN
ZZZ
Finally awake
SORRY.
I LAID MY HEAD DOWN FOR A SECOND...
...AND ENDED UP DOZING OFF...
IF YOU'RE THAT TIRED, YOU SHOULD GET SOME MORE REST.
DON'T WORRY ABOUT IT.
It's fine, really.
YEAH...
I'LL DROP BY SOME OTHER TIME.
What's going on with you lately?

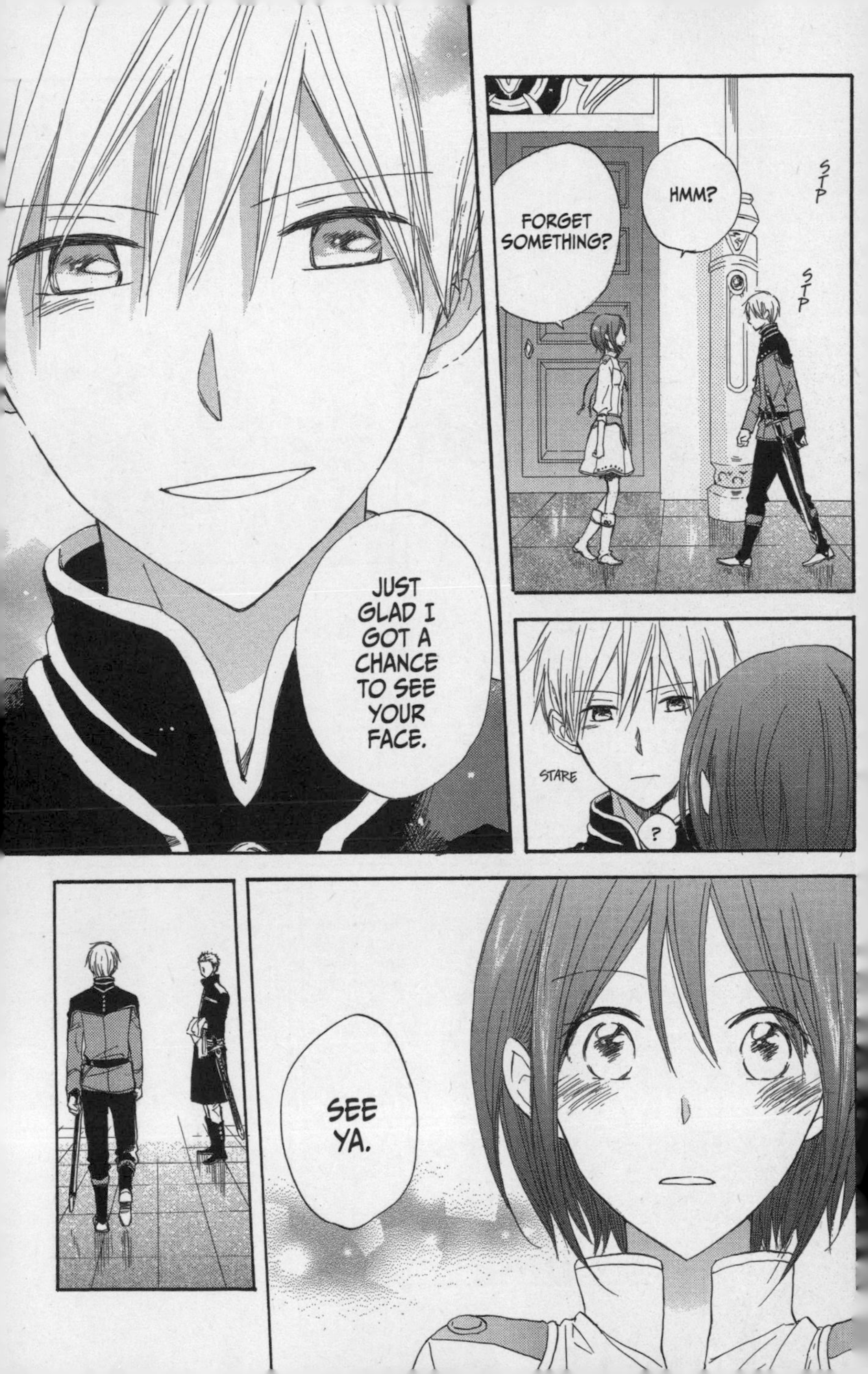
STP
STP
HMM?
FORGET SOMETHING?
STARE
?
JUST GLAD I GOT A CHANCE TO SEE YOUR FACE.
SEE YA.

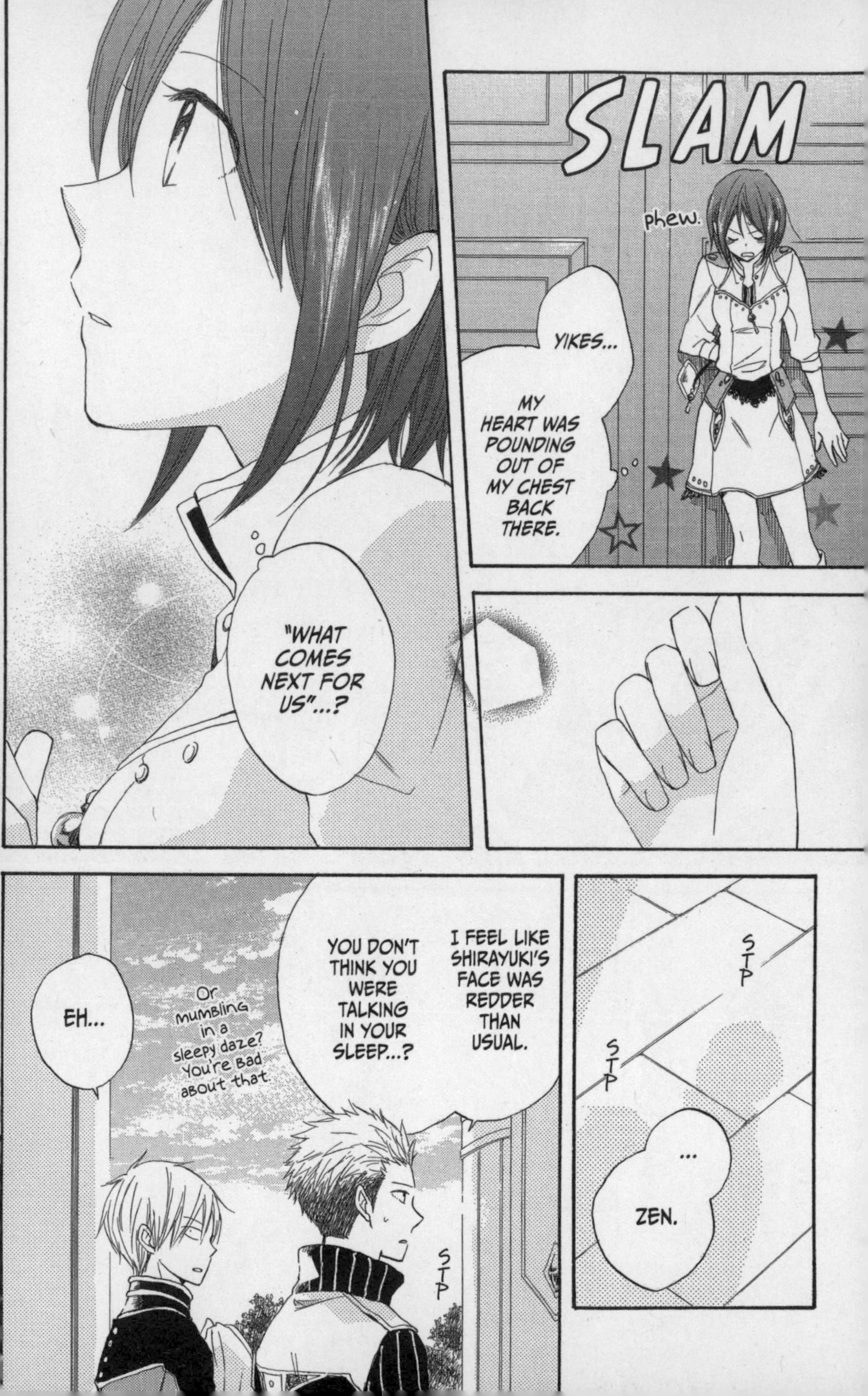
SLAM
phew.
YIKES...
MY HEART WAS POUNDING OUT OF MY CHEST BACK THERE.
"WHAT COMES NEXT FOR US"...?
STP
STP
... ZEN.
I FEEL LIKE SHIRAYUKI'S FACE WAS REDDER THAN USUAL.
YOU DON'T THINK YOU WERE TALKING IN YOUR SLEEP...?
Or mumbling in a sleepy daze? You're Bad about that.
EH...
STP

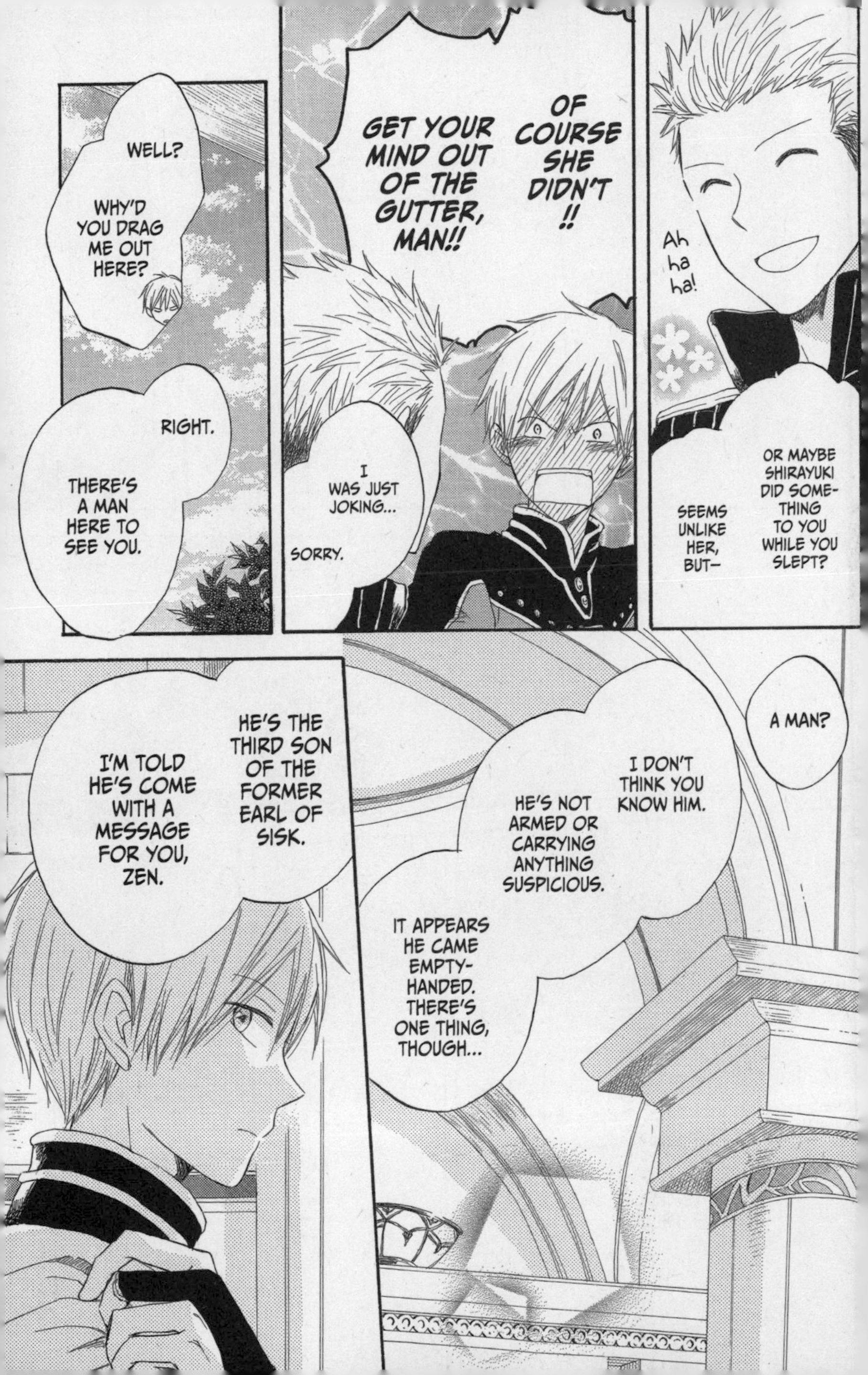
Ah ha ha!
OR MAYBE SHIRAYUKI DID SOMETHING TO YOU WHILE YOU SLEPT?
SEEMS UNLIKE HER, BUT—
OF COURSE SHE DIDN'T!!
GET YOUR MIND OUT OF THE GUTTER, MAN!!
I WAS JUST JOKING...
SORRY.
WELL?
WHY'D YOU DRAG ME OUT HERE?
RIGHT.
THERE'S A MAN HERE TO SEE YOU.
A MAN?
I DON'T THINK YOU KNOW HIM.
HE'S NOT ARMED OR CARRYING ANYTHING SUSPICIOUS.
IT APPEARS HE CAME EMPTY-HANDED. THERE'S ONE THING, THOUGH...
HE'S THE THIRD SON OF THE FORMER EARL OF SISK.
I'M TOLD HE'S COME WITH A MESSAGE FOR YOU, ZEN.

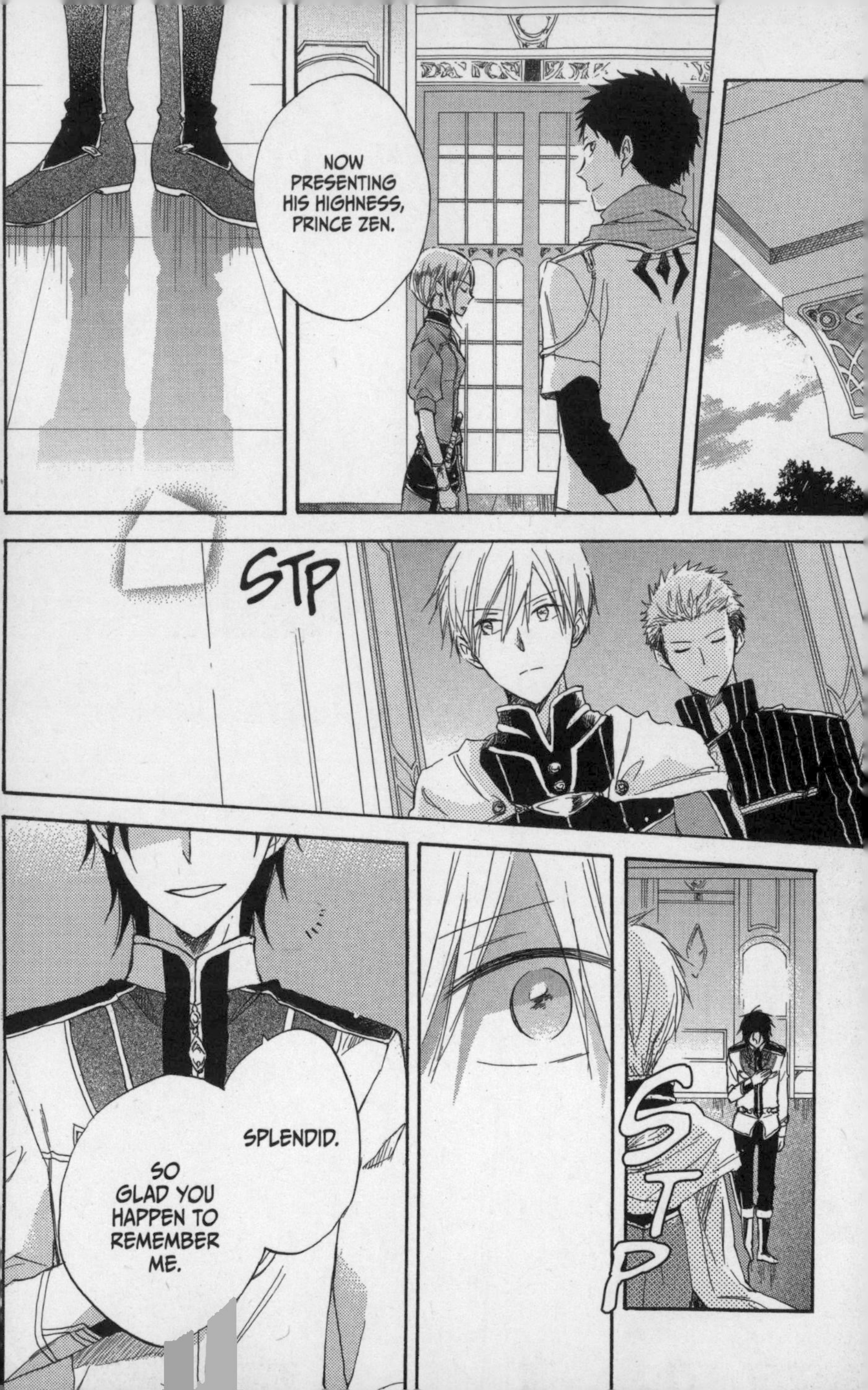
NOW PRESENTING HIS HIGHNESS, PRINCE ZEN.
STP
STP
SPLENDID.
SO GLAD YOU HAPPEN TO REMEMBER ME.

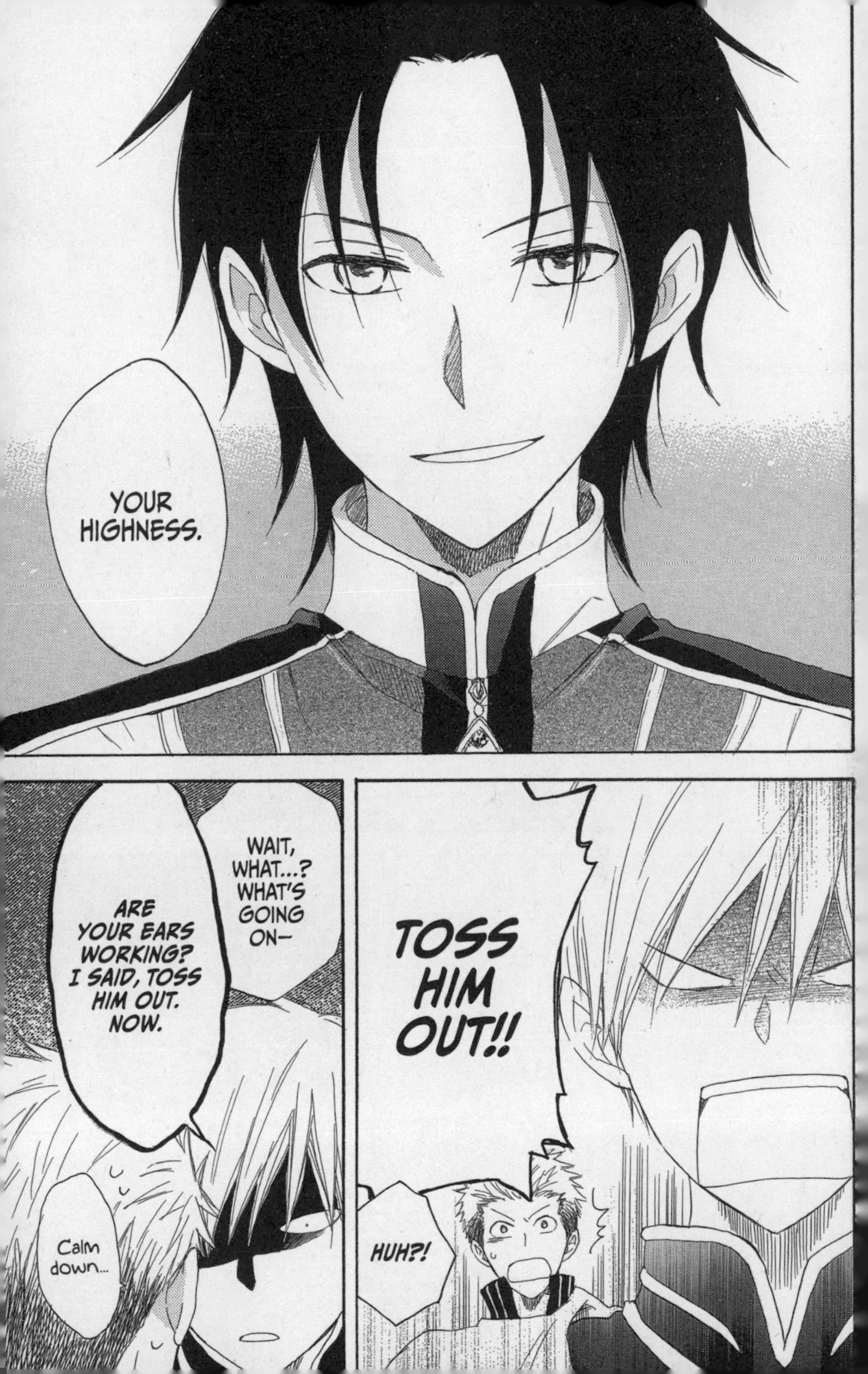
YOUR HIGHNESS.
TOSS HIM OUT!!
HUH?!
WAIT, WHAT...? WHAT'S GOING ON—
ARE YOUR EARS WORKING? I SAID, TOSS HIM OUT. NOW.
Calm down...

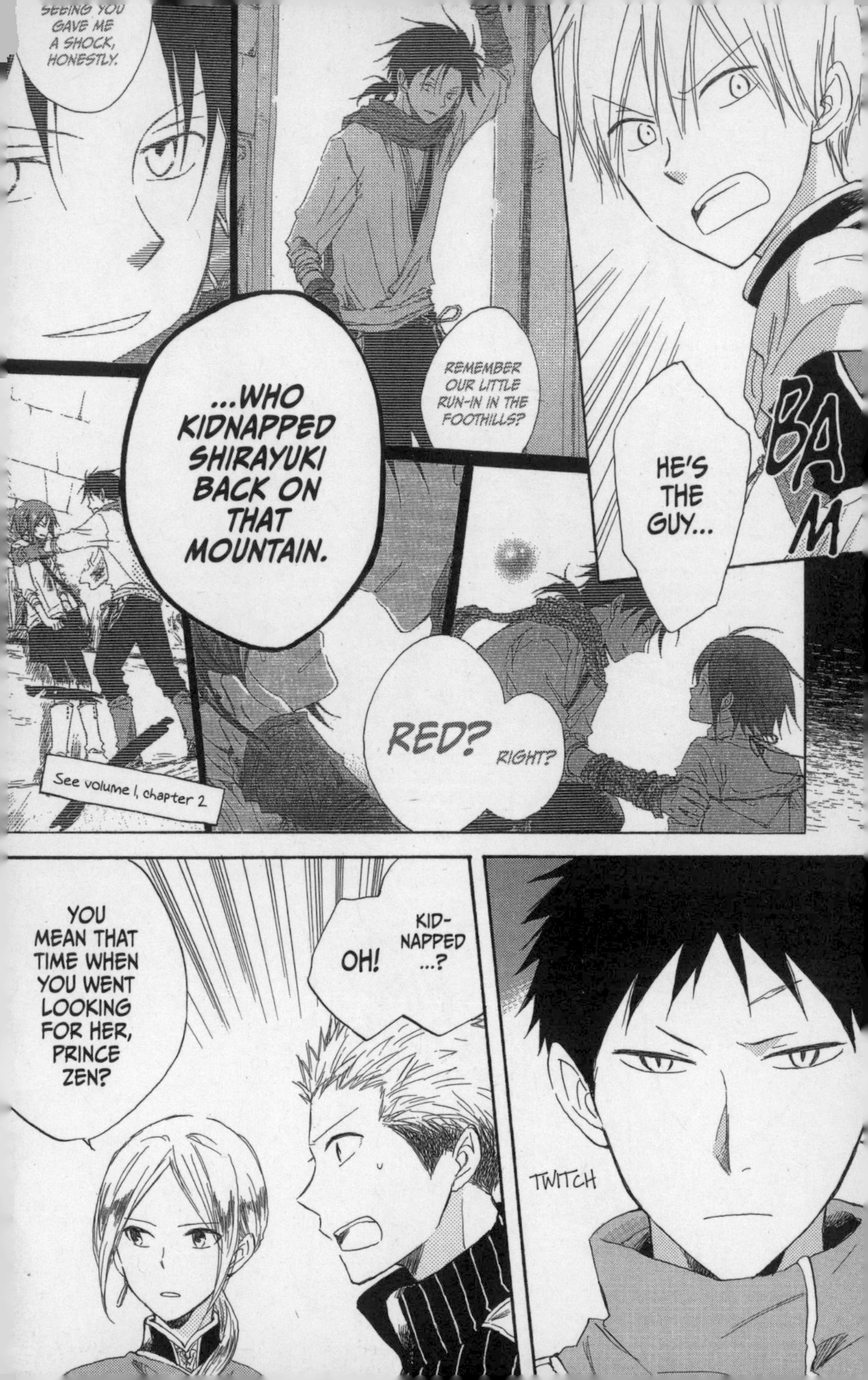
BAM
HE'S THE GUY...
REMEMBER OUR LITTLE RUN-IN IN THE FOOTHILLS?
SEEING YOU GAVE ME A SHOCK, HONESTLY.
...WHO KIDNAPPED SHIRAYUKI BACK ON THAT MOUNTAIN.
RED? RIGHT?
See volume 1, chapter 2
TWITCH
KID-NAPPED ...?
OH!
YOU MEAN THAT TIME WHEN YOU WENT LOOKING FOR HER, PRINCE ZEN?

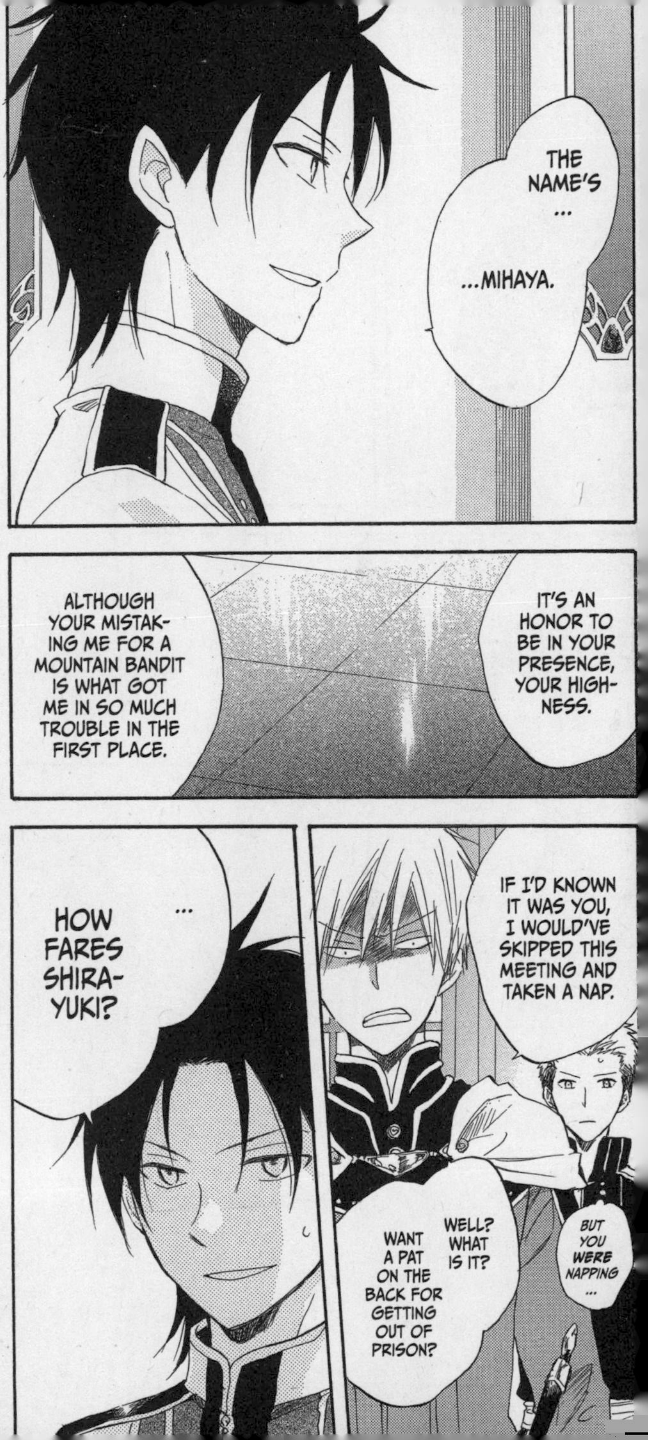
THE NAME'S ...
...MIHAYA.
IT'S AN HONOR TO BE IN YOUR PRESENCE, YOUR HIGHNESS.
ALTHOUGH YOUR MISTAKING ME FOR A MOUNTAIN BANDIT IS WHAT GOT ME IN SO MUCH TROUBLE IN THE FIRST PLACE.
IF I'D KNOWN IT WAS YOU, I WOULD'VE SKIPPED THIS MEETING AND TAKEN A NAP.
BUT YOU WERE NAPPING...
WELL? WHAT IS IT?
WANT A PAT ON THE BACK FOR GETTING OUT OF PRISON?
...
HOW FARES SHIRAYUKI?

GREETINGS

Hello. Akiduki here.

Thank you for purchasing volume 5 of *Snow White with the Red Hair*!

I apologize in advance for this terrible joke, but this is volume f-f-f-f-five.

The stack of books on my desk is growing... Soon this small pile will become a tall, massive tower.

My lady, that tower is pure *Snow White with the Red Hair*, one could say...

Anyhow, thanks again!!

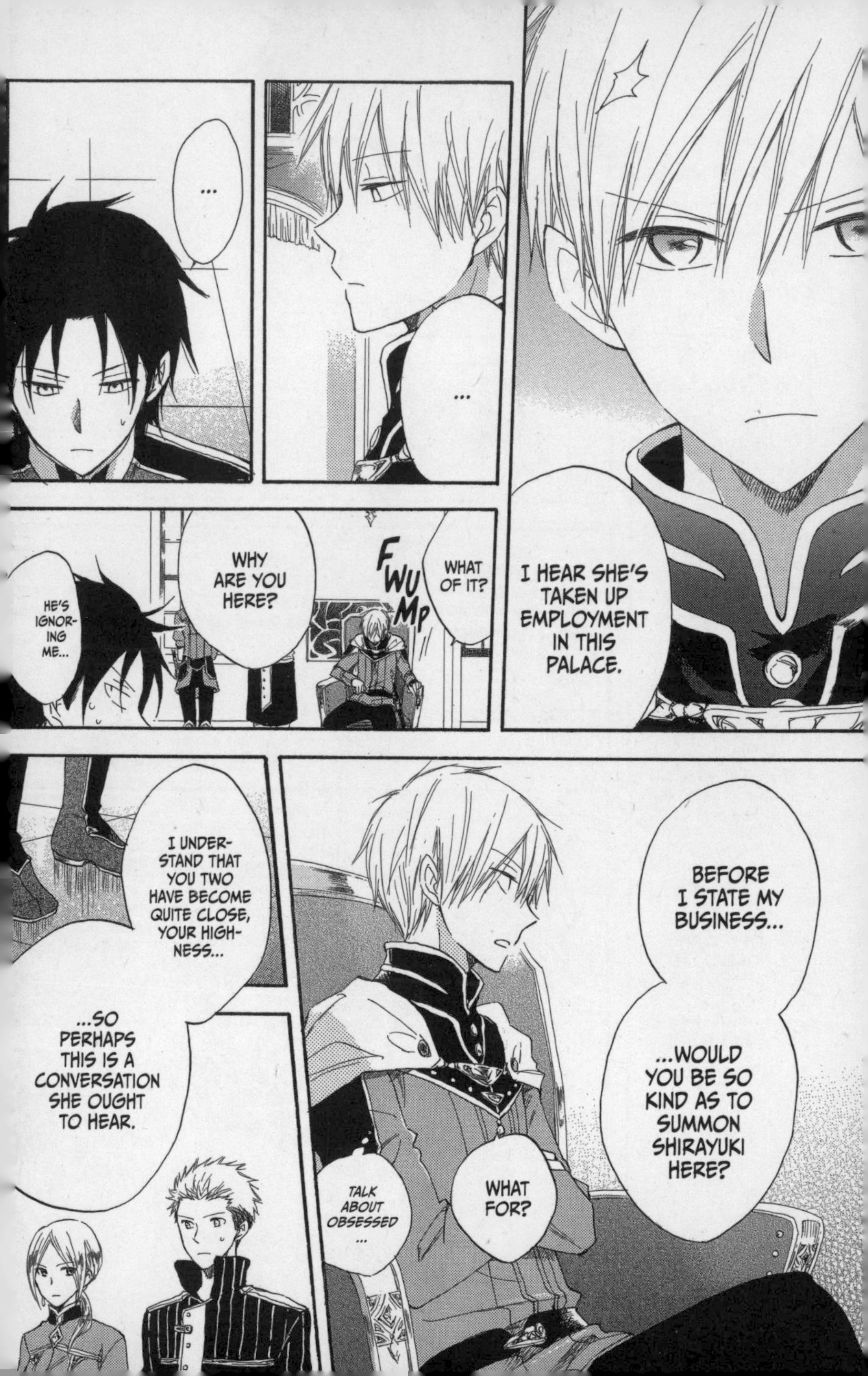
I HEAR SHE'S TAKEN UP EMPLOYMENT IN THIS PALACE.
...
...
WHAT OF IT?
FWUMP
WHY ARE YOU HERE?
HE'S IGNORING ME...
BEFORE I STATE MY BUSINESS...
...WOULD YOU BE SO KIND AS TO SUMMON SHIRAYUKI HERE?
WHAT FOR?
TALK ABOUT OBSESSED ...
I UNDERSTAND THAT YOU TWO HAVE BECOME QUITE CLOSE, YOUR HIGHNESS...
...SO PERHAPS THIS IS A CONVERSATION SHE OUGHT TO HEAR.

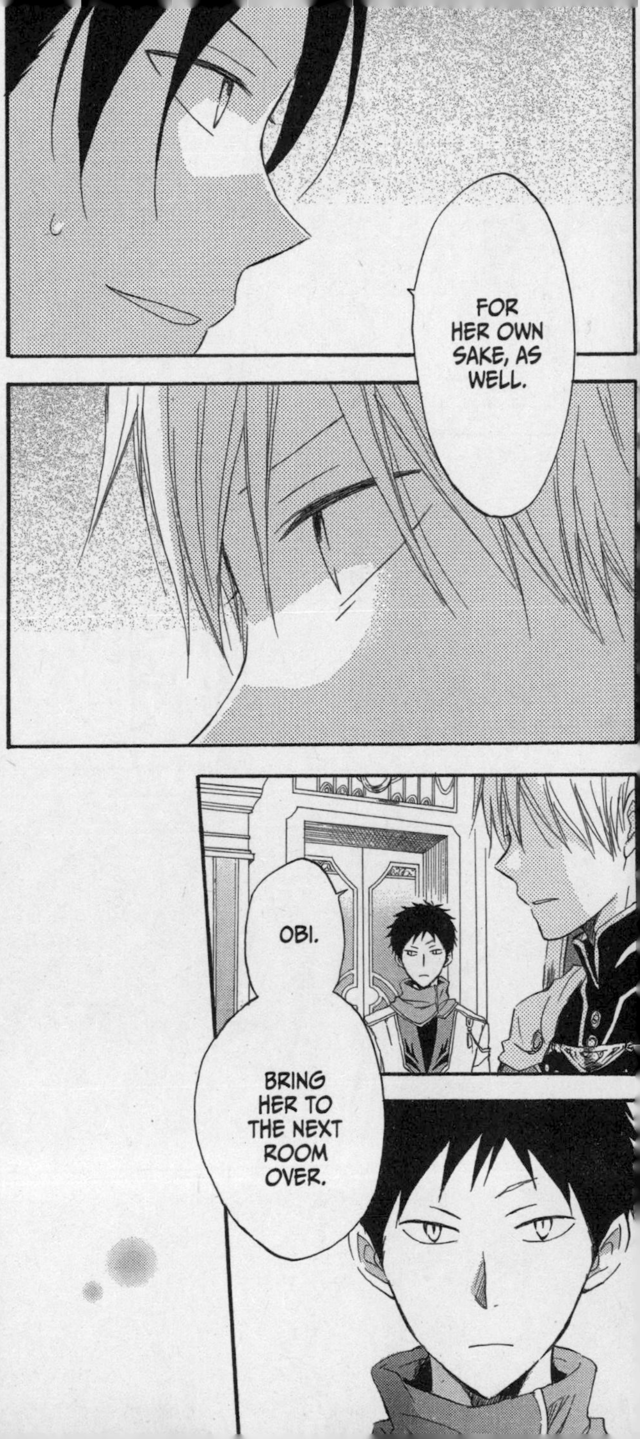
FOR HER OWN SAKE, AS WELL.
OBI.
BRING HER TO THE NEXT ROOM OVER.

Chapter 18

Here we go.
The Mihaya
story arc.

I had a feeling his
reintroduction
would make a good
percentage of
readers go,
"Who's this guy,
again?"

So I
inserted that
single flashback
page to hopefully
jog everyone's
memory...

For anyone
who still doesn't
remember,
just refer back
to volume 1 of
the series!

Snow White with the Red Hair 1

On shelves now!

Uh-oh.
Now people
might think I
brought him back
just to advertise
volume 1.

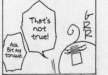

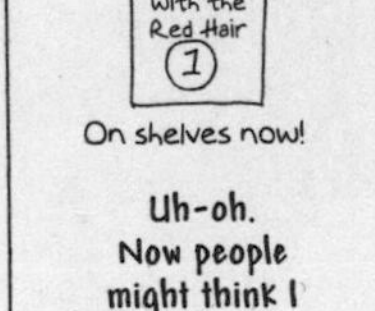
That's not true!
Ack. Bit my tongue.

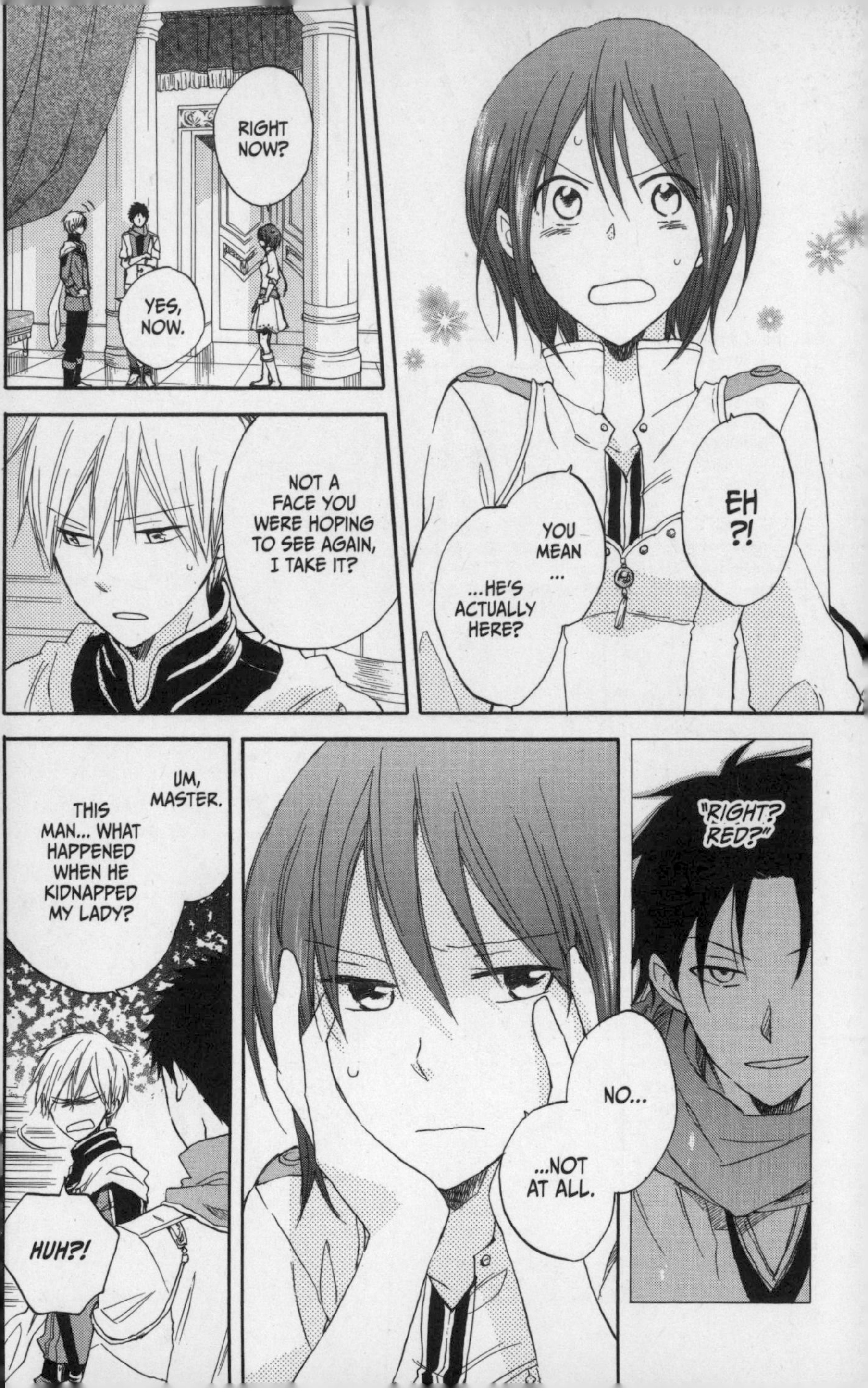
EH ?!
YOU MEAN ...
...HE'S ACTUALLY HERE?
RIGHT NOW?
YES, NOW.
NOT A FACE YOU WERE HOPING TO SEE AGAIN, I TAKE IT?
"RIGHT? RED?"
NO...
...NOT AT ALL.
UM, MASTER.
THIS MAN... WHAT HAPPENED WHEN HE KIDNAPPED MY LADY?
HUH?!

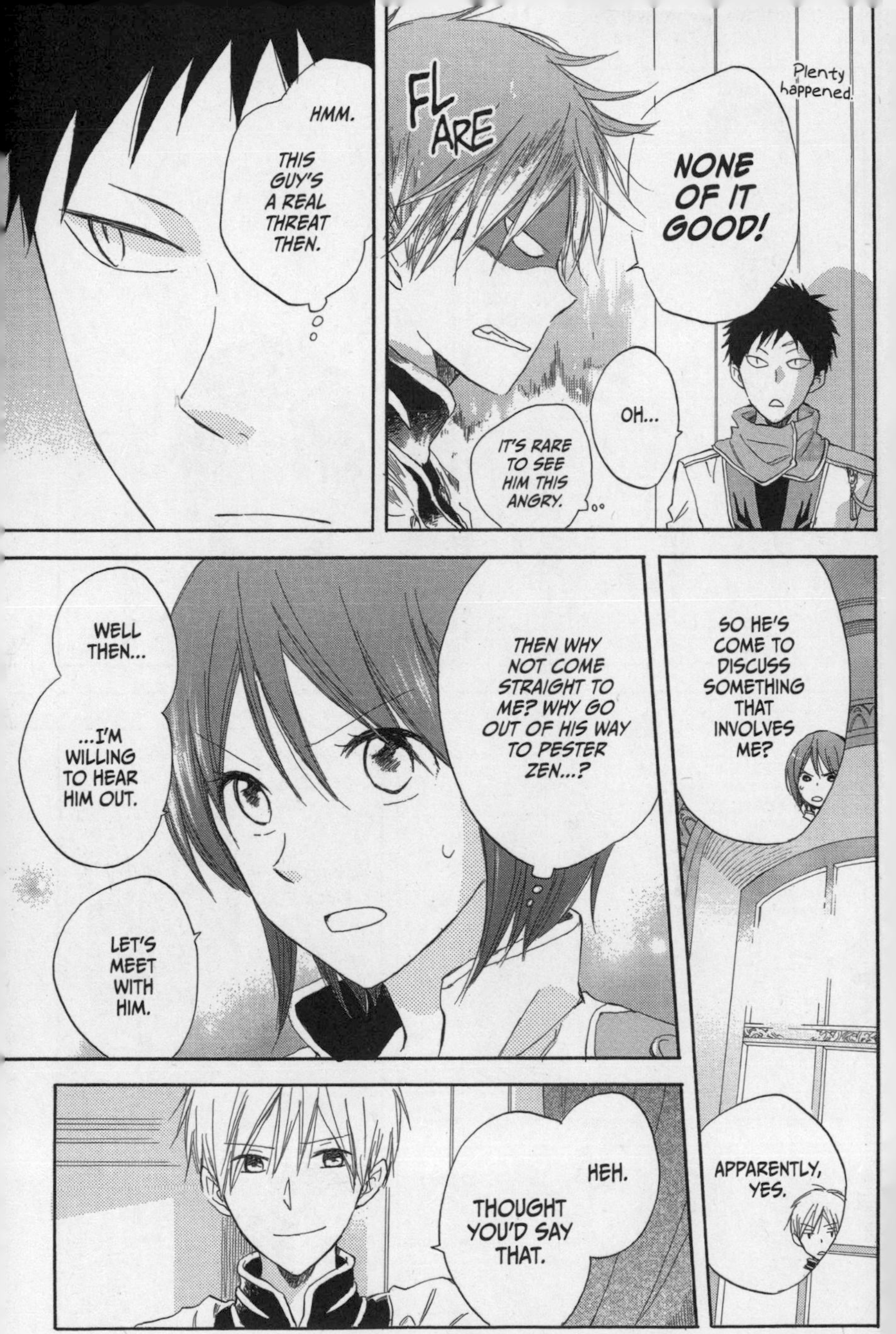
Plenty happened!
FLARE
NONE OF IT GOOD!
OH...
IT'S RARE TO SEE HIM THIS ANGRY.
HMM.
THIS GUY'S A REAL THREAT THEN.
SO HE'S COME TO DISCUSS SOMETHING THAT INVOLVES ME?
THEN WHY NOT COME STRAIGHT TO ME? WHY GO OUT OF HIS WAY TO PESTER ZEN...?
WELL THEN...
...I'M WILLING TO HEAR HIM OUT.
LET'S MEET WITH HIM.
APPARENTLY, YES.
HEH.
THOUGHT YOU'D SAY THAT.

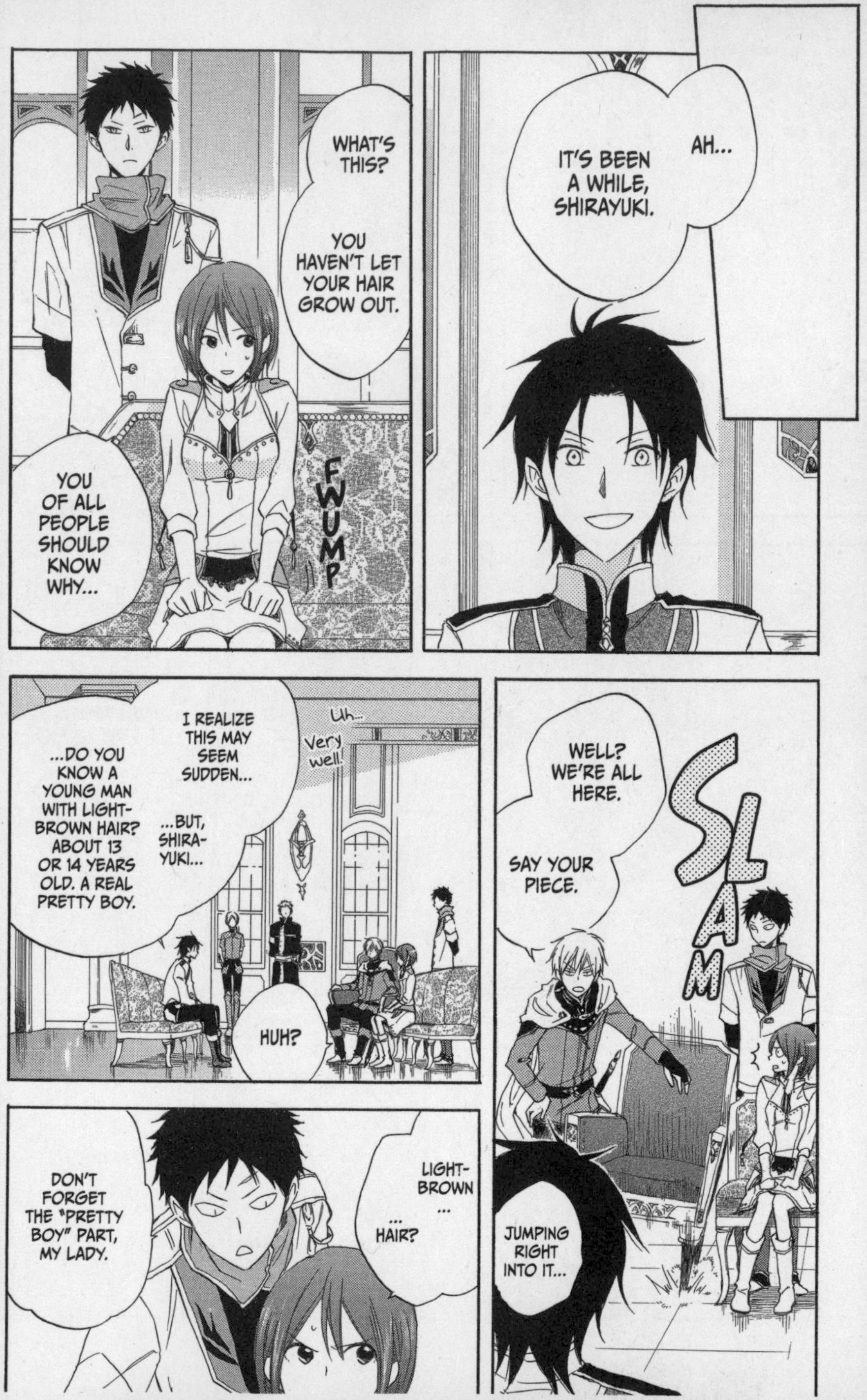
AH...
IT'S BEEN A WHILE, SHIRAYUKI.
WHAT'S THIS?
YOU HAVEN'T LET YOUR HAIR GROW OUT.
FWUMP
YOU OF ALL PEOPLE SHOULD KNOW WHY...
SLAM
WELL? WE'RE ALL HERE.
SAY YOUR PIECE.
JUMPING RIGHT INTO IT...
I REALIZE THIS MAY SEEM SUDDEN...
...BUT, SHIRAYUKI...
Uh...
Very well!
...DO YOU KNOW A YOUNG MAN WITH LIGHT-BROWN HAIR? ABOUT 13 OR 14 YEARS OLD. A REAL PRETTY BOY.
HUH?
LIGHT-BROWN ... ... HAIR?
DON'T FORGET THE "PRETTY BOY" PART, MY LADY.

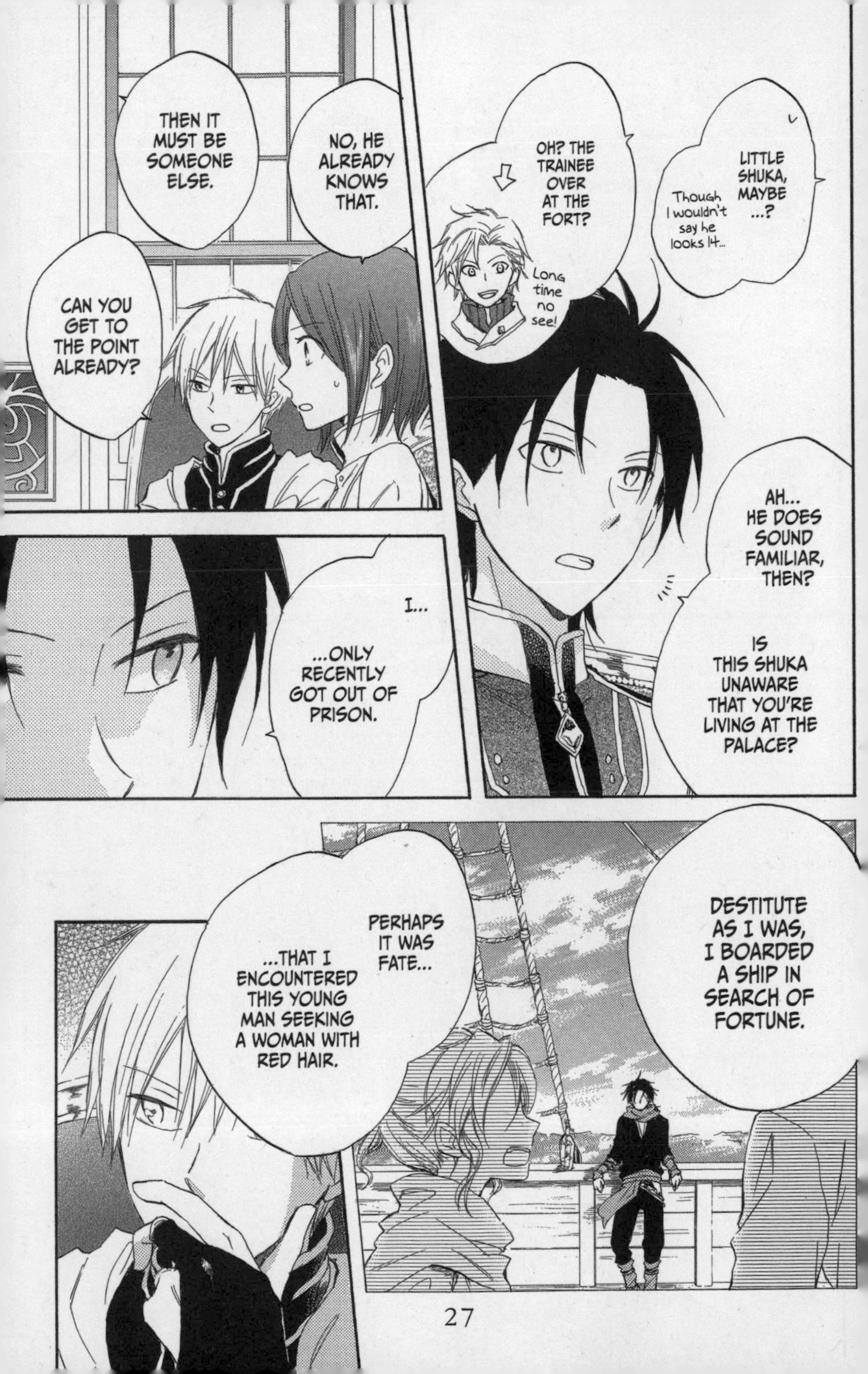
LITTLE SHUKA, MAYBE ...?
Though I wouldn't say he looks 14...
OH? THE TRAINEE OVER AT THE FORT?
Long time no see!
AH... HE DOES SOUND FAMILIAR, THEN?
IS THIS SHUKA UNAWARE THAT YOU'RE LIVING AT THE PALACE?
NO, HE ALREADY KNOWS THAT.
THEN IT MUST BE SOMEONE ELSE.
CAN YOU GET TO THE POINT ALREADY?
I...
...ONLY RECENTLY GOT OUT OF PRISON.
DESTITUTE AS I WAS, I BOARDED A SHIP IN SEARCH OF FORTUNE.
PERHAPS IT WAS FATE...
...THAT I ENCOUNTERED THIS YOUNG MAN SEEKING A WOMAN WITH RED HAIR.

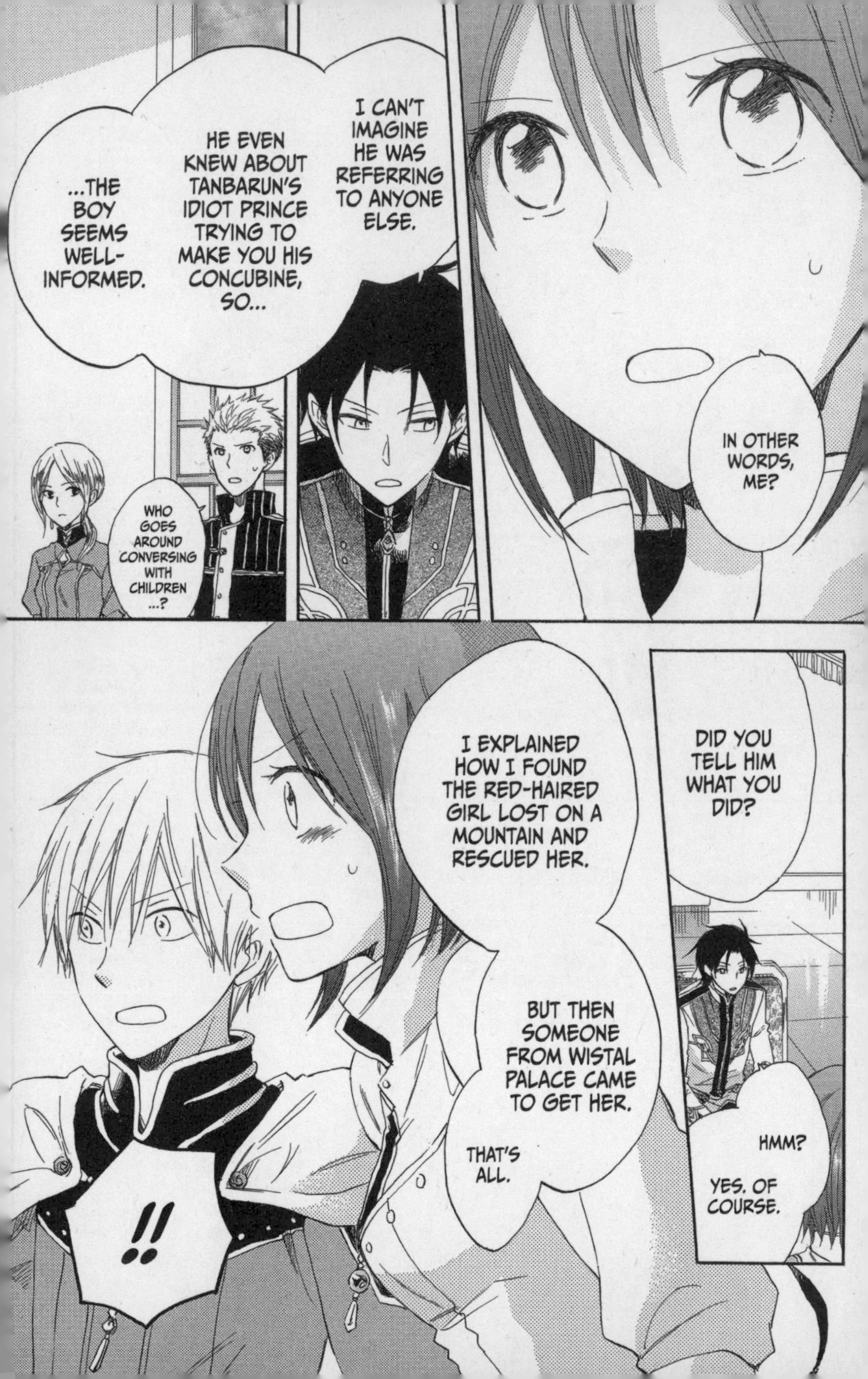
IN OTHER WORDS, ME?
...THE BOY SEEMS WELL-INFORMED.
HE EVEN KNEW ABOUT TANBARUN'S IDIOT PRINCE TRYING TO MAKE YOU HIS CONCUBINE, SO...
I CAN'T IMAGINE HE WAS REFERRING TO ANYONE ELSE.
WHO GOES AROUND CONVERSING WITH CHILDREN ...?
DID YOU TELL HIM WHAT YOU DID?
HMM?
YES. OF COURSE.
I EXPLAINED HOW I FOUND THE RED-HAIRED GIRL LOST ON A MOUNTAIN AND RESCUED HER.
BUT THEN SOMEONE FROM WISTAL PALACE CAME TO GET HER.
THAT'S ALL.
!!

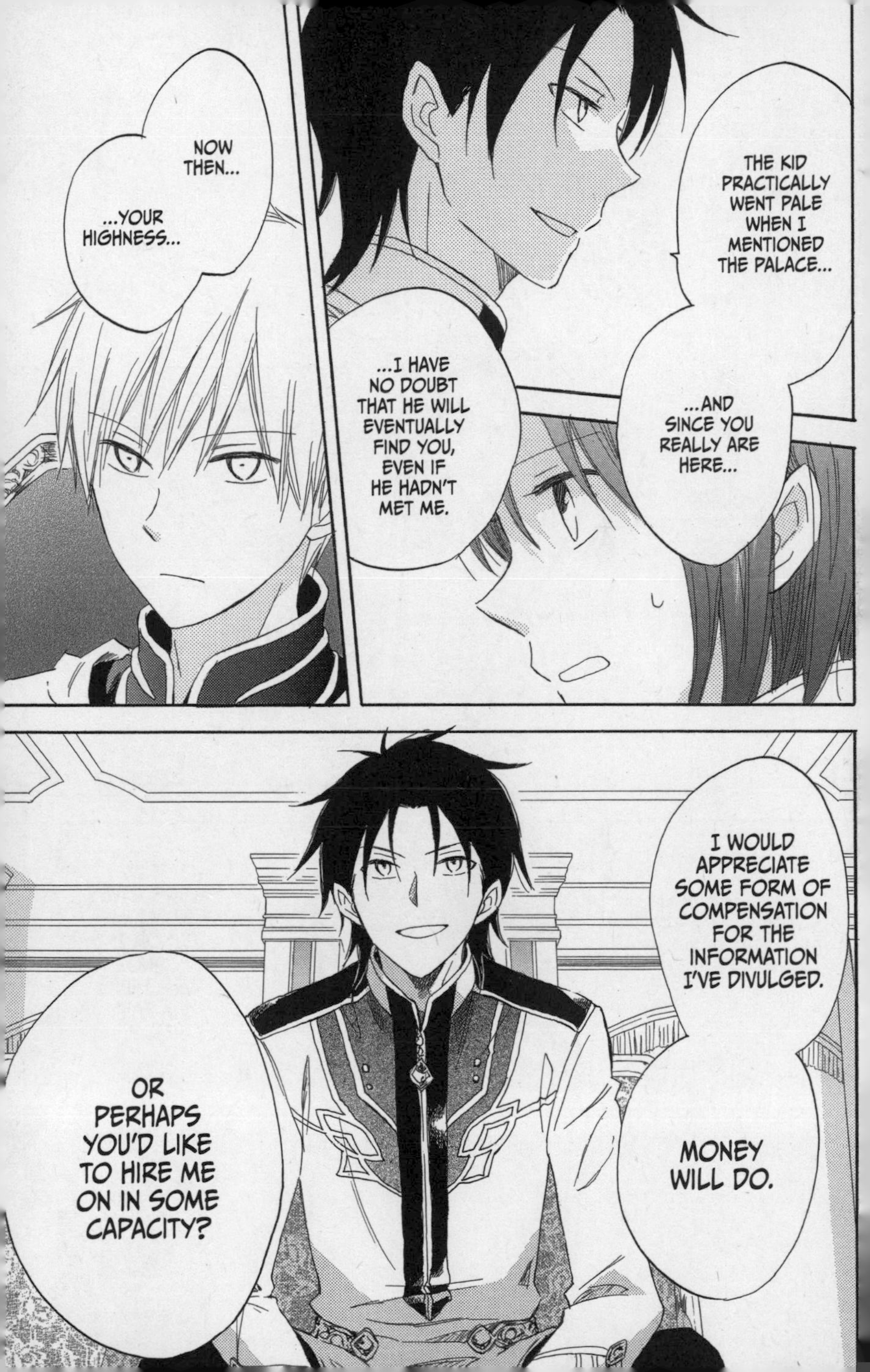
THE KID PRACTICALLY WENT PALE WHEN I MENTIONED THE PALACE...
...AND SINCE YOU REALLY ARE HERE...
...I HAVE NO DOUBT THAT HE WILL EVENTUALLY FIND YOU, EVEN IF HE HADN'T MET ME.
NOW THEN...
...YOUR HIGHNESS...
I WOULD APPRECIATE SOME FORM OF COMPENSATION FOR THE INFORMATION I'VE DIVULGED.
MONEY WILL DO.
OR PERHAPS YOU'D LIKE TO HIRE ME ON IN SOME CAPACITY?

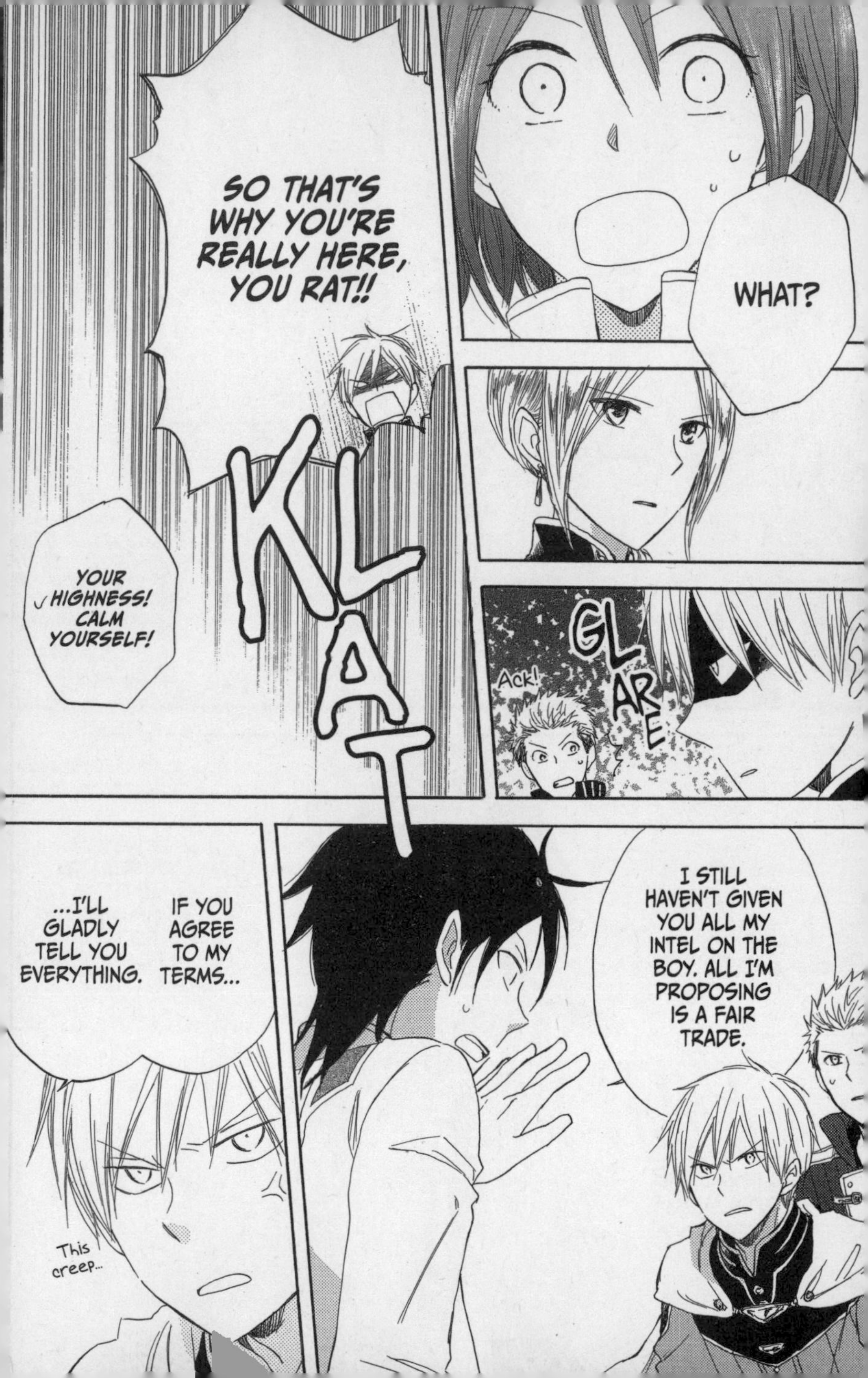
WHAT?
GLARE
Ack!
SO THAT'S WHY YOU'RE REALLY HERE, YOU RAT!!
KLAT
YOUR HIGHNESS! CALM YOURSELF!
I STILL HAVEN'T GIVEN YOU ALL MY INTEL ON THE BOY. ALL I'M PROPOSING IS A FAIR TRADE.
IF YOU AGREE TO MY TERMS...
...I'LL GLADLY TELL YOU EVERYTHING.
This creep...

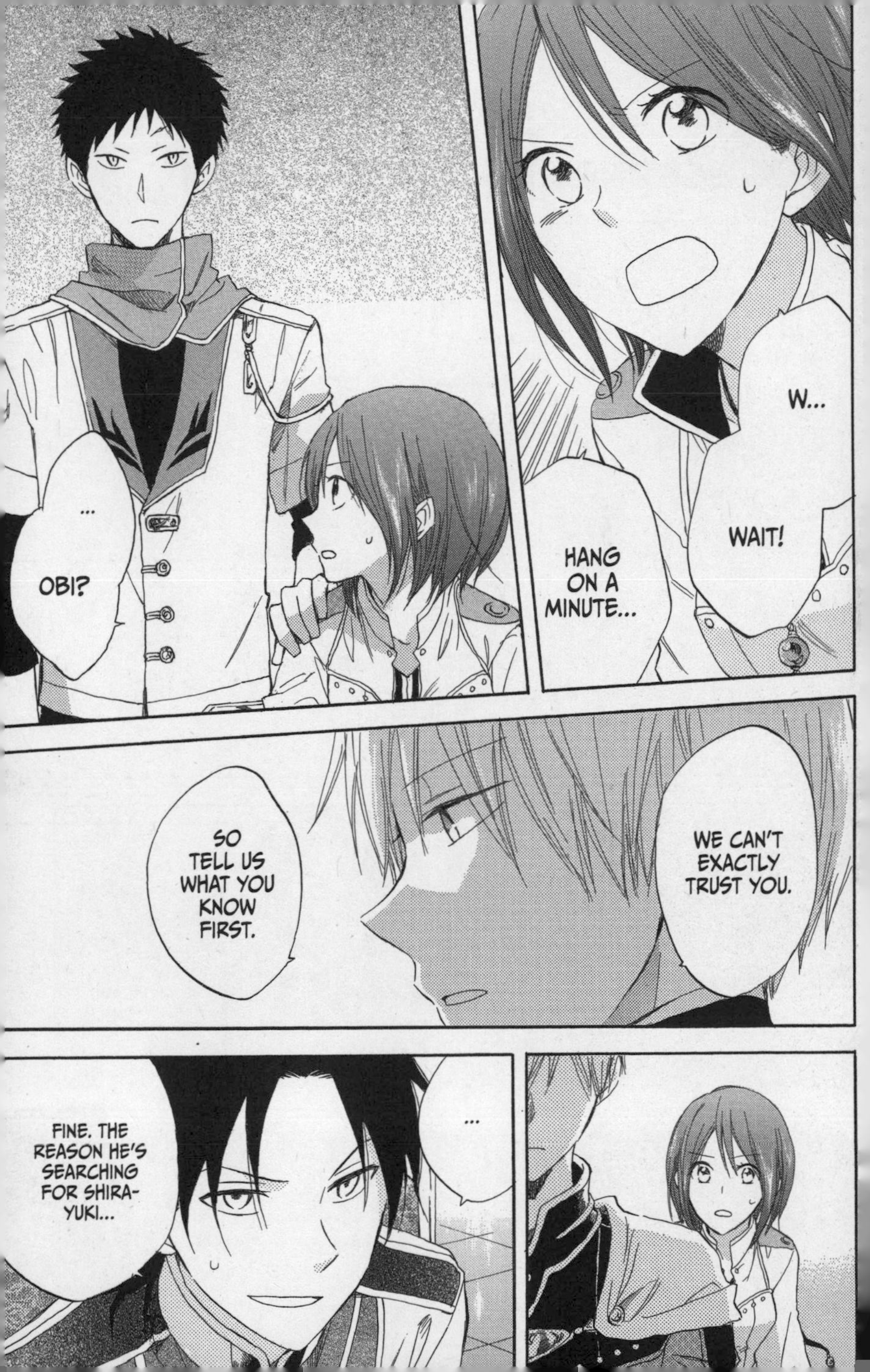
W...
WAIT!
HANG ON A MINUTE...
...
OBI?
WE CAN'T EXACTLY TRUST YOU.
SO TELL US WHAT YOU KNOW FIRST.
...
FINE. THE REASON HE'S SEARCHING FOR SHIRA-YUKI...

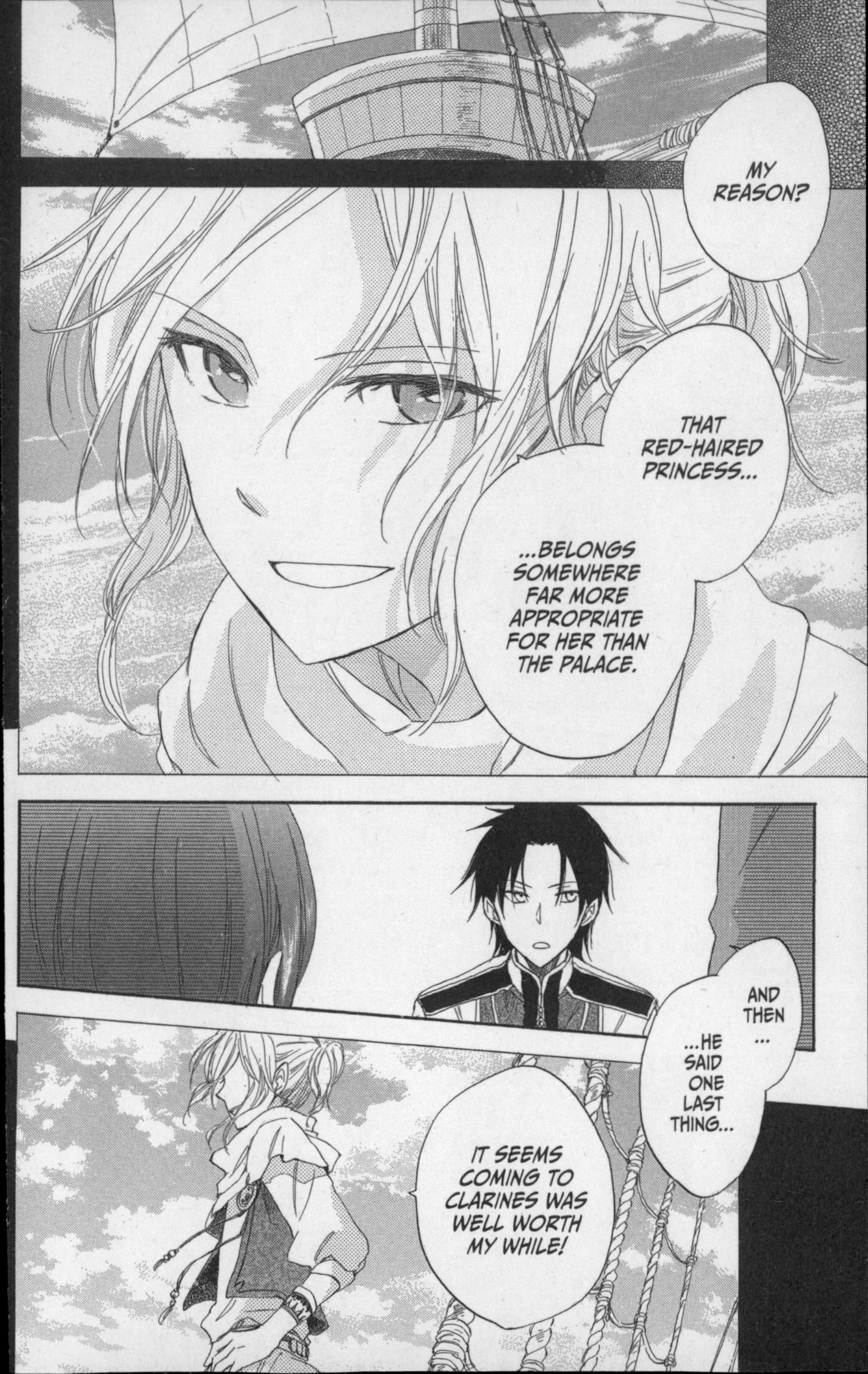
MY REASON?
THAT RED-HAIRED PRINCESS...
...BELONGS SOMEWHERE FAR MORE APPROPRIATE FOR HER THAN THE PALACE.
AND THEN ...
...HE SAID ONE LAST THING...
IT SEEMS COMING TO CLARINES WAS WELL WORTH MY WHILE!

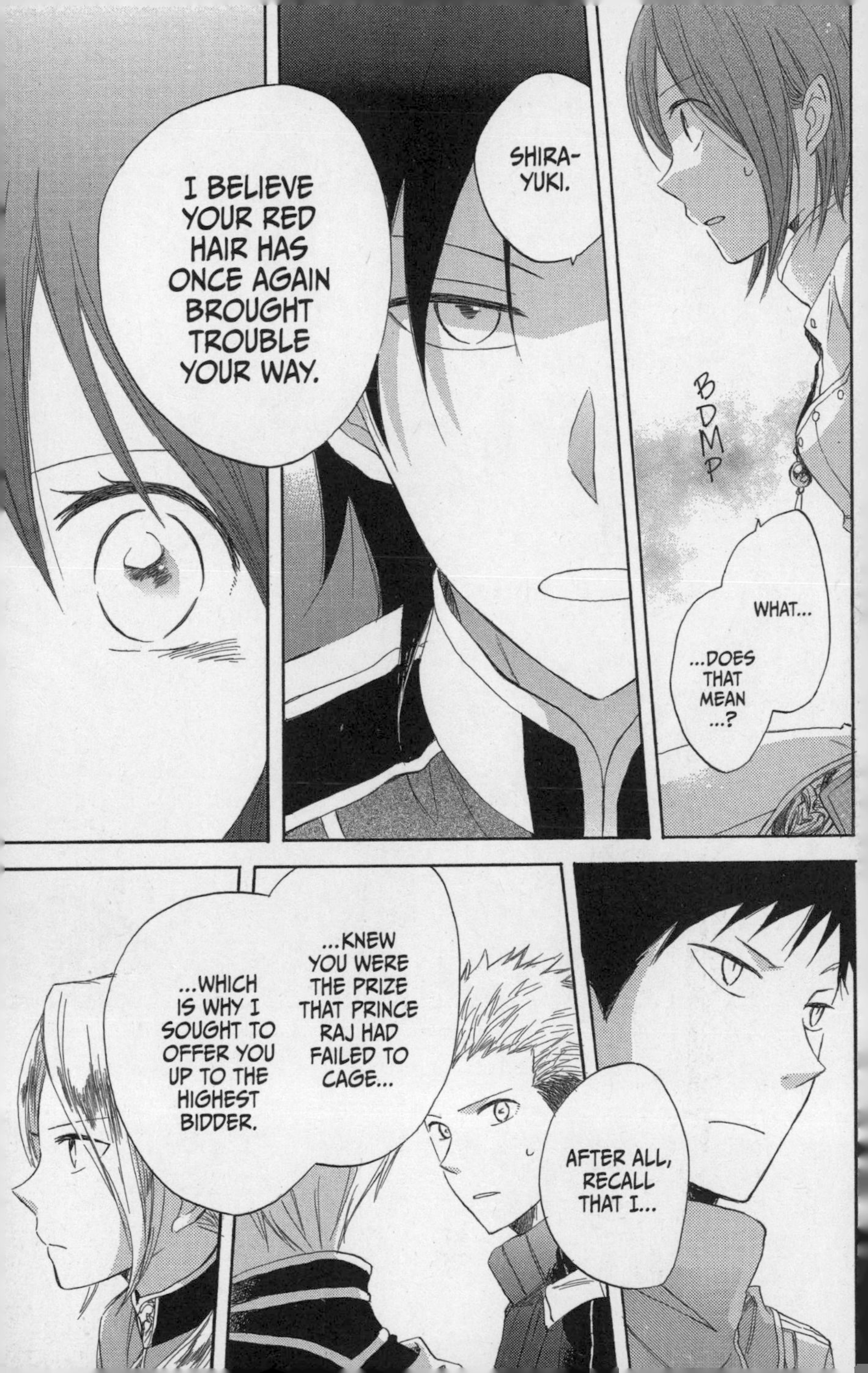
BDMP
WHAT...
...DOES THAT MEAN ...?
SHIRA-YUKI.
I BELIEVE YOUR RED HAIR HAS ONCE AGAIN BROUGHT TROUBLE YOUR WAY.
AFTER ALL, RECALL THAT I...
...KNEW YOU WERE THE PRIZE THAT PRINCE RAJ HAD FAILED TO CAGE...
...WHICH IS WHY I SOUGHT TO OFFER YOU UP TO THE HIGHEST BIDDER.

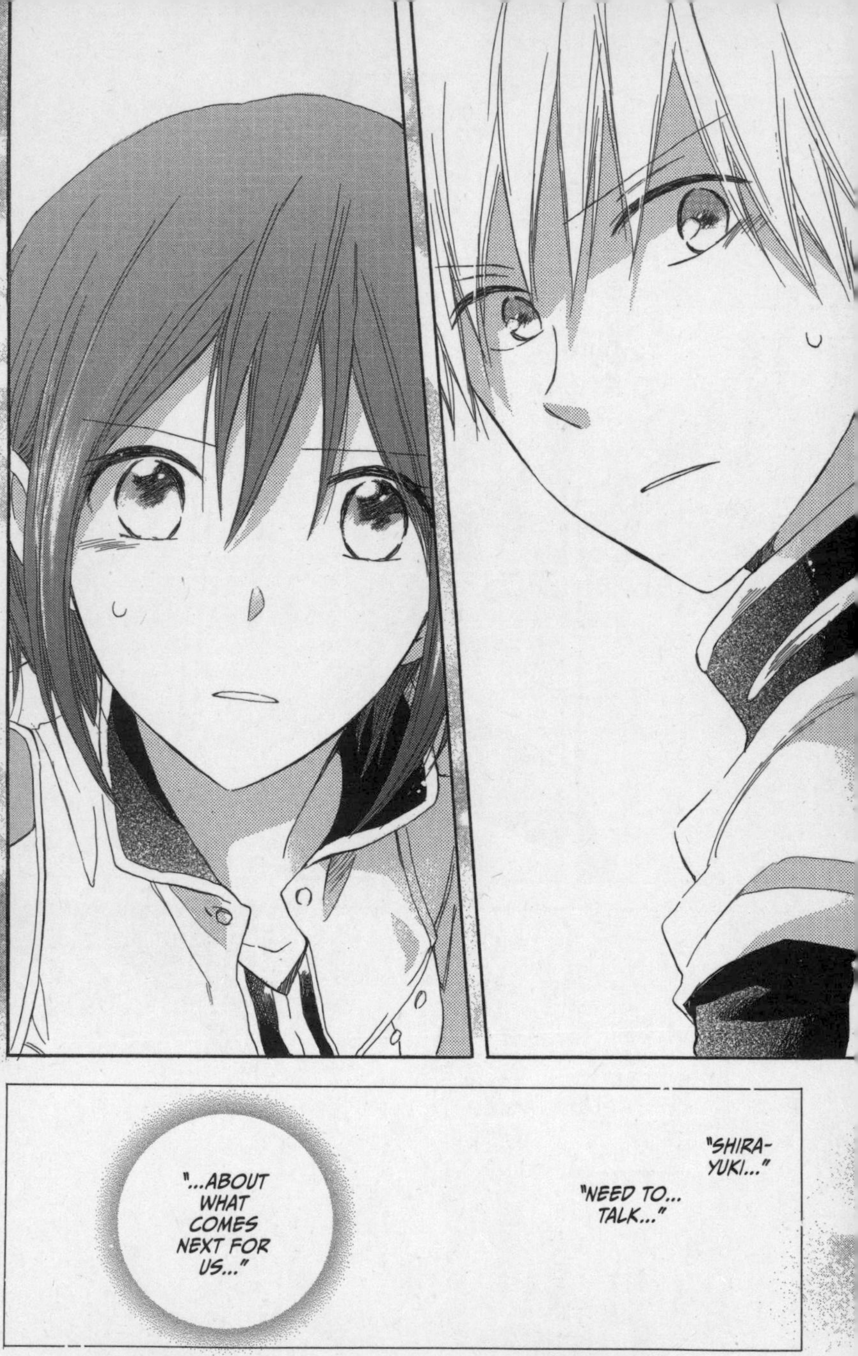
"SHIRA-YUKI..."
"NEED TO... TALK..."
"...ABOUT WHAT COMES NEXT FOR US..."

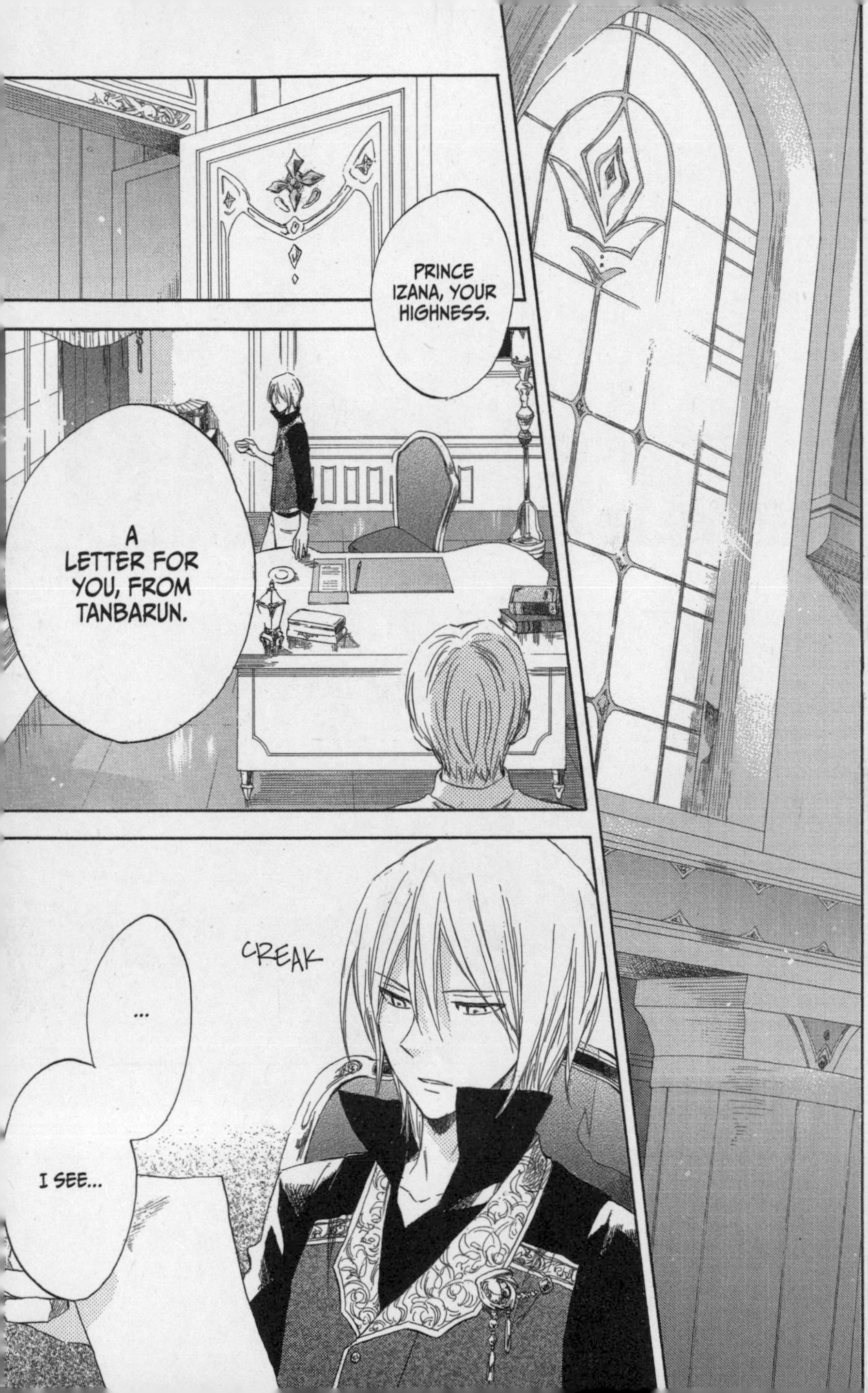
PRINCE IZANA, YOUR HIGHNESS.
A LETTER FOR YOU, FROM TANBARUN.
CREAK
...
I SEE...

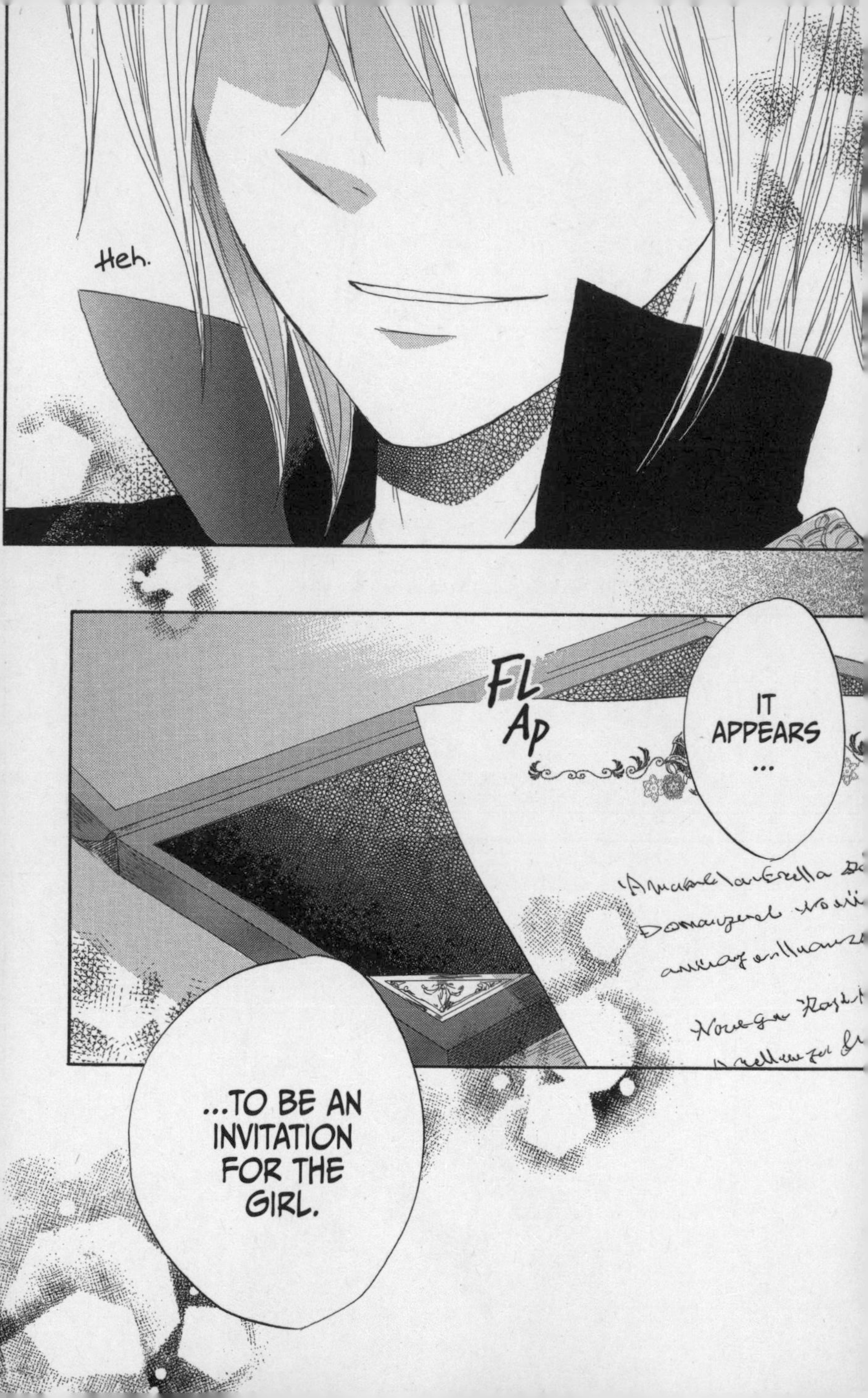
Heh.
FLAP
IT APPEARS ...
...TO BE AN INVITATION FOR THE GIRL.

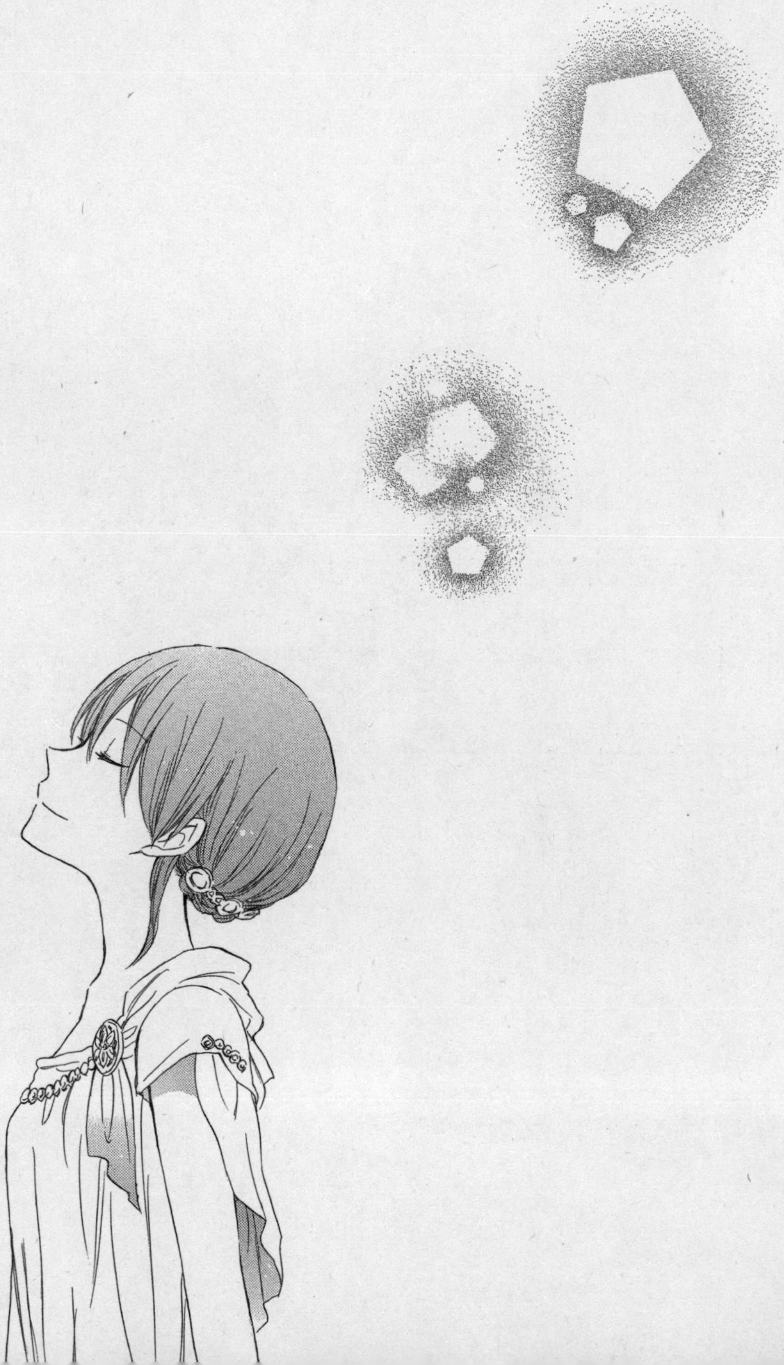

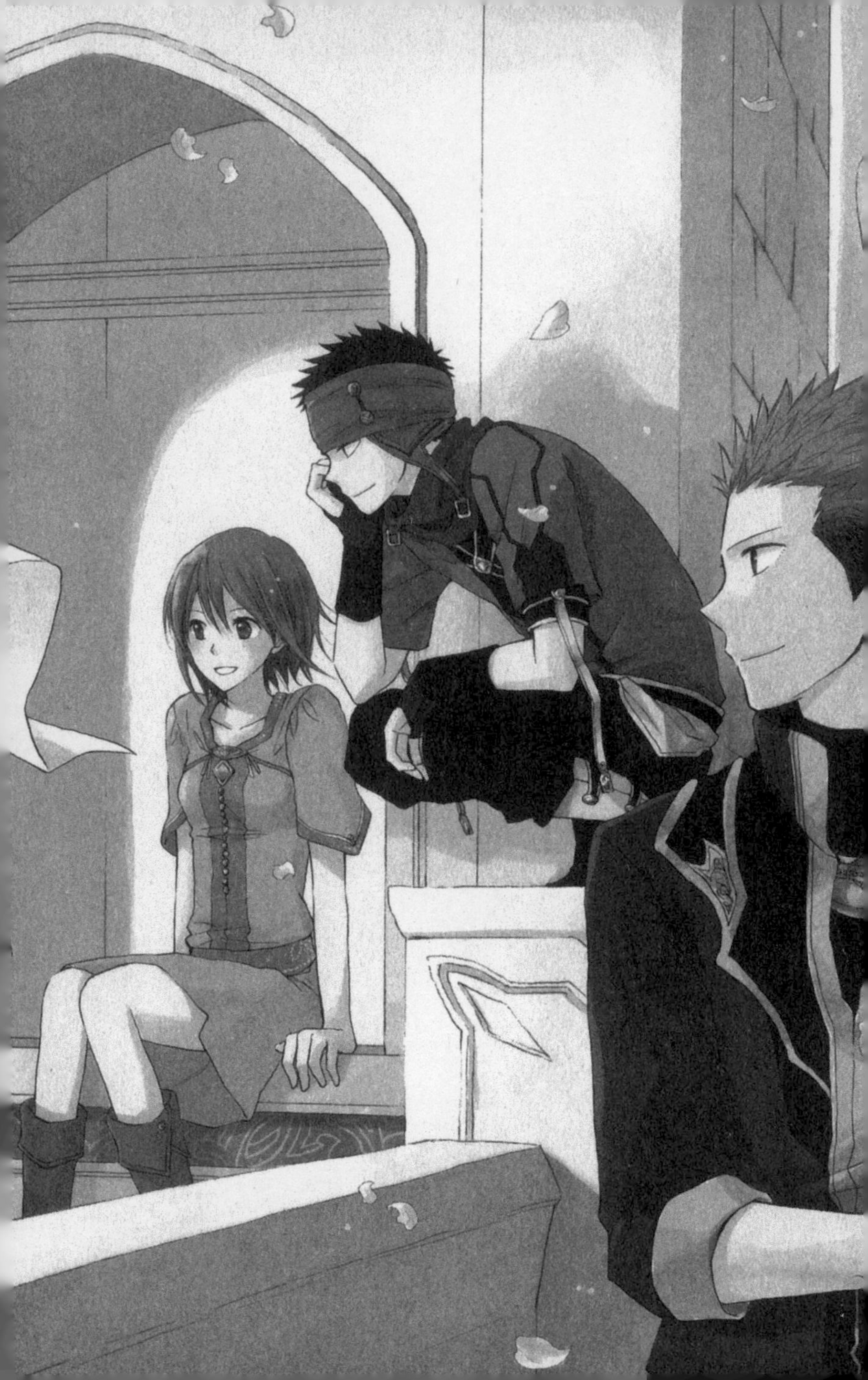

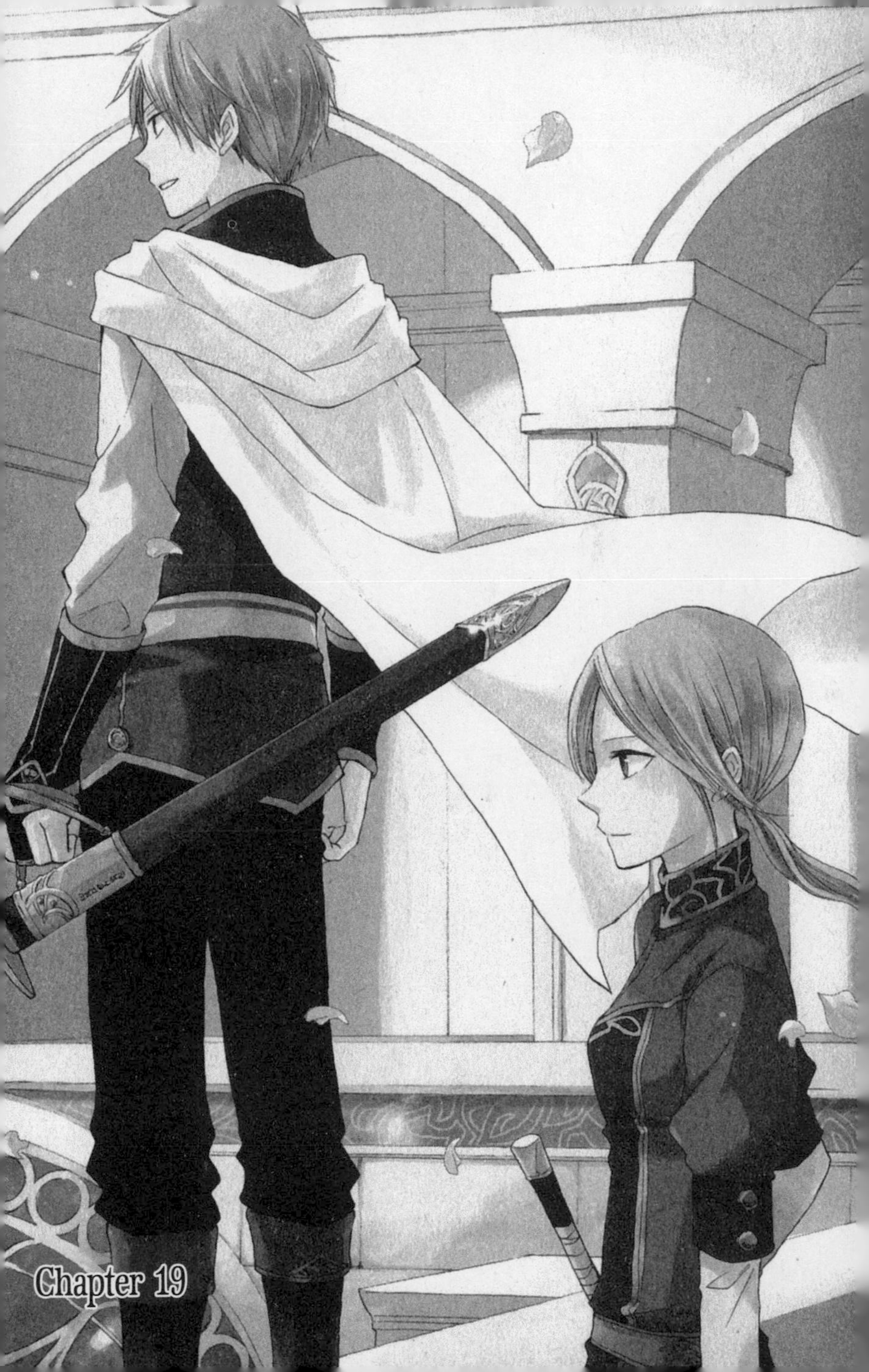
Chapter 19

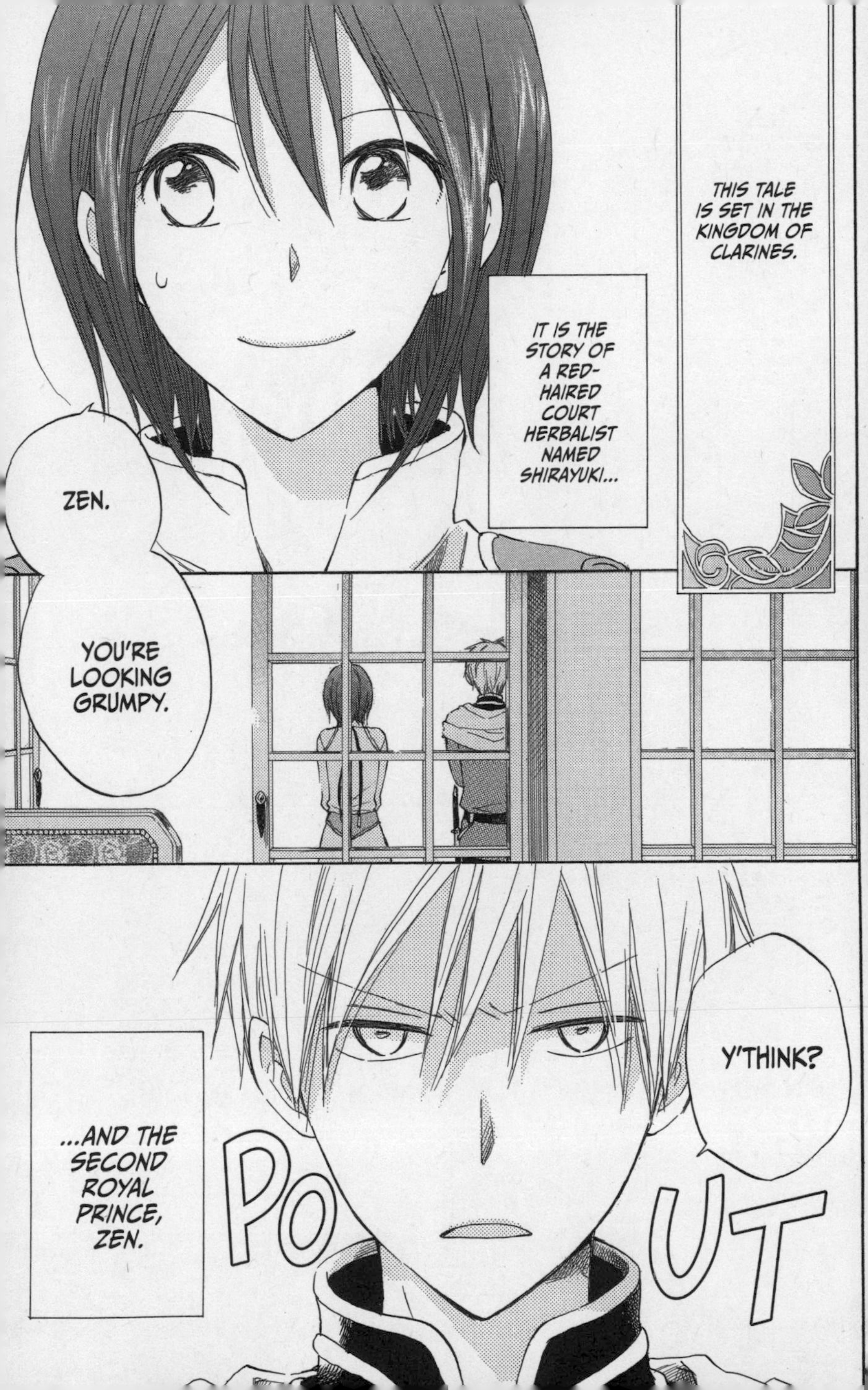
THIS TALE IS SET IN THE KINGDOM OF CLARINES.
IT IS THE STORY OF A RED-HAIRED COURT HERBALIST NAMED SHIRAYUKI...
ZEN.
YOU'RE LOOKING GRUMPY.
Y'THINK?
POUT
...AND THE SECOND ROYAL PRINCE, ZEN.

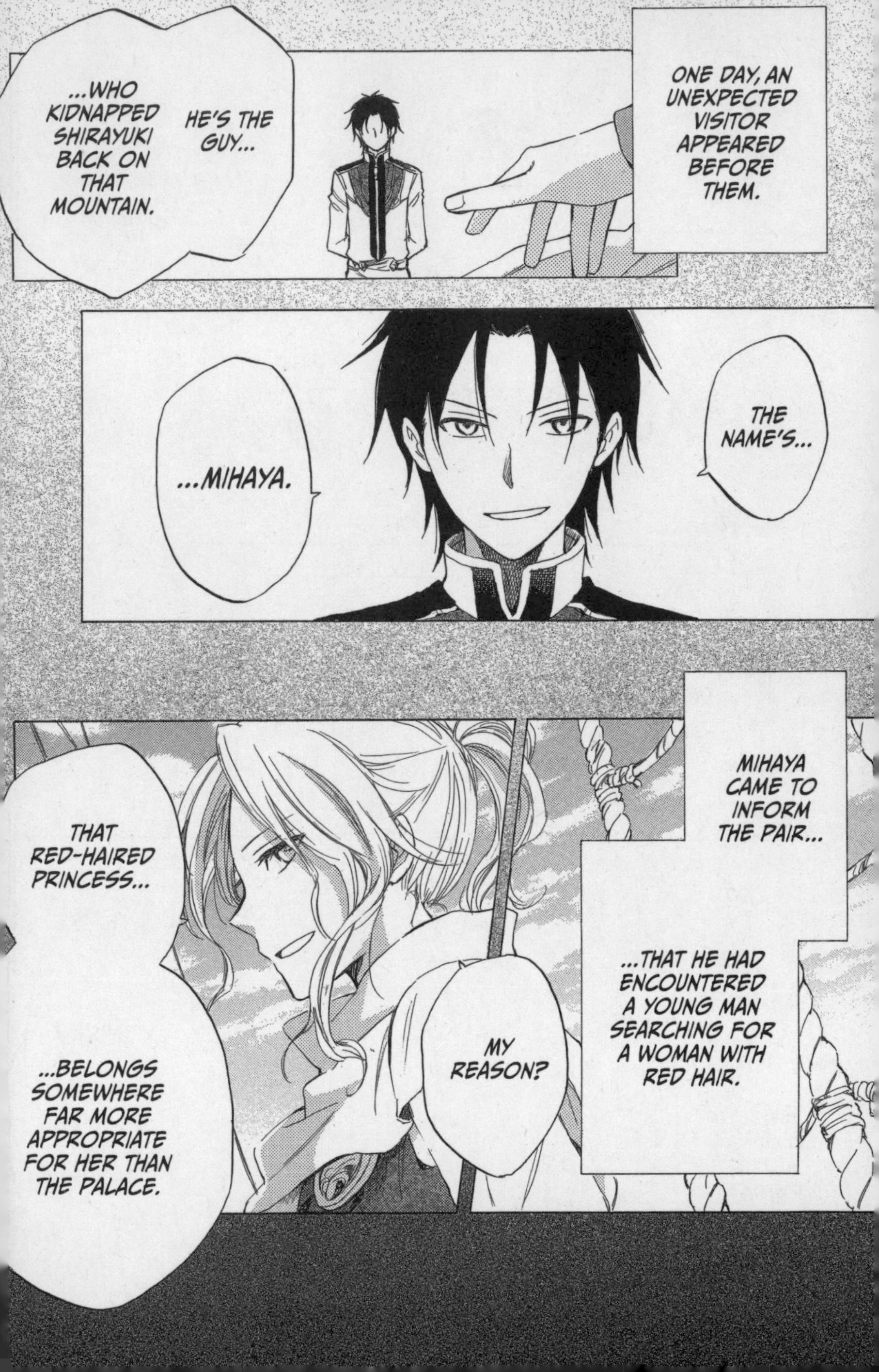
ONE DAY, AN UNEXPECTED VISITOR APPEARED BEFORE THEM.
HE'S THE GUY...
...WHO KIDNAPPED SHIRAYUKI BACK ON THAT MOUNTAIN.
THE NAME'S...
...MIHAYA.
MIHAYA CAME TO INFORM THE PAIR...
...THAT HE HAD ENCOUNTERED A YOUNG MAN SEARCHING FOR A WOMAN WITH RED HAIR.
MY REASON?
THAT RED-HAIRED PRINCESS...
...BELONGS SOMEWHERE FAR MORE APPROPRIATE FOR HER THAN THE PALACE.

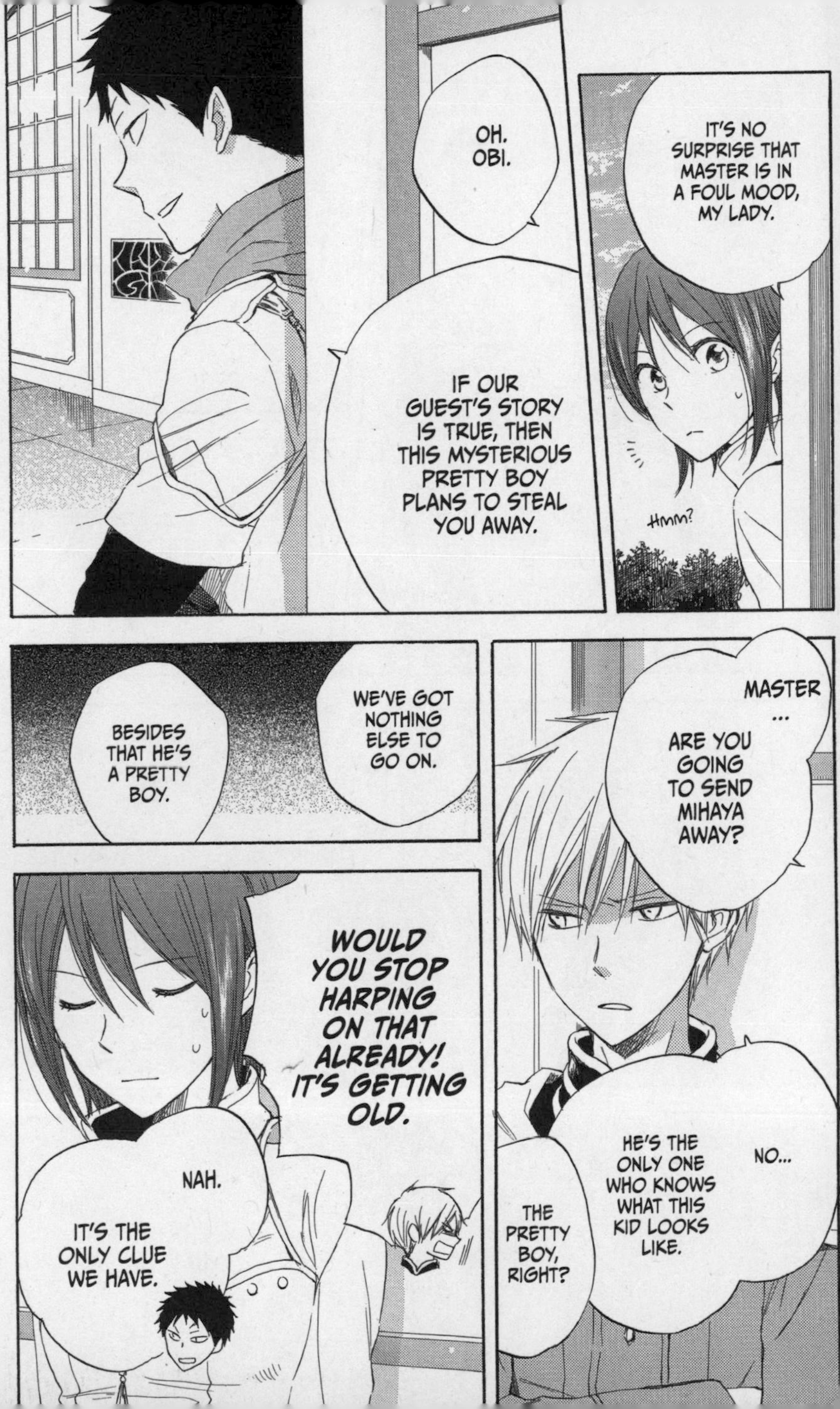
IT'S NO SURPRISE THAT MASTER IS IN A FOUL MOOD, MY LADY.
Hmm?
OH. OBI.
IF OUR GUEST'S STORY IS TRUE, THEN THIS MYSTERIOUS PRETTY BOY PLANS TO STEAL YOU AWAY.
MASTER ... ARE YOU GOING TO SEND MIHAYA AWAY?
NO...
HE'S THE ONLY ONE WHO KNOWS WHAT THIS KID LOOKS LIKE.
THE PRETTY BOY, RIGHT?
WE'VE GOT NOTHING ELSE TO GO ON.
BESIDES THAT HE'S A PRETTY BOY.
WOULD YOU STOP HARPING ON THAT ALREADY! IT'S GETTING OLD.
NAH.
IT'S THE ONLY CLUE WE HAVE.

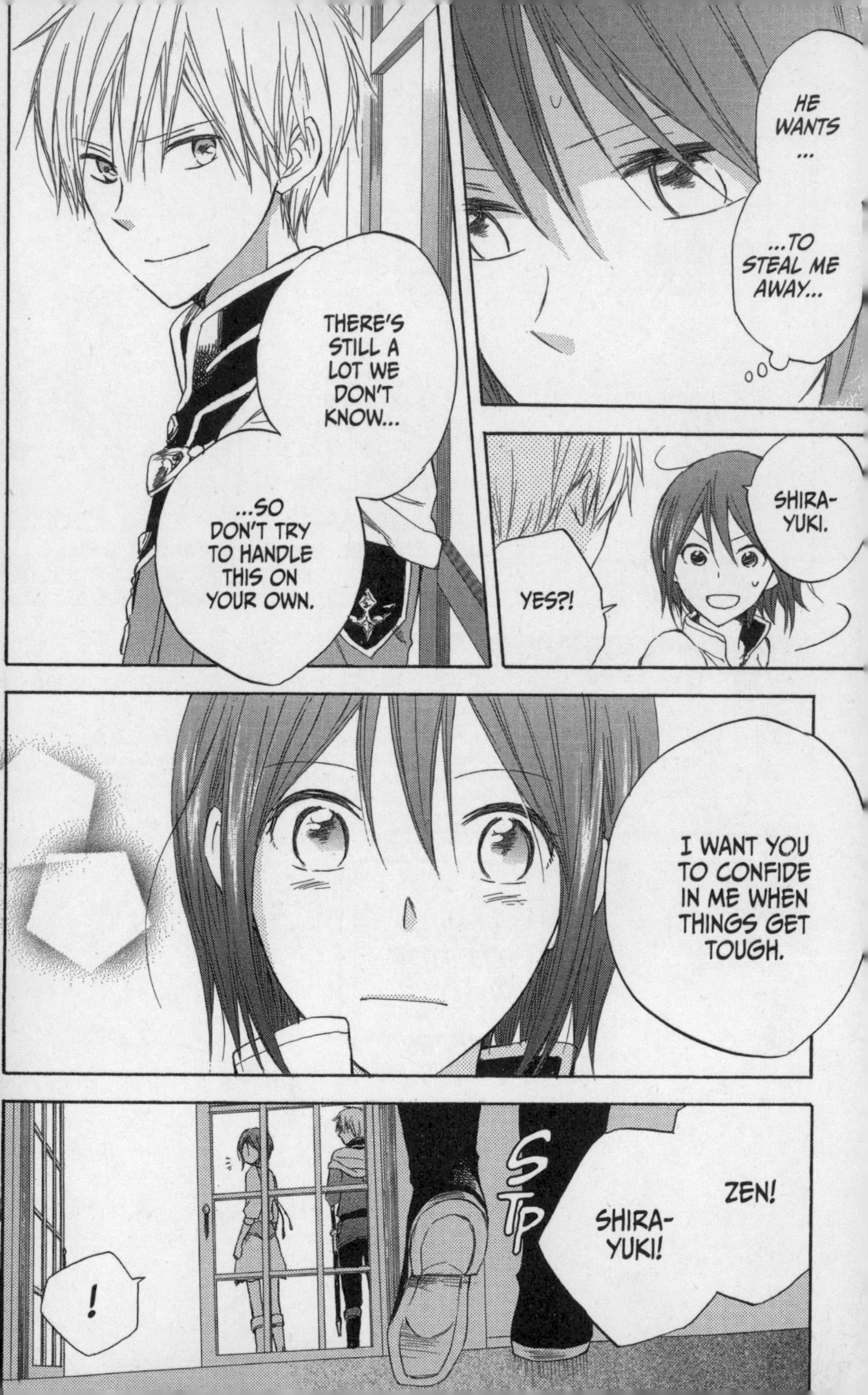
HE WANTS ...
...TO STEAL ME AWAY...
SHIRA-YUKI.
YES?!
THERE'S STILL A LOT WE DON'T KNOW...
...SO DON'T TRY TO HANDLE THIS ON YOUR OWN.
I WANT YOU TO CONFIDE IN ME WHEN THINGS GET TOUGH.
ZEN!
SHIRA-YUKI!
STP
!

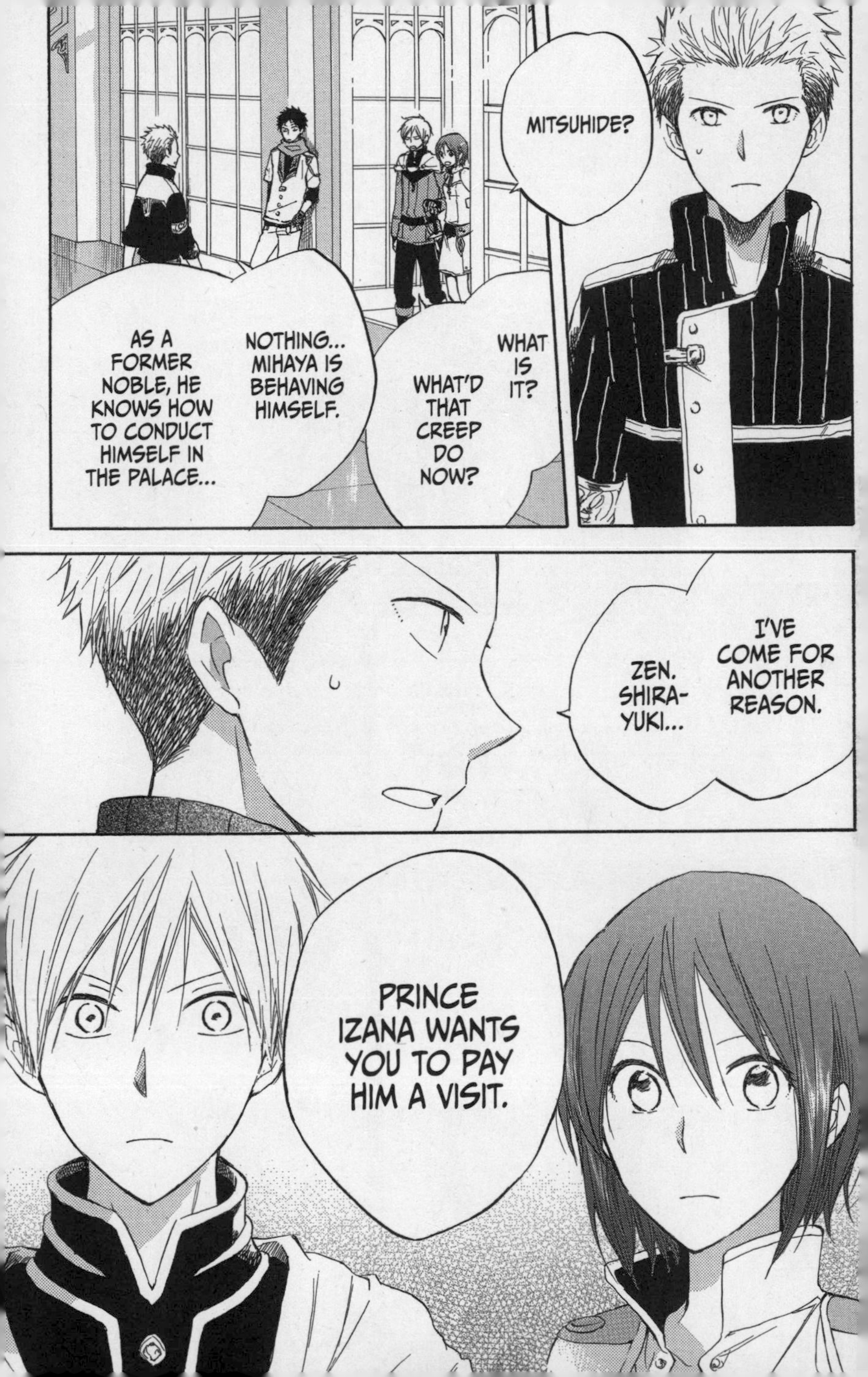
MITSUHIDE?
WHAT IS IT?
WHAT'D THAT CREEP DO NOW?
NOTHING... MIHAYA IS BEHAVING HIMSELF.
AS A FORMER NOBLE, HE KNOWS HOW TO CONDUCT HIMSELF IN THE PALACE...
I'VE COME FOR ANOTHER REASON.
ZEN. SHIRA-YUKI...
PRINCE IZANA WANTS YOU TO PAY HIM A VISIT.

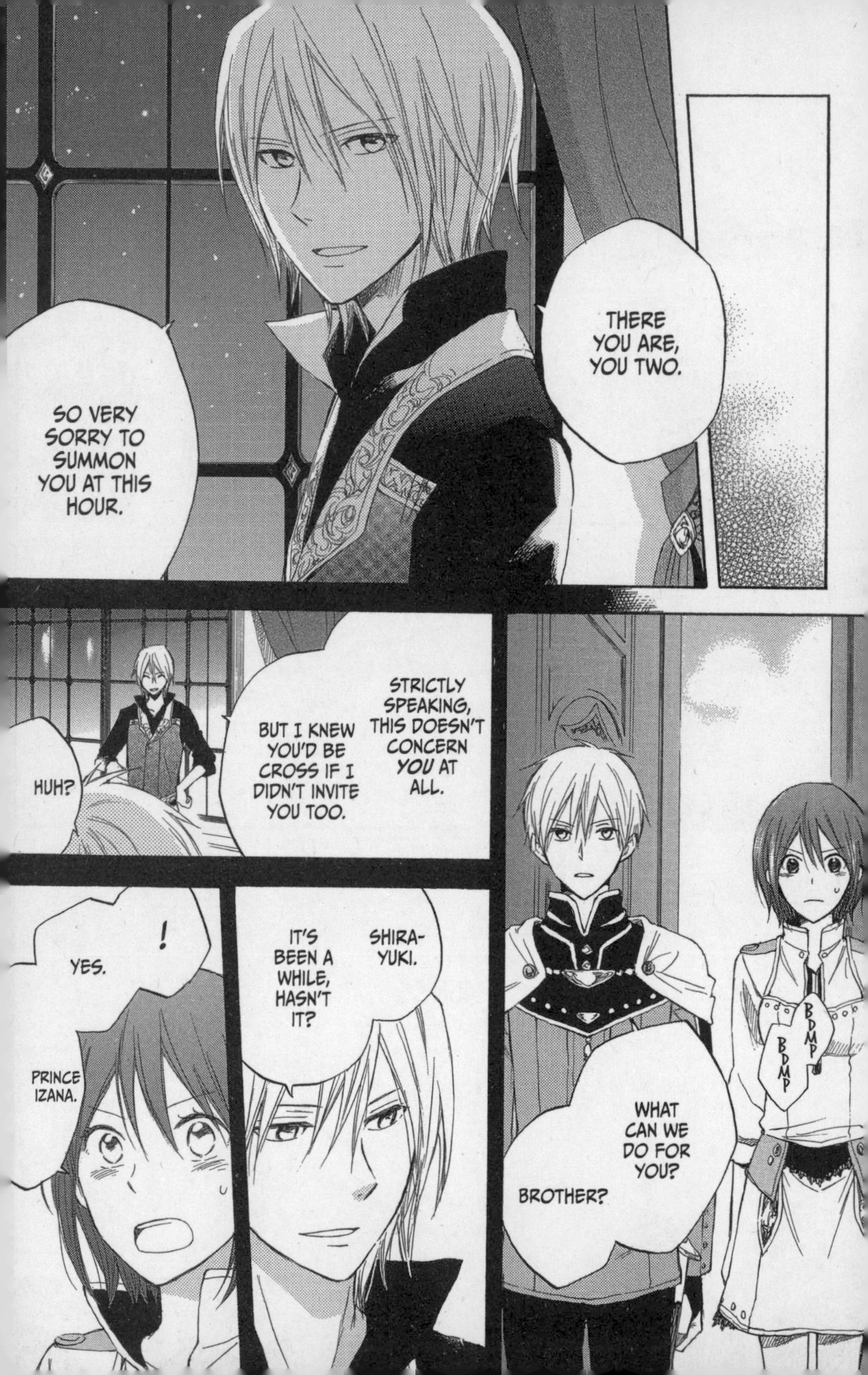
THERE YOU ARE, YOU TWO.
SO VERY SORRY TO SUMMON YOU AT THIS HOUR.
WHAT CAN WE DO FOR YOU?
BROTHER?
BDMP BDMP
STRICTLY SPEAKING, THIS DOESN'T CONCERN *YOU* AT ALL.
BUT I KNEW YOU'D BE CROSS IF I DIDN'T INVITE YOU TOO.
HUH?
SHIRAYUKI.
IT'S BEEN A WHILE, HASN'T IT?
!
YES.
PRINCE IZANA.

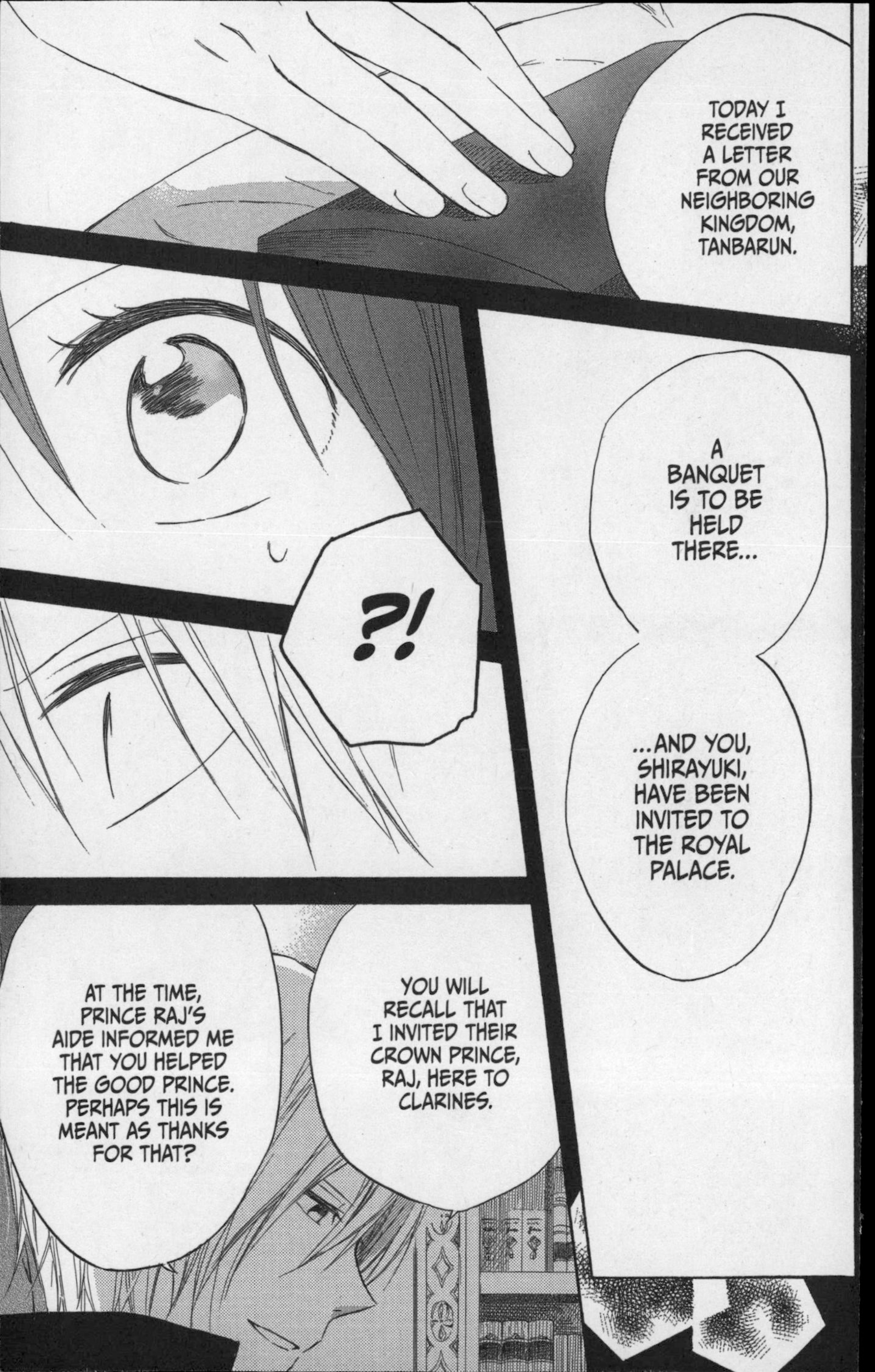
TODAY I RECEIVED A LETTER FROM OUR NEIGHBORING KINGDOM, TANBARUN.
A BANQUET IS TO BE HELD THERE...
...AND YOU, SHIRAYUKI, HAVE BEEN INVITED TO THE ROYAL PALACE.
?!
YOU WILL RECALL THAT I INVITED THEIR CROWN PRINCE, RAJ, HERE TO CLARINES.
AT THE TIME, PRINCE RAJ'S AIDE INFORMED ME THAT YOU HELPED THE GOOD PRINCE. PERHAPS THIS IS MEANT AS THANKS FOR THAT?

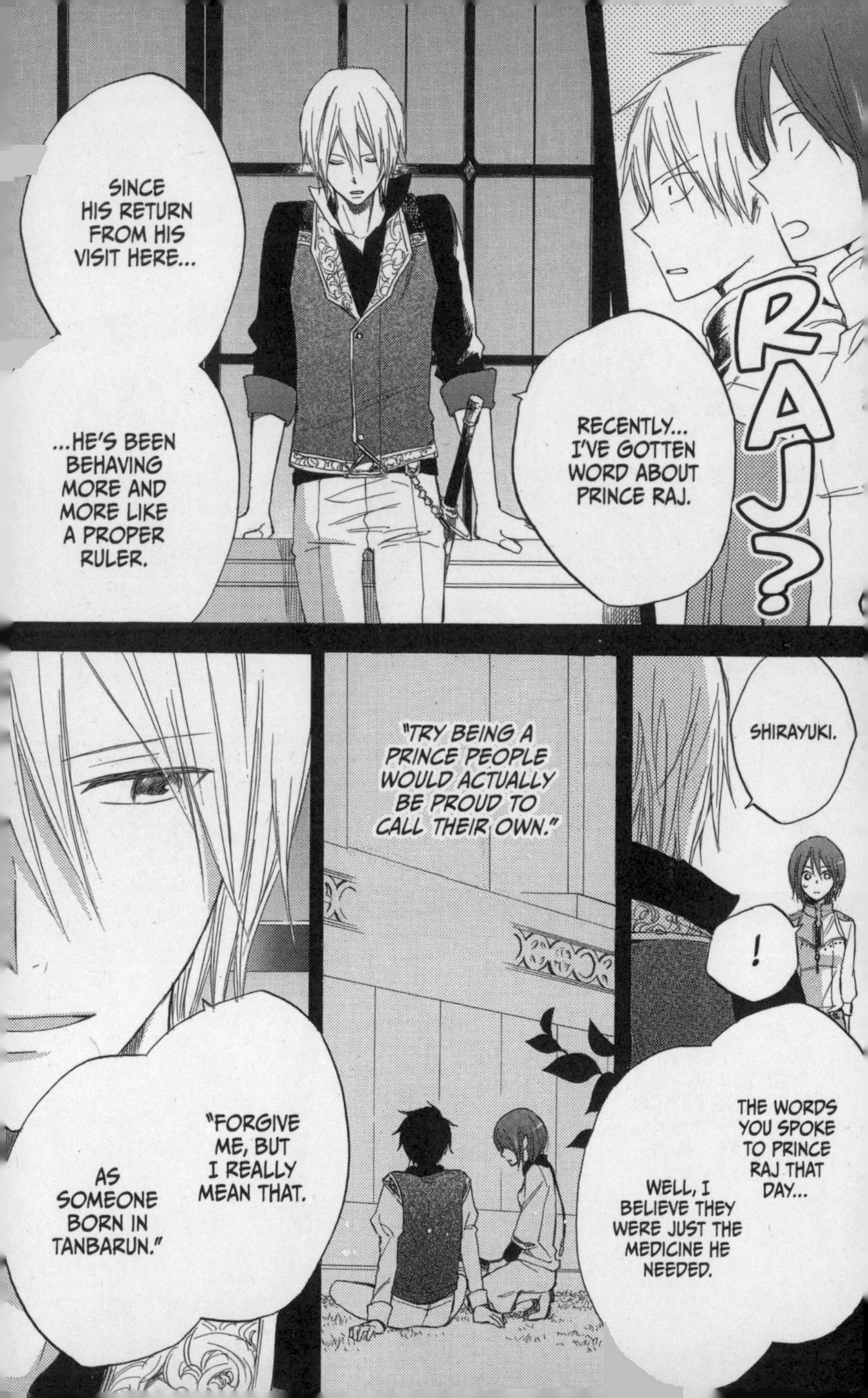
RECENTLY... I'VE GOTTEN WORD ABOUT PRINCE RAJ.
RAJ?
SINCE HIS RETURN FROM HIS VISIT HERE...
...HE'S BEEN BEHAVING MORE AND MORE LIKE A PROPER RULER.
SHIRAYUKI.
!
THE WORDS YOU SPOKE TO PRINCE RAJ THAT DAY...
WELL, I BELIEVE THEY WERE JUST THE MEDICINE HE NEEDED.
"TRY BEING A PRINCE PEOPLE WOULD ACTUALLY BE PROUD TO CALL THEIR OWN."
"FORGIVE ME, BUT I REALLY MEAN THAT.
AS SOMEONE BORN IN TANBARUN."

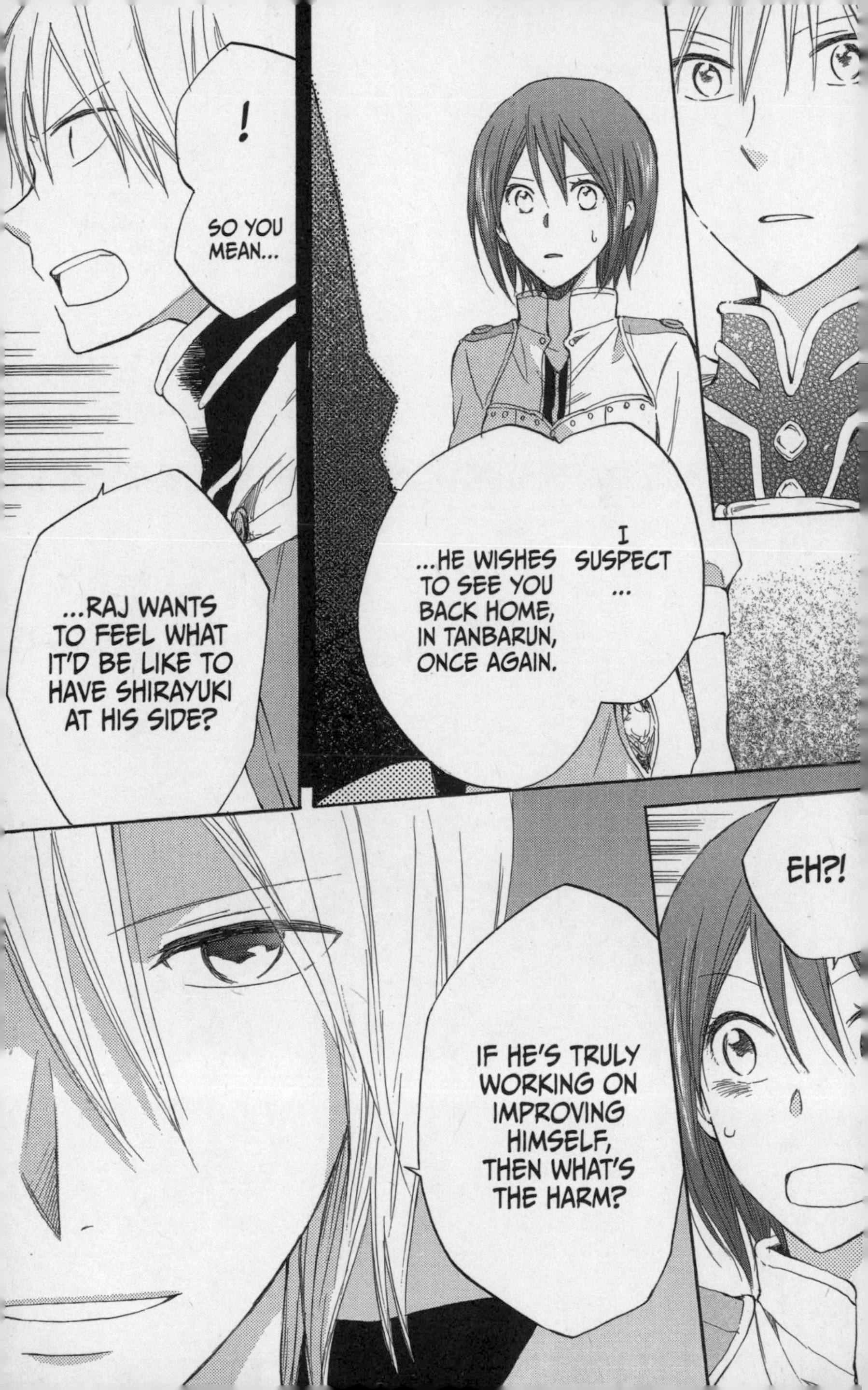
I SUSPECT ...
...HE WISHES TO SEE YOU BACK HOME, IN TANBARUN, ONCE AGAIN.
!
SO YOU MEAN...
...RAJ WANTS TO FEEL WHAT IT'D BE LIKE TO HAVE SHIRAYUKI AT HIS SIDE?
EH?!
IF HE'S TRULY WORKING ON IMPROVING HIMSELF, THEN WHAT'S THE HARM?

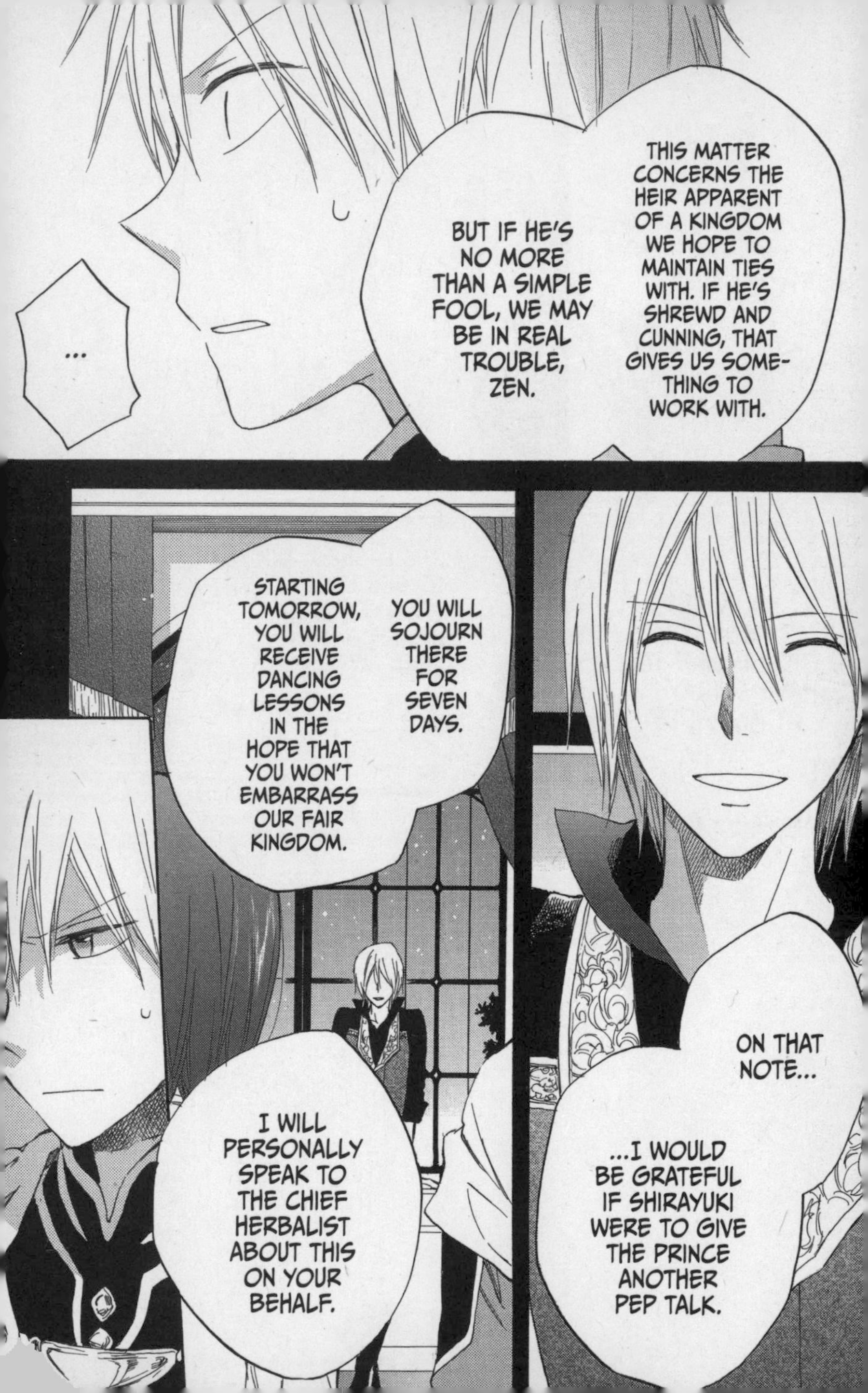
THIS MATTER CONCERNS THE HEIR APPARENT OF A KINGDOM WE HOPE TO MAINTAIN TIES WITH. IF HE'S SHREWD AND CUNNING, THAT GIVES US SOMETHING TO WORK WITH.
BUT IF HE'S NO MORE THAN A SIMPLE FOOL, WE MAY BE IN REAL TROUBLE, ZEN.
...
ON THAT NOTE...
...I WOULD BE GRATEFUL IF SHIRAYUKI WERE TO GIVE THE PRINCE ANOTHER PEP TALK.
YOU WILL SOJOURN THERE FOR SEVEN DAYS.
STARTING TOMORROW, YOU WILL RECEIVE DANCING LESSONS IN THE HOPE THAT YOU WON'T EMBARRASS OUR FAIR KINGDOM.
I WILL PERSONALLY SPEAK TO THE CHIEF HERBALIST ABOUT THIS ON YOUR BEHALF.

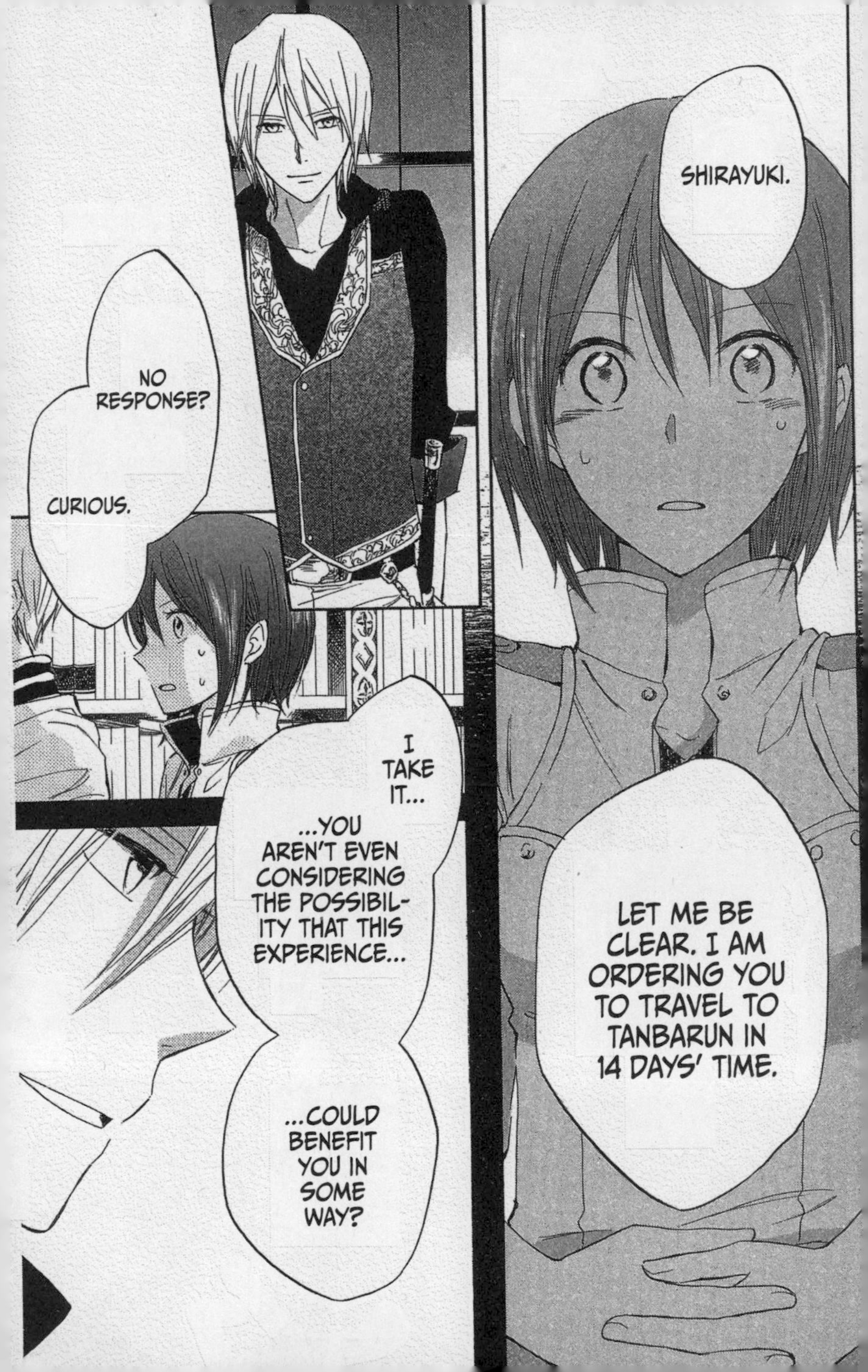
SHIRAYUKI.
LET ME BE CLEAR. I AM ORDERING YOU TO TRAVEL TO TANBARUN IN 14 DAYS' TIME.
NO RESPONSE?
CURIOUS.
I TAKE IT...
...YOU AREN'T EVEN CONSIDERING THE POSSIBIL-ITY THAT THIS EXPERIENCE...
...COULD BENEFIT YOU IN SOME WAY?

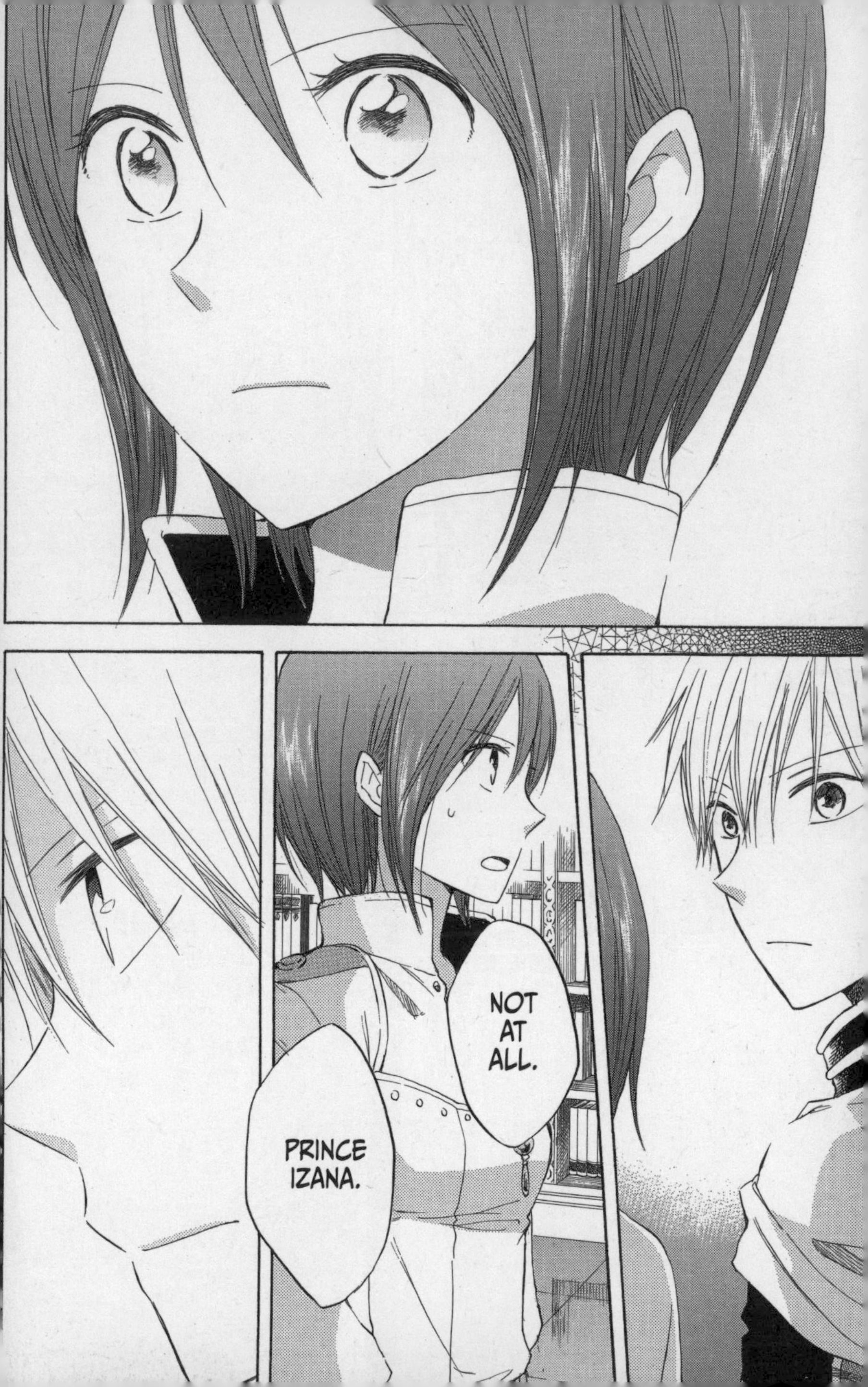
NOT AT ALL.
PRINCE IZANA.

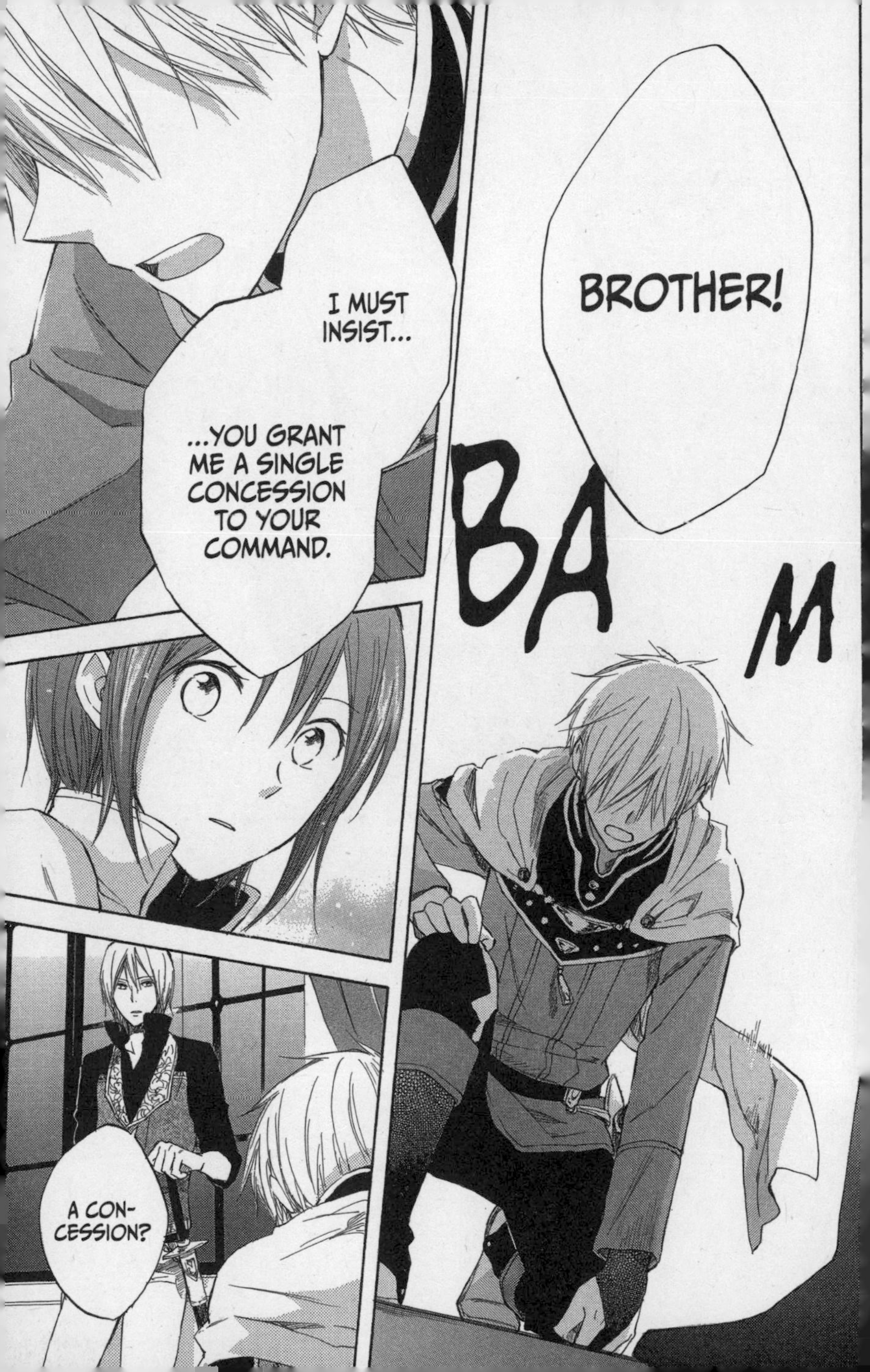
BROTHER!
BAM
I MUST INSIST...
...YOU GRANT ME A SINGLE CONCESSION TO YOUR COMMAND.
A CON-CESSION?

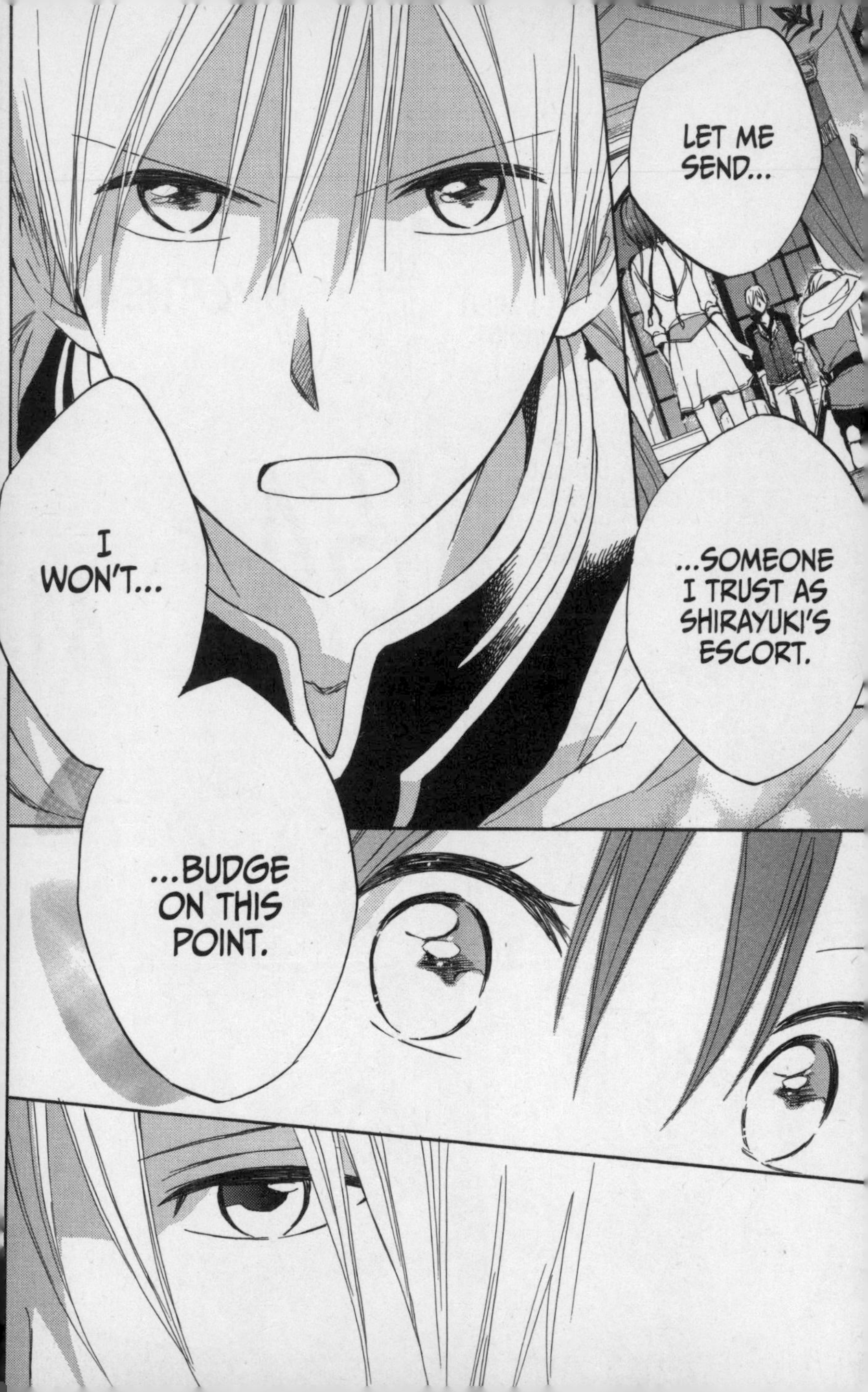
LET ME SEND...
...SOMEONE I TRUST AS SHIRAYUKI'S ESCORT.
I WON'T...
...BUDGE ON THIS POINT.

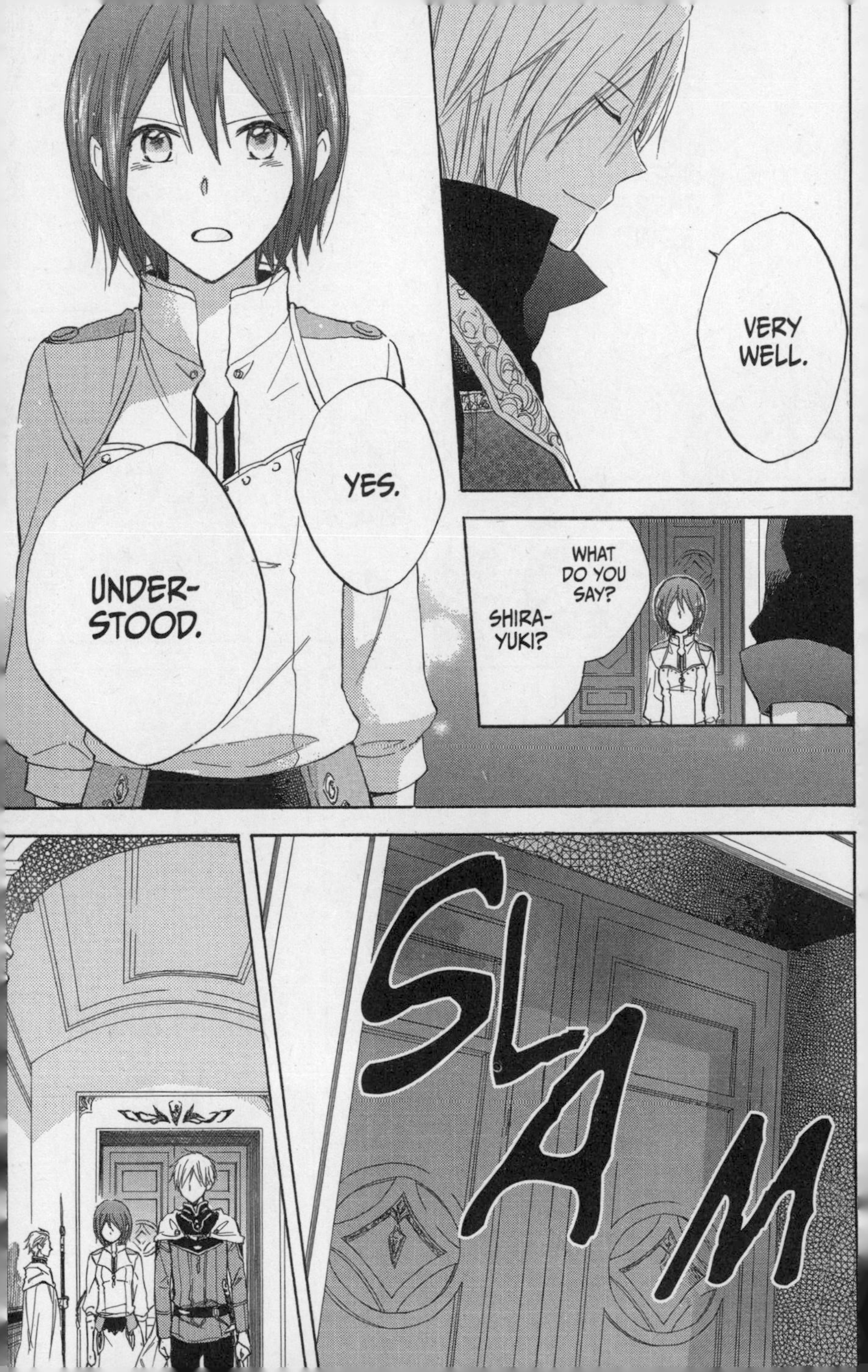
VERY WELL.
WHAT DO YOU SAY? SHIRA-YUKI?
YES.
UNDER-STOOD.
SLAM

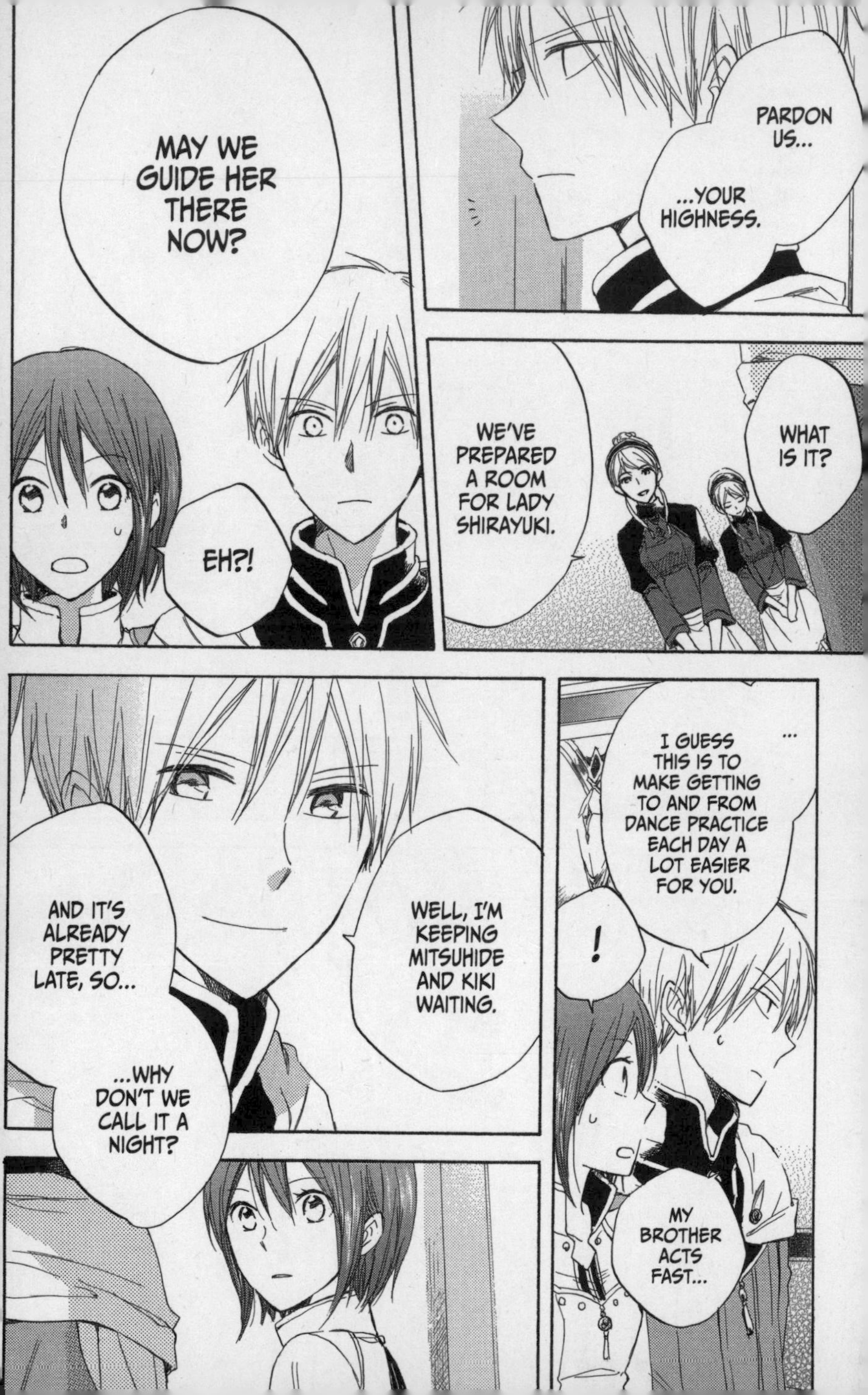
PARDON US...
...YOUR HIGHNESS.
WHAT IS IT?
WE'VE PREPARED A ROOM FOR LADY SHIRAYUKI.
MAY WE GUIDE HER THERE NOW?
EH?!
...
I GUESS THIS IS TO MAKE GETTING TO AND FROM DANCE PRACTICE EACH DAY A LOT EASIER FOR YOU.
!
MY BROTHER ACTS FAST...
WELL, I'M KEEPING MITSUHIDE AND KIKI WAITING.
AND IT'S ALREADY PRETTY LATE, SO...
...WHY DON'T WE CALL IT A NIGHT?

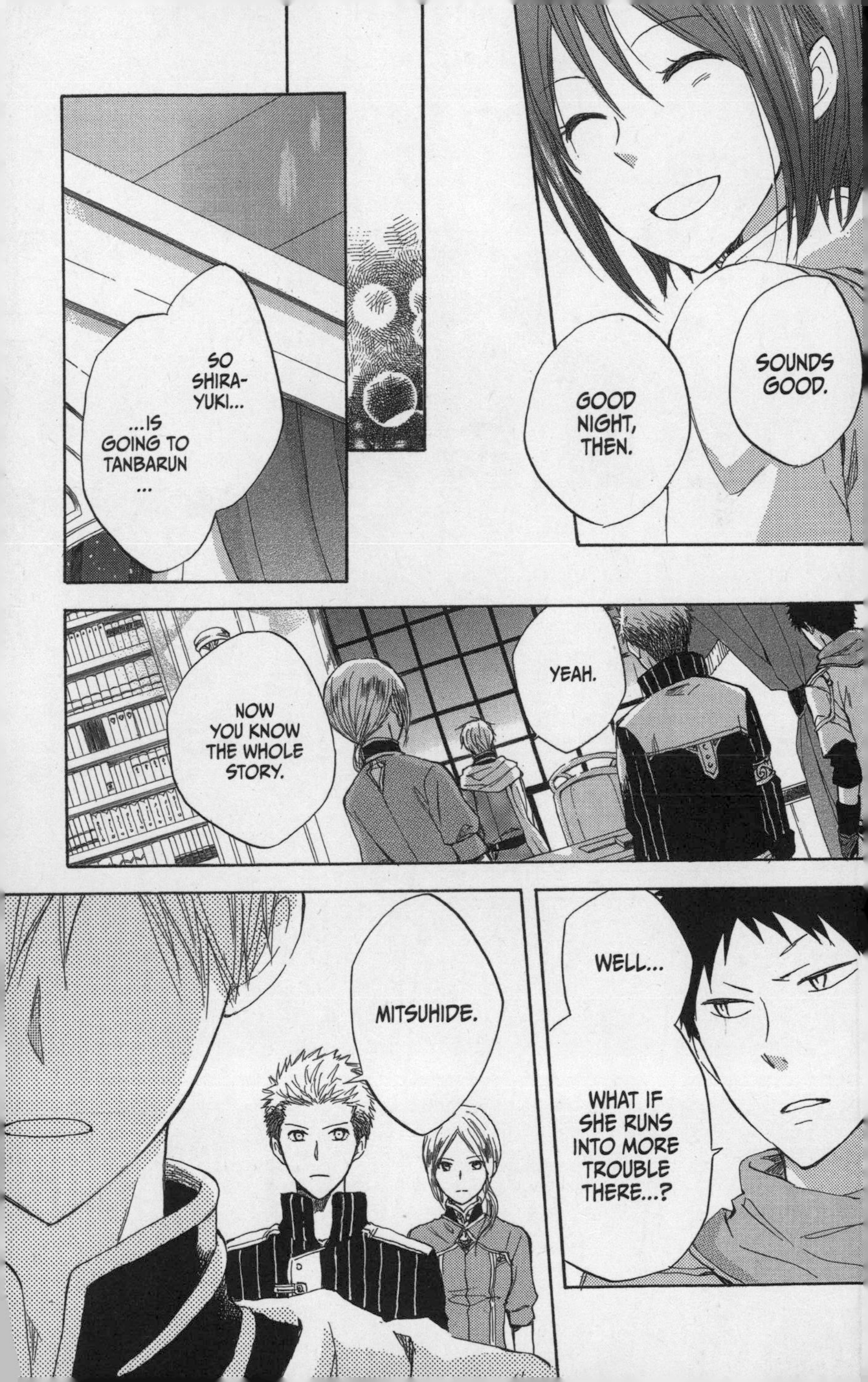
SOUNDS GOOD.
GOOD NIGHT, THEN.
SO SHIRA-YUKI...
...IS GOING TO TANBARUN ...
NOW YOU KNOW THE WHOLE STORY.
YEAH.
WELL...
WHAT IF SHE RUNS INTO MORE TROUBLE THERE...?
MITSUHIDE.

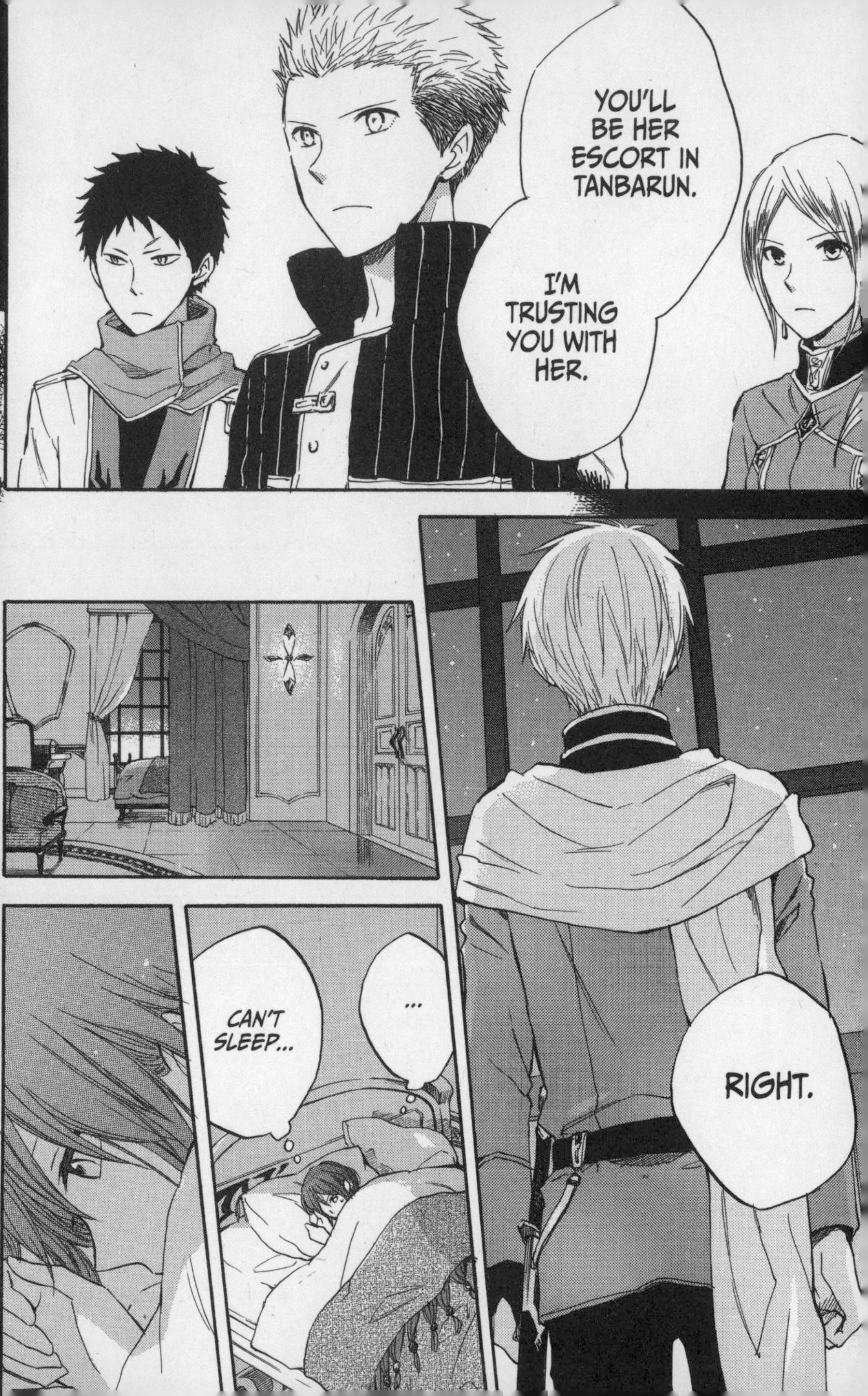
YOU'LL BE HER ESCORT IN TANBARUN.
I'M TRUSTING YOU WITH HER.
RIGHT.
...
CAN'T SLEEP...

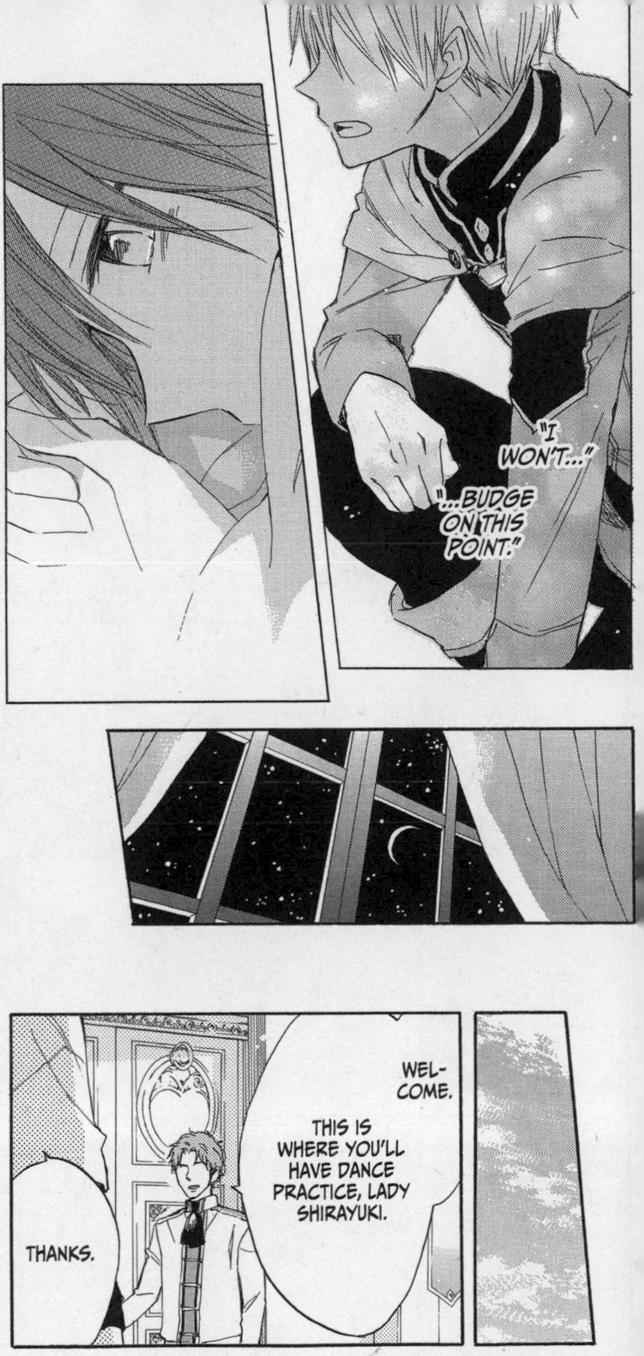
"I WON'T..."
"...BUDGE ON THIS POINT."
WEL-COME.
THIS IS WHERE YOU'LL HAVE DANCE PRACTICE, LADY SHIRAYUKI.
THANKS.

A little while back, my sister was binging rom-coms, and I ended up watching some of them with her.

During the climax of one, the lovers kiss and the camera spins 360 degrees around them three times. Then, "fin."

This type of ending seems pretty common in those films, so I tried replicating that camerawork in manga panel form...and...

It turned out like this.

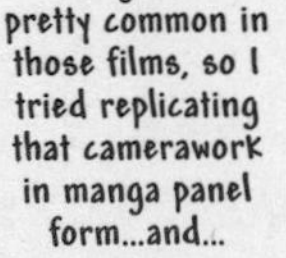

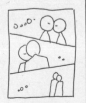

Looks like a private eye caught them smooching.

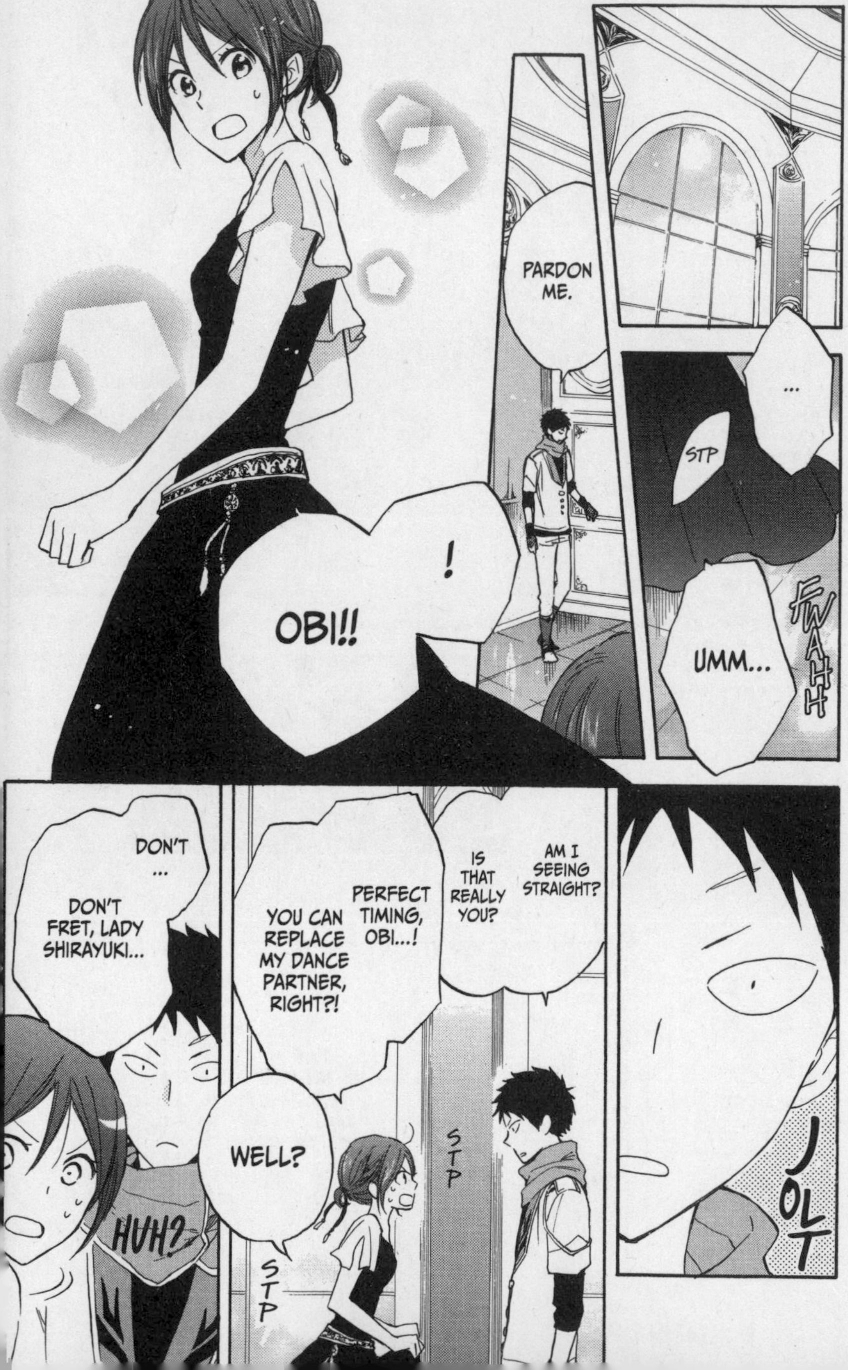
...
STP
UMM...
FWAHH
PARDON ME.
!
OBI!!
JOLT
AM I SEEING STRAIGHT?
IS THAT REALLY YOU?
PERFECT TIMING, OBI...!
YOU CAN REPLACE MY DANCE PARTNER, RIGHT?!
WELL?
STP
STP
DON'T ...
DON'T FRET, LADY SHIRAYUKI...
HUH?

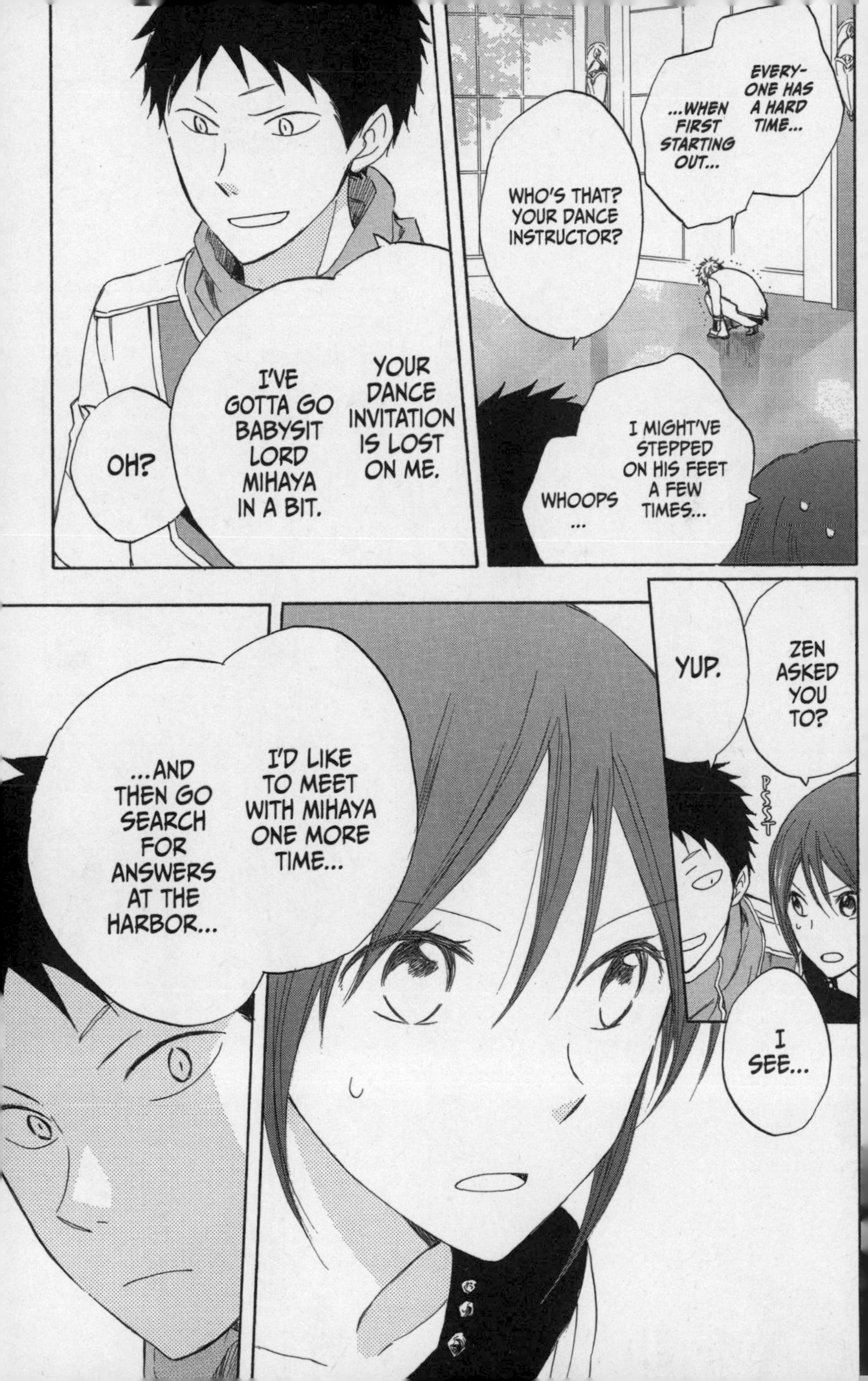
EVERY-ONE HAS A HARD TIME...
...WHEN FIRST STARTING OUT...
WHO'S THAT? YOUR DANCE INSTRUCTOR?
I MIGHT'VE STEPPED ON HIS FEET A FEW TIMES...
WHOOPS...
YOUR DANCE INVITATION IS LOST ON ME.
I'VE GOTTA GO BABYSIT LORD MIHAYA IN A BIT.
OH?
ZEN ASKED YOU TO?
YUP.
PSST
I SEE...
I'D LIKE TO MEET WITH MIHAYA ONE MORE TIME...
...AND THEN GO SEARCH FOR ANSWERS AT THE HARBOR...

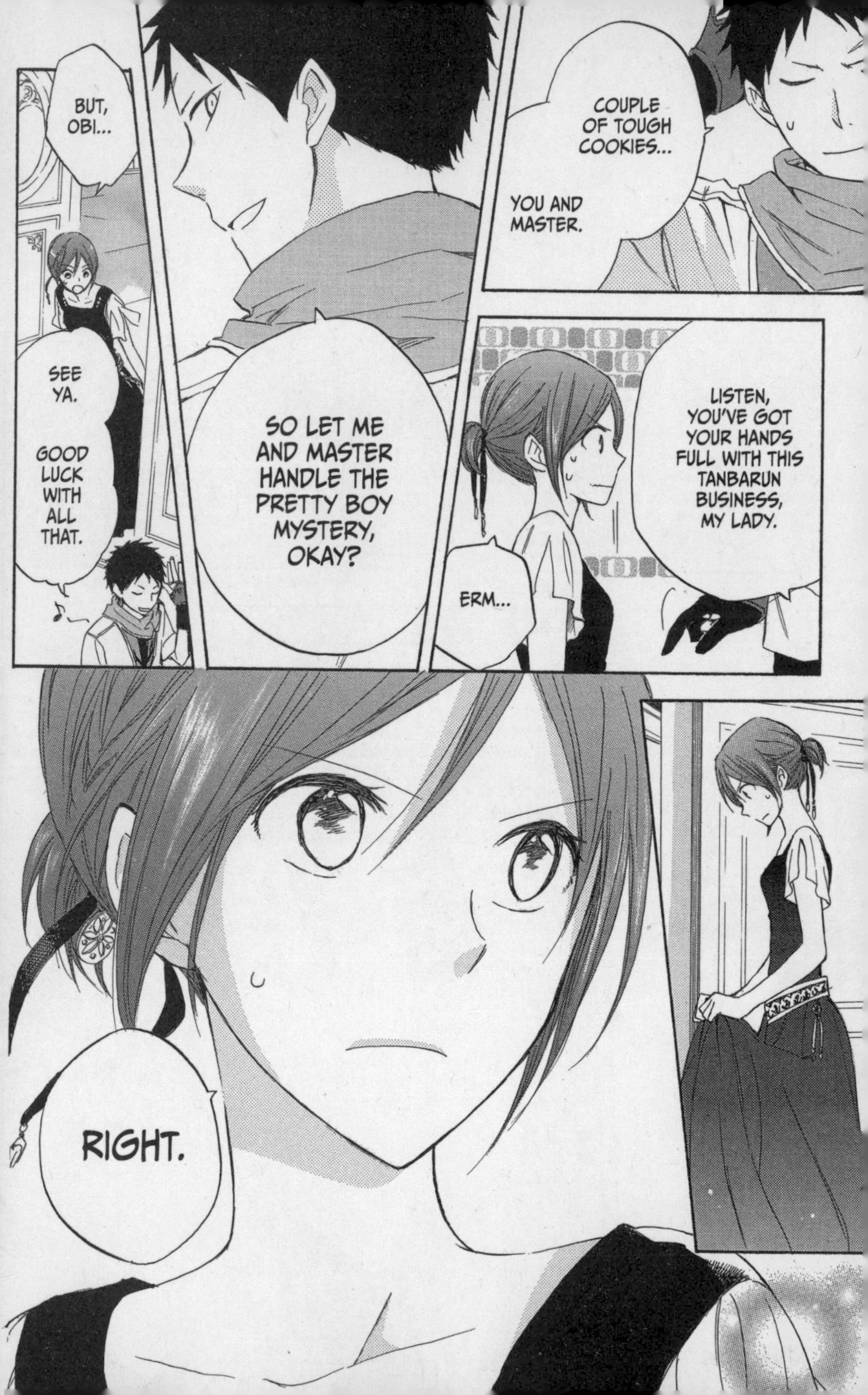
COUPLE OF TOUGH COOKIES...
YOU AND MASTER.
LISTEN, YOU'VE GOT YOUR HANDS FULL WITH THIS TANBARUN BUSINESS, MY LADY.
ERM...
SO LET ME AND MASTER HANDLE THE PRETTY BOY MYSTERY, OKAY?
BUT, OBI...
SEE YA.
GOOD LUCK WITH ALL THAT.
RIGHT.

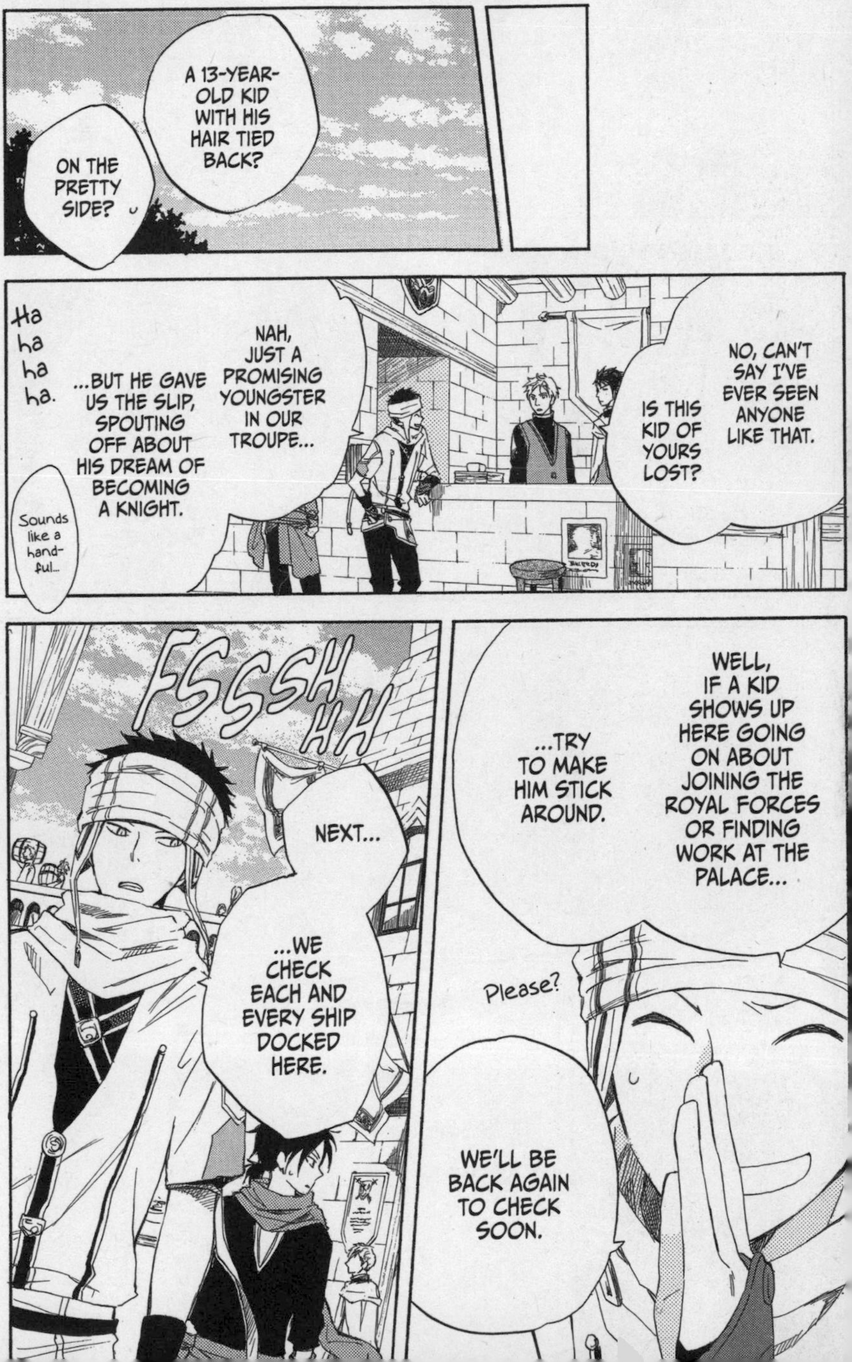
A 13-YEAR-OLD KID WITH HIS HAIR TIED BACK?
ON THE PRETTY SIDE?
NO, CAN'T SAY I'VE EVER SEEN ANYONE LIKE THAT.
IS THIS KID OF YOURS LOST?
NAH, JUST A PROMISING YOUNGSTER IN OUR TROUPE...
...BUT HE GAVE US THE SLIP, SPOUTING OFF ABOUT HIS DREAM OF BECOMING A KNIGHT.
Ha ha ha ha.
Sounds like a hand-ful...
WELL, IF A KID SHOWS UP HERE GOING ON ABOUT JOINING THE ROYAL FORCES OR FINDING WORK AT THE PALACE...
...TRY TO MAKE HIM STICK AROUND.
Please?
WE'LL BE BACK AGAIN TO CHECK SOON.
FSSSHHH
NEXT...
...WE CHECK EACH AND EVERY SHIP DOCKED HERE.

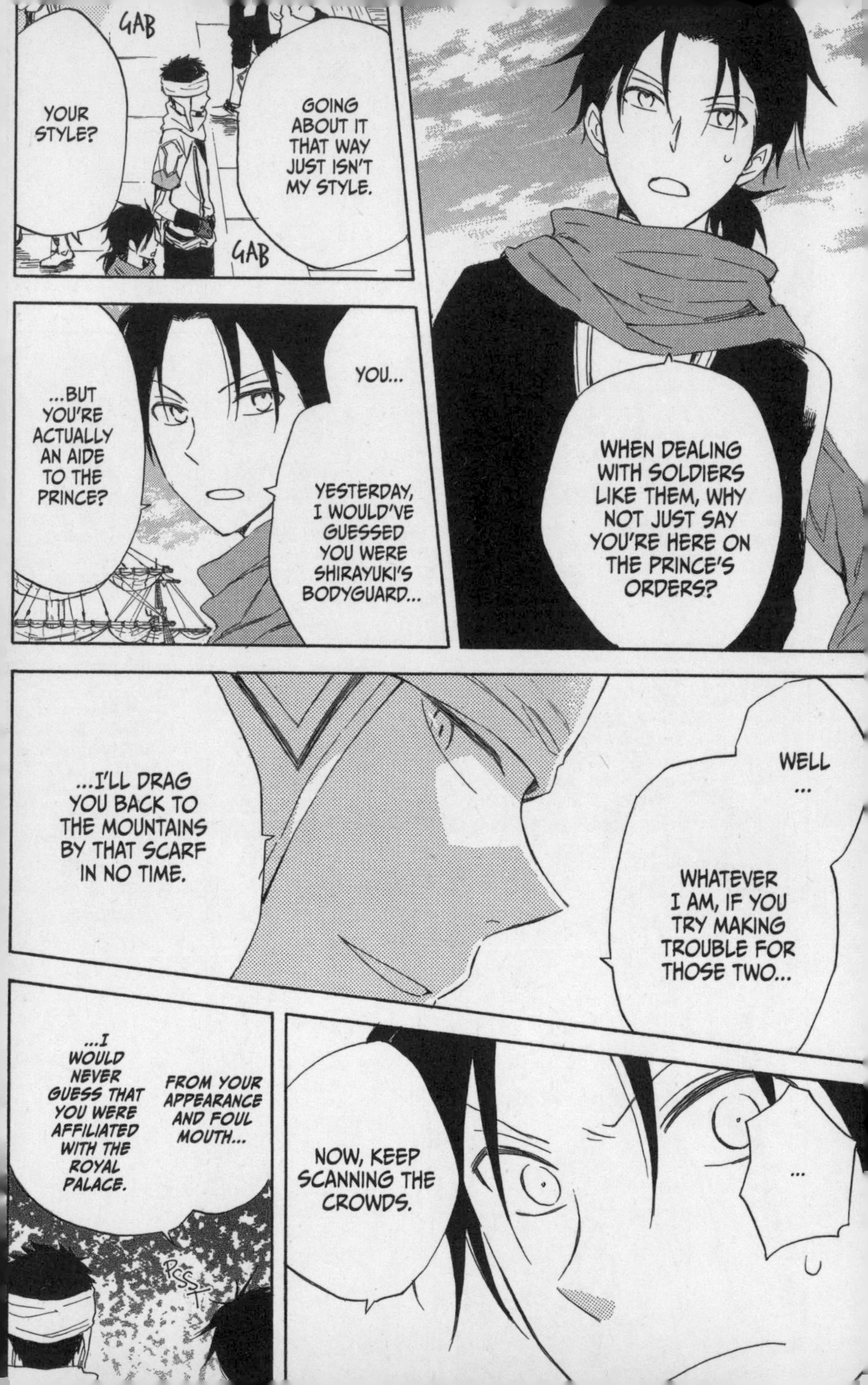
WHEN DEALING WITH SOLDIERS LIKE THEM, WHY NOT JUST SAY YOU'RE HERE ON THE PRINCE'S ORDERS?
GAB
GOING ABOUT IT THAT WAY JUST ISN'T MY STYLE.
YOUR STYLE?
GAB
YOU...
YESTERDAY, I WOULD'VE GUESSED YOU WERE SHIRAYUKI'S BODYGUARD...
...BUT YOU'RE ACTUALLY AN AIDE TO THE PRINCE?
WELL ...
WHATEVER I AM, IF YOU TRY MAKING TROUBLE FOR THOSE TWO...
...I'LL DRAG YOU BACK TO THE MOUNTAINS BY THAT SCARF IN NO TIME.
...
NOW, KEEP SCANNING THE CROWDS.
FROM YOUR APPEARANCE AND FOUL MOUTH...
...I WOULD NEVER GUESS THAT YOU WERE AFFILIATED WITH THE ROYAL PALACE.
PSST

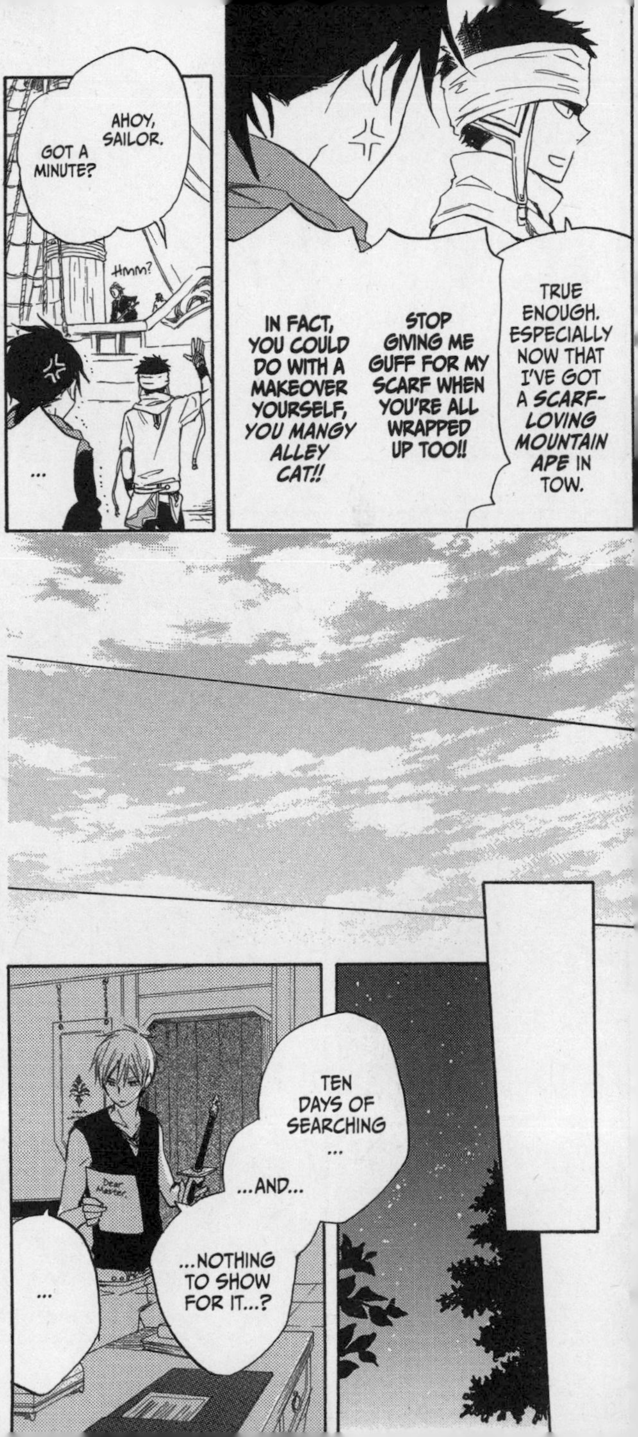
TRUE ENOUGH. ESPECIALLY NOW THAT I'VE GOT A *SCARF-LOVING MOUNTAIN APE* IN TOW.
STOP GIVING ME GUFF FOR MY SCARF WHEN YOU'RE ALL WRAPPED UP TOO!!
IN FACT, YOU COULD DO WITH A MAKEOVER YOURSELF, *YOU MANGY ALLEY CAT!!*
AHOY, SAILOR.
GOT A MINUTE?
Hmm?
...
TEN DAYS OF SEARCHING ...
...AND...
...NOTHING TO SHOW FOR IT...?
Dear Master,
...

Chapter 19

Note that Izana has begun to address Shirayuki more casually.

Beyond that, this chapter has Obi and Mihaya squabbling with each other. I doubt they'll ever get along.

Most of the characters in this series are on good terms, so it's actually fun for me when two of them don't see eye to eye.

I wonder if they'll ever show up together again?

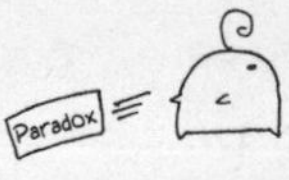
Paradox

I also like it when a boy and a girl don't get along. Those relationships are weirdly cute, once you step away and give them some time.

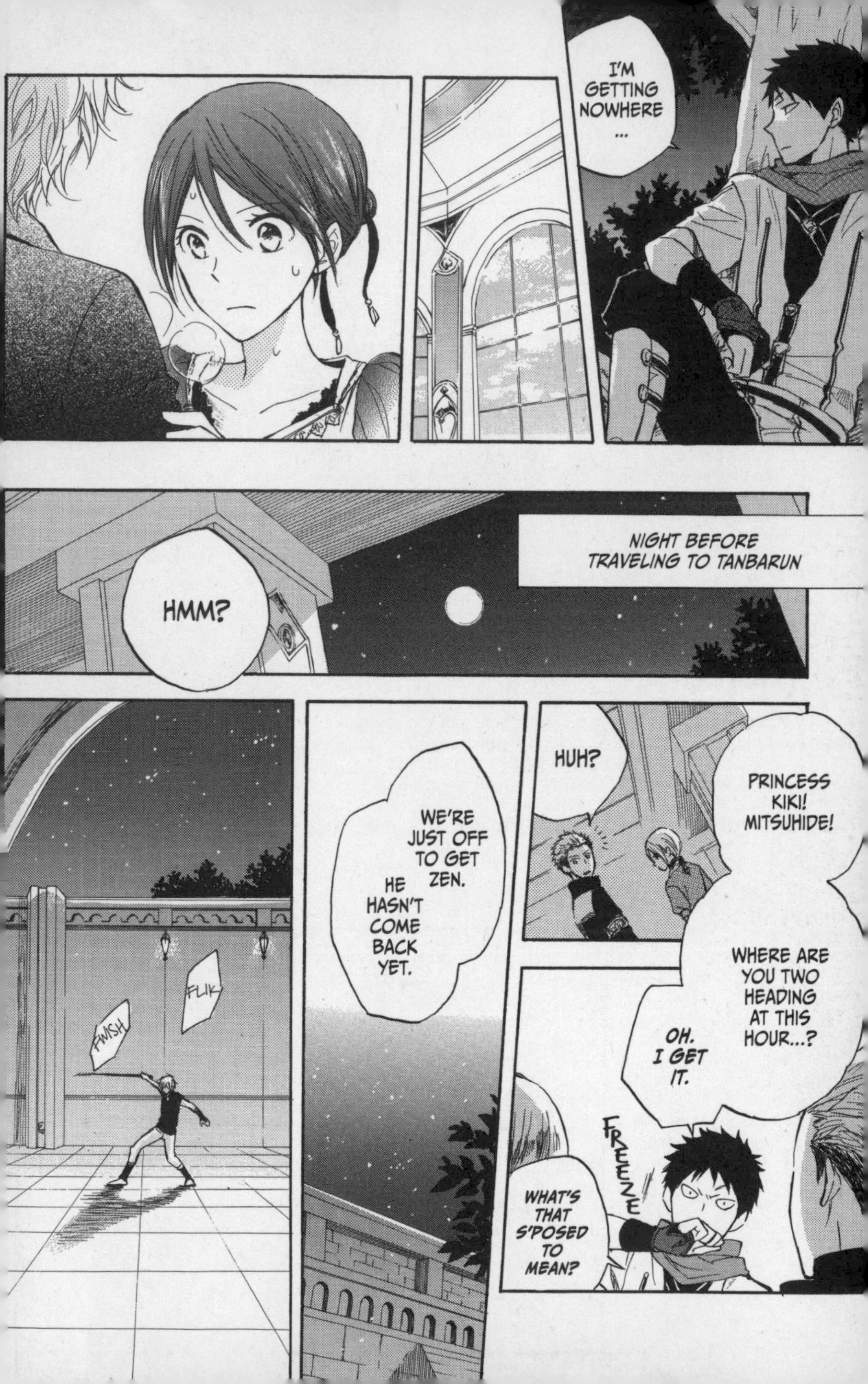
I'M GETTING NOWHERE ...
NIGHT BEFORE TRAVELING TO TANBARUN
HMM?
PRINCESS KIKI! MITSUHIDE!
HUH?
WHERE ARE YOU TWO HEADING AT THIS HOUR...?
WE'RE JUST OFF TO GET ZEN.
HE HASN'T COME BACK YET.
OH. I GET IT.
FREEZE
WHAT'S THAT S'POSED TO MEAN?
FLIK
FWISH

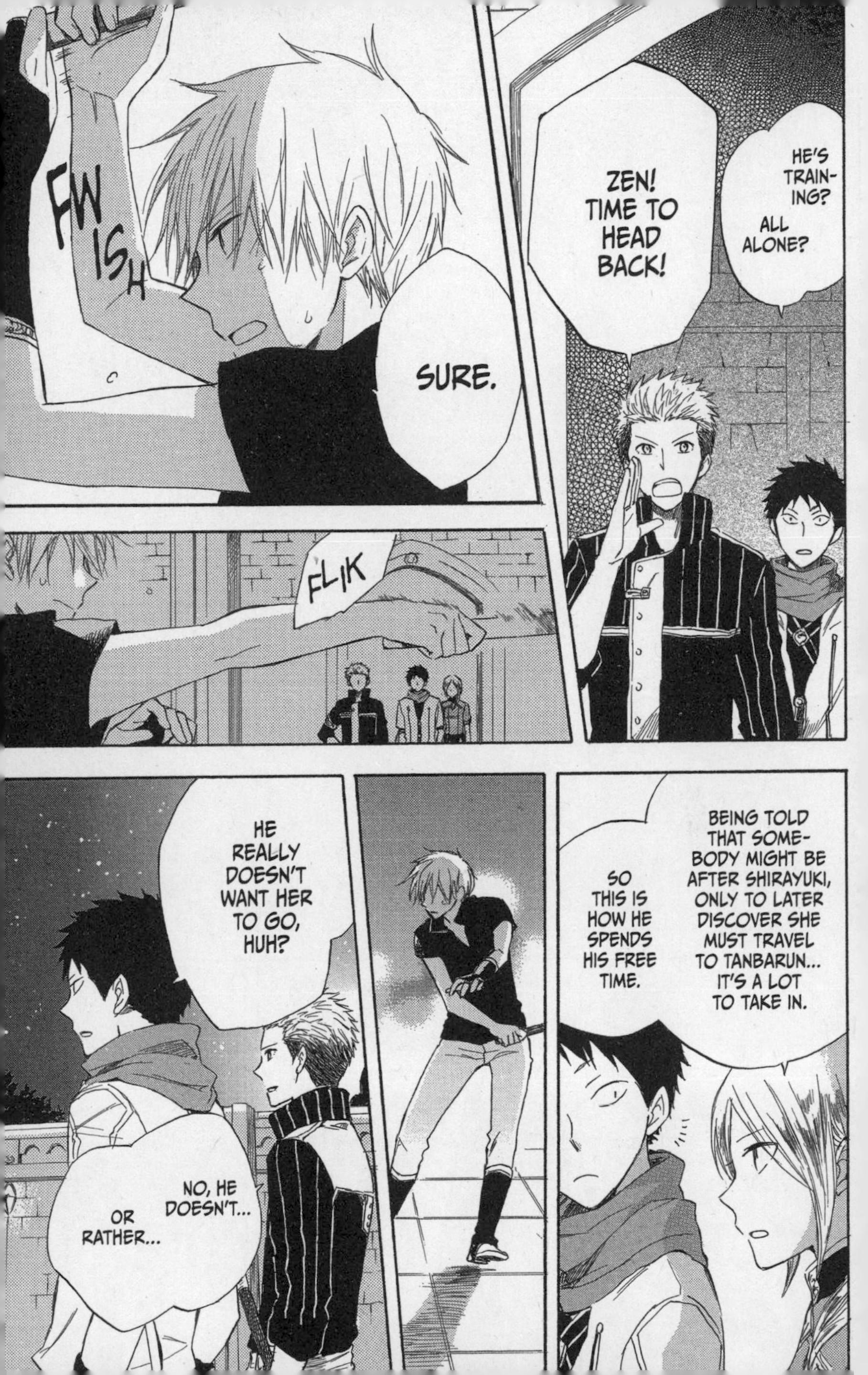
HE'S TRAIN-ING?
ALL ALONE?
ZEN! TIME TO HEAD BACK!
FWISH
SURE.
FLIK
BEING TOLD THAT SOME-BODY MIGHT BE AFTER SHIRAYUKI, ONLY TO LATER DISCOVER SHE MUST TRAVEL TO TANBARUN... IT'S A LOT TO TAKE IN.
SO THIS IS HOW HE SPENDS HIS FREE TIME.
HE REALLY DOESN'T WANT HER TO GO, HUH?
NO, HE DOESN'T...
OR RATHER...

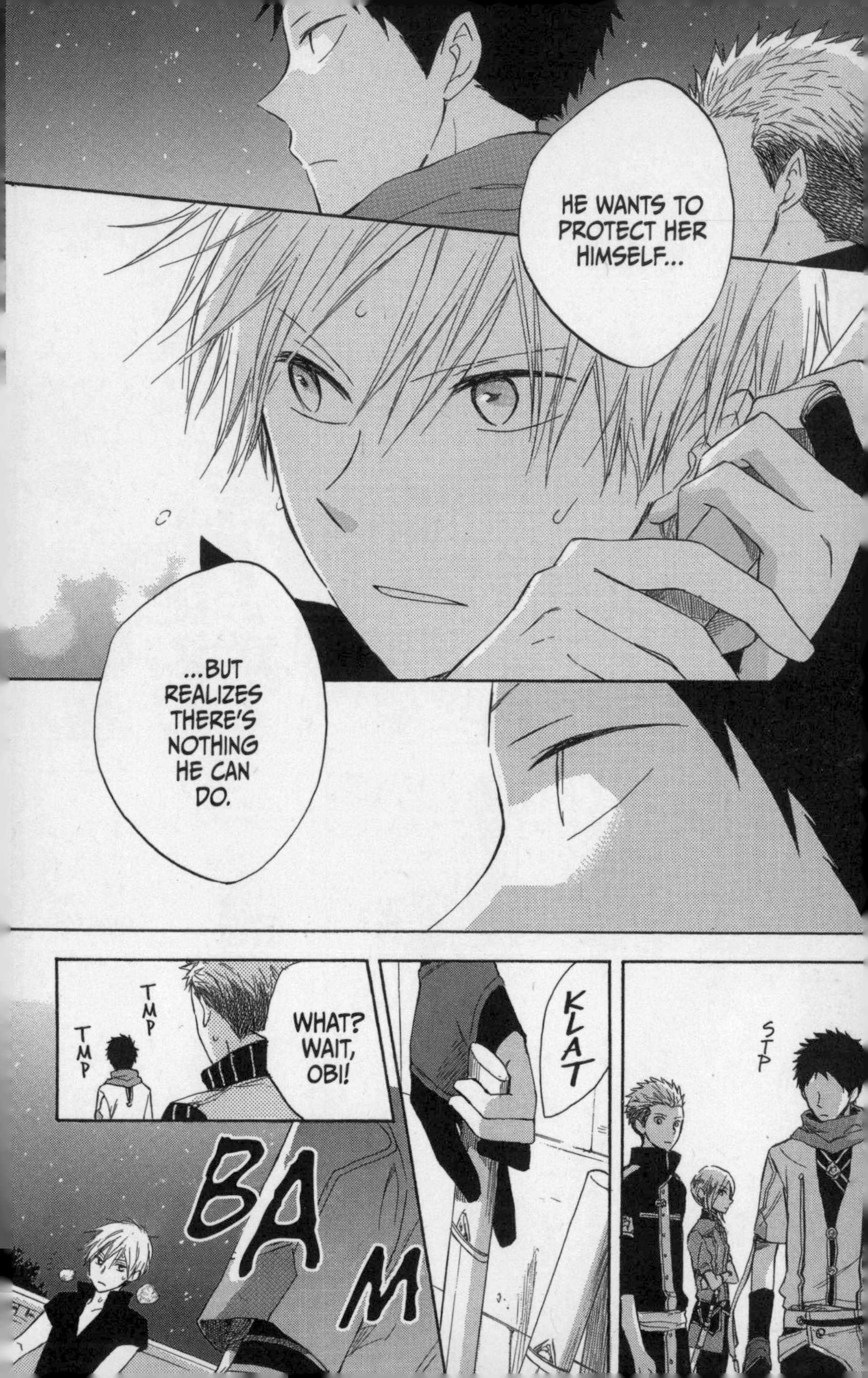
HE WANTS TO PROTECT HER HIMSELF...
...BUT REALIZES THERE'S NOTHING HE CAN DO.
STP
KLAT
WHAT? WAIT, OBI!
TMP
TMP
BAM

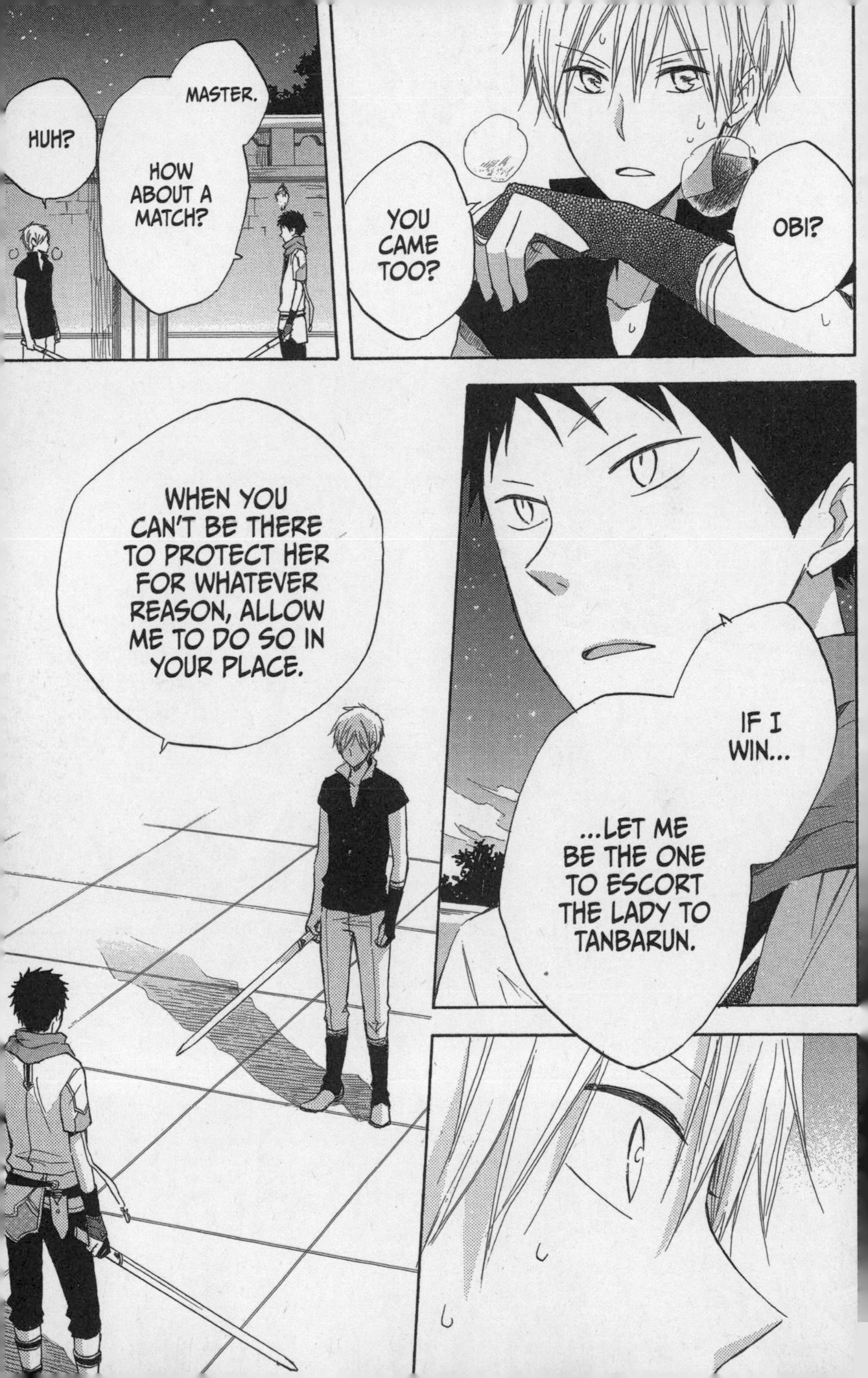
OBI?
YOU CAME TOO?
MASTER. HOW ABOUT A MATCH?
HUH?
IF I WIN...
...LET ME BE THE ONE TO ESCORT THE LADY TO TANBARUN.
WHEN YOU CAN'T BE THERE TO PROTECT HER FOR WHATEVER REASON, ALLOW ME TO DO SO IN YOUR PLACE.

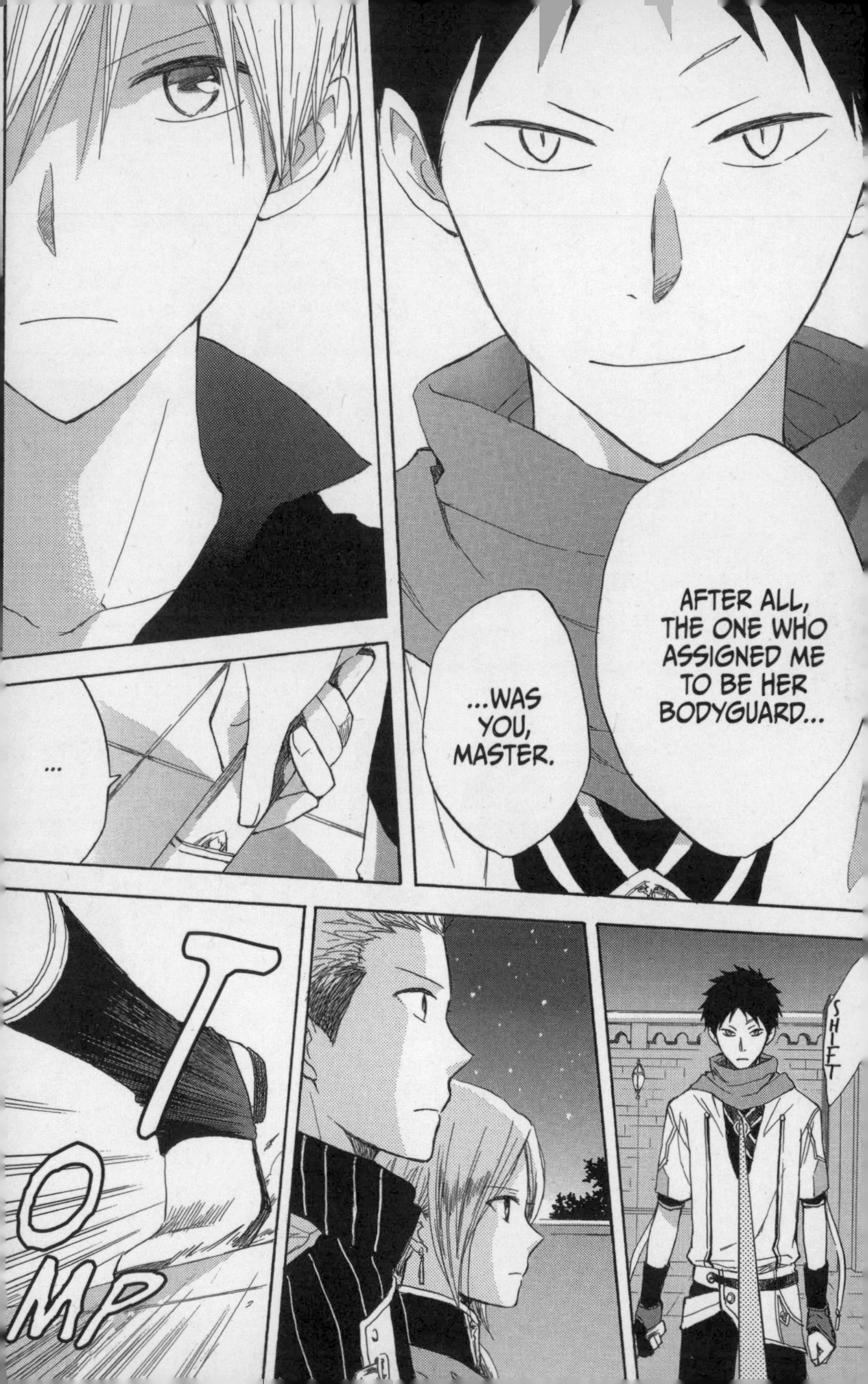
AFTER ALL, THE ONE WHO ASSIGNED ME TO BE HER BODYGUARD...
...WAS YOU, MASTER.
...
SHIFT
TOMP

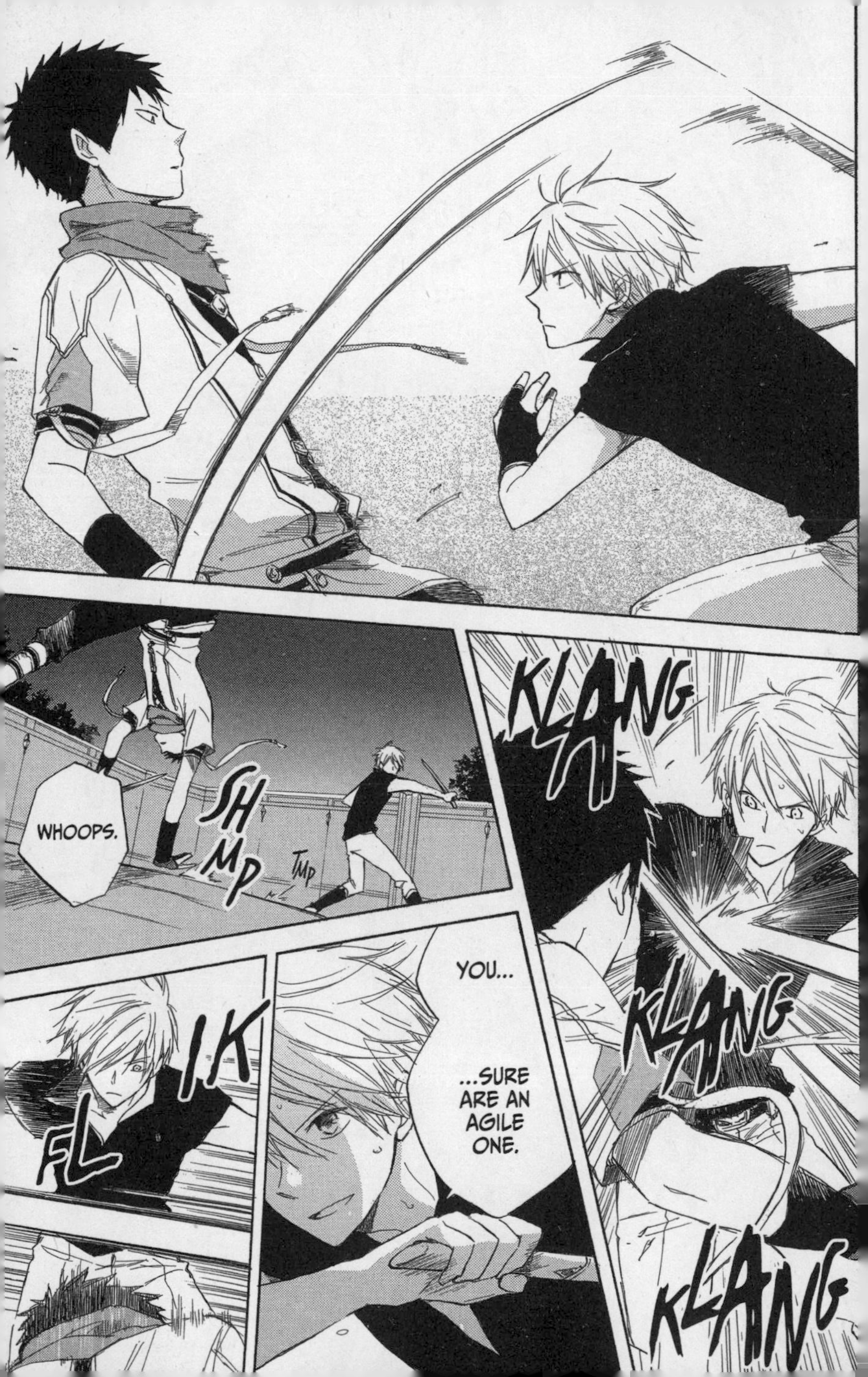
KLANG
KLANG
KLANG
WHOOPS.
SHMP
TMP
YOU...
...SURE ARE AN AGILE ONE.
FLIK

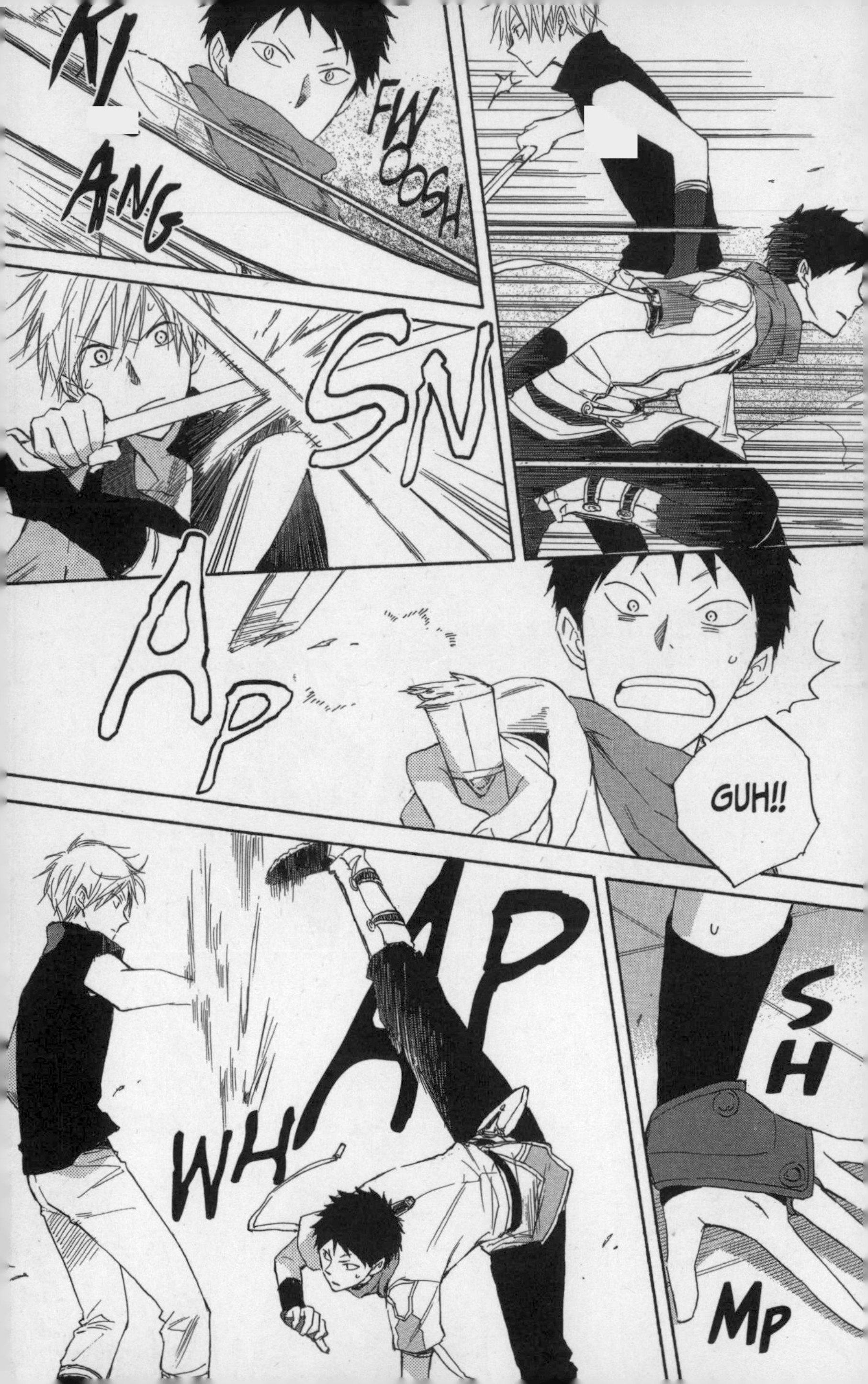
KI ANG
FWOOSH
SNAP
GUH!!
SHMp
WHAP

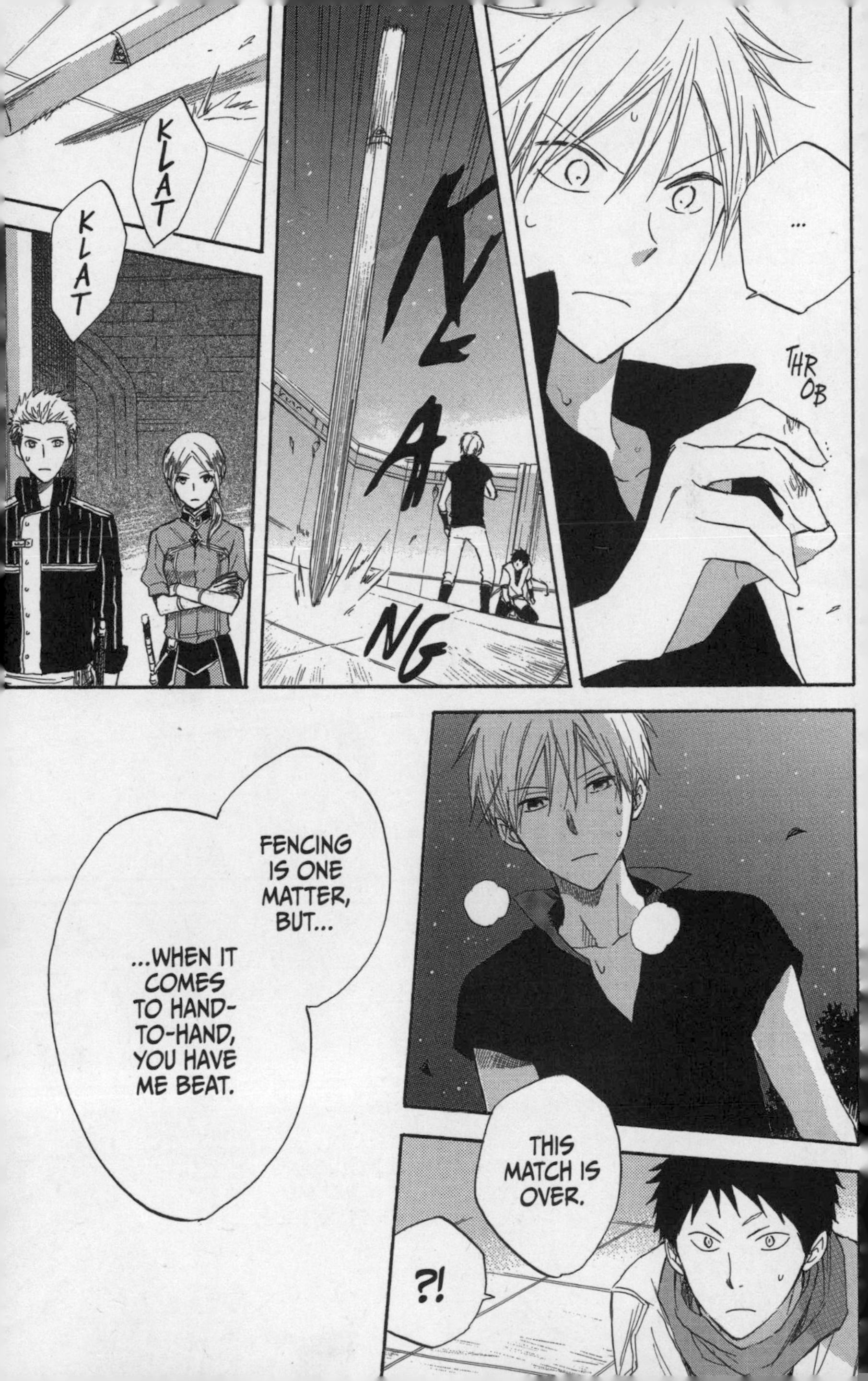
...
THROB
KLANG
KLAT
KLAT
FENCING IS ONE MATTER, BUT...
...WHEN IT COMES TO HAND-TO-HAND, YOU HAVE ME BEAT.
THIS MATCH IS OVER.
?!

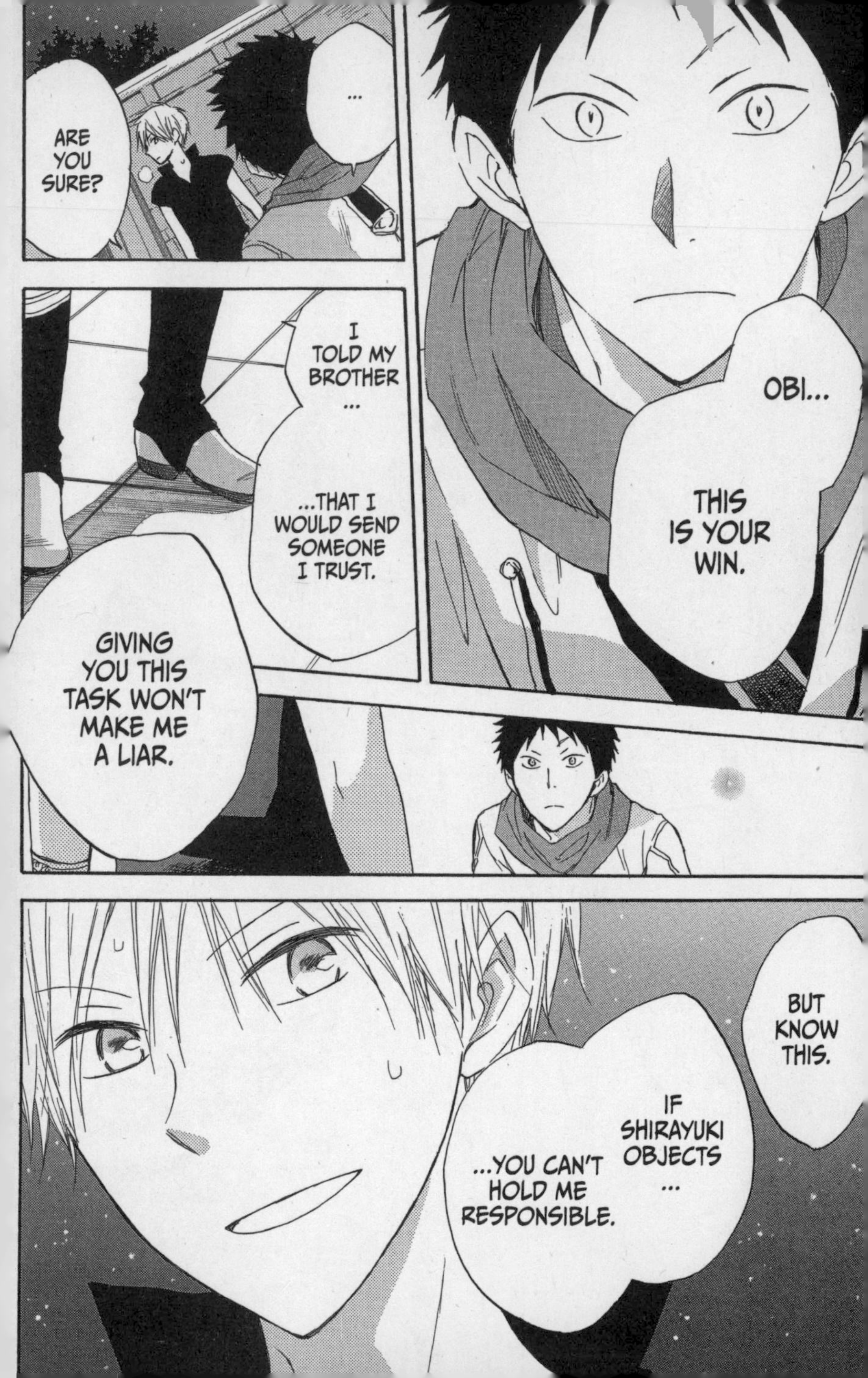
OBI...
THIS IS YOUR WIN.
...
ARE YOU SURE?
I TOLD MY BROTHER...
...THAT I WOULD SEND SOMEONE I TRUST.
GIVING YOU THIS TASK WON'T MAKE ME A LIAR.
BUT KNOW THIS.
IF SHIRAYUKI OBJECTS...
...YOU CAN'T HOLD ME RESPONSIBLE.

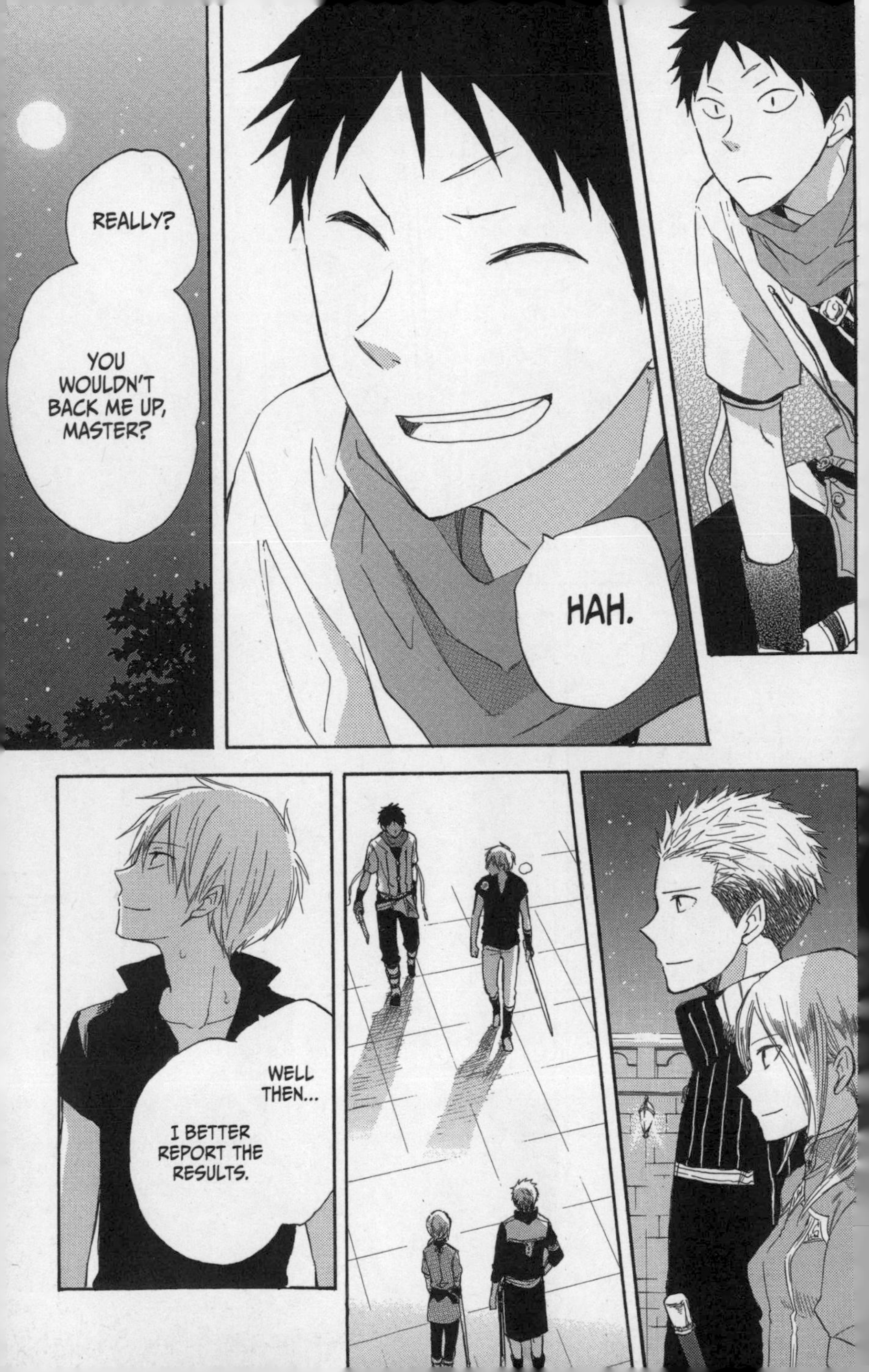
HAH.
REALLY?
YOU WOULDN'T BACK ME UP, MASTER?
WELL THEN...
I BETTER REPORT THE RESULTS.

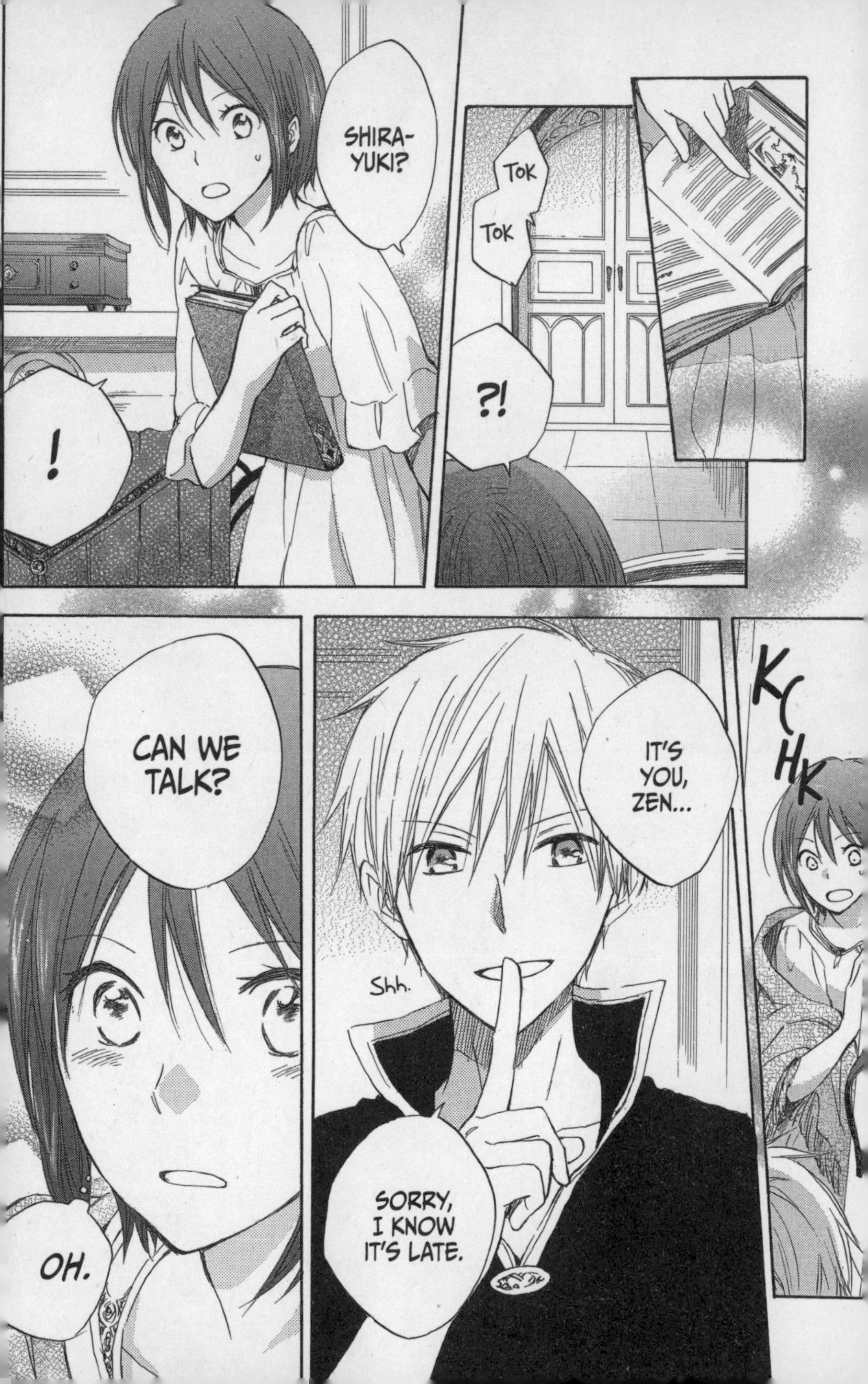
TOK
TOK
?!
SHIRA-YUKI?
!
K(HK
IT'S YOU, ZEN...
Shh.
SORRY, I KNOW IT'S LATE.
CAN WE TALK?
OH.

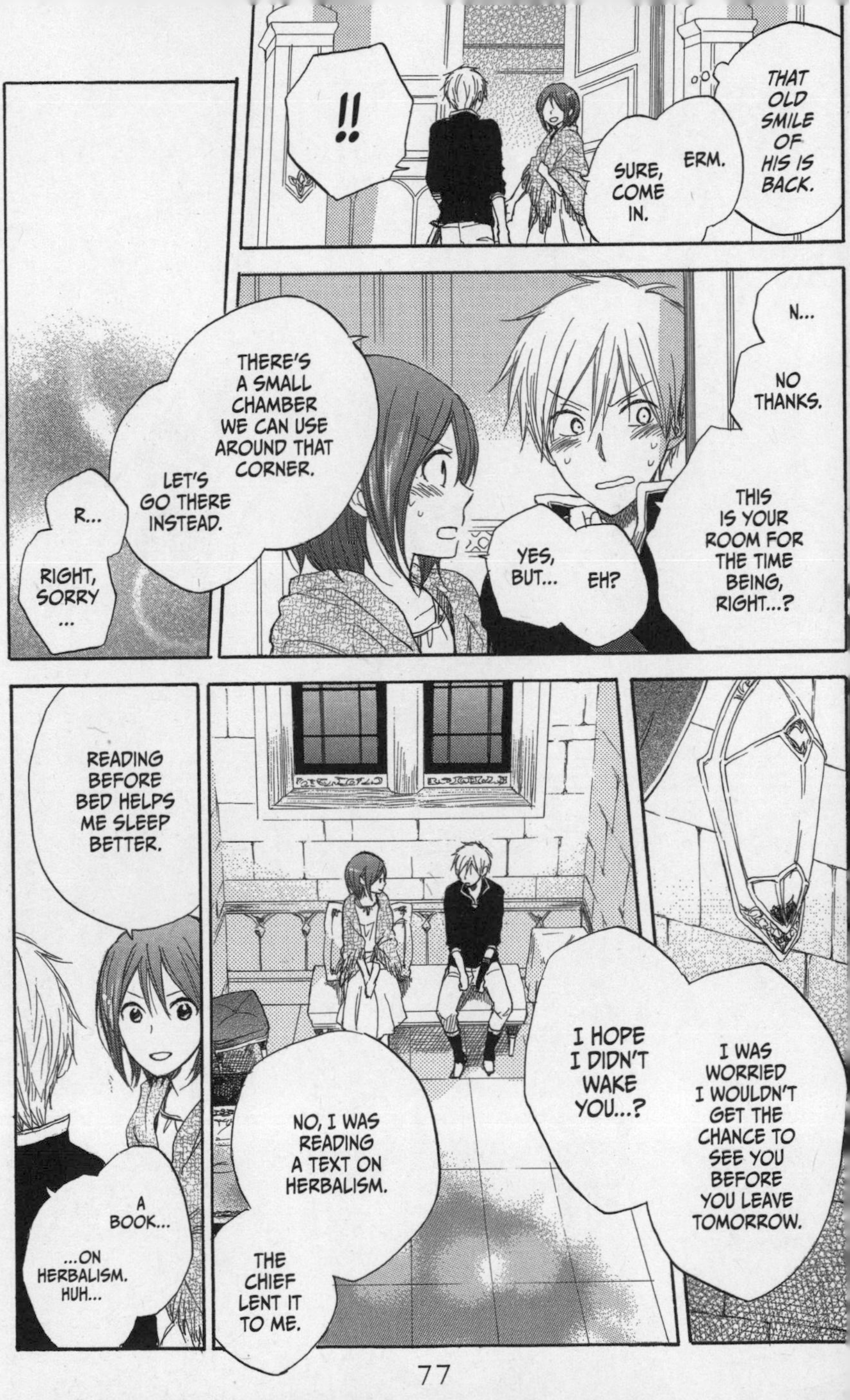
THAT OLD SMILE OF HIS IS BACK.
ERM.
SURE, COME IN.
!!
N...
NO THANKS.
THIS IS YOUR ROOM FOR THE TIME BEING, RIGHT...?
EH?
YES, BUT...
THERE'S A SMALL CHAMBER WE CAN USE AROUND THAT CORNER.
LET'S GO THERE INSTEAD.
R...
RIGHT, SORRY ...
I WAS WORRIED I WOULDN'T GET THE CHANCE TO SEE YOU BEFORE YOU LEAVE TOMORROW.
I HOPE I DIDN'T WAKE YOU...?
NO, I WAS READING A TEXT ON HERBALISM.
THE CHIEF LENT IT TO ME.
READING BEFORE BED HELPS ME SLEEP BETTER.
A BOOK...
...ON HERBALISM. HUH...

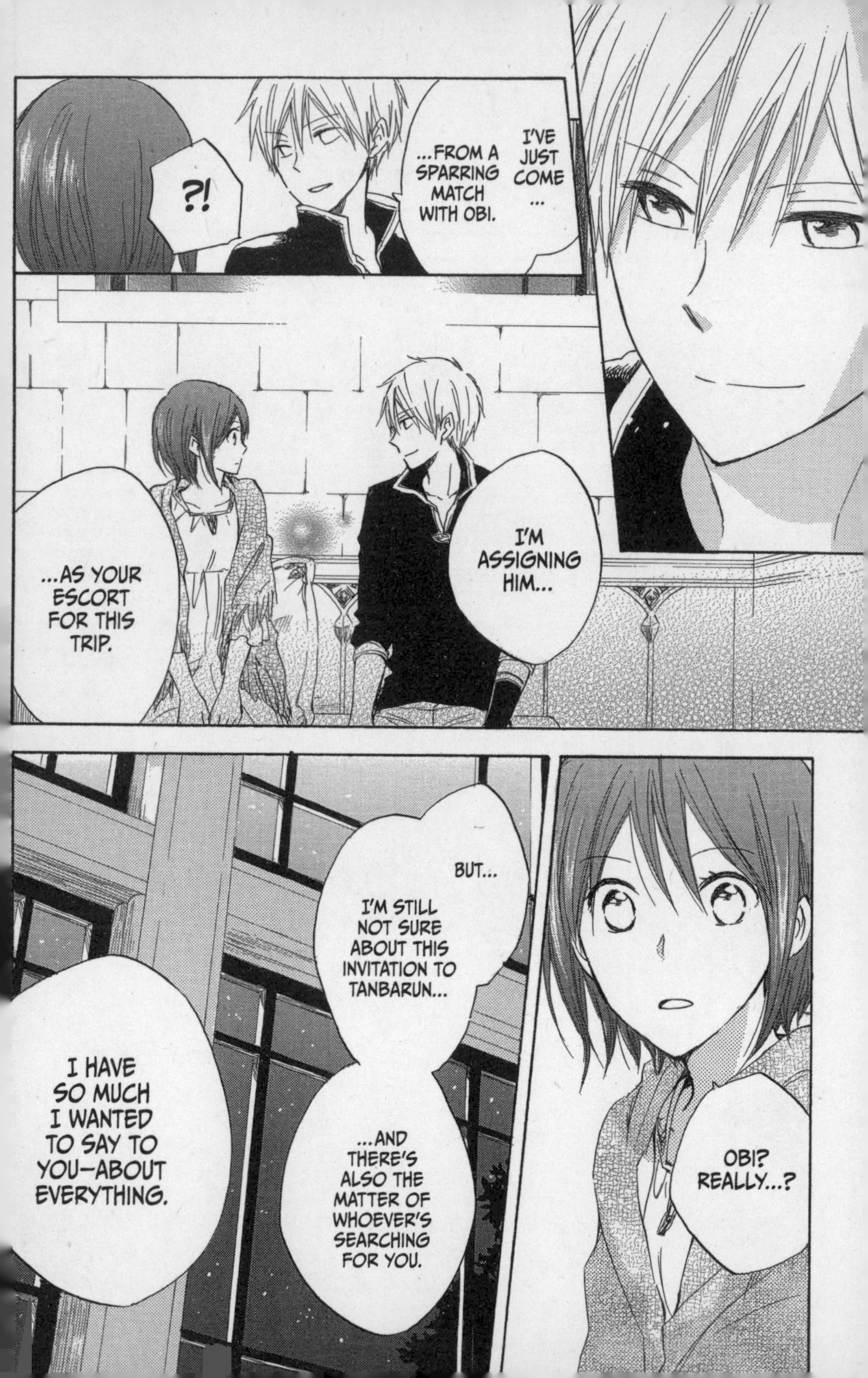
I'VE JUST COME ...
...FROM A SPARRING MATCH WITH OBI.
?!
I'M ASSIGNING HIM...
...AS YOUR ESCORT FOR THIS TRIP.
OBI? REALLY...?
BUT...
I'M STILL NOT SURE ABOUT THIS INVITATION TO TANBARUN...
...AND THERE'S ALSO THE MATTER OF WHOEVER'S SEARCHING FOR YOU.
I HAVE SO MUCH I WANTED TO SAY TO YOU—ABOUT EVERYTHING.

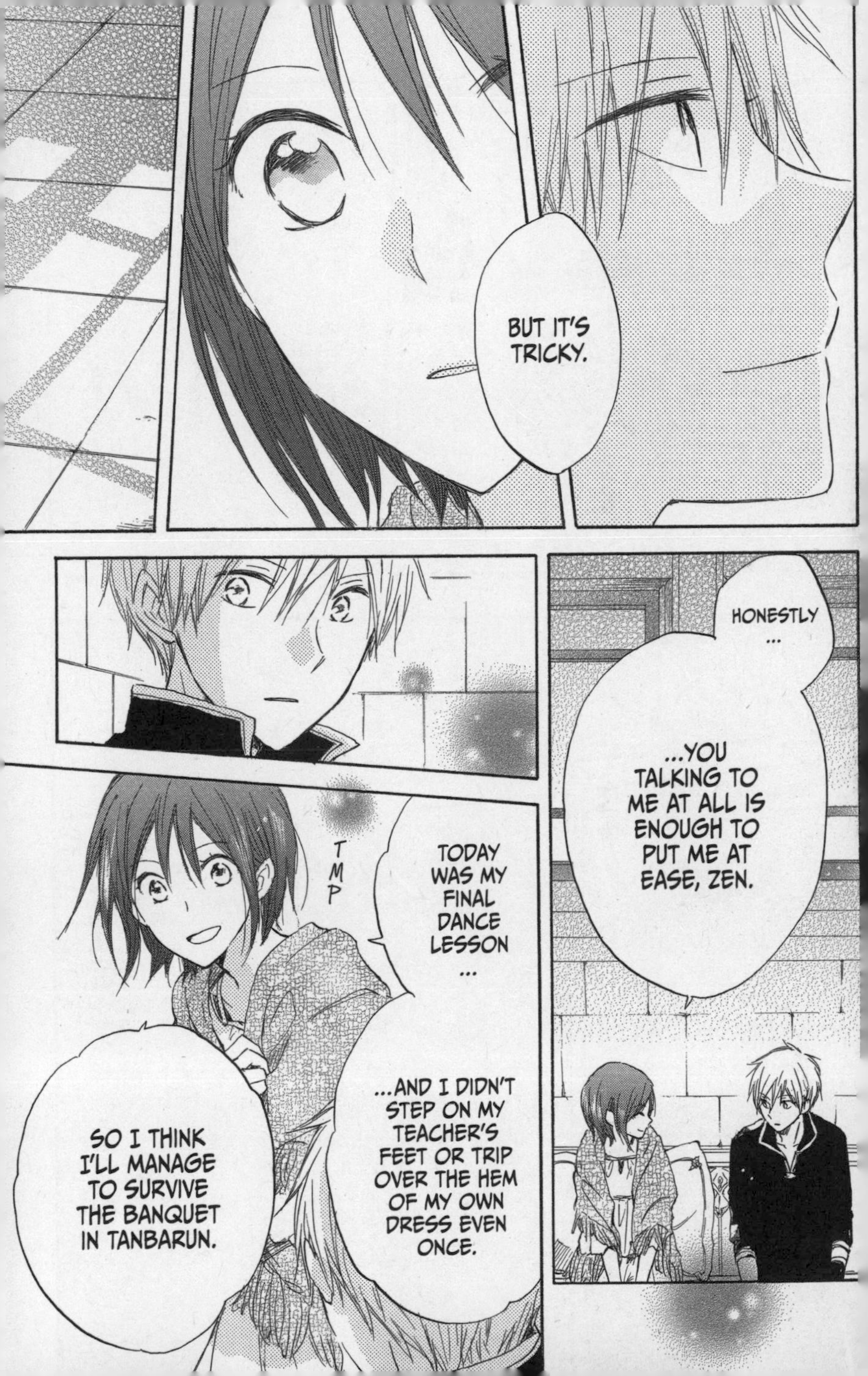
BUT IT'S TRICKY.
HONESTLY ...
...YOU TALKING TO ME AT ALL IS ENOUGH TO PUT ME AT EASE, ZEN.
TMP
TODAY WAS MY FINAL DANCE LESSON ...
...AND I DIDN'T STEP ON MY TEACHER'S FEET OR TRIP OVER THE HEM OF MY OWN DRESS EVEN ONCE.
SO I THINK I'LL MANAGE TO SURVIVE THE BANQUET IN TANBARUN.

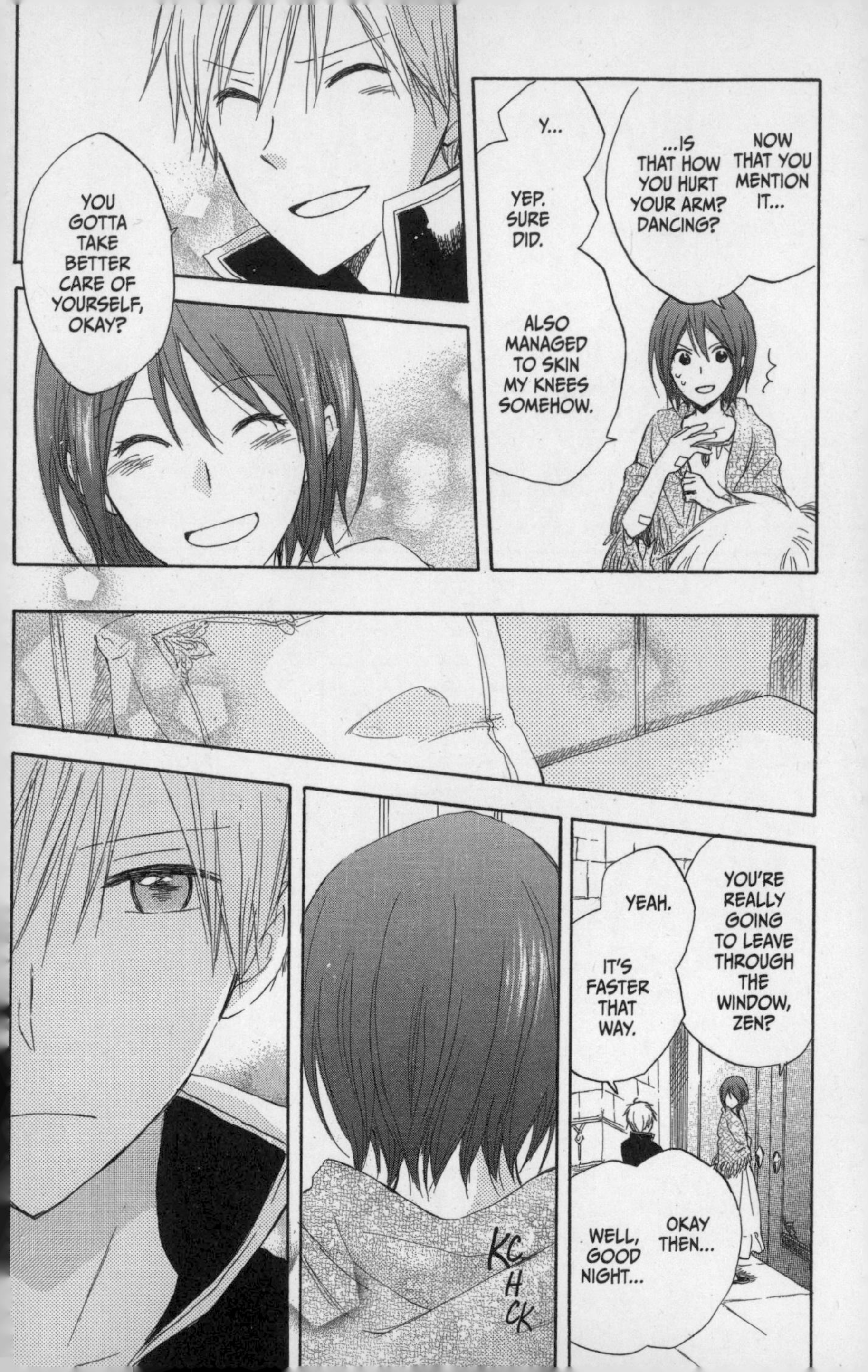
NOW THAT YOU MENTION IT...
...IS THAT HOW YOU HURT YOUR ARM? DANCING?
Y...
YEP. SURE DID.
ALSO MANAGED TO SKIN MY KNEES SOMEHOW.
YOU GOTTA TAKE BETTER CARE OF YOURSELF, OKAY?
YOU'RE REALLY GOING TO LEAVE THROUGH THE WINDOW, ZEN?
YEAH.
IT'S FASTER THAT WAY.
OKAY THEN...
WELL, GOOD NIGHT...
KCHCK

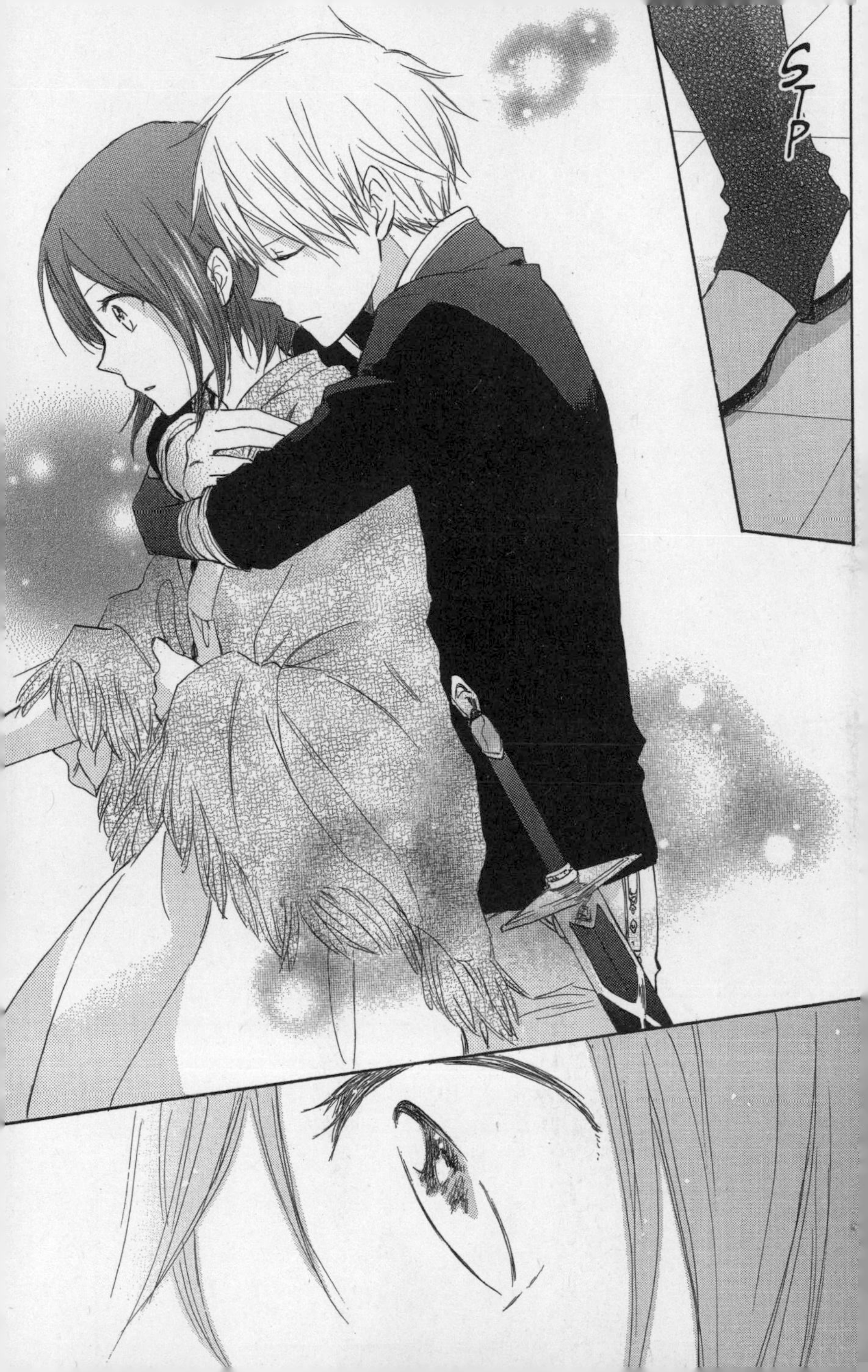
STP

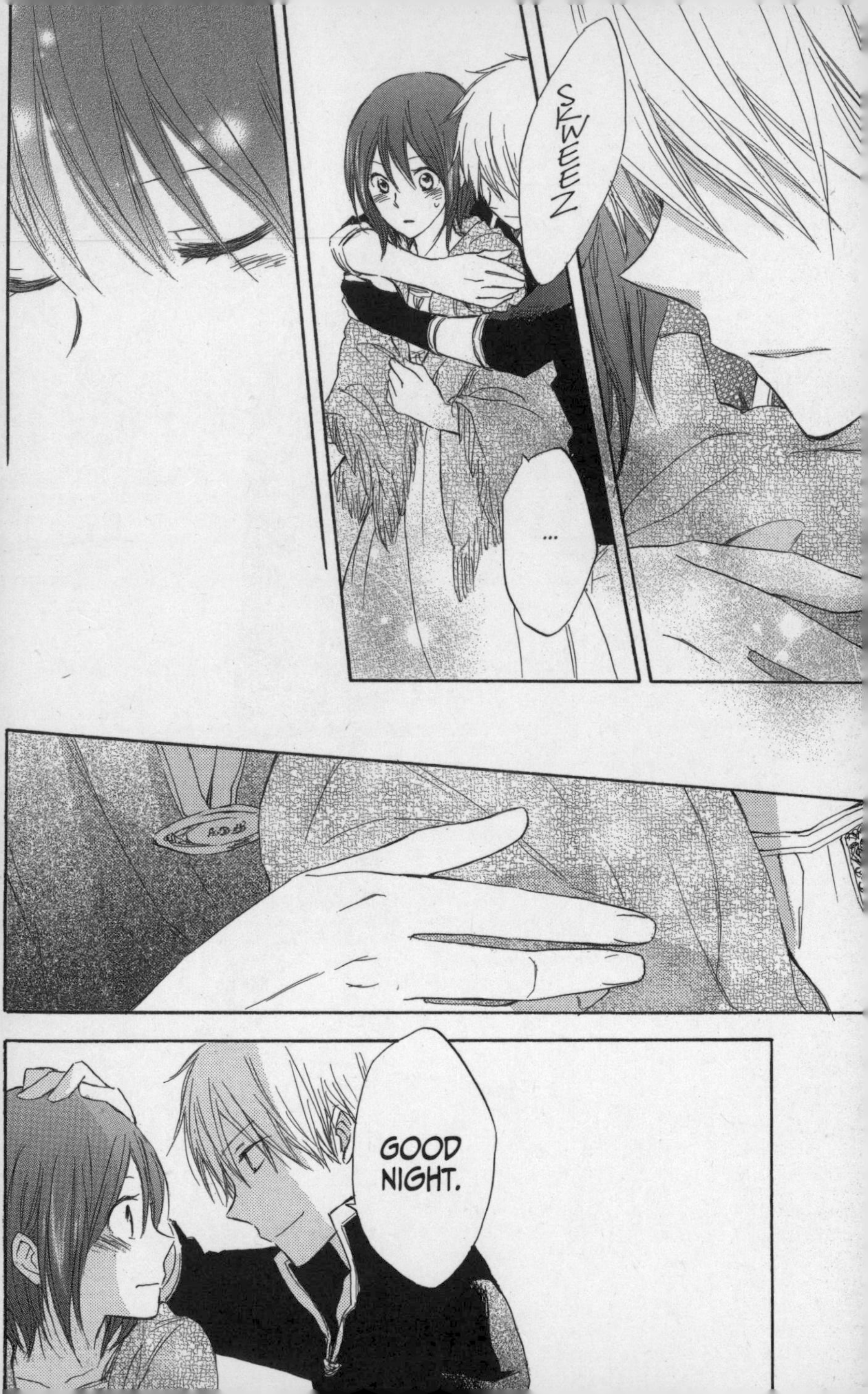
SKWEEZ
...
GOOD NIGHT.

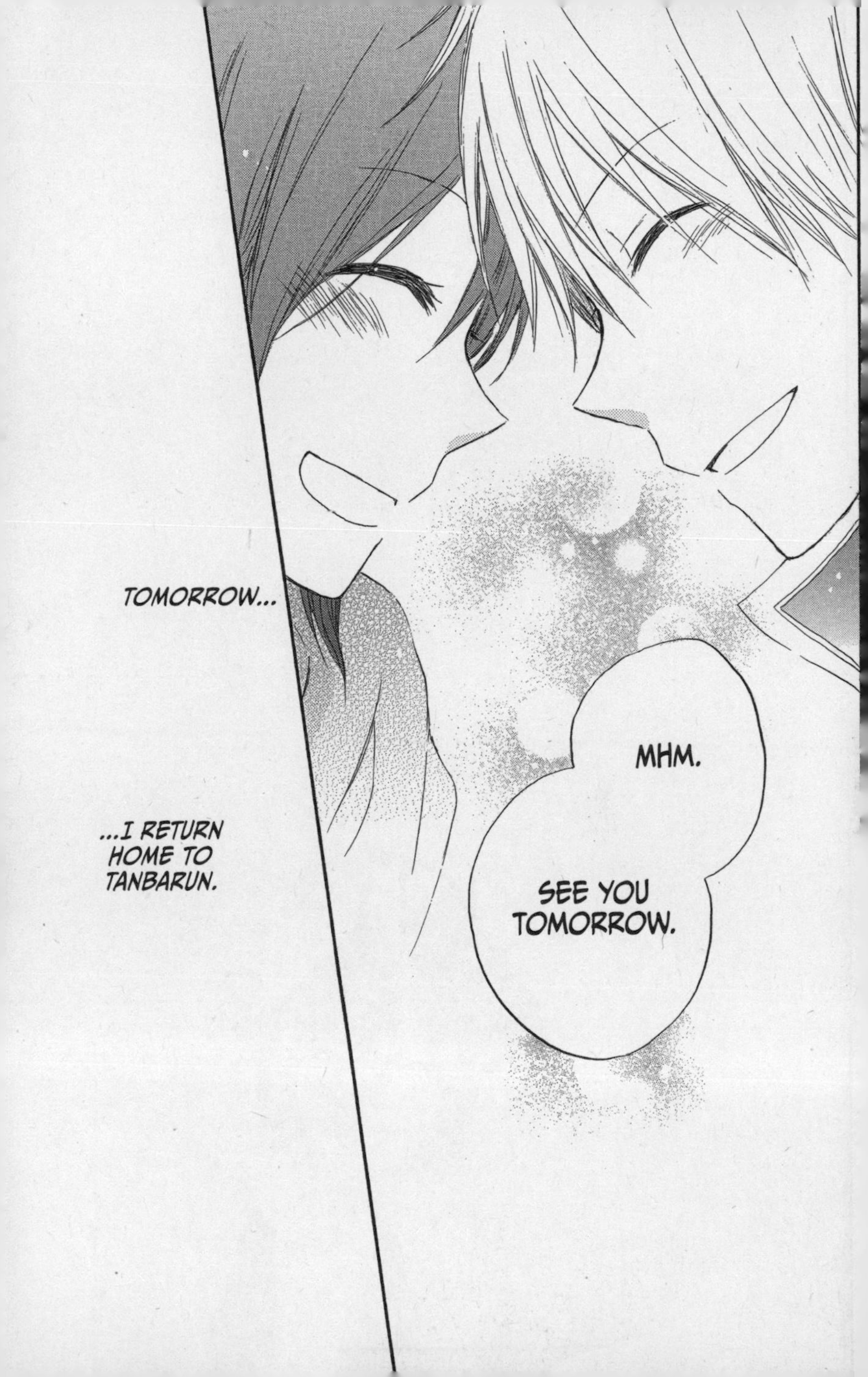
MHM.
SEE YOU TOMORROW.
TOMORROW...
...I RETURN HOME TO TANBARUN.

Chapter 20

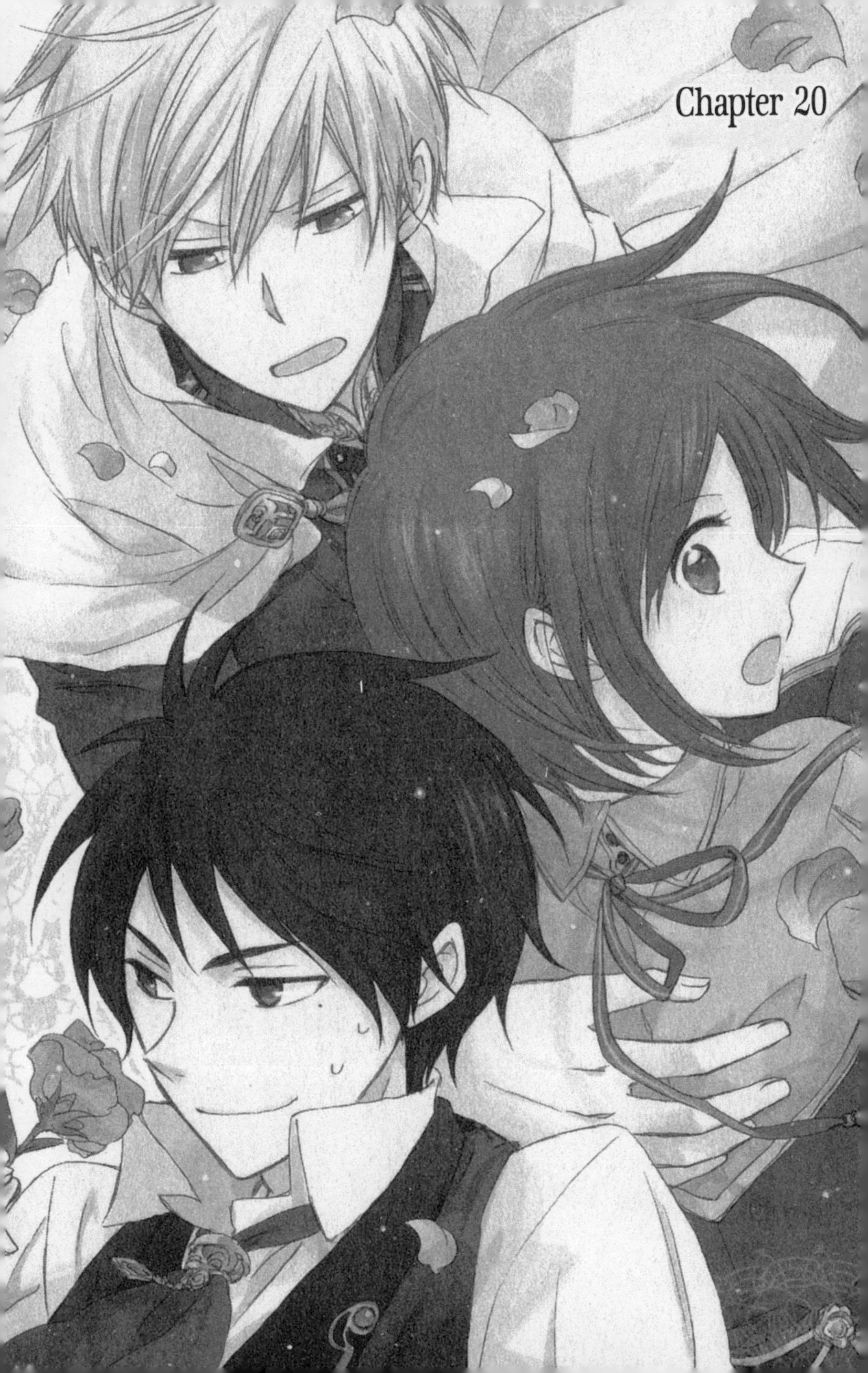

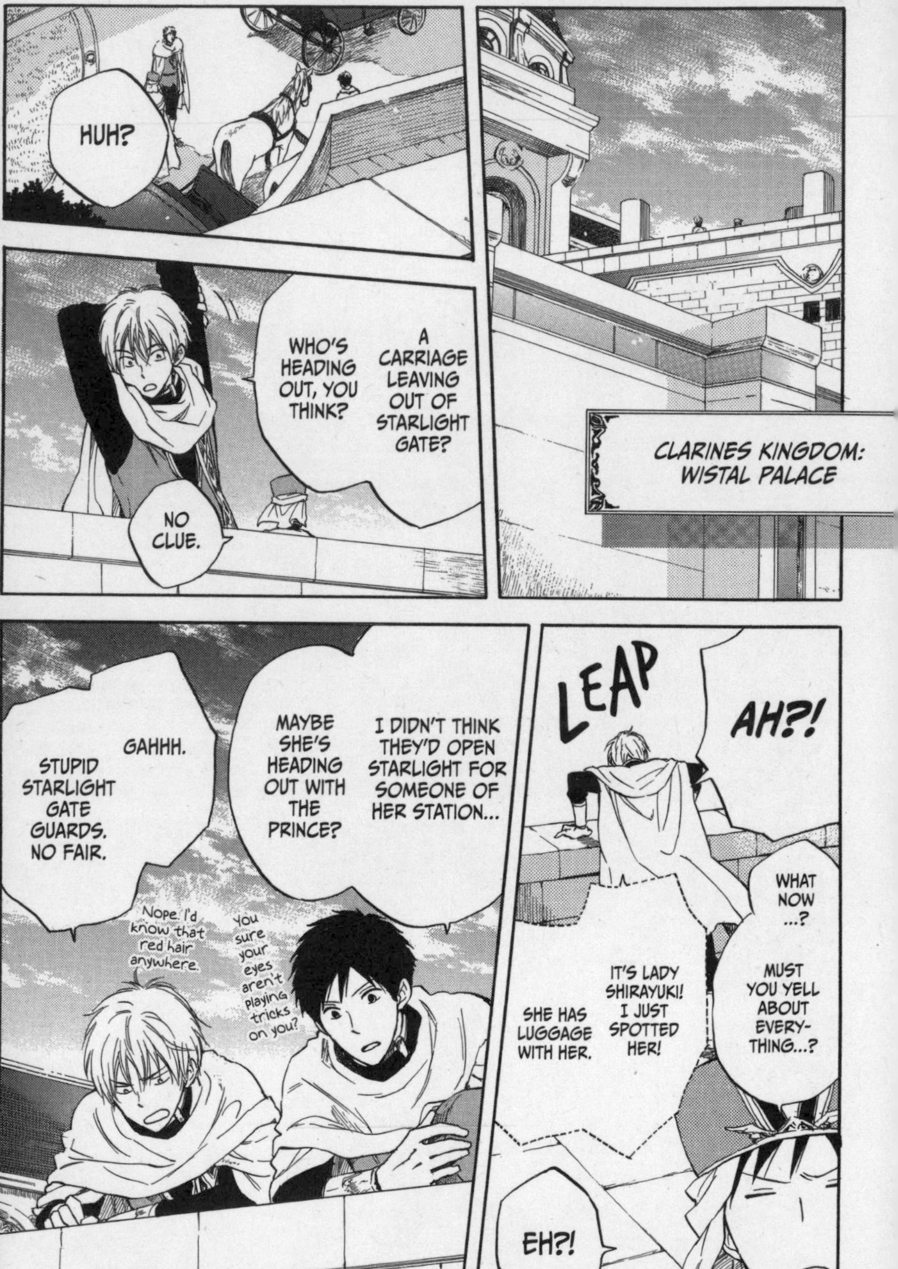
CLARINES KINGDOM: WISTAL PALACE
HUH?
A CARRIAGE LEAVING OUT OF STARLIGHT GATE?
WHO'S HEADING OUT, YOU THINK?
NO CLUE.
AH?!
LEAP
WHAT NOW ...?
MUST YOU YELL ABOUT EVERY-THING...?
IT'S LADY SHIRAYUKI! I JUST SPOTTED HER!
SHE HAS LUGGAGE WITH HER.
EH?!
I DIDN'T THINK THEY'D OPEN STARLIGHT FOR SOMEONE OF HER STATION...
MAYBE SHE'S HEADING OUT WITH THE PRINCE?
GAHHH.
STUPID STARLIGHT GATE GUARDS. NO FAIR.
You sure your eyes aren't playing tricks on you?
Nope. I'd know that red hair anywhere.

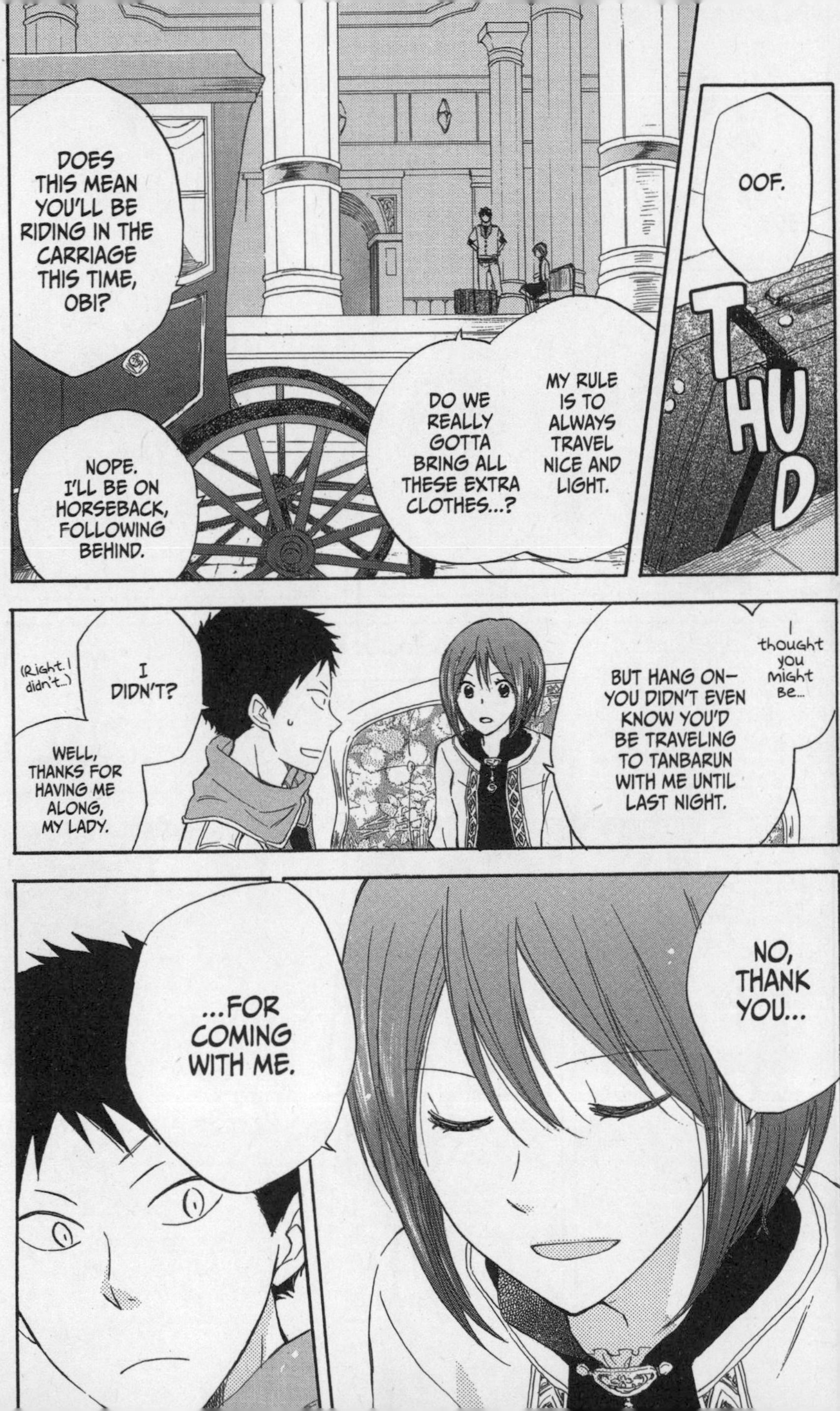
OOF.
THUD
MY RULE IS TO ALWAYS TRAVEL NICE AND LIGHT.
DO WE REALLY GOTTA BRING ALL THESE EXTRA CLOTHES...?
DOES THIS MEAN YOU'LL BE RIDING IN THE CARRIAGE THIS TIME, OBI?
NOPE. I'LL BE ON HORSEBACK, FOLLOWING BEHIND.
I thought you might be...
BUT HANG ON— YOU DIDN'T EVEN KNOW YOU'D BE TRAVELING TO TANBARUN WITH ME UNTIL LAST NIGHT.
I DIDN'T?
(Right. I didn't...)
WELL, THANKS FOR HAVING ME ALONG, MY LADY.
NO, THANK YOU...
...FOR COMING WITH ME.

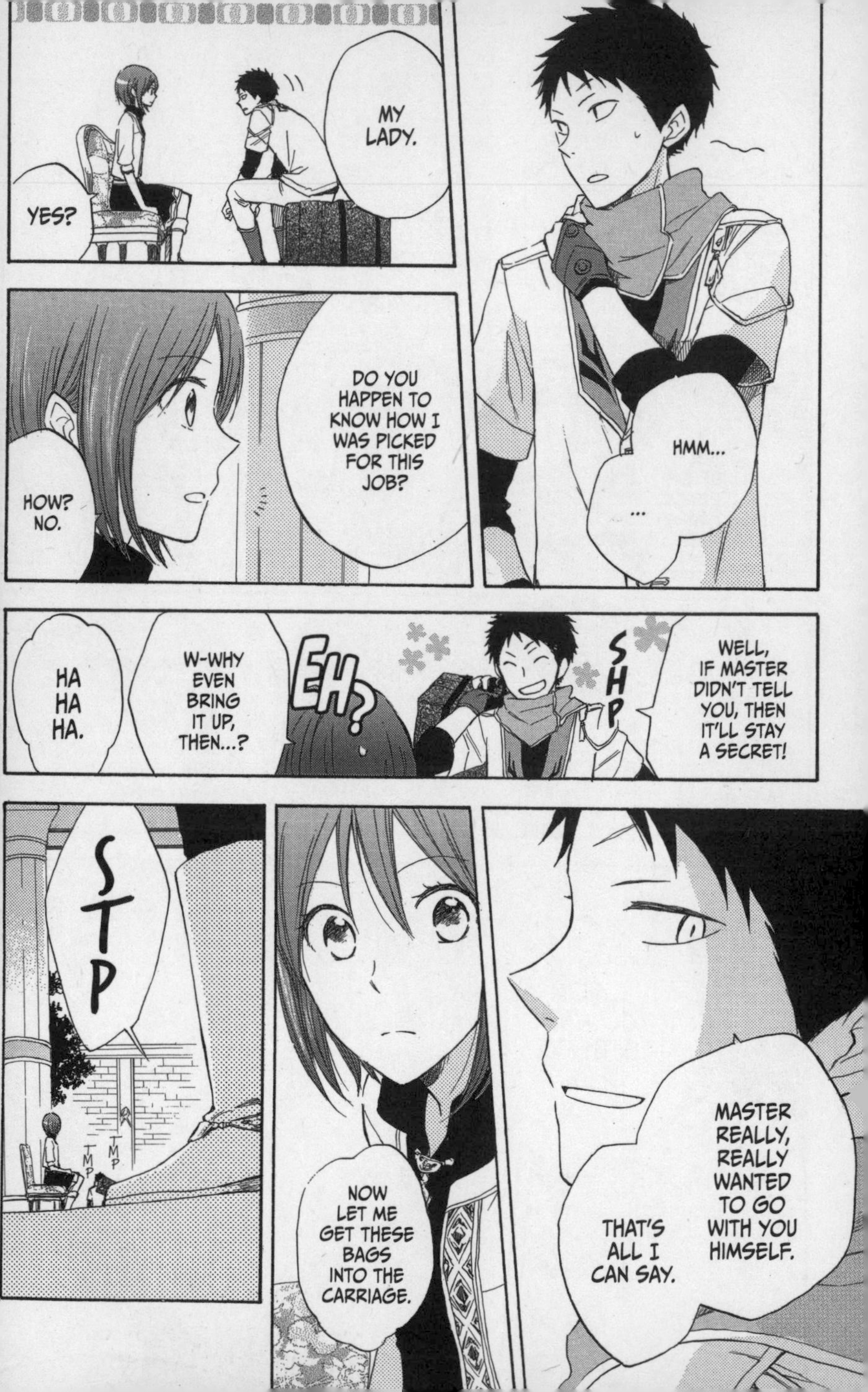
HMM...
...
MY LADY.
YES?
DO YOU HAPPEN TO KNOW HOW I WAS PICKED FOR THIS JOB?
HOW? NO.
WELL, IF MASTER DIDN'T TELL YOU, THEN IT'LL STAY A SECRET!
SHP
EH?
W-WHY EVEN BRING IT UP, THEN...?
HA HA HA.
MASTER REALLY, REALLY WANTED TO GO WITH YOU HIMSELF.
THAT'S ALL I CAN SAY.
NOW LET ME GET THESE BAGS INTO THE CARRIAGE.
STP
TMP
TMP

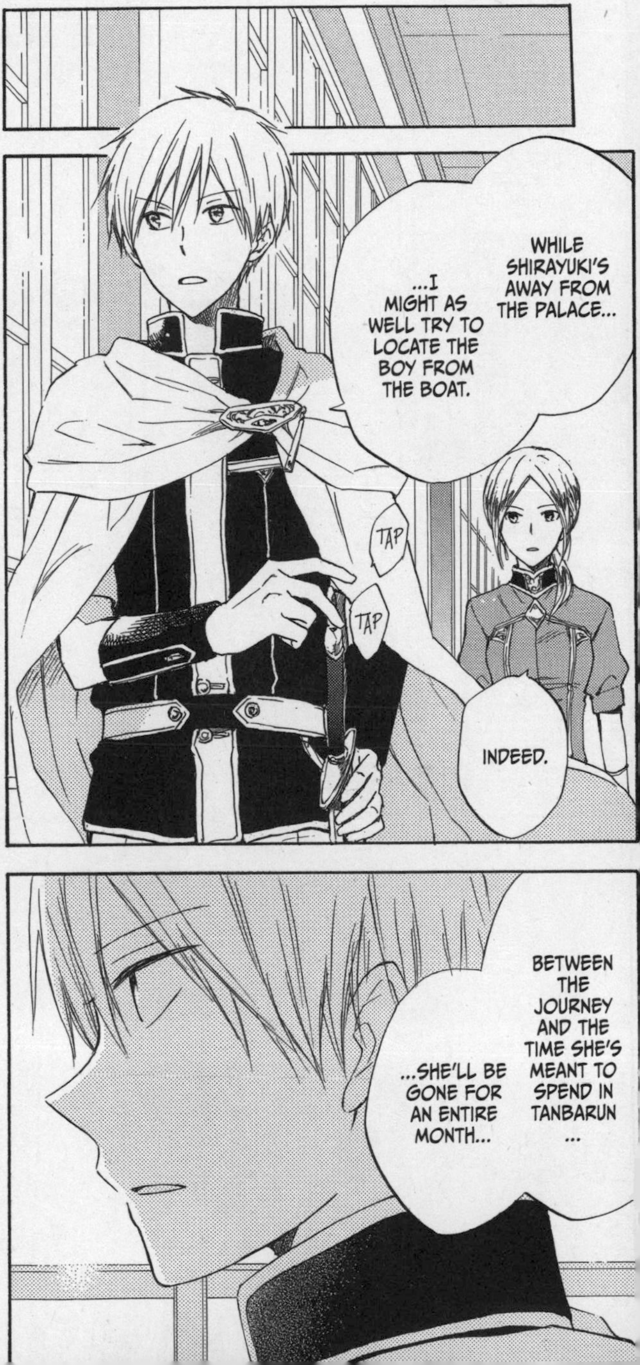
WHILE SHIRAYUKI'S AWAY FROM THE PALACE...
...I MIGHT AS WELL TRY TO LOCATE THE BOY FROM THE BOAT.
TAP
TAP
INDEED.
BETWEEN THE JOURNEY AND THE TIME SHE'S MEANT TO SPEND IN TANBARUN ...
...SHE'LL BE GONE FOR AN ENTIRE MONTH...

With Shirayuki traveling to Tanbarun, she won't be showing up in the medical wing for a while. How might her colleagues feel about that?

I like thinking about scenes that I don't get a chance to draw out in the story.

You could almost call it a habit of mine.

I want more scenes for Chief Garak.

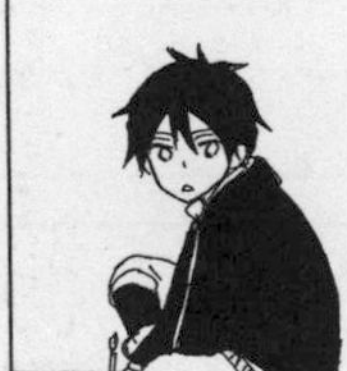

↑

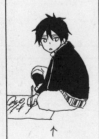

Ryu has a habit of starting to talk to Shirayuki before realizing she's not there.

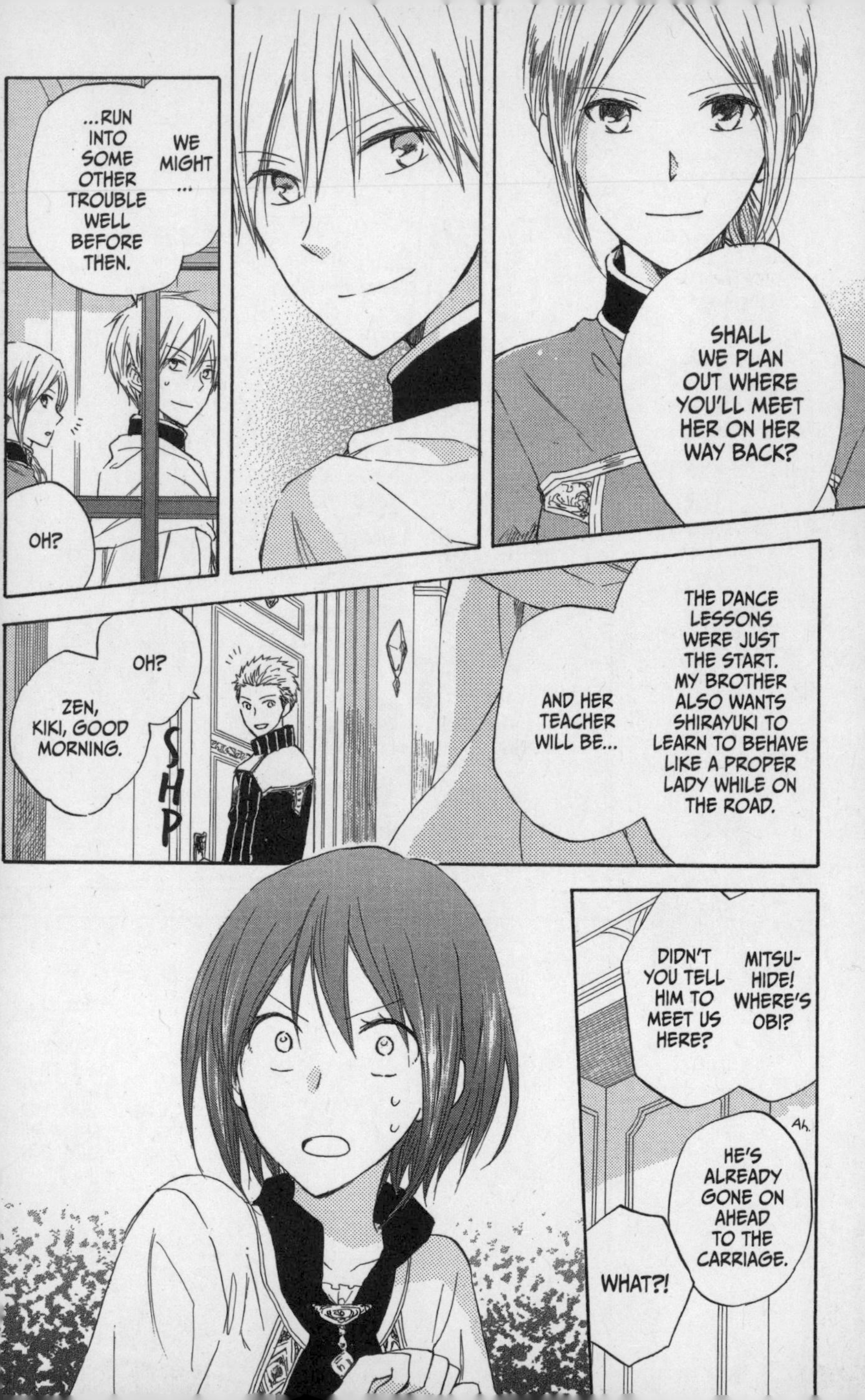
SHALL WE PLAN OUT WHERE YOU'LL MEET HER ON HER WAY BACK?
WE MIGHT ...
...RUN INTO SOME OTHER TROUBLE WELL BEFORE THEN.
OH?
THE DANCE LESSONS WERE JUST THE START. MY BROTHER ALSO WANTS SHIRAYUKI TO LEARN TO BEHAVE LIKE A PROPER LADY WHILE ON THE ROAD.
AND HER TEACHER WILL BE...
OH?
ZEN, KIKI, GOOD MORNING.
SHP
MITSU-HIDE! WHERE'S OBI?
DIDN'T YOU TELL HIM TO MEET US HERE?
Ah.
HE'S ALREADY GONE ON AHEAD TO THE CARRIAGE.
WHAT?!

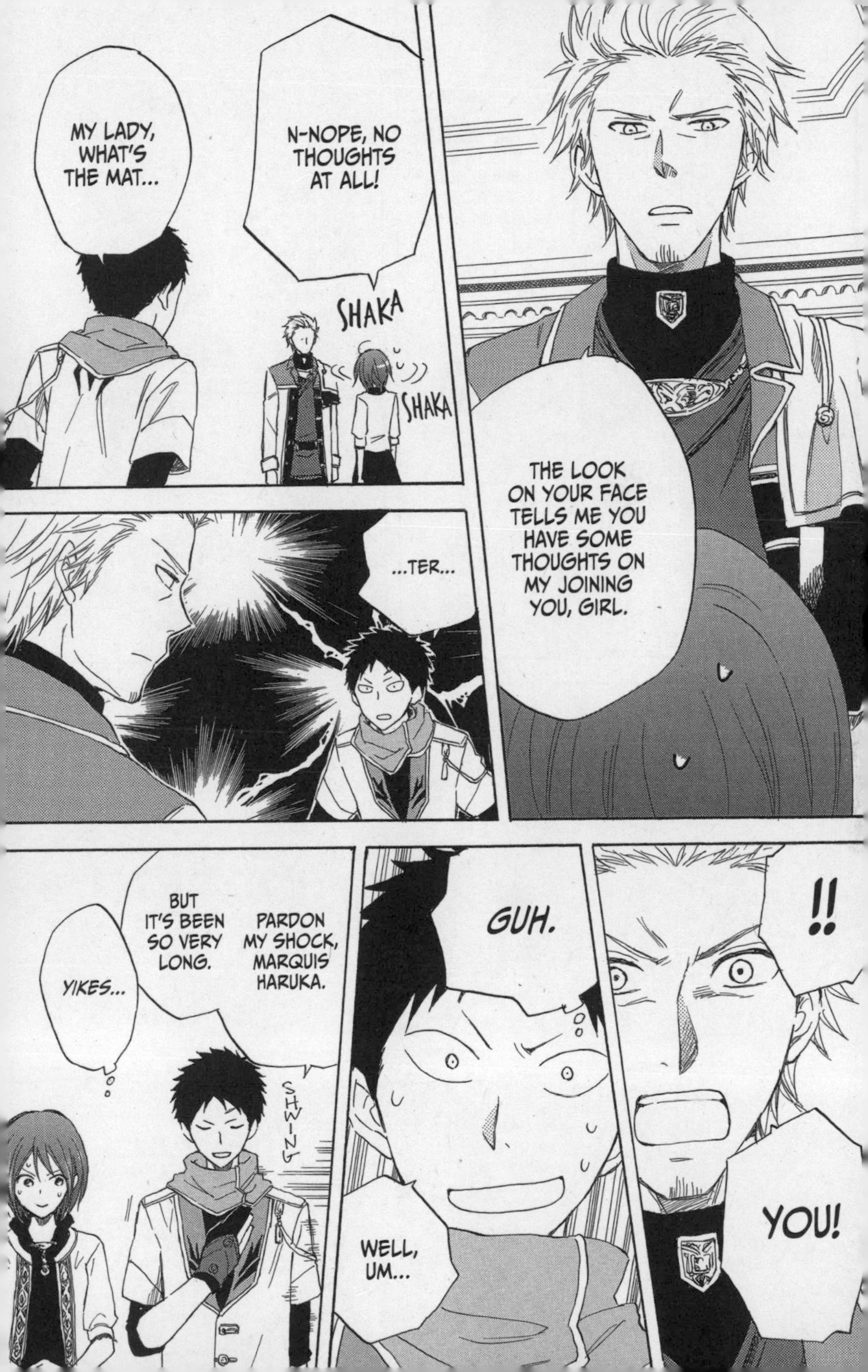
THE LOOK ON YOUR FACE TELLS ME YOU HAVE SOME THOUGHTS ON MY JOINING YOU, GIRL.
N-NOPE, NO THOUGHTS AT ALL!
SHAKA
SHAKA
MY LADY, WHAT'S THE MAT...
...TER...
!!
YOU!
GUH.
WELL, UM...
PARDON MY SHOCK, MARQUIS HARUKA.
BUT IT'S BEEN SO VERY LONG.
SHWING
YIKES...

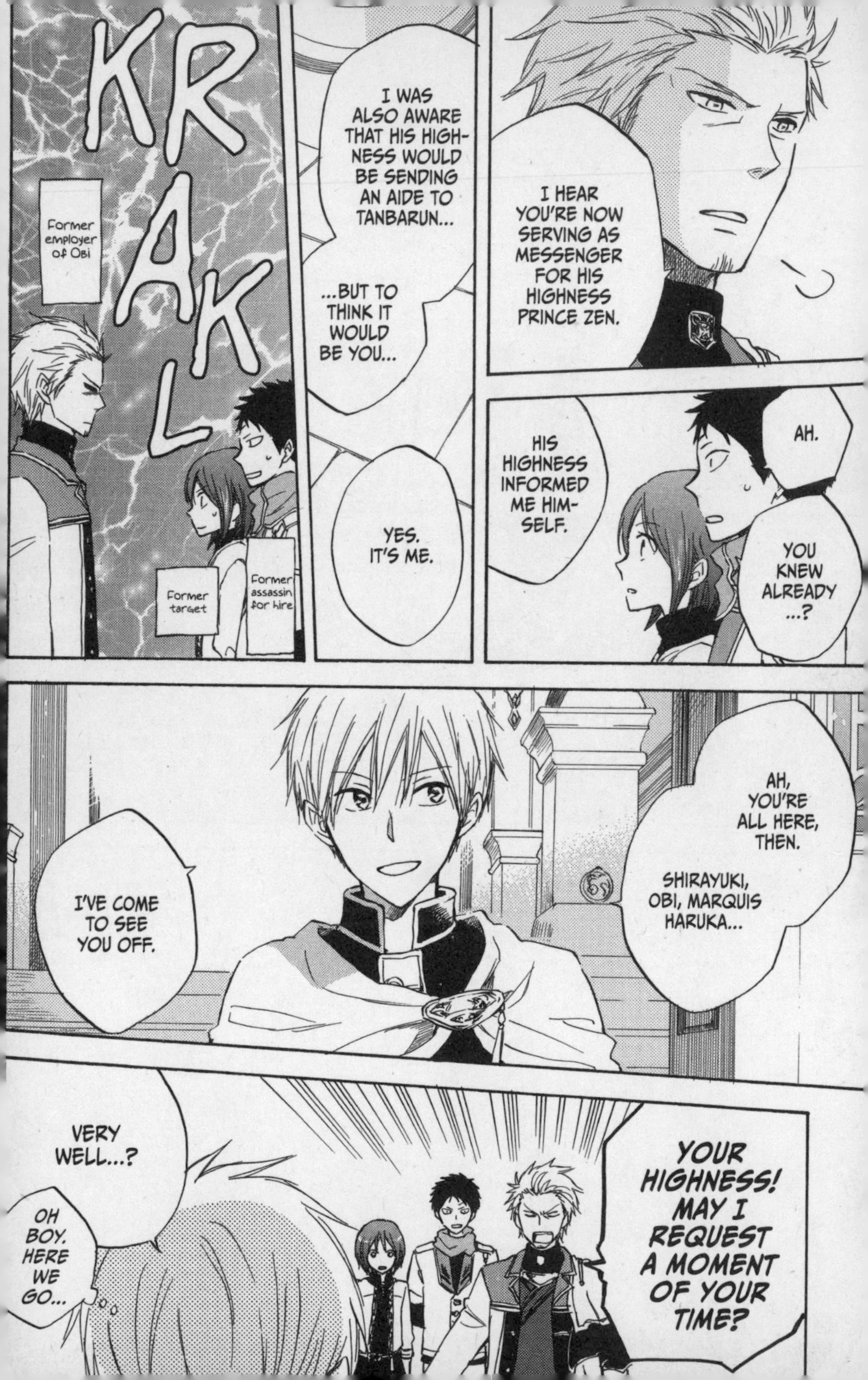
I HEAR YOU'RE NOW SERVING AS MESSENGER FOR HIS HIGHNESS PRINCE ZEN.
AH.
YOU KNEW ALREADY ...?
HIS HIGHNESS INFORMED ME HIM-SELF.
I WAS ALSO AWARE THAT HIS HIGH-NESS WOULD BE SENDING AN AIDE TO TANBARUN...
...BUT TO THINK IT WOULD BE YOU...
YES. IT'S ME.
KRAKL
Former employer of Obi
Former assassin for hire
Former target
AH, YOU'RE ALL HERE, THEN.
SHIRAYUKI, OBI, MARQUIS HARUKA...
I'VE COME TO SEE YOU OFF.
YOUR HIGHNESS! MAY I REQUEST A MOMENT OF YOUR TIME?
VERY WELL...?
OH BOY. HERE WE GO...

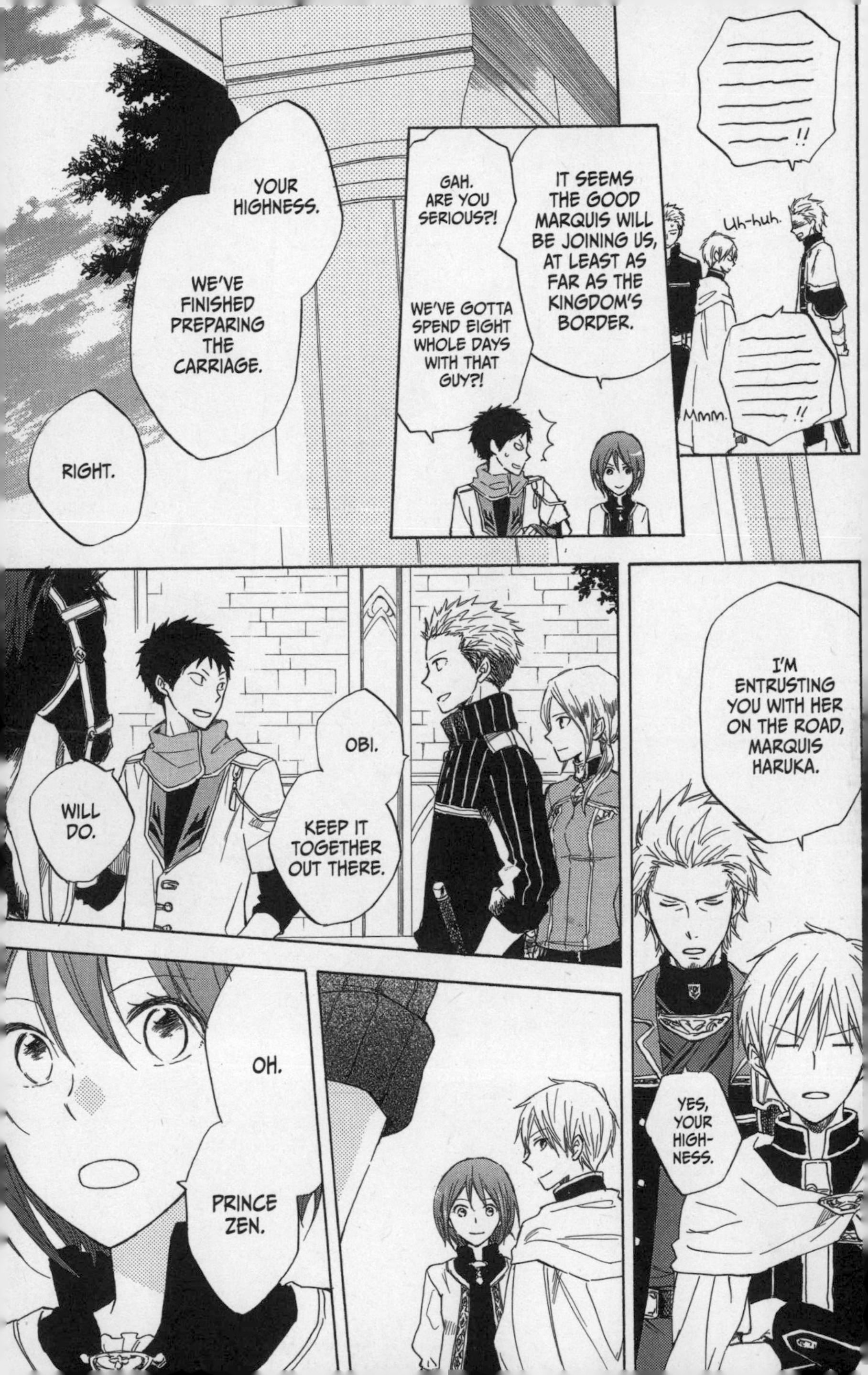
Uh-huh.
Mmm.
IT SEEMS THE GOOD MARQUIS WILL BE JOINING US, AT LEAST AS FAR AS THE KINGDOM'S BORDER.
GAH. ARE YOU SERIOUS?!
WE'VE GOTTA SPEND EIGHT WHOLE DAYS WITH THAT GUY?!
YOUR HIGHNESS.
WE'VE FINISHED PREPARING THE CARRIAGE.
RIGHT.
I'M ENTRUSTING YOU WITH HER ON THE ROAD, MARQUIS HARUKA.
YES, YOUR HIGH-NESS.
OBI.
KEEP IT TOGETHER OUT THERE.
WILL DO.
OH.
PRINCE ZEN.

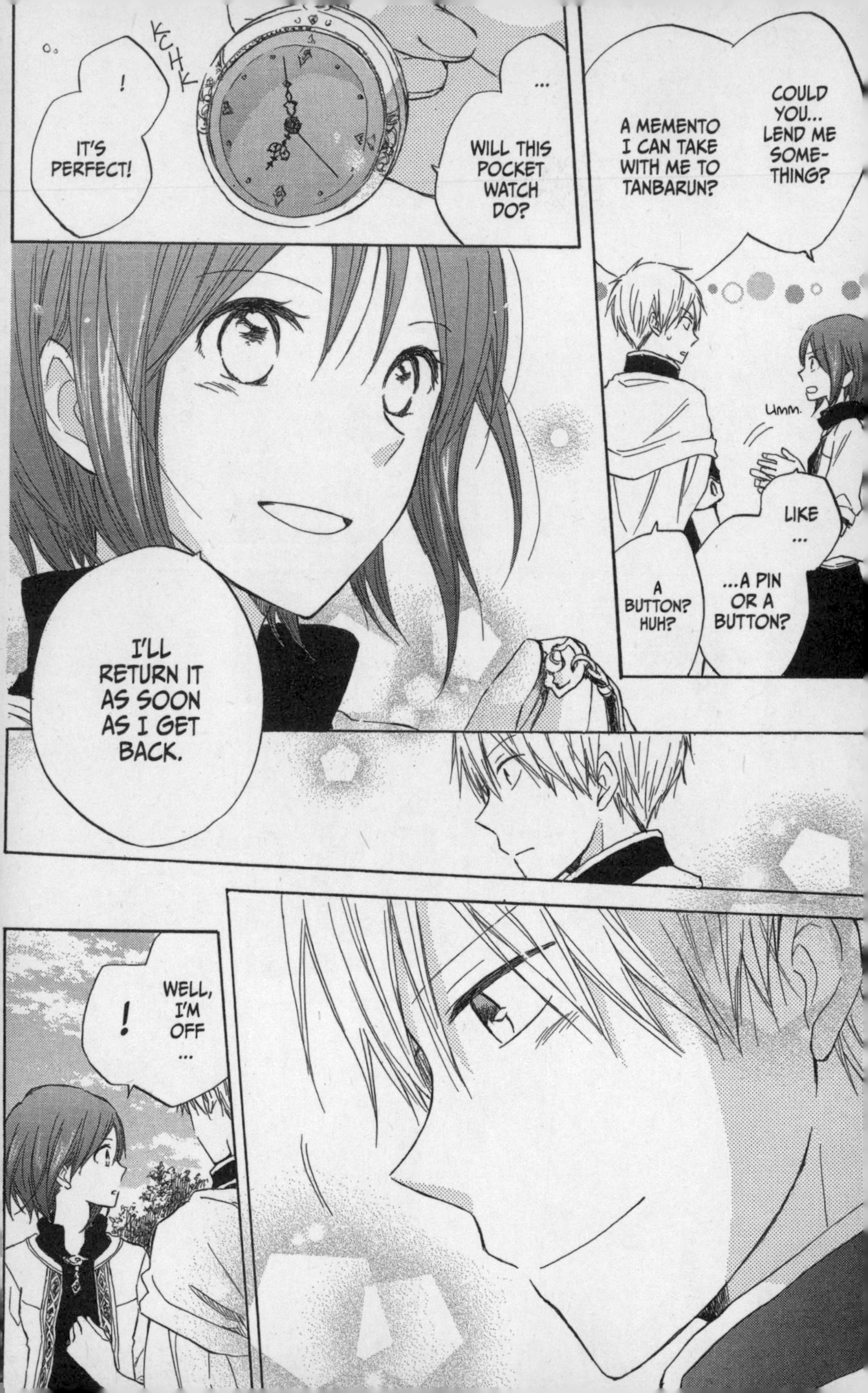
COULD YOU... LEND ME SOME-THING?
A MEMENTO I CAN TAKE WITH ME TO TANBARUN?
Umm.
LIKE ...
...A PIN OR A BUTTON?
A BUTTON? HUH?
...
WILL THIS POCKET WATCH DO?
KCHK
!
IT'S PERFECT!
I'LL RETURN IT AS SOON AS I GET BACK.
WELL, I'M OFF ...
!

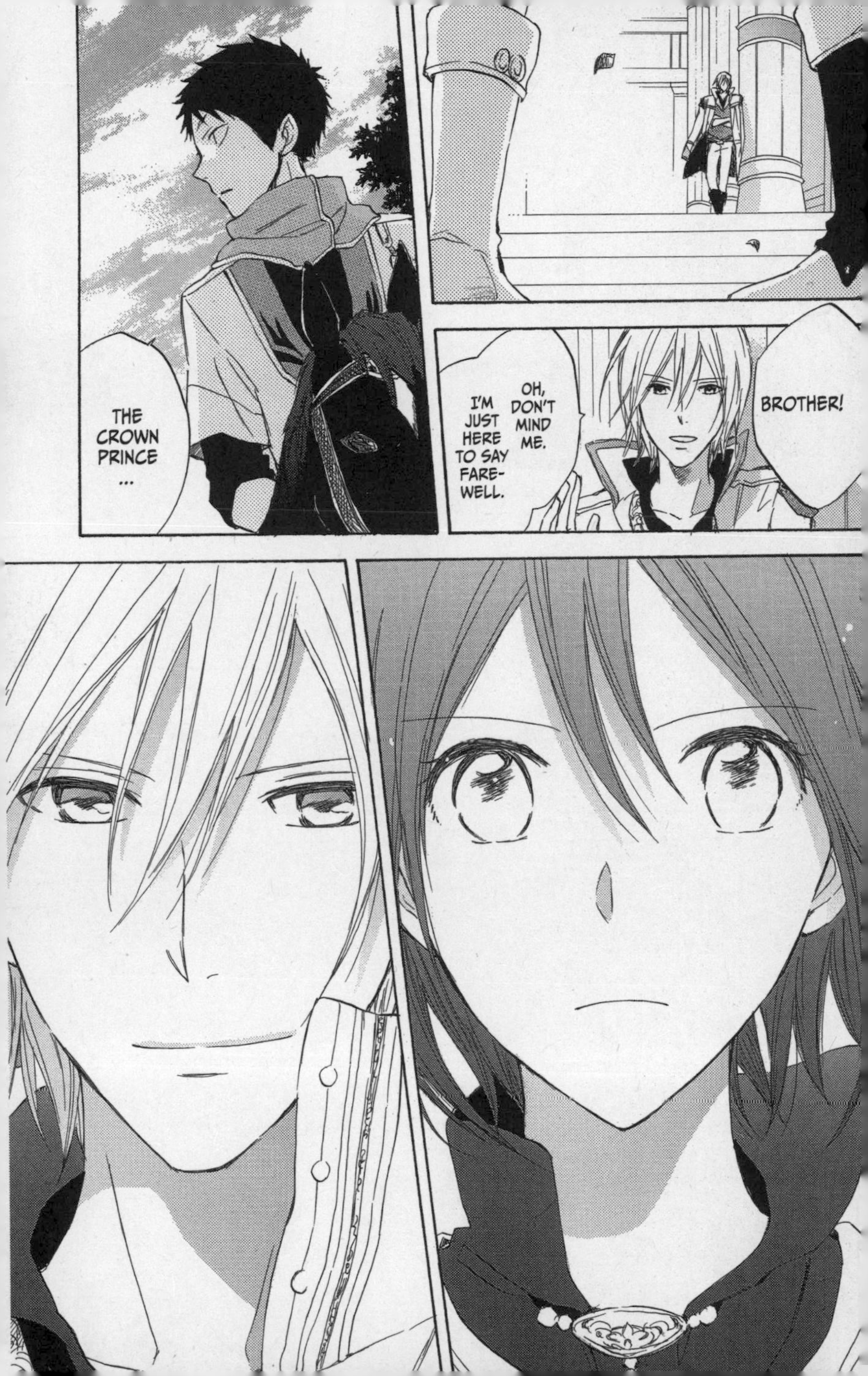
BROTHER!
OH, DON'T MIND ME.
I'M JUST HERE TO SAY FAREWELL.
THE CROWN PRINCE ...

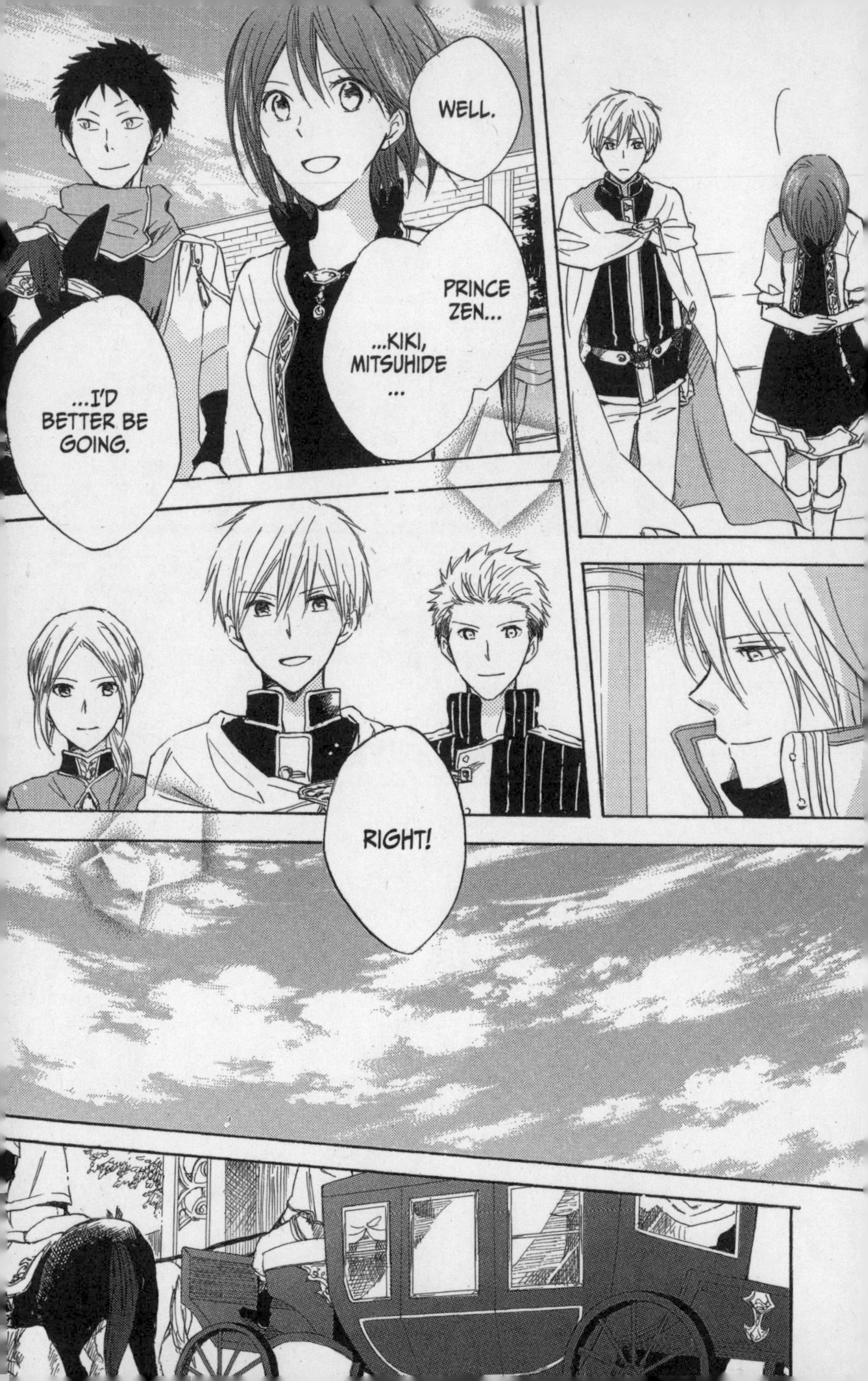
WELL.
PRINCE ZEN...
...KIKI, MITSUHIDE ...
...I'D BETTER BE GOING.
RIGHT!

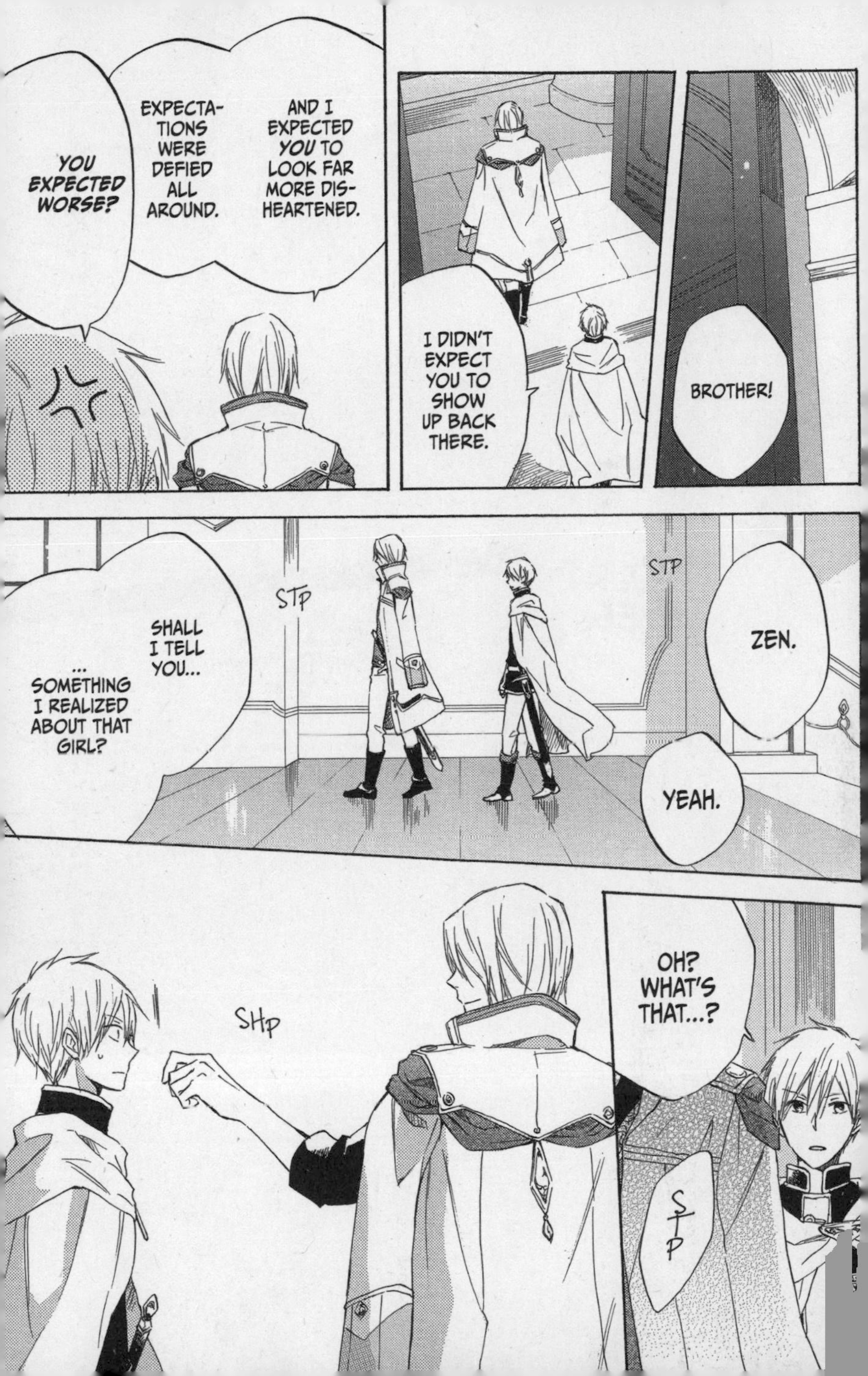
BROTHER!
I DIDN'T EXPECT YOU TO SHOW UP BACK THERE.
AND I EXPECTED *YOU* TO LOOK FAR MORE DIS-HEARTENED.
EXPECTA-TIONS WERE DEFIED ALL AROUND.
YOU EXPECTED WORSE?
ZEN.
STP
YEAH.
STP
SHALL I TELL YOU...
...SOMETHING I REALIZED ABOUT THAT GIRL?
OH? WHAT'S THAT...?
STP
SHP

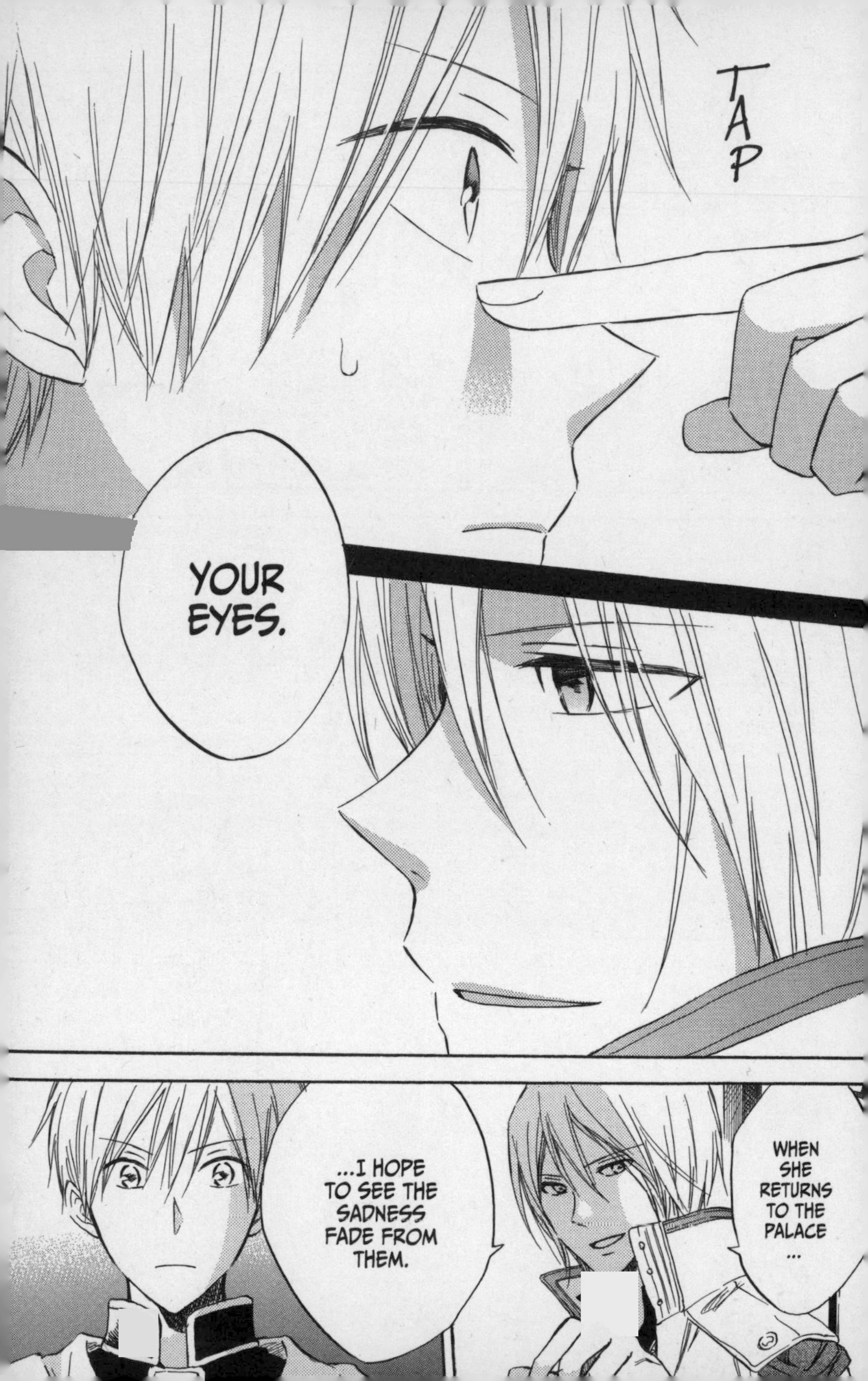
TAP
YOUR EYES.
WHEN SHE RETURNS TO THE PALACE ...
...I HOPE TO SEE THE SADNESS FADE FROM THEM.

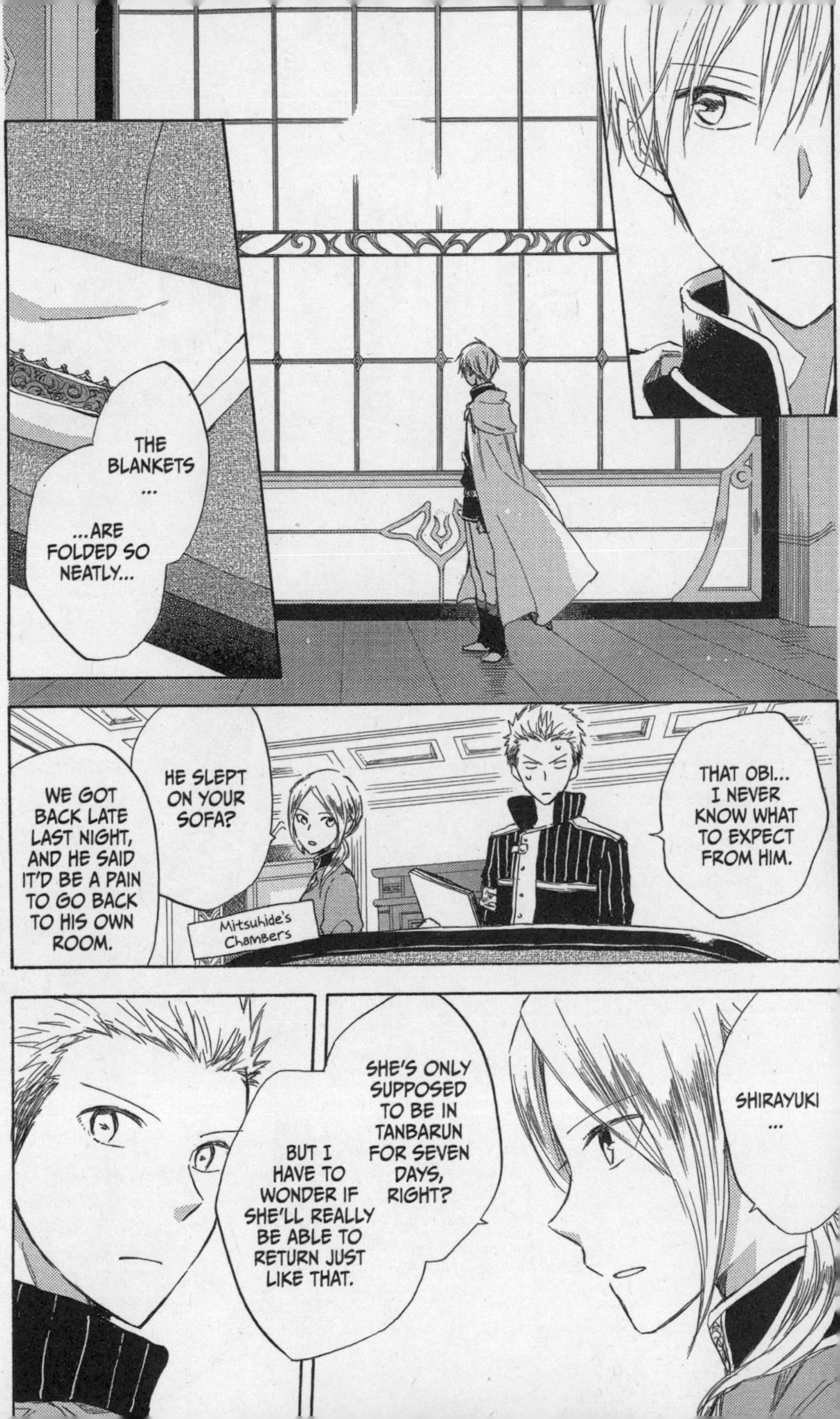
THE BLANKETS ...
...ARE FOLDED SO NEATLY...
Mitsuhide's Chambers
THAT OBI... I NEVER KNOW WHAT TO EXPECT FROM HIM.
HE SLEPT ON YOUR SOFA?
WE GOT BACK LATE LAST NIGHT, AND HE SAID IT'D BE A PAIN TO GO BACK TO HIS OWN ROOM.
SHIRAYUKI ...
SHE'S ONLY SUPPOSED TO BE IN TANBARUN FOR SEVEN DAYS, RIGHT?
BUT I HAVE TO WONDER IF SHE'LL REALLY BE ABLE TO RETURN JUST LIKE THAT.

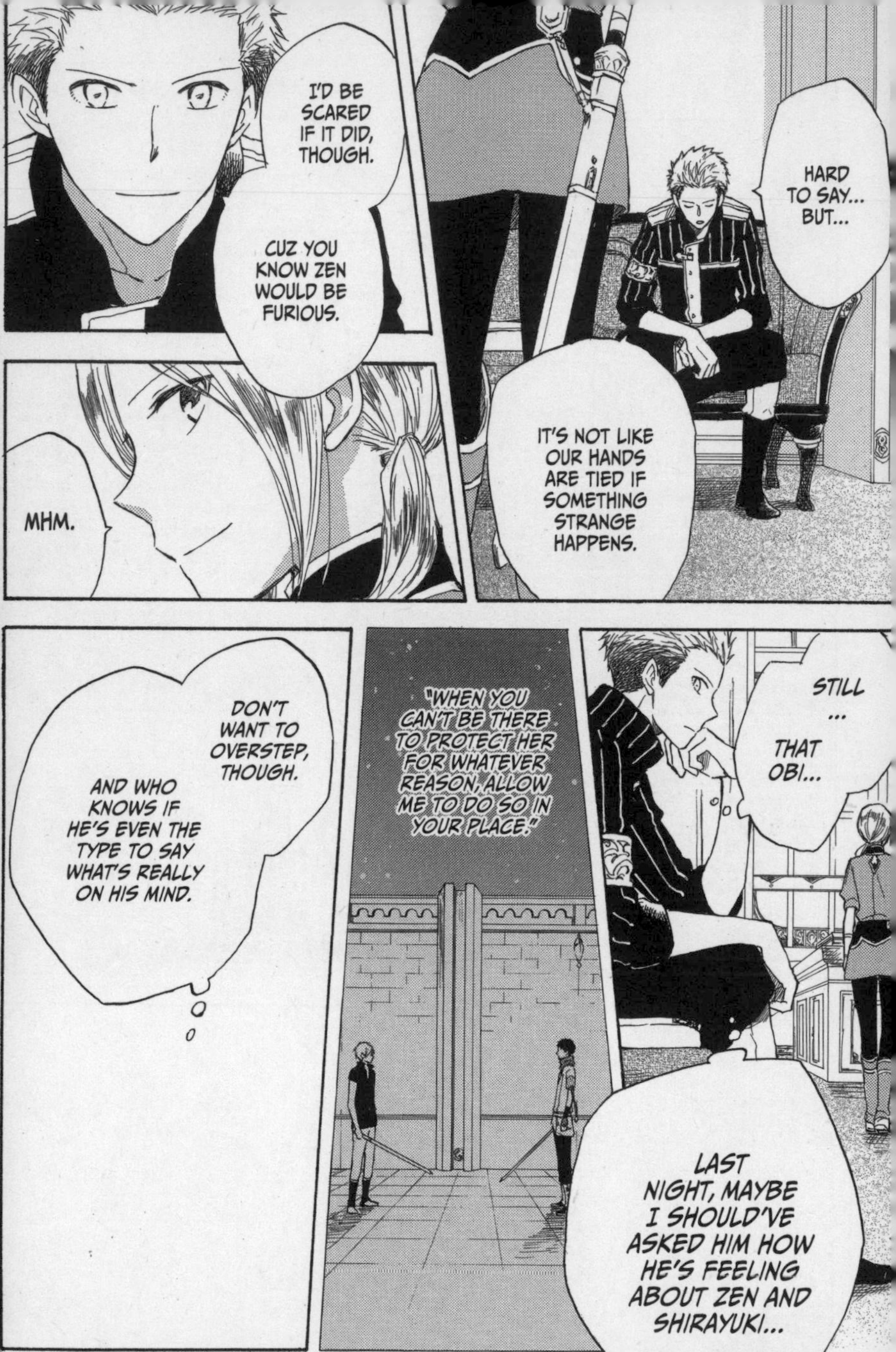
HARD TO SAY... BUT...
IT'S NOT LIKE OUR HANDS ARE TIED IF SOMETHING STRANGE HAPPENS.
I'D BE SCARED IF IT DID, THOUGH.
CUZ YOU KNOW ZEN WOULD BE FURIOUS.
MHM.
STILL ... THAT OBI...
LAST NIGHT, MAYBE I SHOULD'VE ASKED HIM HOW HE'S FEELING ABOUT ZEN AND SHIRAYUKI...
"WHEN YOU CAN'T BE THERE TO PROTECT HER FOR WHATEVER REASON, ALLOW ME TO DO SO IN YOUR PLACE."
DON'T WANT TO OVERSTEP, THOUGH.
AND WHO KNOWS IF HE'S EVEN THE TYPE TO SAY WHAT'S REALLY ON HIS MIND.

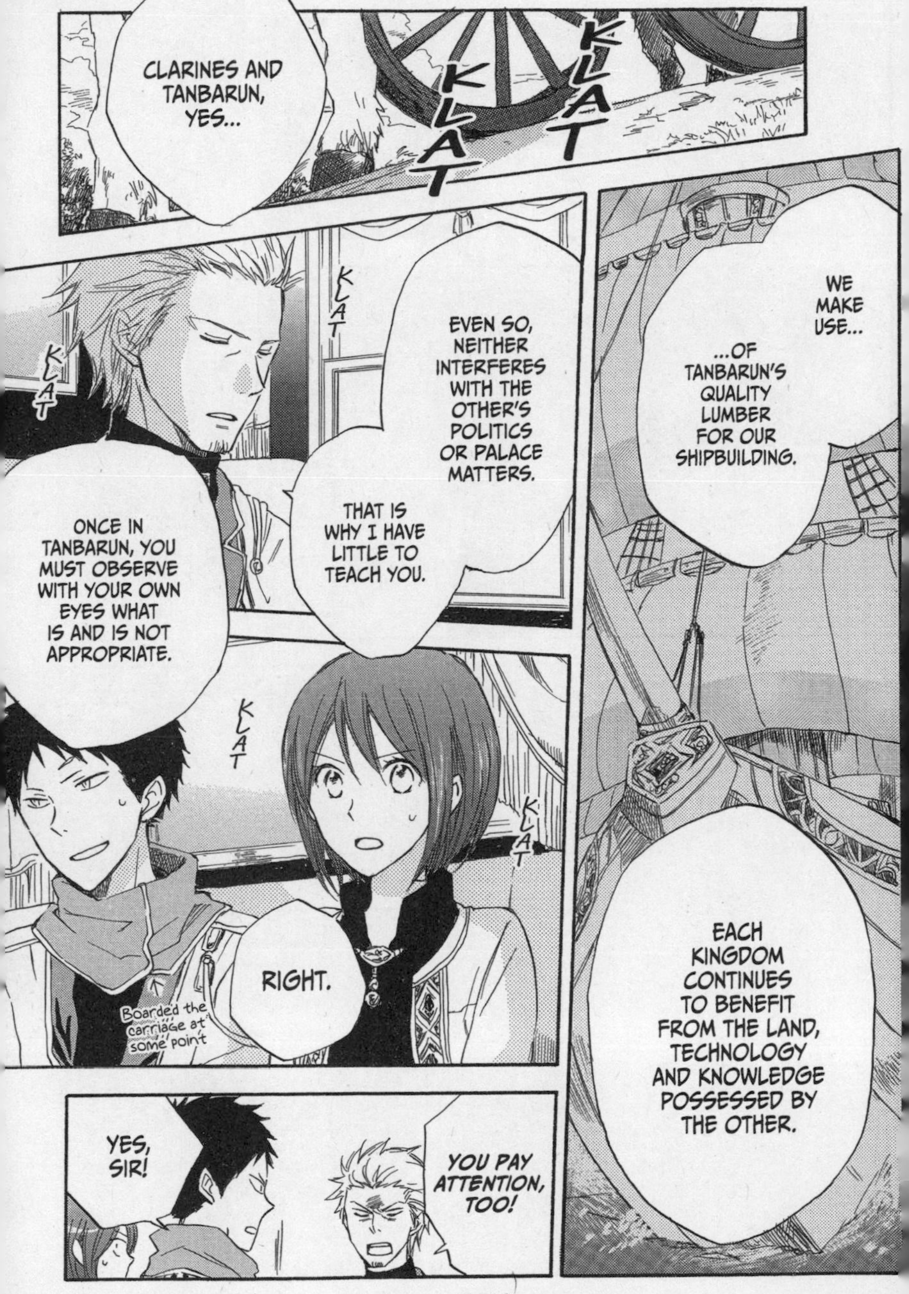
KLAT
KLAT
CLARINES AND TANBARUN, YES...
WE MAKE USE...
...OF TANBARUN'S QUALITY LUMBER FOR OUR SHIPBUILDING.
EACH KINGDOM CONTINUES TO BENEFIT FROM THE LAND, TECHNOLOGY AND KNOWLEDGE POSSESSED BY THE OTHER.
EVEN SO, NEITHER INTERFERES WITH THE OTHER'S POLITICS OR PALACE MATTERS.
KLAT
KLAT
THAT IS WHY I HAVE LITTLE TO TEACH YOU.
ONCE IN TANBARUN, YOU MUST OBSERVE WITH YOUR OWN EYES WHAT IS AND IS NOT APPROPRIATE.
KLAT
KLAT
RIGHT.
Boarded the carriage at some point
YOU PAY ATTENTION, TOO!
YES, SIR!

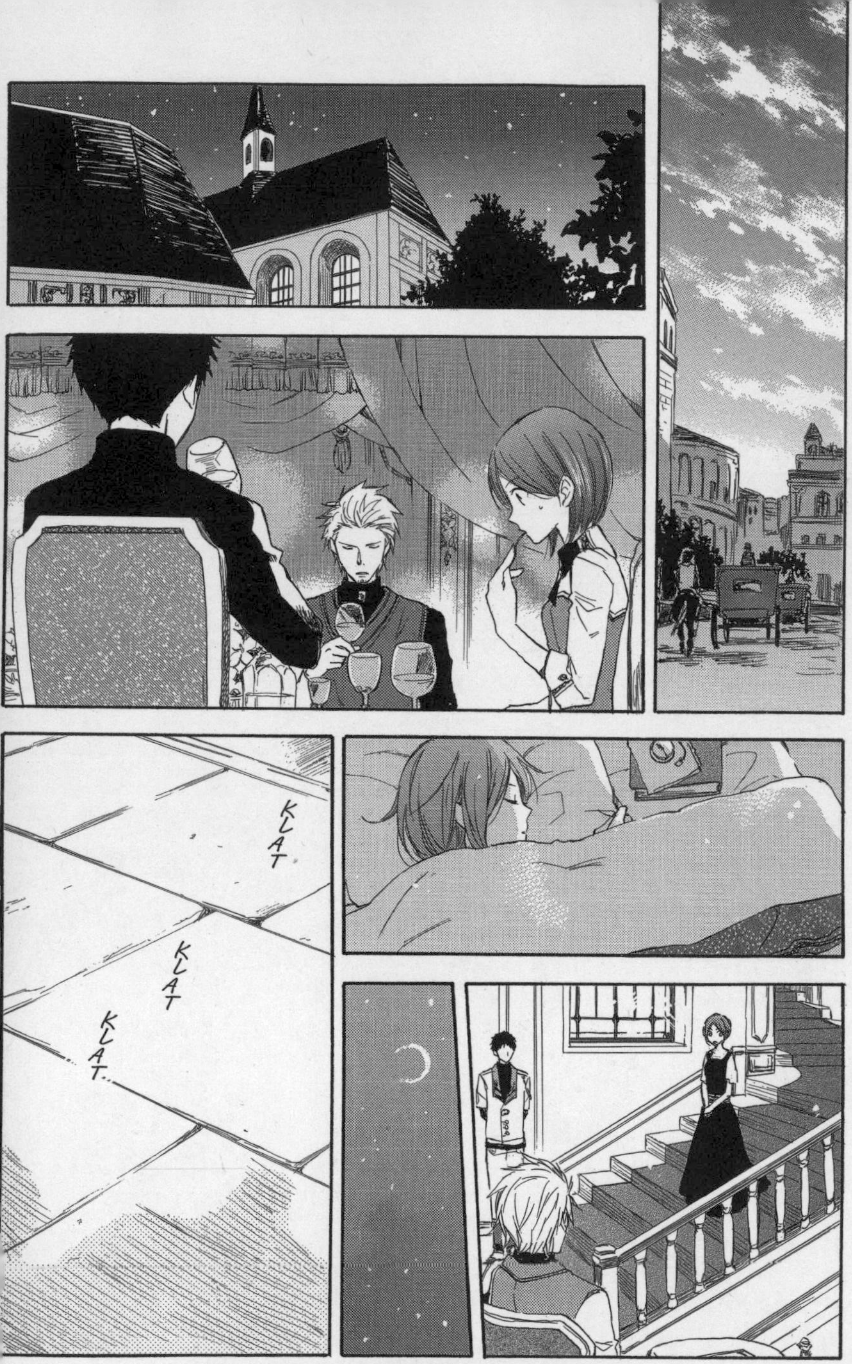
KLAT
KLAT
KLAT

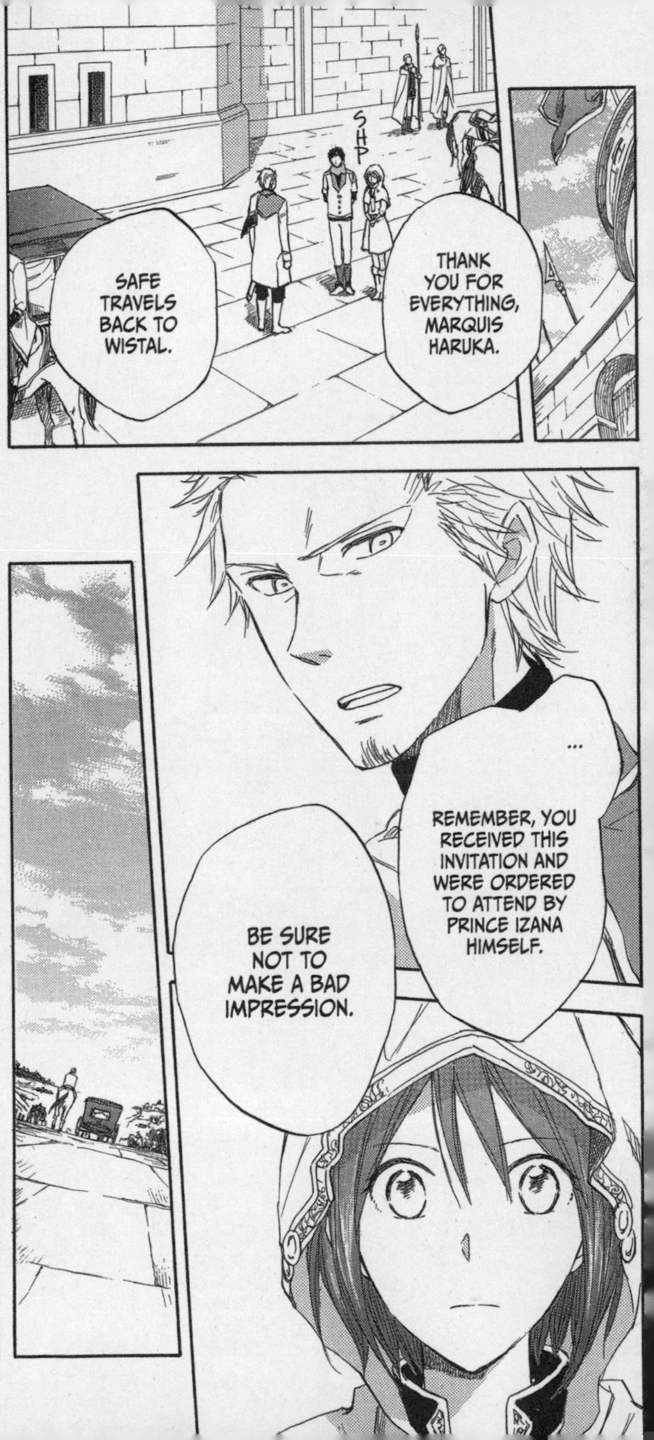
SHP
THANK YOU FOR EVERYTHING, MARQUIS HARUKA.
SAFE TRAVELS BACK TO WISTAL.
...
REMEMBER, YOU RECEIVED THIS INVITATION AND WERE ORDERED TO ATTEND BY PRINCE IZANA HIMSELF.
BE SURE NOT TO MAKE A BAD IMPRESSION.

Chapter 20

Ever since around volume 3, Marquis Haruka has had his role stolen by Zakura (the guy hanging out with Mitsuhide and Kiki during the story arc about the birds).

Now he makes his triumphant return, at least for a few pages.

Stomp, stomp, harrumph.

Hopefully, we'll get to see him smile someday.

Right?

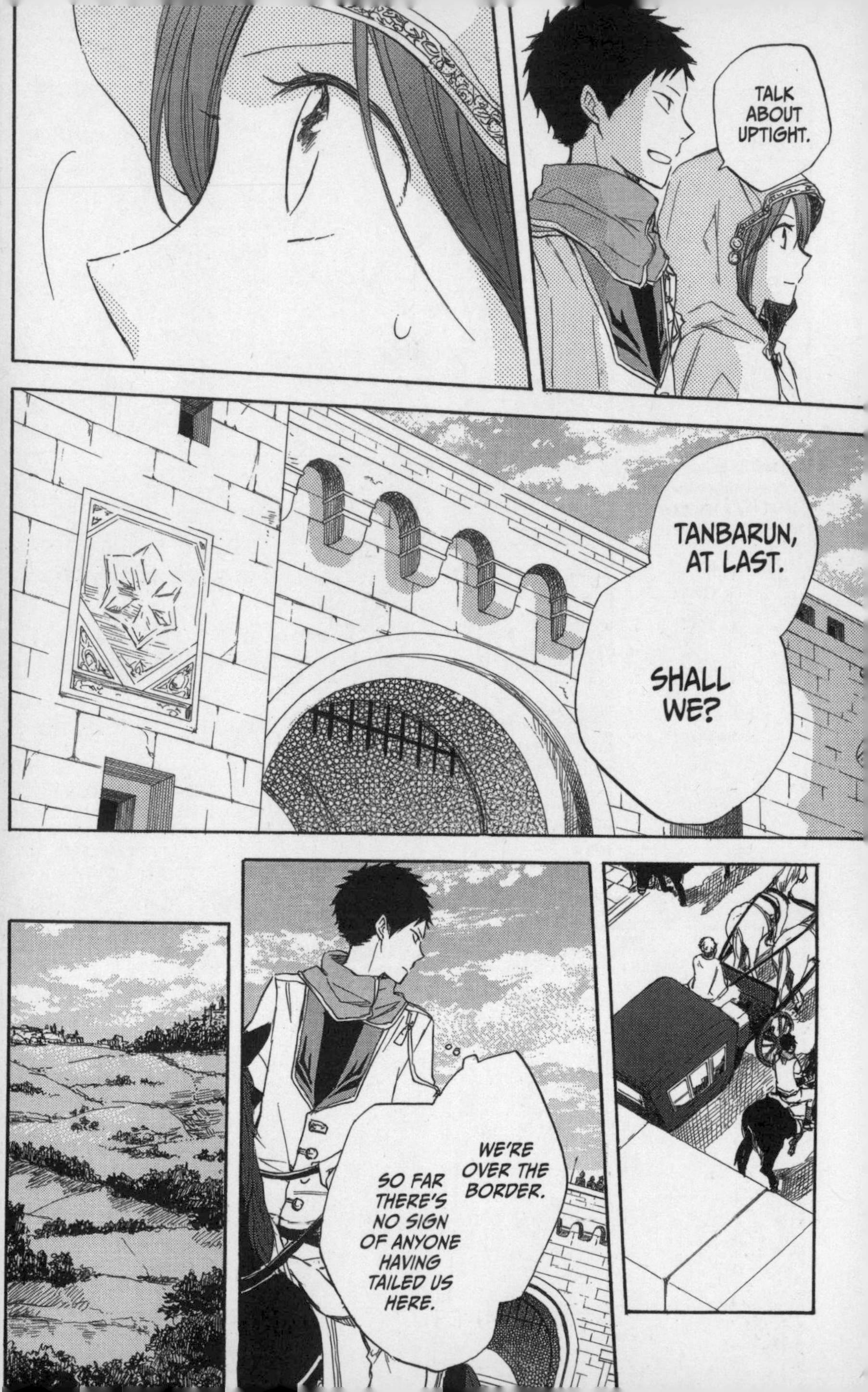
TALK ABOUT UPTIGHT.
TANBARUN, AT LAST.
SHALL WE?
WE'RE OVER THE BORDER.
SO FAR THERE'S NO SIGN OF ANYONE HAVING TAILED US HERE.

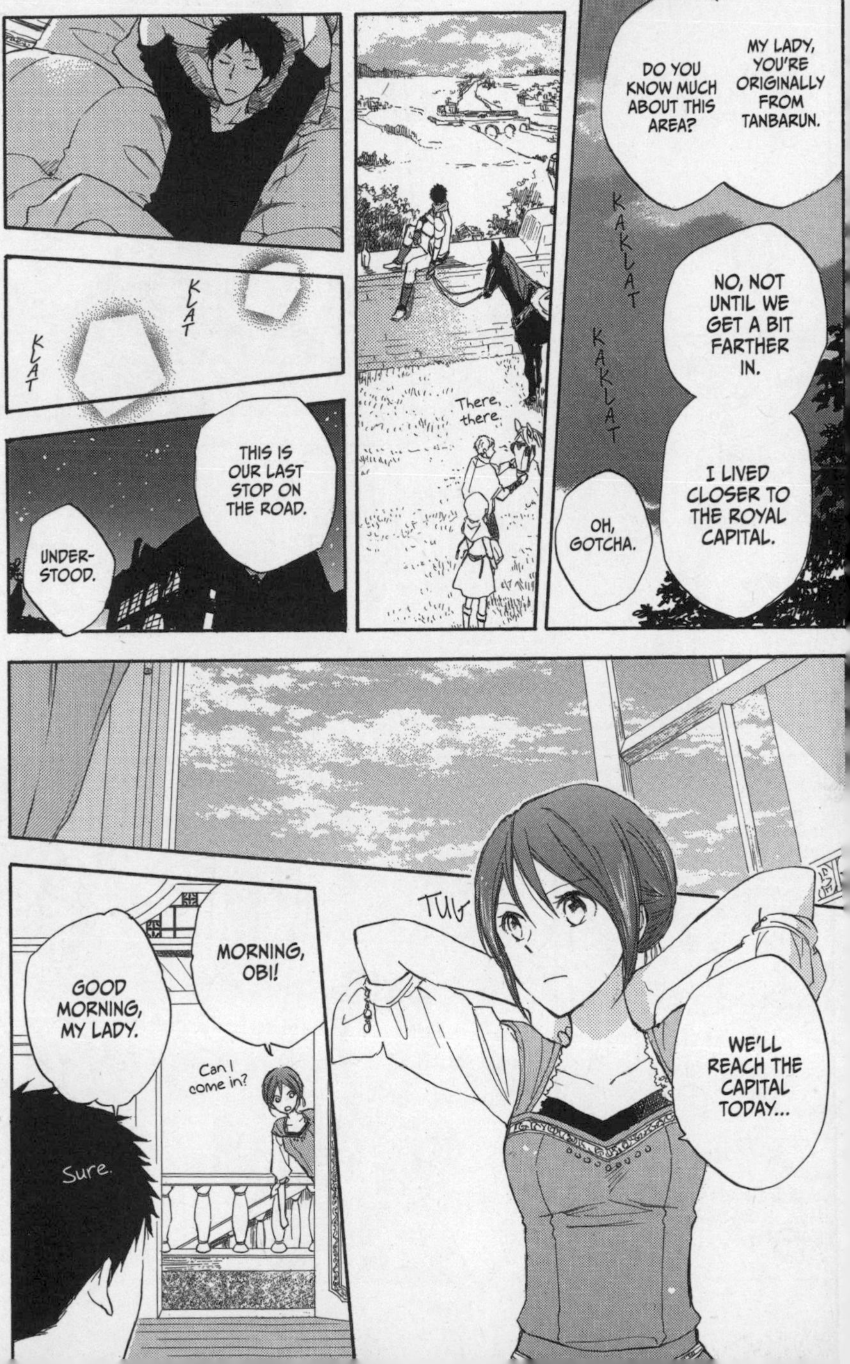
MY LADY, YOU'RE ORIGINALLY FROM TANBARUN.
DO YOU KNOW MUCH ABOUT THIS AREA?
KAKLAT
KAKLAT
NO, NOT UNTIL WE GET A BIT FARTHER IN.
I LIVED CLOSER TO THE ROYAL CAPITAL.
OH, GOTCHA.
There, there.
KLAT
KLAT
THIS IS OUR LAST STOP ON THE ROAD.
UNDER-STOOD.
TUG
WE'LL REACH THE CAPITAL TODAY...
MORNING, OBI!
GOOD MORNING, MY LADY.
Can I come in?
Sure.

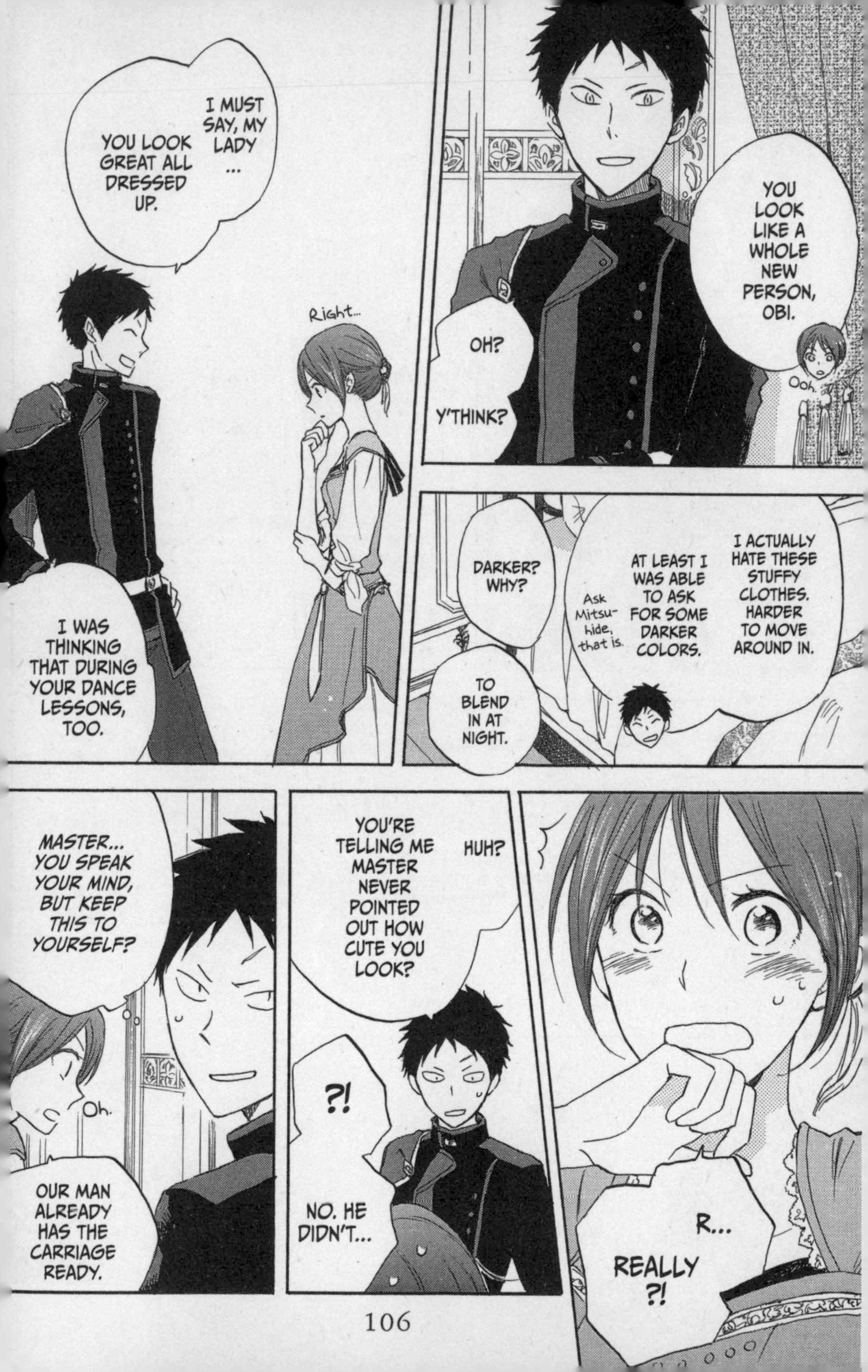
YOU LOOK LIKE A WHOLE NEW PERSON, OBI.
Ooh.
OH?
Y'THINK?
I ACTUALLY HATE THESE STUFFY CLOTHES. HARDER TO MOVE AROUND IN.
AT LEAST I WAS ABLE TO ASK FOR SOME DARKER COLORS.
Ask Mitsu-hide, that is.
DARKER? WHY?
TO BLEND IN AT NIGHT.
I MUST SAY, MY LADY ...
YOU LOOK GREAT ALL DRESSED UP.
Right...
I WAS THINKING THAT DURING YOUR DANCE LESSONS, TOO.
R...
REALLY ?!
HUH?
YOU'RE TELLING ME MASTER NEVER POINTED OUT HOW CUTE YOU LOOK?
?!
NO. HE DIDN'T...
MASTER... YOU SPEAK YOUR MIND, BUT KEEP THIS TO YOURSELF?
Oh.
OUR MAN ALREADY HAS THE CARRIAGE READY.

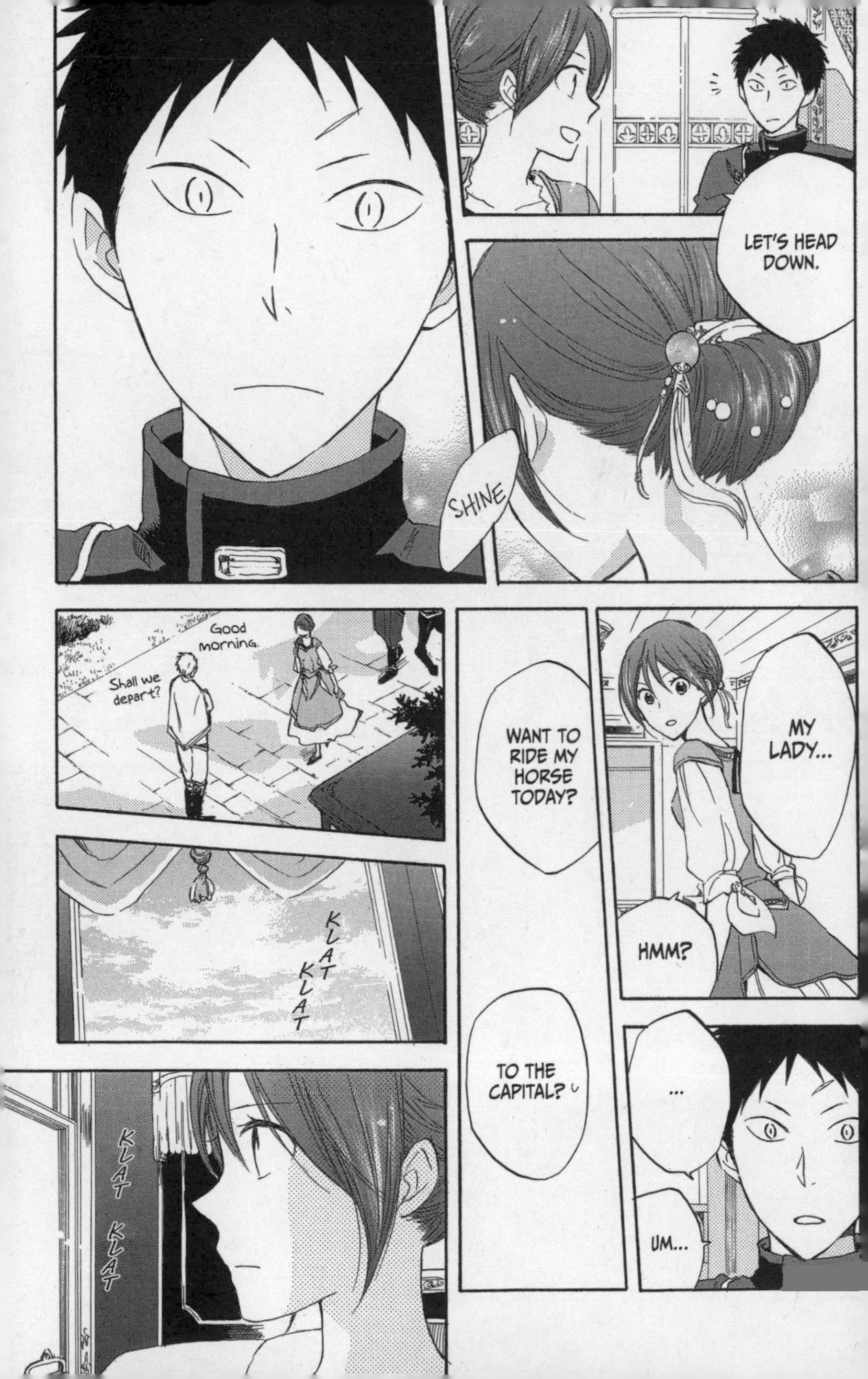
LET'S HEAD DOWN.
SHINE
MY LADY...
HMM?
...
UM...
WANT TO RIDE MY HORSE TODAY?
TO THE CAPITAL?
Good morning.
Shall we depart?
KLAT KLAT
KLAT KLAT

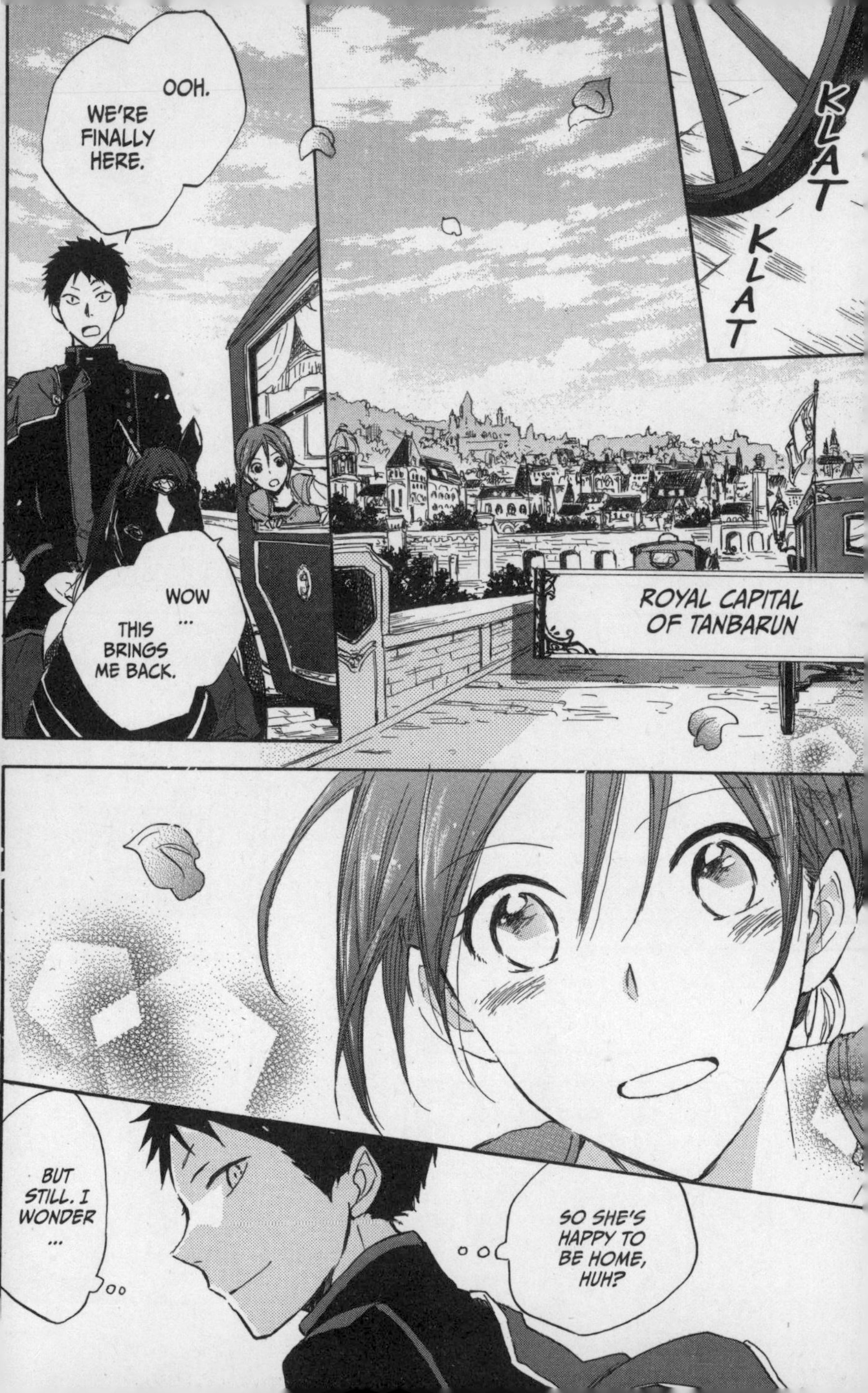
KLAT
KLAT
ROYAL CAPITAL OF TANBARUN
OOH. WE'RE FINALLY HERE.
WOW... THIS BRINGS ME BACK.
SO SHE'S HAPPY TO BE HOME, HUH?
BUT STILL. I WONDER...

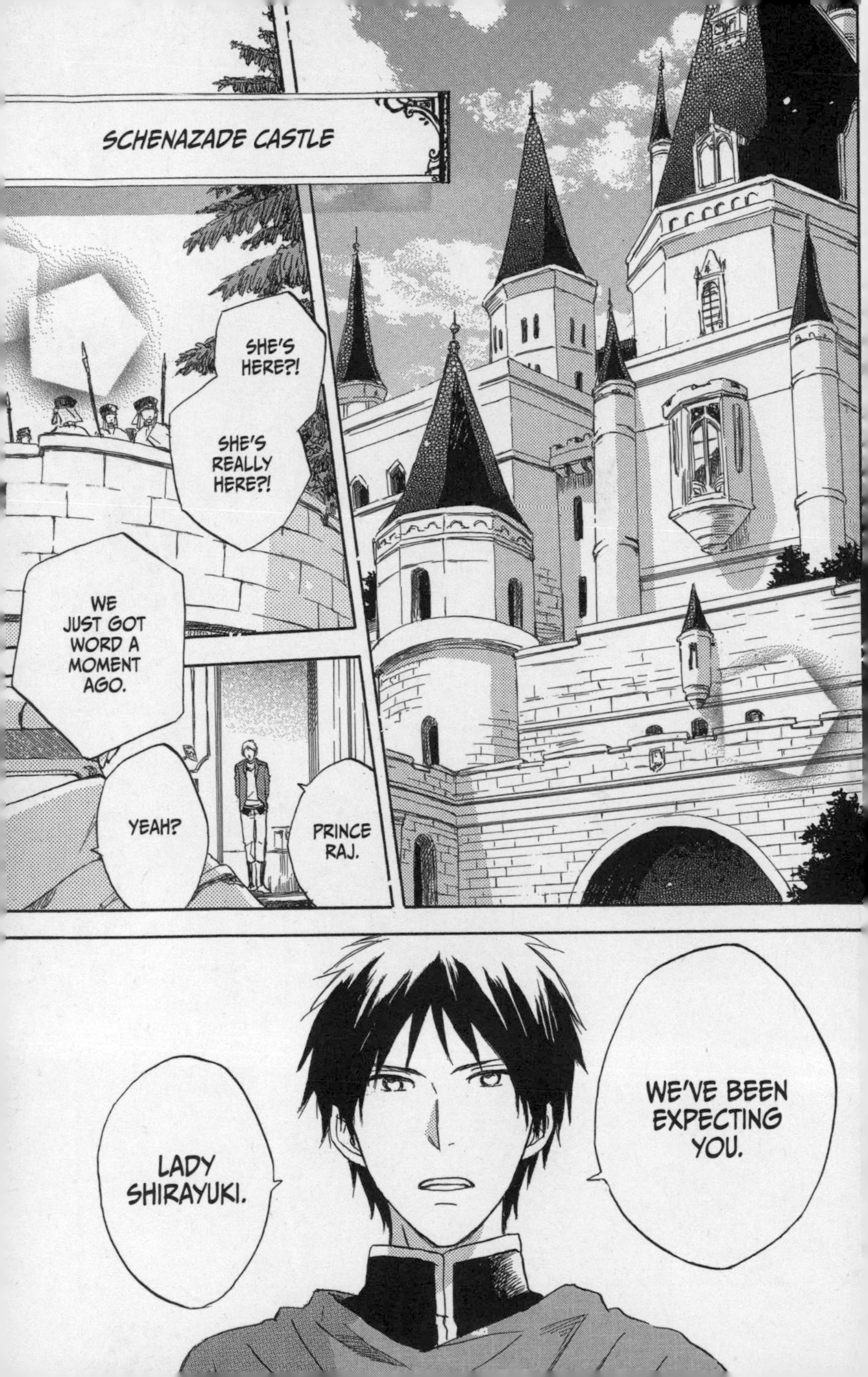
SCHENAZADE CASTLE
SHE'S HERE?!
SHE'S REALLY HERE?!
PRINCE RAJ.
YEAH?
WE JUST GOT WORD A MOMENT AGO.
WE'VE BEEN EXPECTING YOU.
LADY SHIRAYUKI.

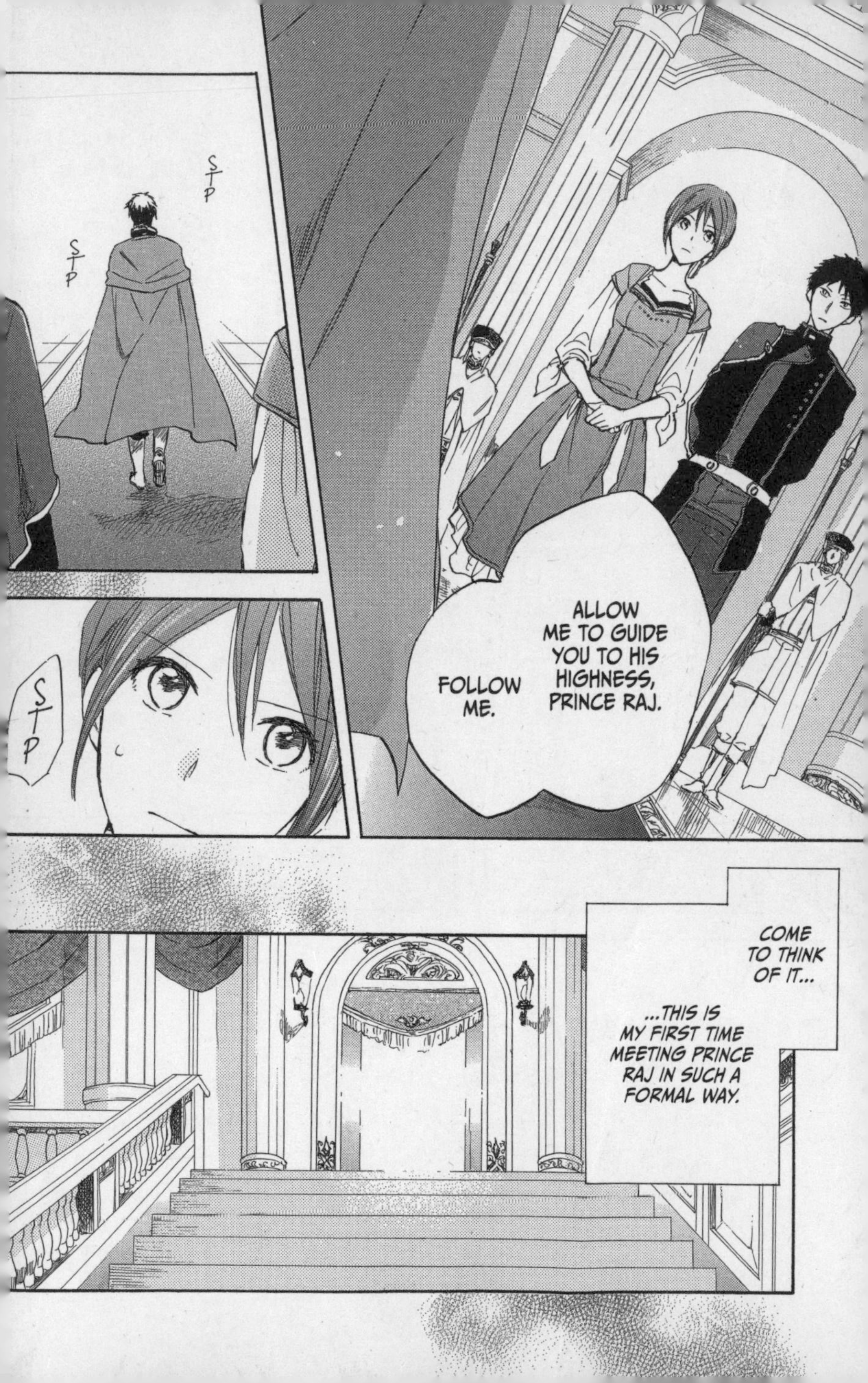
ALLOW ME TO GUIDE YOU TO HIS HIGHNESS, PRINCE RAJ.
FOLLOW ME.
STP
STP
STP
COME TO THINK OF IT...
...THIS IS MY FIRST TIME MEETING PRINCE RAJ IN SUCH A FORMAL WAY.

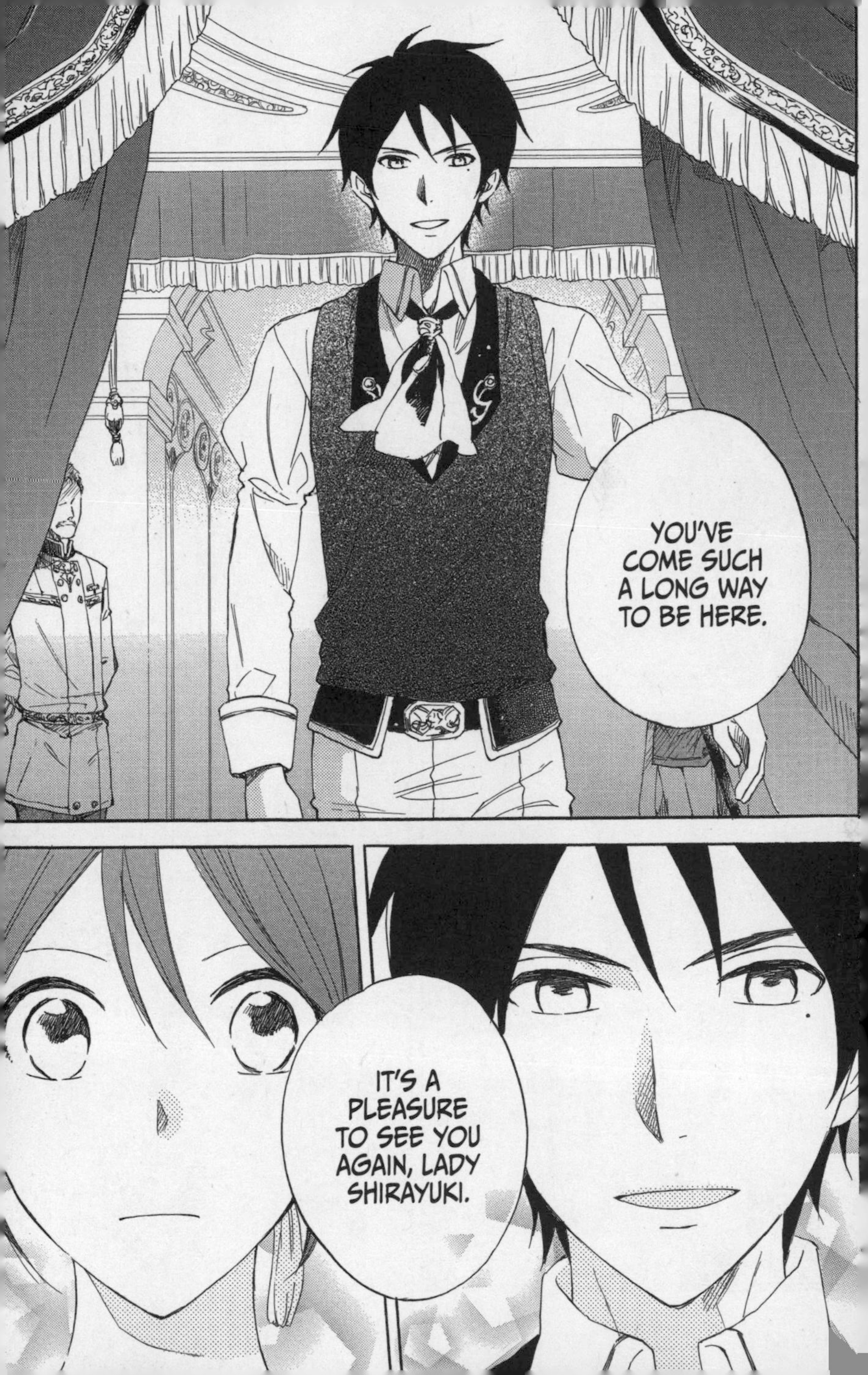
YOU'VE COME SUCH A LONG WAY TO BE HERE.
IT'S A PLEASURE TO SEE YOU AGAIN, LADY SHIRAYUKI.

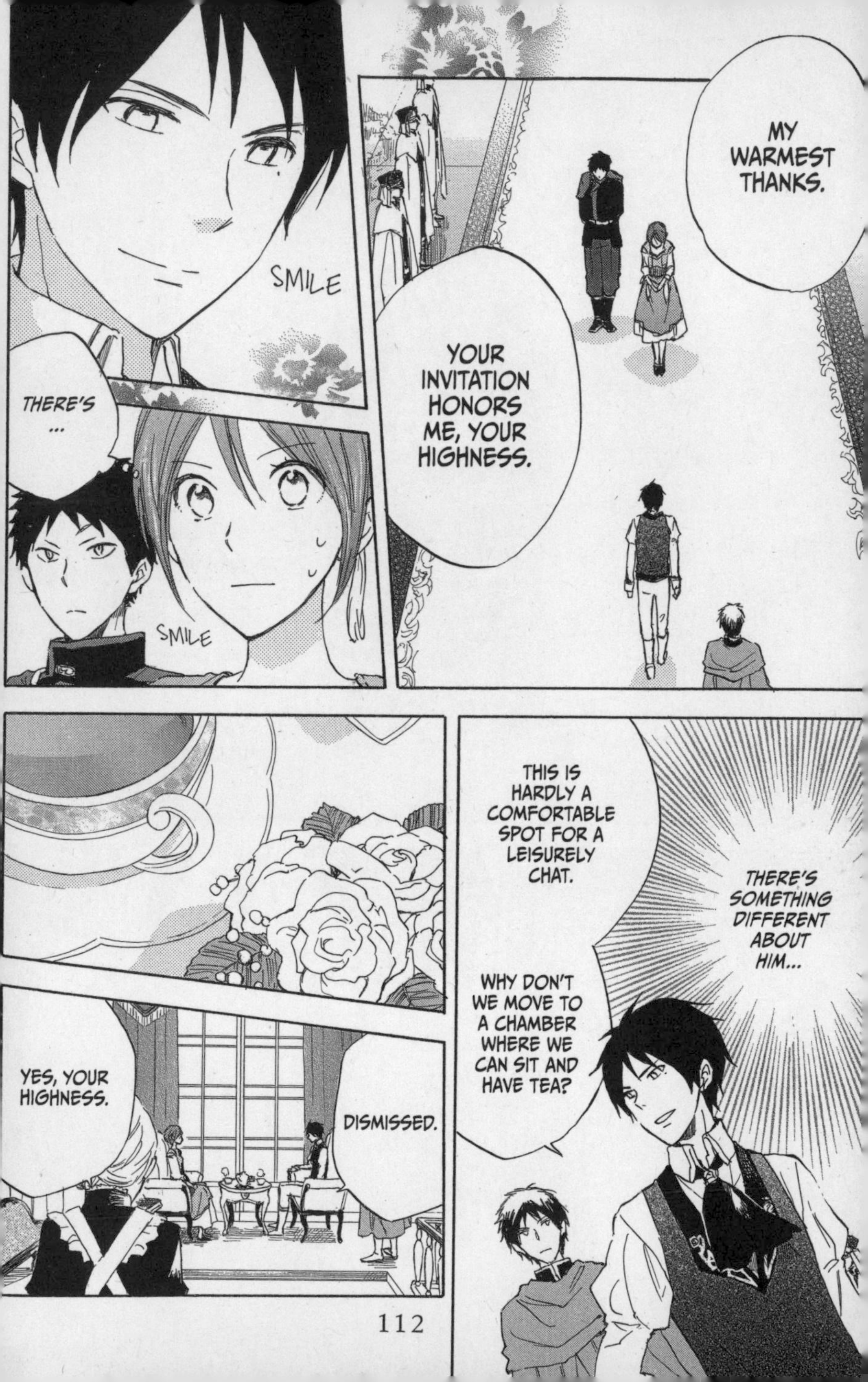
MY WARMEST THANKS.
YOUR INVITATION HONORS ME, YOUR HIGHNESS.
SMILE
THERE'S ...
SMILE
THIS IS HARDLY A COMFORTABLE SPOT FOR A LEISURELY CHAT.
THERE'S SOMETHING DIFFERENT ABOUT HIM...
WHY DON'T WE MOVE TO A CHAMBER WHERE WE CAN SIT AND HAVE TEA?
DISMISSED.
YES, YOUR HIGHNESS.

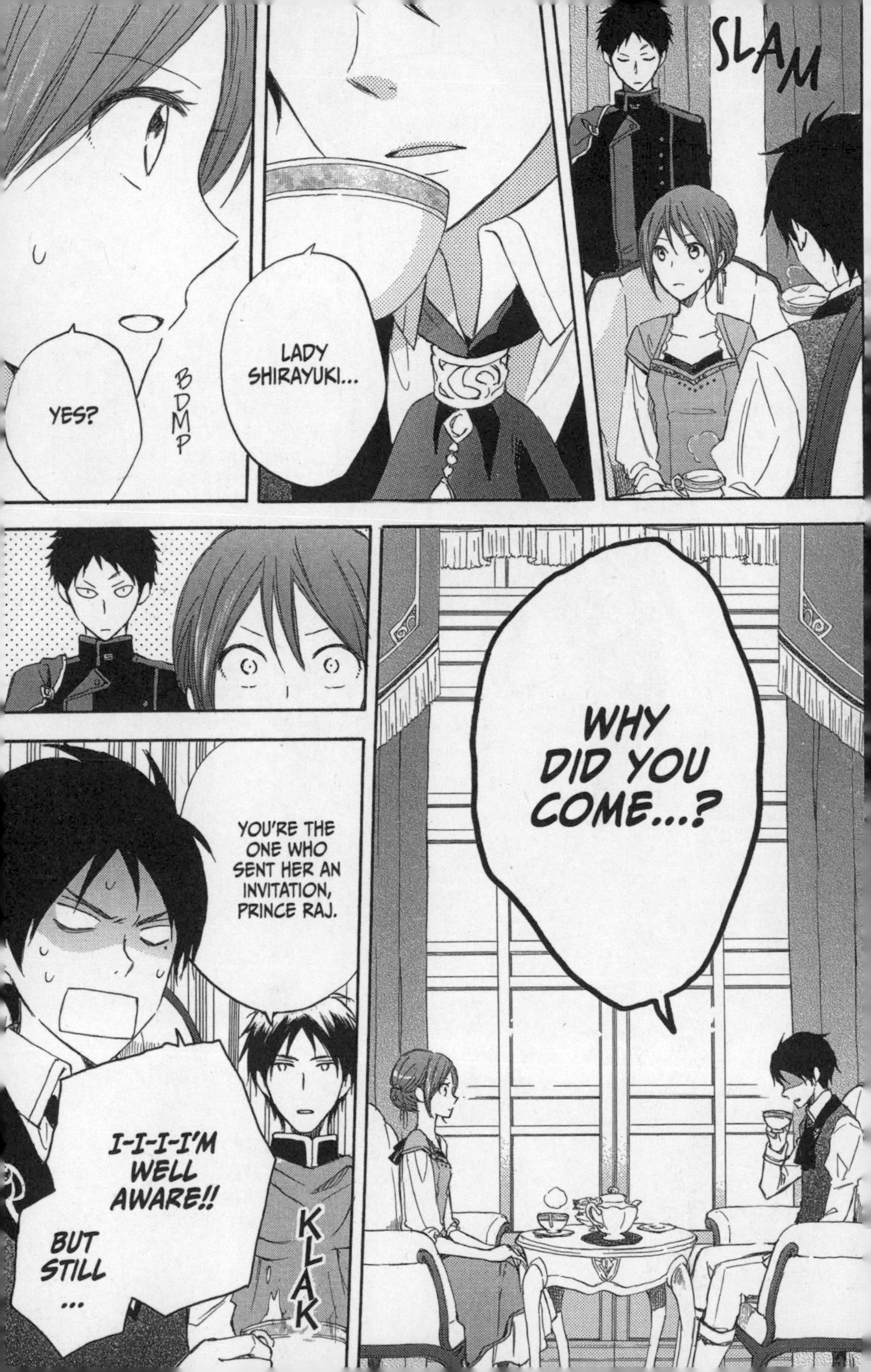
SLAM
LADY SHIRAYUKI...
YES?
BDMP
WHY DID YOU COME...?
YOU'RE THE ONE WHO SENT HER AN INVITATION, PRINCE RAJ.
KLAK
I-I-I-I'M WELL AWARE!!
BUT STILL ...

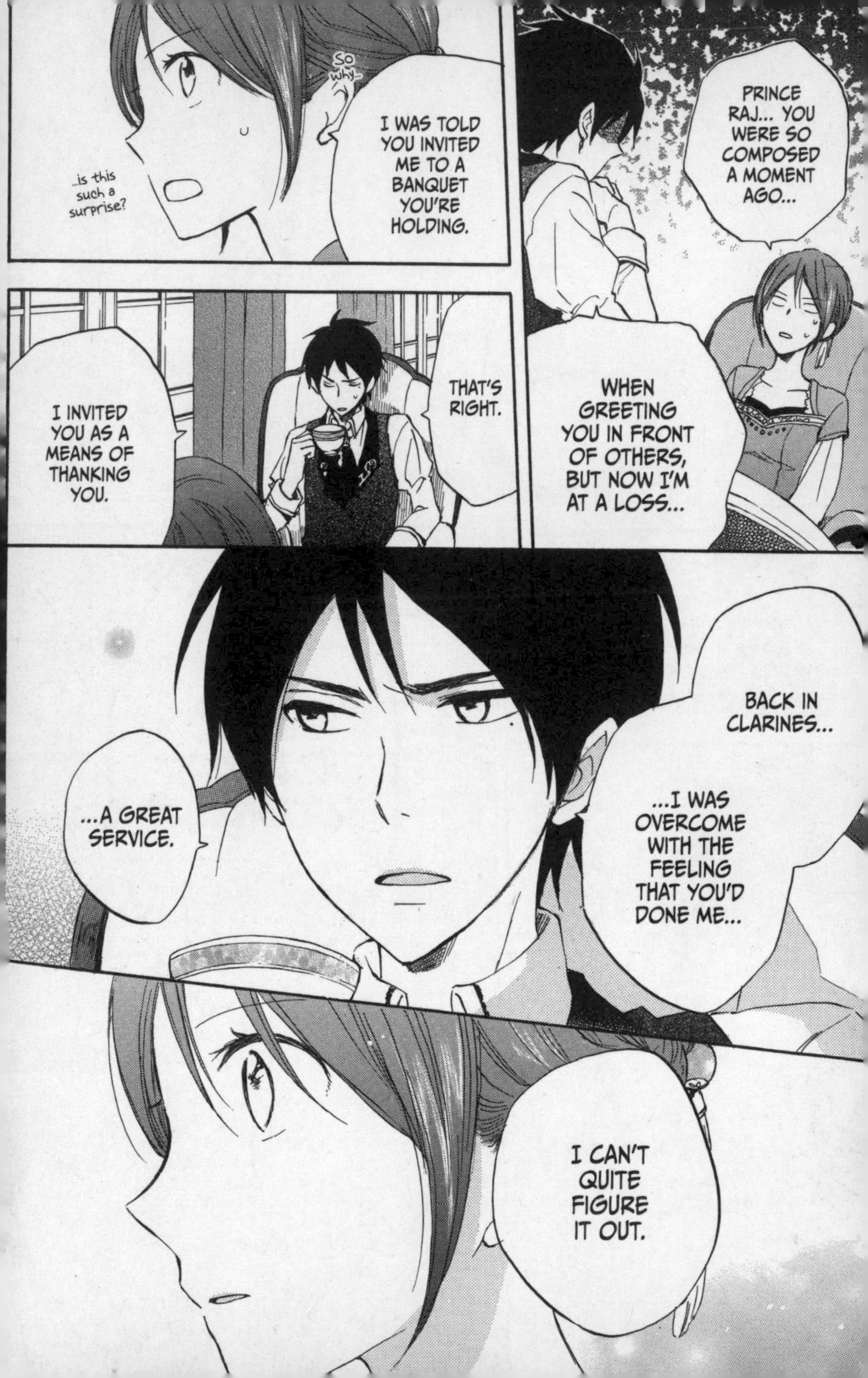
PRINCE RAJ... YOU WERE SO COMPOSED A MOMENT AGO...
WHEN GREETING YOU IN FRONT OF OTHERS, BUT NOW I'M AT A LOSS...
I WAS TOLD YOU INVITED ME TO A BANQUET YOU'RE HOLDING.
So why...
...is this such a surprise?
THAT'S RIGHT.
I INVITED YOU AS A MEANS OF THANKING YOU.
BACK IN CLARINES...
...I WAS OVERCOME WITH THE FEELING THAT YOU'D DONE ME...
...A GREAT SERVICE.
I CAN'T QUITE FIGURE IT OUT.

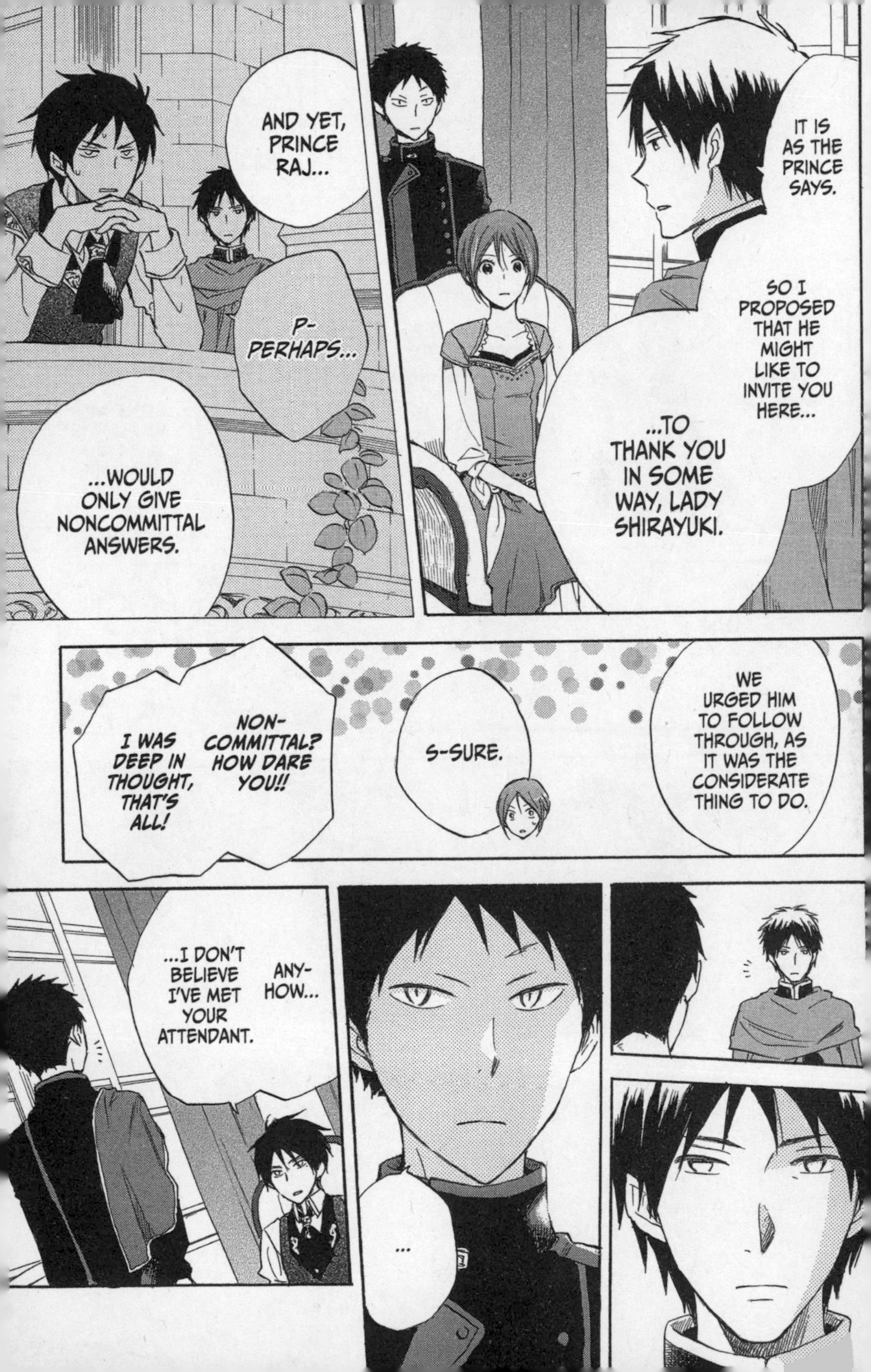
IT IS AS THE PRINCE SAYS.
SO I PROPOSED THAT HE MIGHT LIKE TO INVITE YOU HERE...
...TO THANK YOU IN SOME WAY, LADY SHIRAYUKI.
AND YET, PRINCE RAJ...
P-PERHAPS...
...WOULD ONLY GIVE NONCOMMITTAL ANSWERS.
WE URGED HIM TO FOLLOW THROUGH, AS IT WAS THE CONSIDERATE THING TO DO.
S-SURE.
NON-COMMITTAL? HOW DARE YOU!!
I WAS DEEP IN THOUGHT, THAT'S ALL!
...
ANY-HOW...
...I DON'T BELIEVE I'VE MET YOUR ATTENDANT.

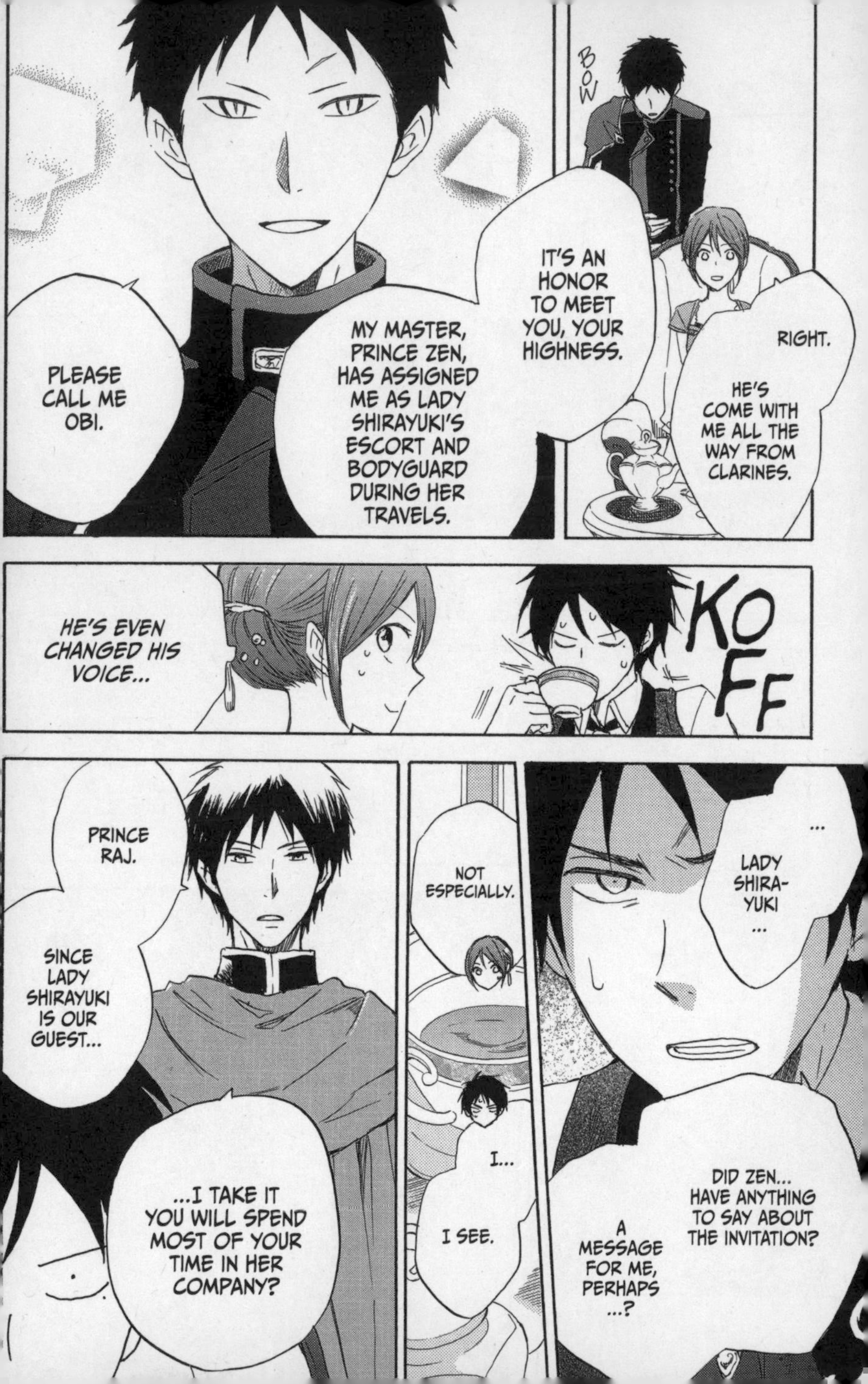

BOW
IT'S AN HONOR TO MEET YOU, YOUR HIGHNESS.
RIGHT.
HE'S COME WITH ME ALL THE WAY FROM CLARINES.
MY MASTER, PRINCE ZEN, HAS ASSIGNED ME AS LADY SHIRAYUKI'S ESCORT AND BODYGUARD DURING HER TRAVELS.
PLEASE CALL ME OBI.
KOFF
HE'S EVEN CHANGED HIS VOICE...
...
LADY SHIRAYUKI...
DID ZEN... HAVE ANYTHING TO SAY ABOUT THE INVITATION?
A MESSAGE FOR ME, PERHAPS...?
NOT ESPECIALLY.
I...
I SEE.
PRINCE RAJ.
SINCE LADY SHIRAYUKI IS OUR GUEST...
...I TAKE IT YOU WILL SPEND MOST OF YOUR TIME IN HER COMPANY?

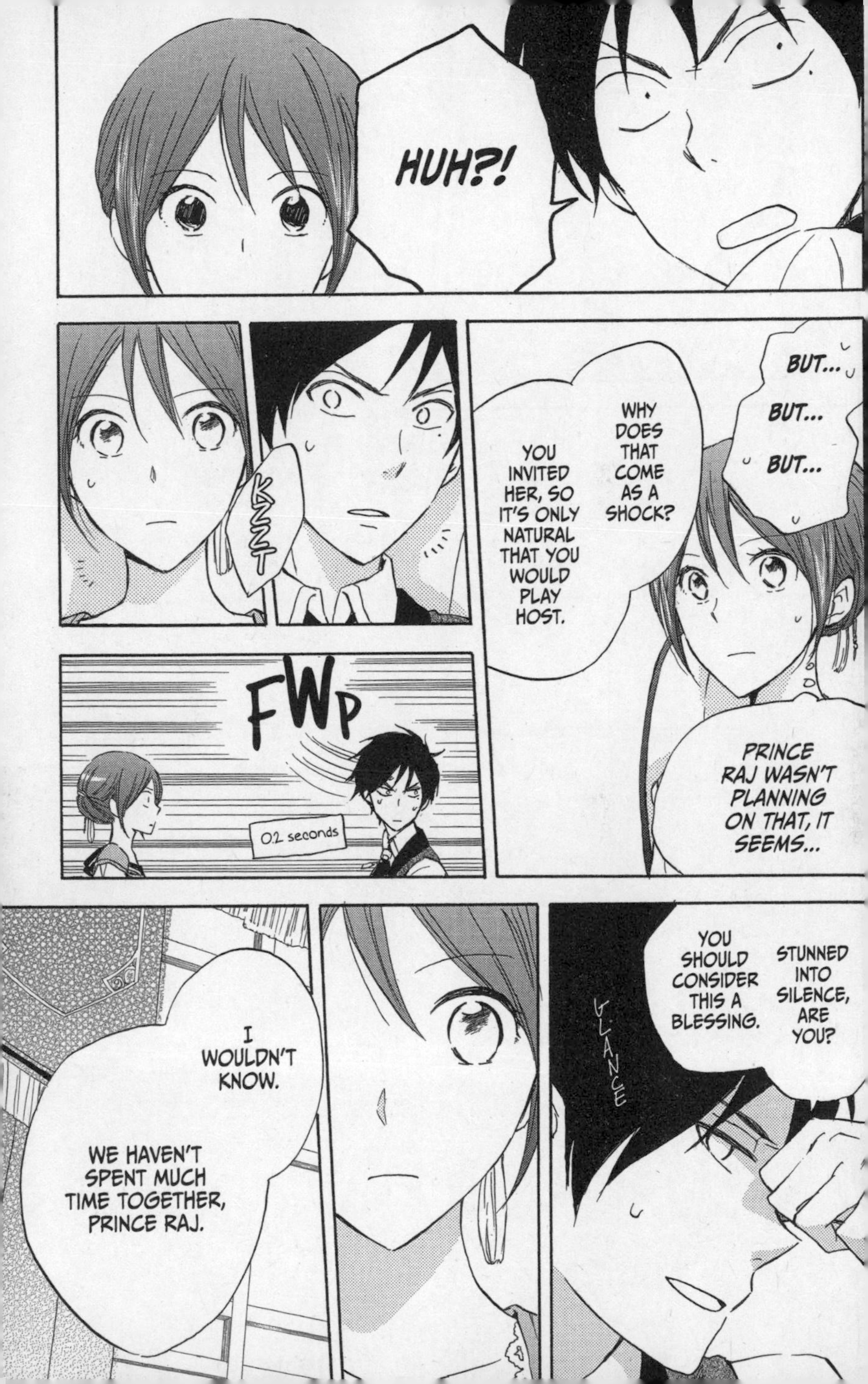
HUH?!
BUT... BUT... BUT...
WHY DOES THAT COME AS A SHOCK?
YOU INVITED HER, SO IT'S ONLY NATURAL THAT YOU WOULD PLAY HOST.
PRINCE RAJ WASN'T PLANNING ON THAT, IT SEEMS...
KZZT
FWP
0.2 seconds
STUNNED INTO SILENCE, ARE YOU?
YOU SHOULD CONSIDER THIS A BLESSING.
GLANCE
I WOULDN'T KNOW.
WE HAVEN'T SPENT MUCH TIME TOGETHER, PRINCE RAJ.

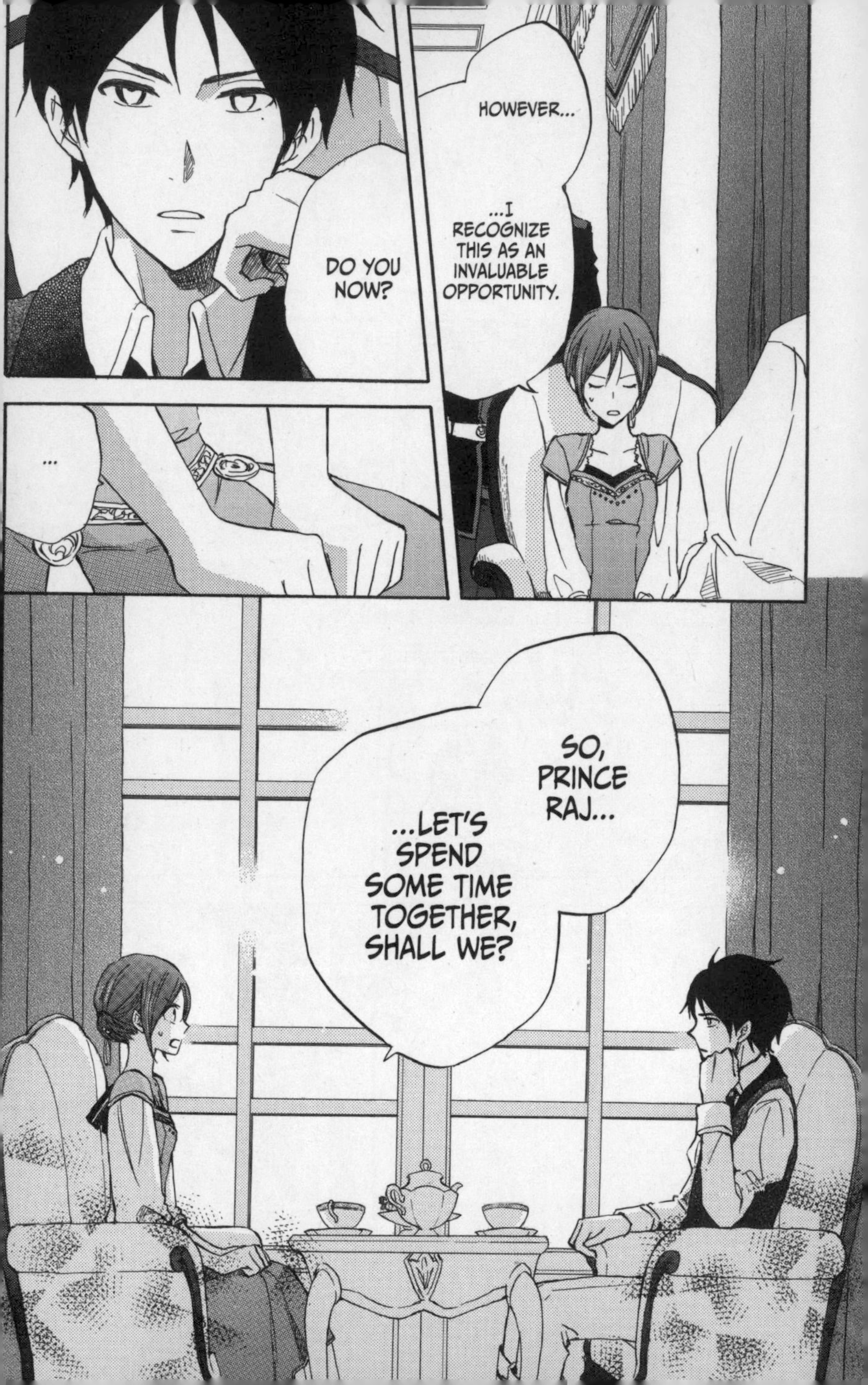
HOWEVER...
...I RECOGNIZE THIS AS AN INVALUABLE OPPORTUNITY.
DO YOU NOW?
...
SO, PRINCE RAJ...
...LET'S SPEND SOME TIME TOGETHER, SHALL WE?

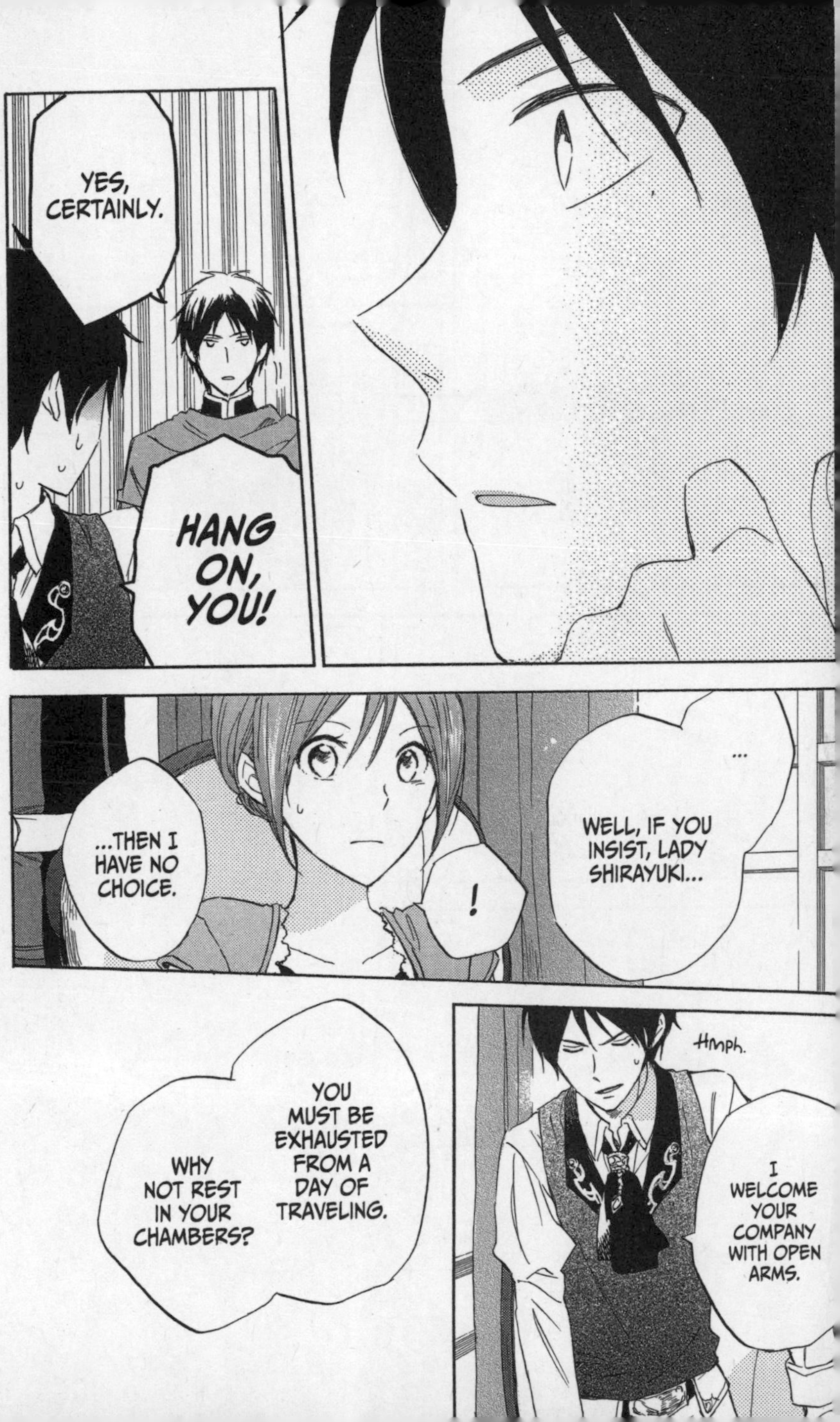
YES, CERTAINLY.
HANG ON, YOU!
...
WELL, IF YOU INSIST, LADY SHIRAYUKI...
!
...THEN I HAVE NO CHOICE.
Hmph.
I WELCOME YOUR COMPANY WITH OPEN ARMS.
YOU MUST BE EXHAUSTED FROM A DAY OF TRAVELING.
WHY NOT REST IN YOUR CHAMBERS?

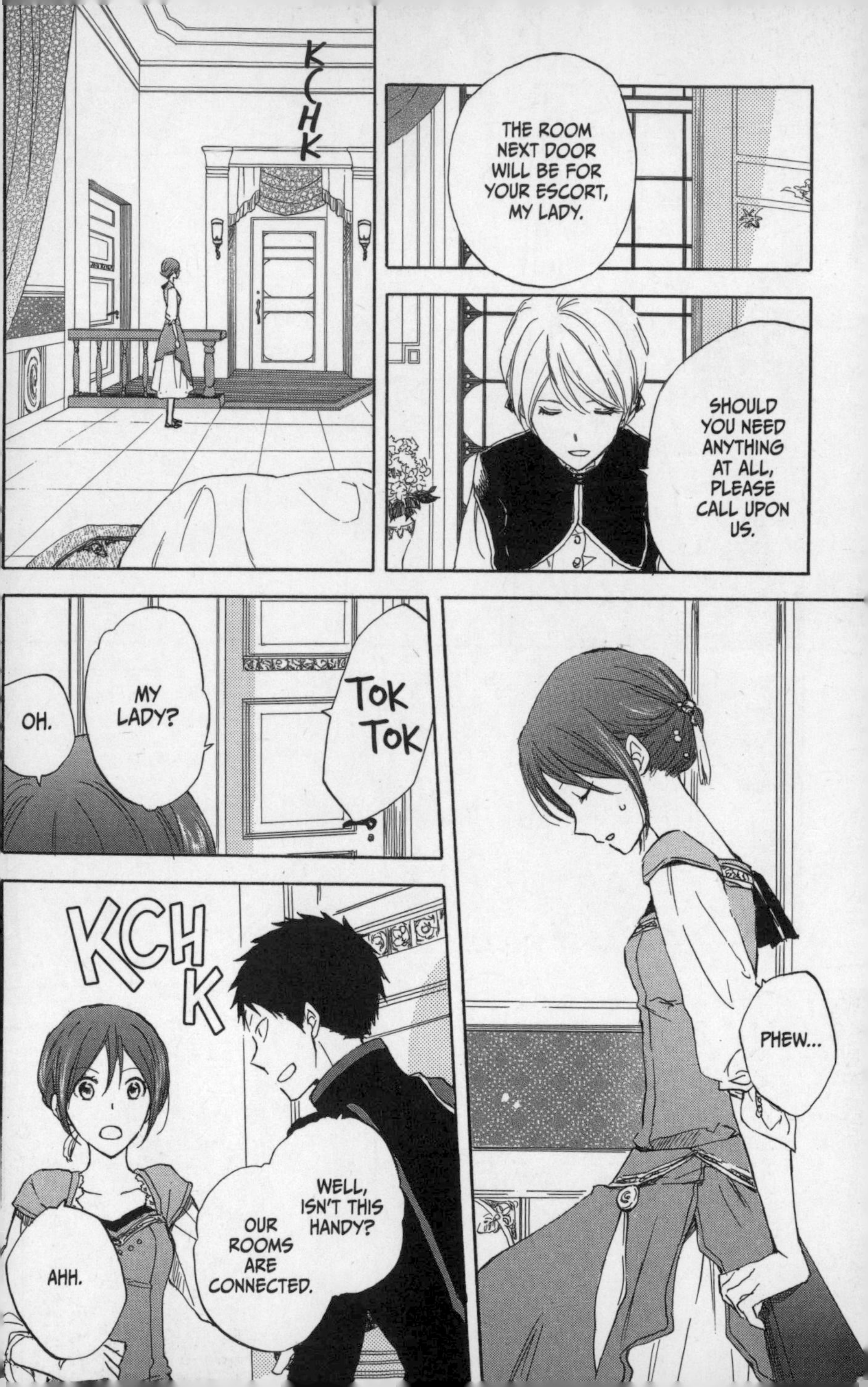
THE ROOM NEXT DOOR WILL BE FOR YOUR ESCORT, MY LADY.
SHOULD YOU NEED ANYTHING AT ALL, PLEASE CALL UPON US.
KCHK
PHEW...
TOK TOK
MY LADY?
OH.
KCHK
WELL, ISN'T THIS HANDY?
OUR ROOMS ARE CONNECTED.
AHH.

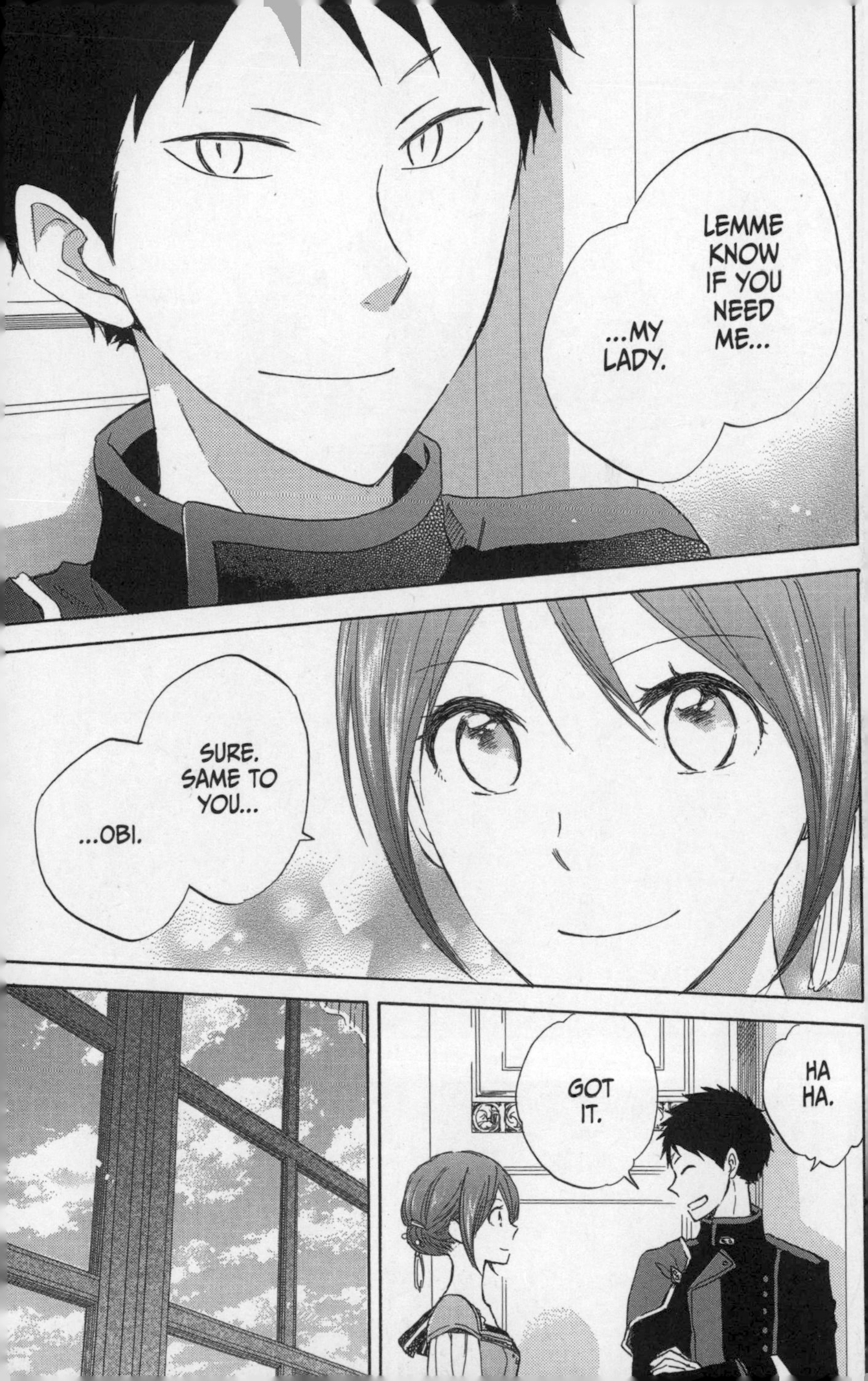
LEMME KNOW IF YOU NEED ME...
...MY LADY.
SURE. SAME TO YOU...
...OBI.
HA HA.
GOT IT.

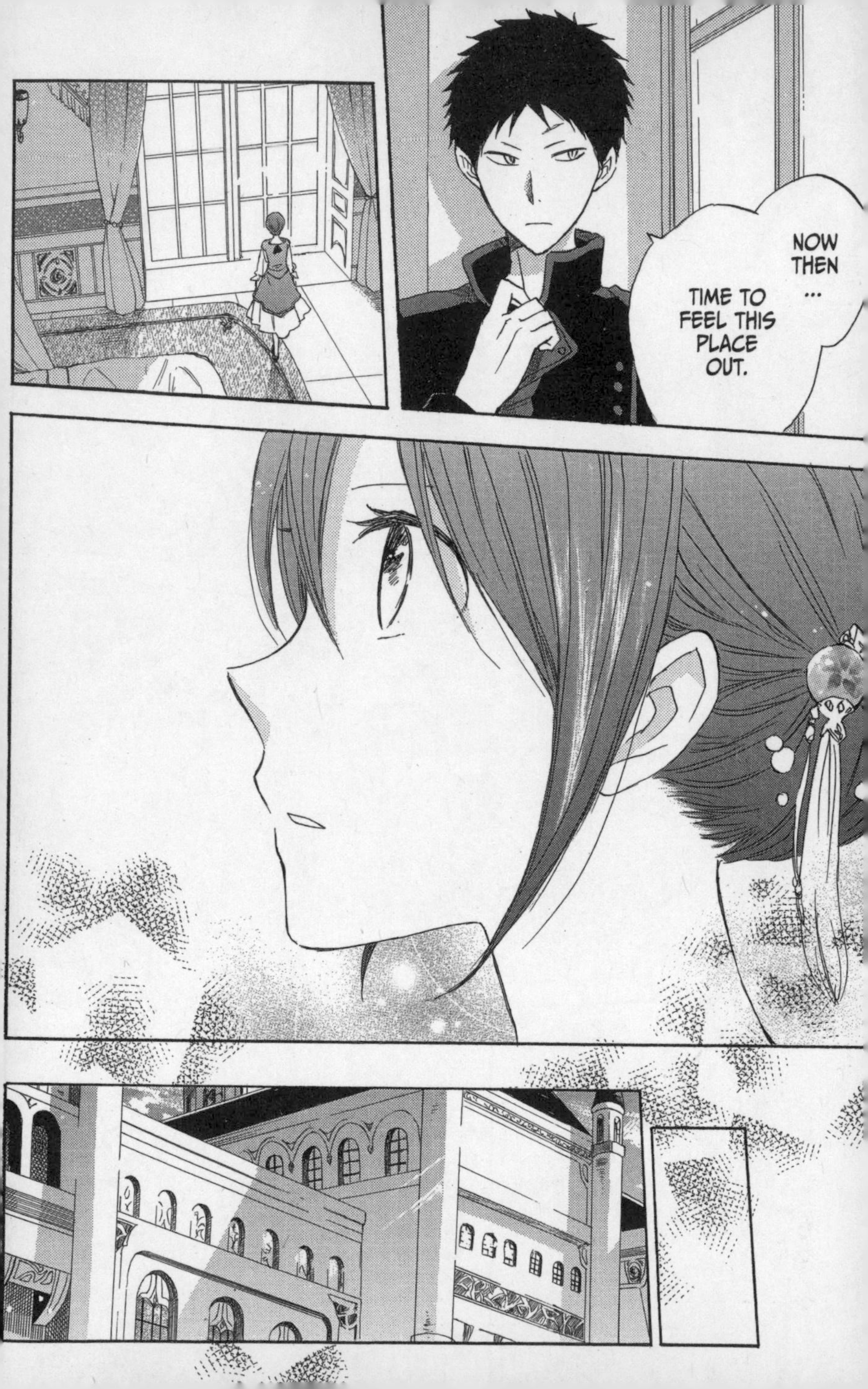
NOW THEN ...
TIME TO FEEL THIS PLACE OUT.

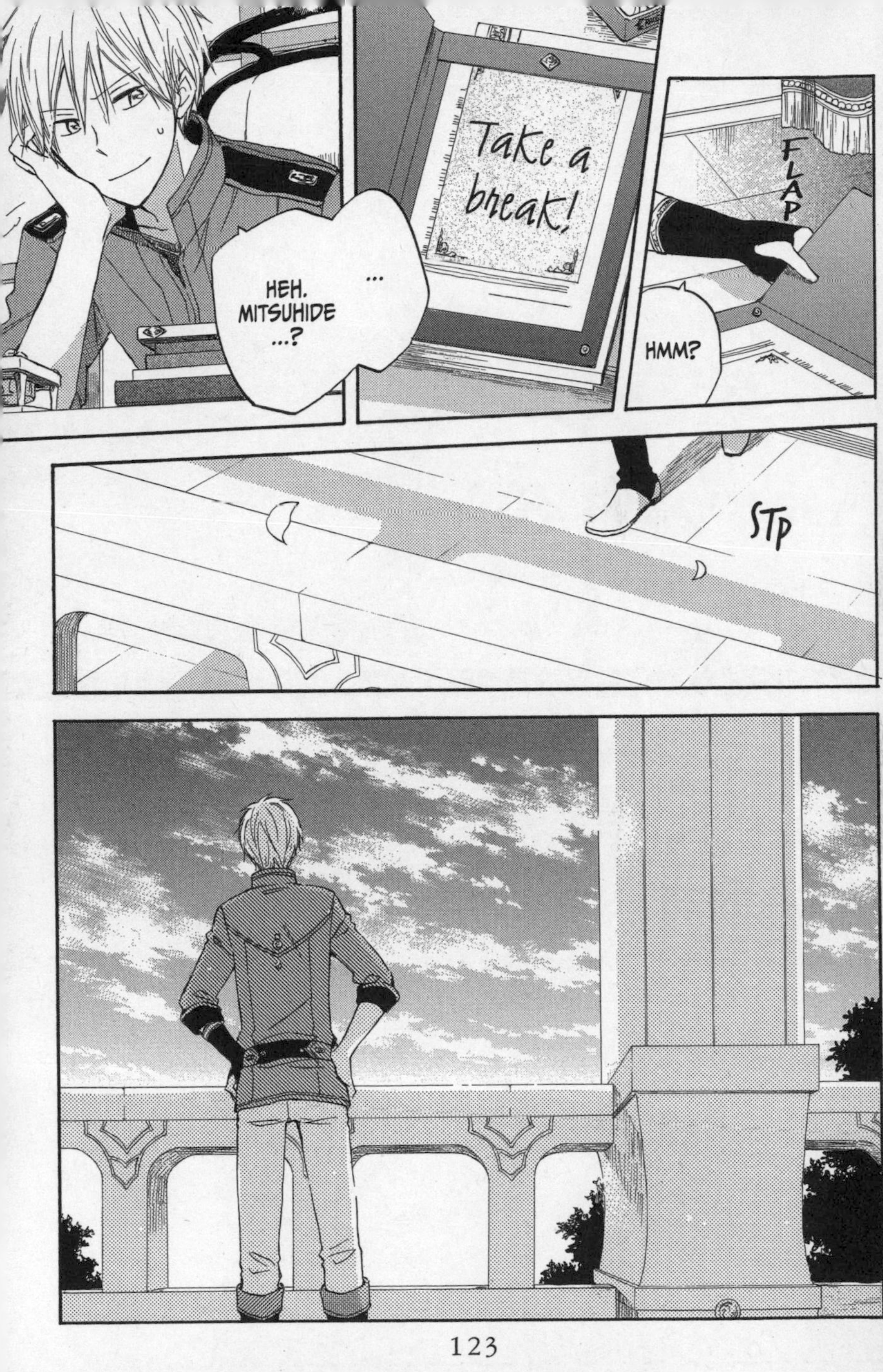
FLAP
HMM?
Take a break!
...
HEH. MITSUHIDE ...?
STP

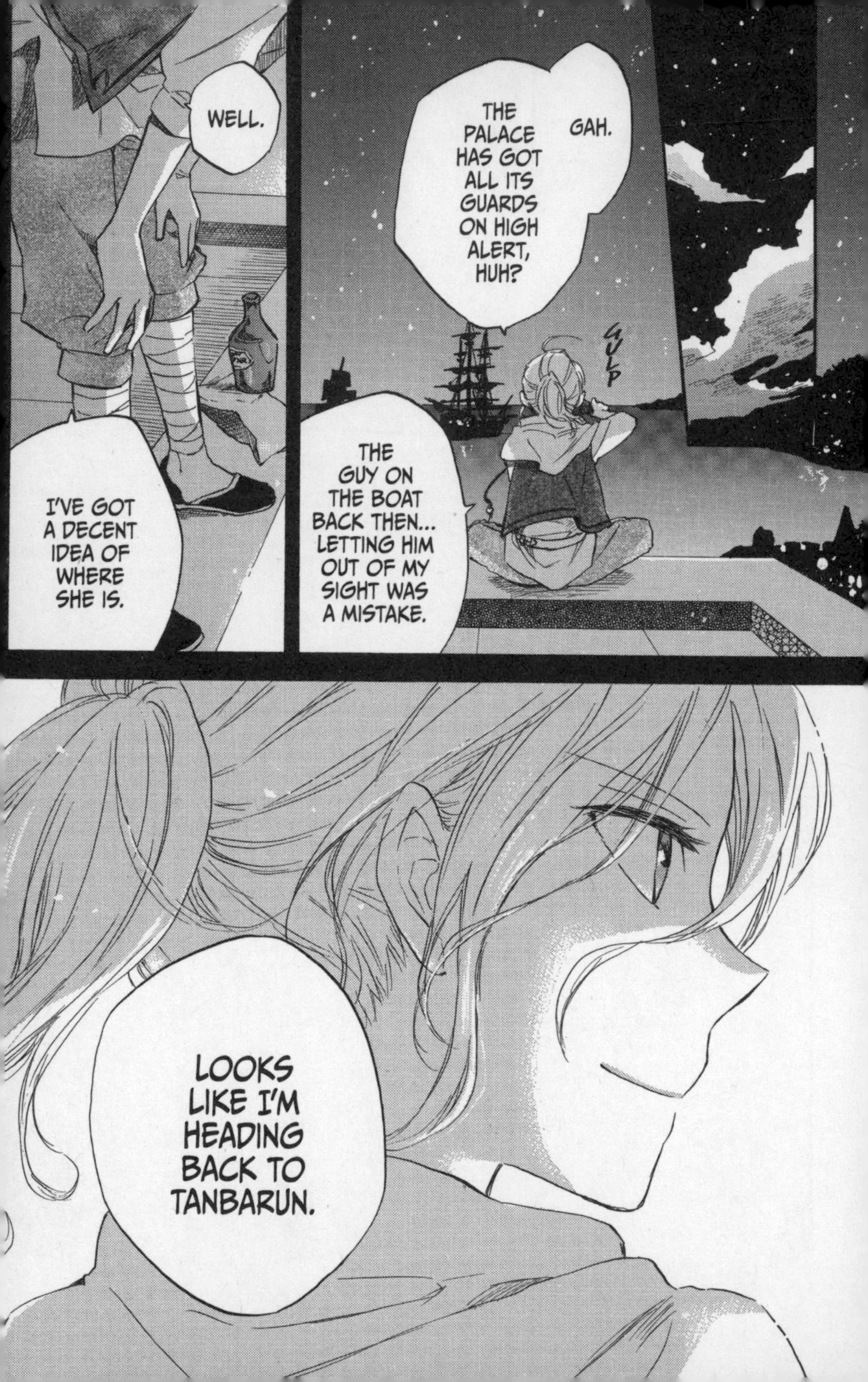
GAH.
THE PALACE HAS GOT ALL ITS GUARDS ON HIGH ALERT, HUH?
GULP
THE GUY ON THE BOAT BACK THEN... LETTING HIM OUT OF MY SIGHT WAS A MISTAKE.
WELL.
I'VE GOT A DECENT IDEA OF WHERE SHE IS.
LOOKS LIKE I'M HEADING BACK TO TANBARUN.

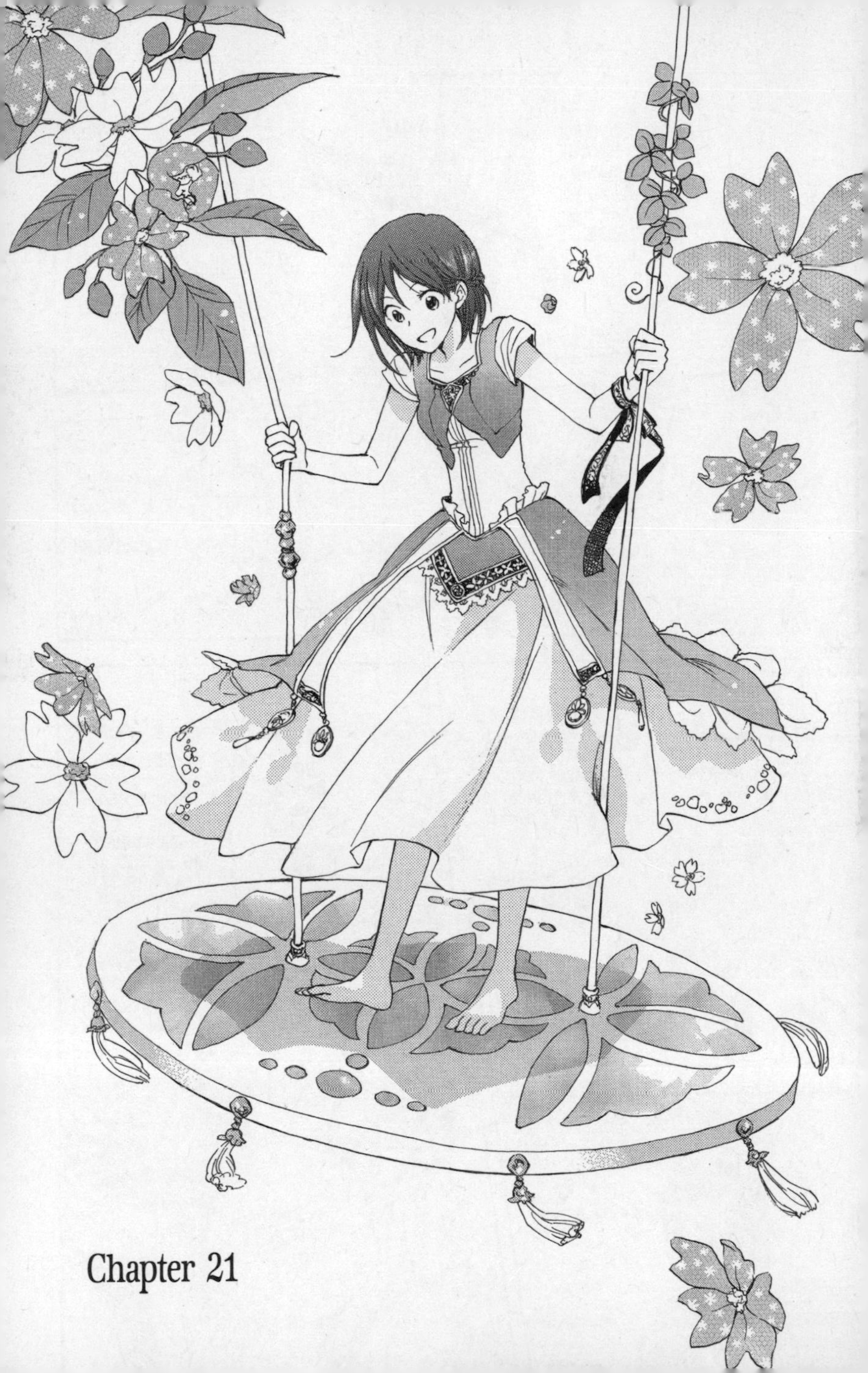

Chapter 21

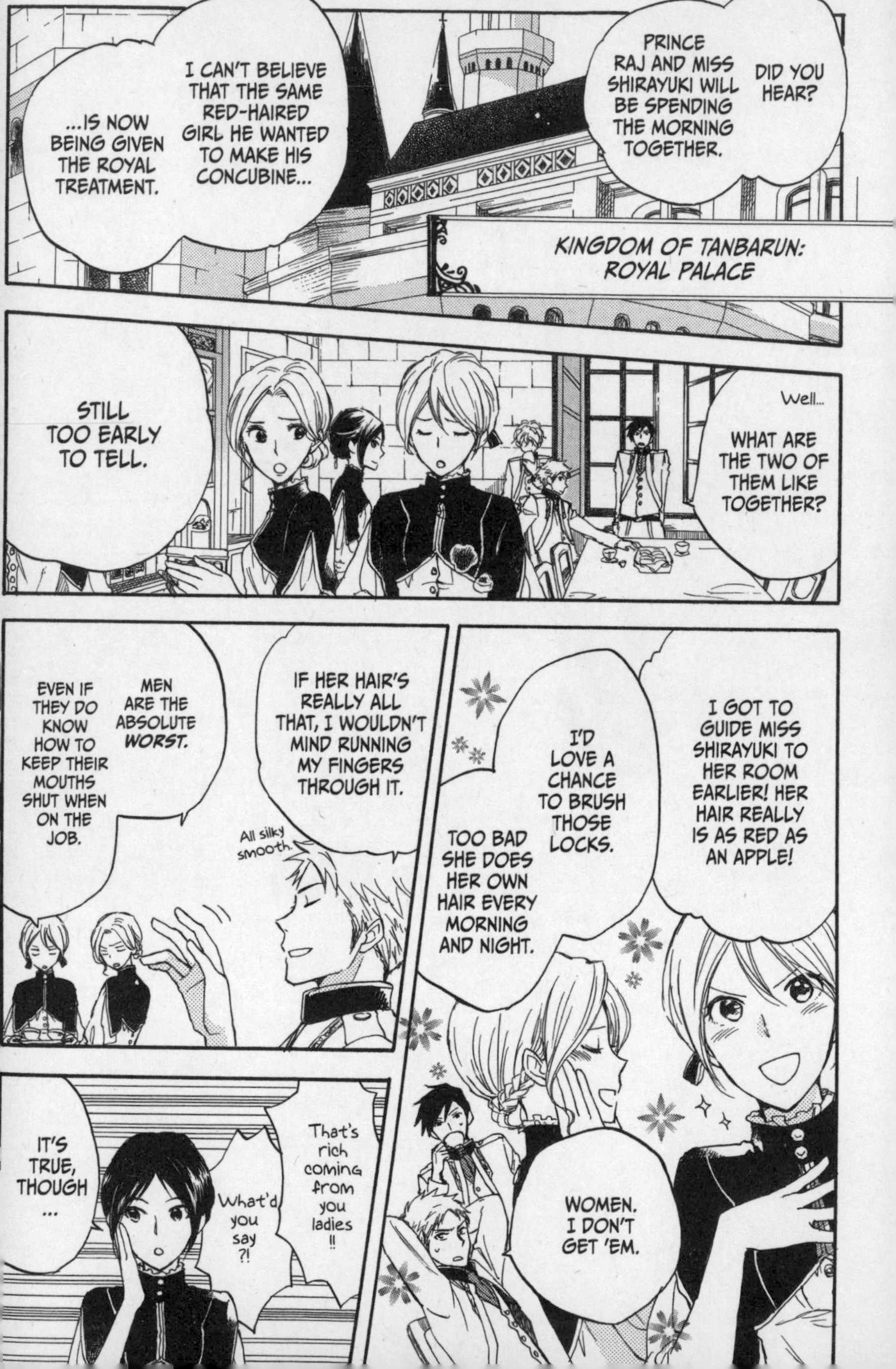
DID YOU HEAR?
PRINCE RAJ AND MISS SHIRAYUKI WILL BE SPENDING THE MORNING TOGETHER.
KINGDOM OF TANBARUN: ROYAL PALACE
I CAN'T BELIEVE THAT THE SAME RED-HAIRED GIRL HE WANTED TO MAKE HIS CONCUBINE...
...IS NOW BEING GIVEN THE ROYAL TREATMENT.
Well...
WHAT ARE THE TWO OF THEM LIKE TOGETHER?
STILL TOO EARLY TO TELL.
I GOT TO GUIDE MISS SHIRAYUKI TO HER ROOM EARLIER! HER HAIR REALLY IS AS RED AS AN APPLE!
I'D LOVE A CHANCE TO BRUSH THOSE LOCKS.
TOO BAD SHE DOES HER OWN HAIR EVERY MORNING AND NIGHT.
WOMEN. I DON'T GET 'EM.
IF HER HAIR'S REALLY ALL THAT, I WOULDN'T MIND RUNNING MY FINGERS THROUGH IT.
All silky smooth.
MEN ARE THE ABSOLUTE *WORST.*
EVEN IF THEY DO KNOW HOW TO KEEP THEIR MOUTHS SHUT WHEN ON THE JOB.
That's rich coming from you ladies!!
What'd you say?!
IT'S TRUE, THOUGH...

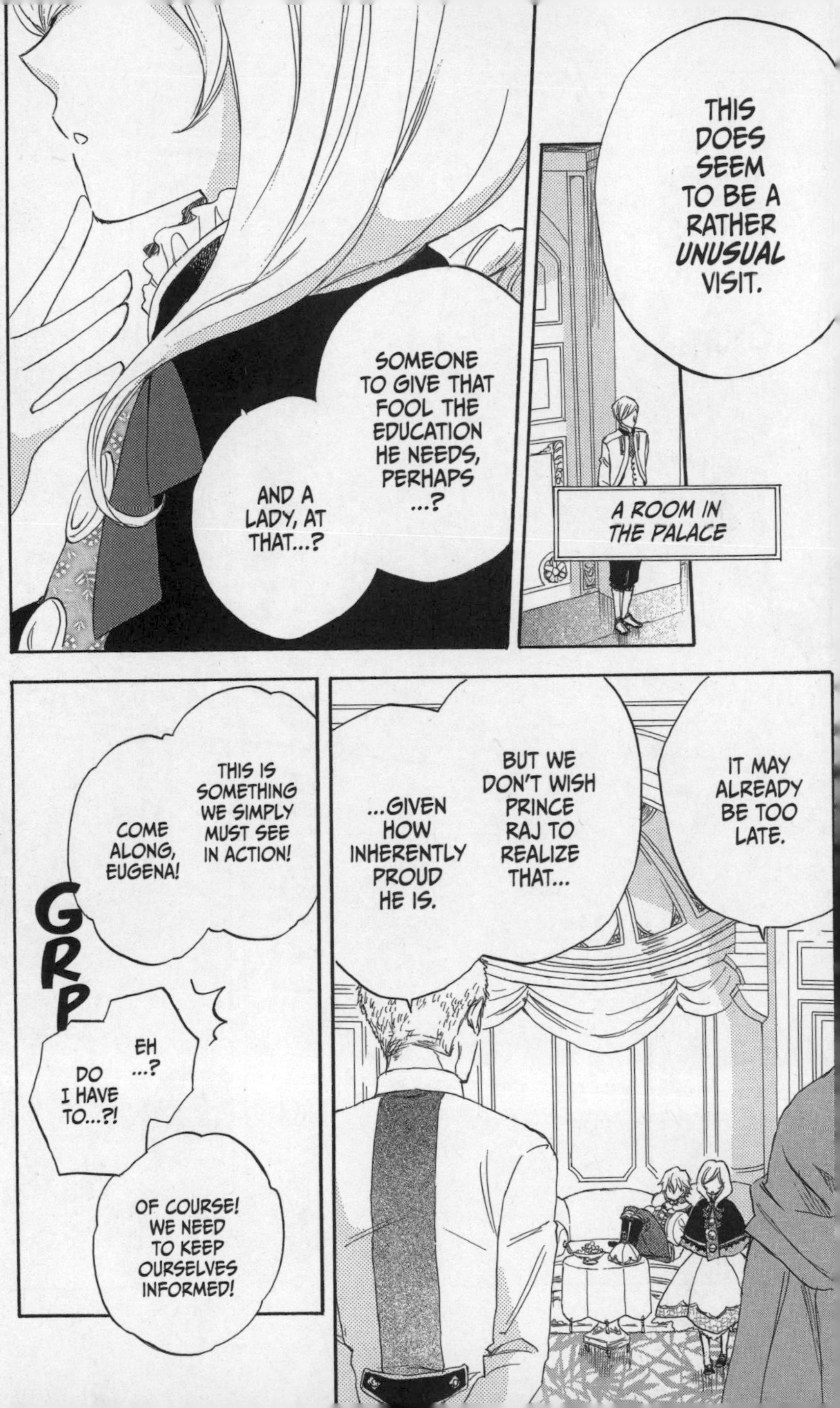
THIS DOES SEEM TO BE A RATHER *UNUSUAL* VISIT.
A ROOM IN THE PALACE
SOMEONE TO GIVE THAT FOOL THE EDUCATION HE NEEDS, PERHAPS ...?
AND A LADY, AT THAT...?
IT MAY ALREADY BE TOO LATE.
BUT WE DON'T WISH PRINCE RAJ TO REALIZE THAT...
...GIVEN HOW INHERENTLY PROUD HE IS.
THIS IS SOMETHING WE SIMPLY MUST SEE IN ACTION!
COME ALONG, EUGENA!
GRP
EH ...?
DO I HAVE TO...?!
OF COURSE! WE NEED TO KEEP OURSELVES INFORMED!

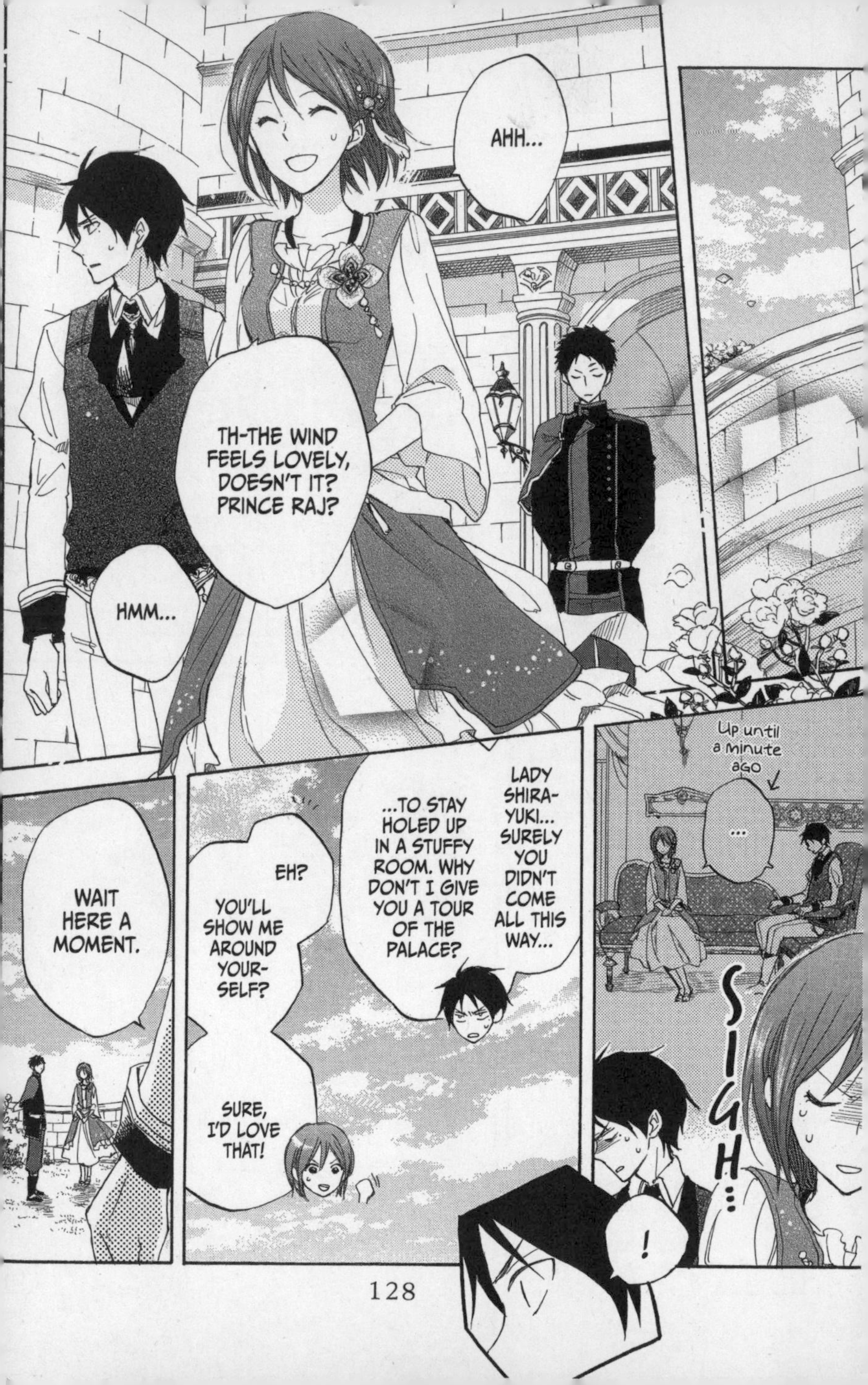
AHH...
TH-THE WIND FEELS LOVELY, DOESN'T IT? PRINCE RAJ?
HMM...
Up until a minute ago
...
SIGH...
!
LADY SHIRAYUKI... SURELY YOU DIDN'T COME ALL THIS WAY...
...TO STAY HOLED UP IN A STUFFY ROOM. WHY DON'T I GIVE YOU A TOUR OF THE PALACE?
EH?
YOU'LL SHOW ME AROUND YOURSELF?
SURE, I'D LOVE THAT!
WAIT HERE A MOMENT.

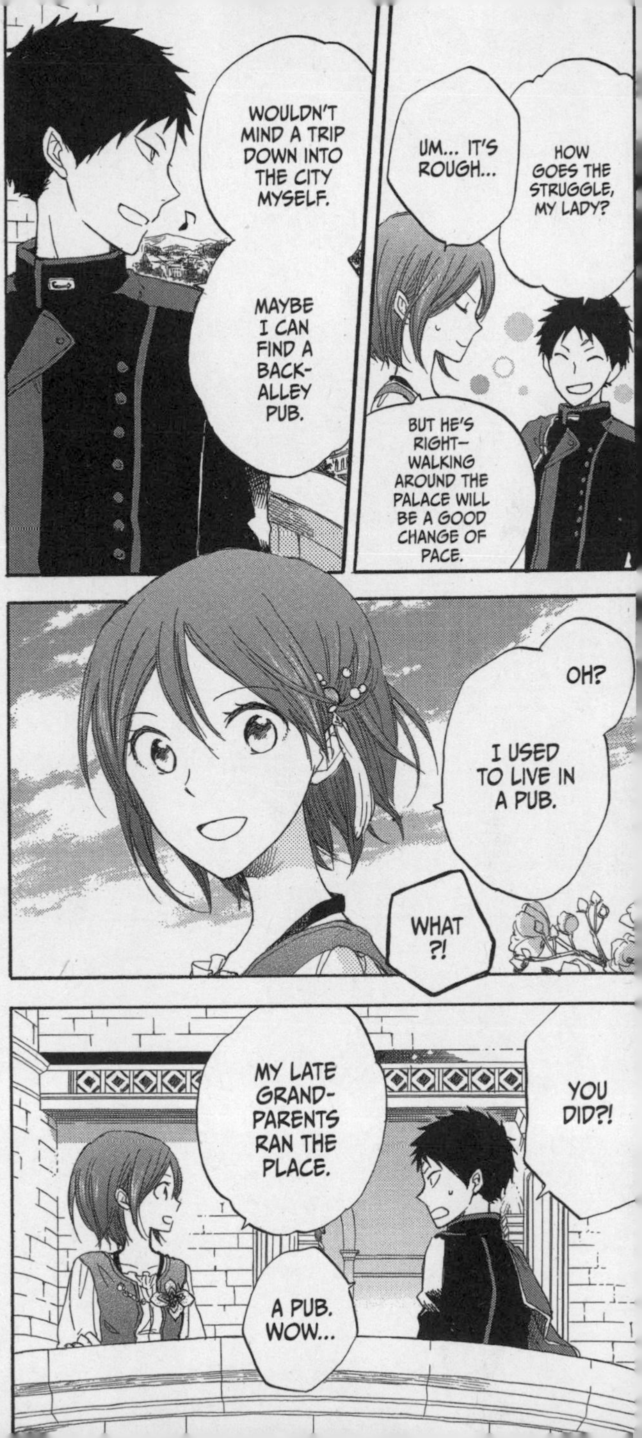
HOW GOES THE STRUGGLE, MY LADY?
UM... IT'S ROUGH...
BUT HE'S RIGHT—WALKING AROUND THE PALACE WILL BE A GOOD CHANGE OF PACE.
WOULDN'T MIND A TRIP DOWN INTO THE CITY MYSELF.
MAYBE I CAN FIND A BACK-ALLEY PUB.
OH?
I USED TO LIVE IN A PUB.
WHAT?!
YOU DID?!
MY LATE GRAND-PARENTS RAN THE PLACE.
A PUB. WOW...

The other day, I was doing some pen work on way too little sleep.

My sister, who was helping out with the toning, asked,

"What on earth are you doing?"

It turned out I wasn't even holding a pen.

I-I call this move... "air pen"...

Luckily, this silly mistake meant I didn't have to do a bunch of corrections.

Get good sleep, everyone.

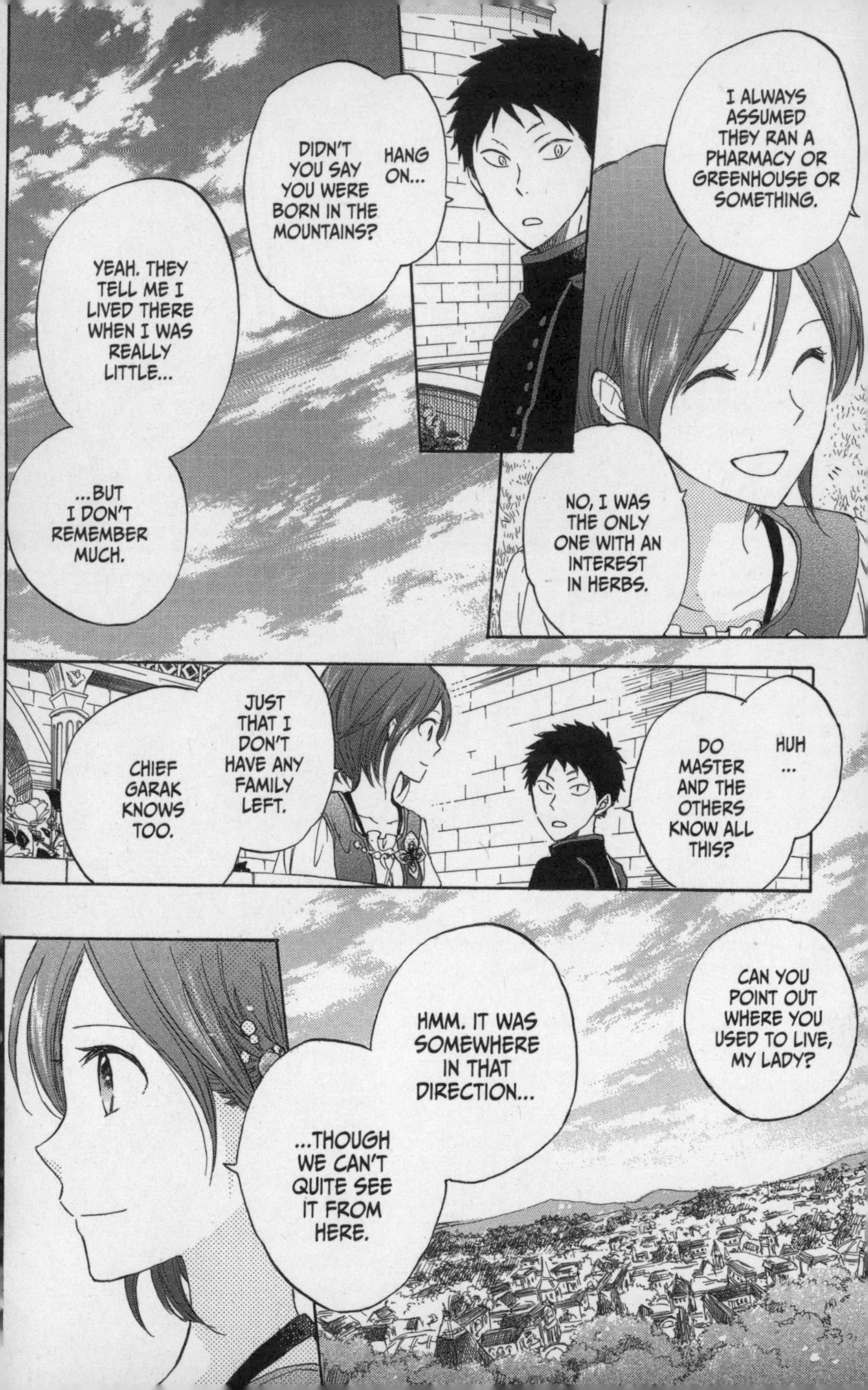
I ALWAYS ASSUMED THEY RAN A PHARMACY OR GREENHOUSE OR SOMETHING.
NO, I WAS THE ONLY ONE WITH AN INTEREST IN HERBS.
HANG ON...
DIDN'T YOU SAY YOU WERE BORN IN THE MOUNTAINS?
YEAH. THEY TELL ME I LIVED THERE WHEN I WAS REALLY LITTLE...
...BUT I DON'T REMEMBER MUCH.
HUH ...
DO MASTER AND THE OTHERS KNOW ALL THIS?
JUST THAT I DON'T HAVE ANY FAMILY LEFT.
CHIEF GARAK KNOWS TOO.
CAN YOU POINT OUT WHERE YOU USED TO LIVE, MY LADY?
HMM. IT WAS SOMEWHERE IN THAT DIRECTION...
...THOUGH WE CAN'T QUITE SEE IT FROM HERE.

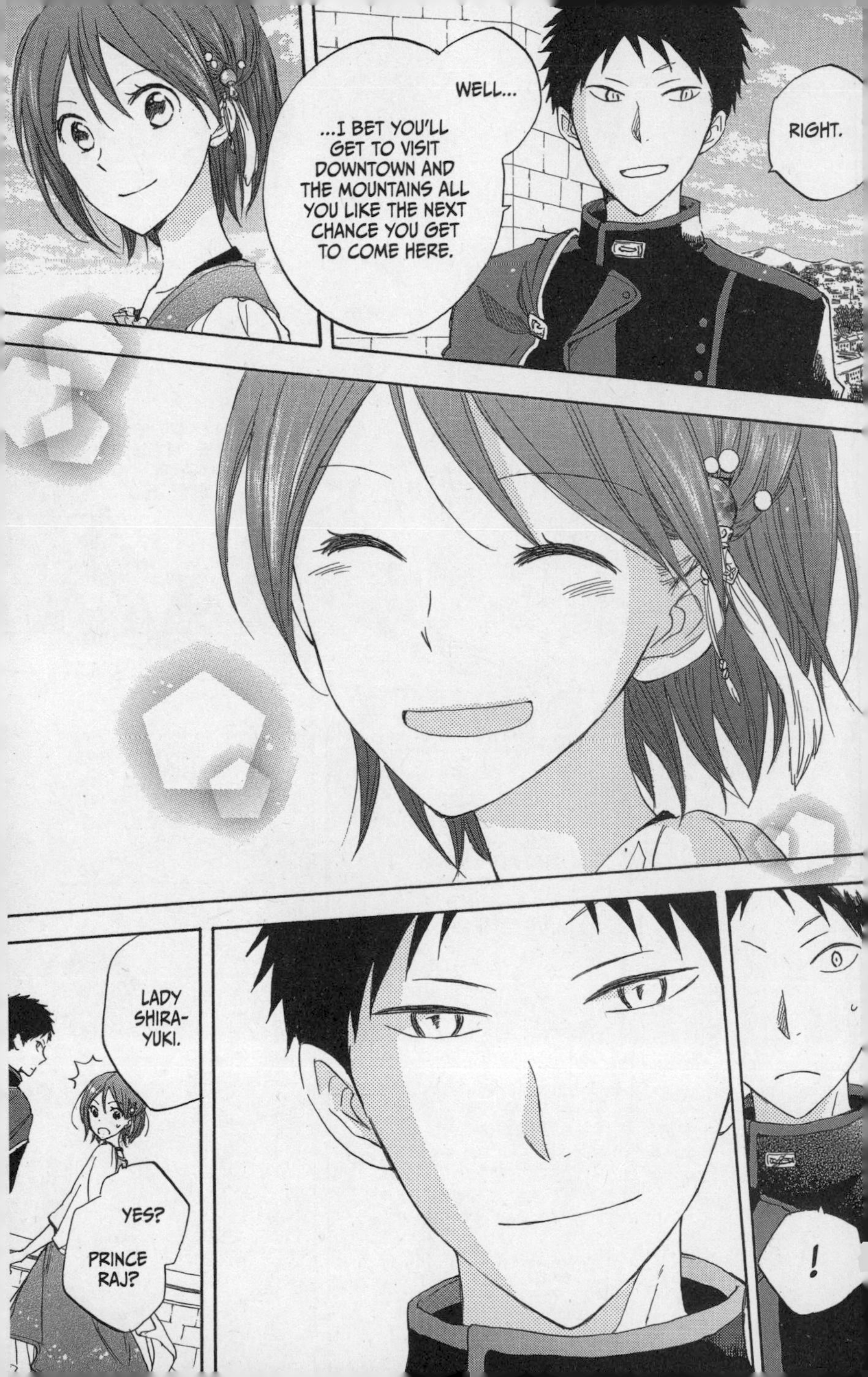
RIGHT.
WELL...
...I BET YOU'LL GET TO VISIT DOWNTOWN AND THE MOUNTAINS ALL YOU LIKE THE NEXT CHANCE YOU GET TO COME HERE.
!
LADY SHIRA-YUKI.
YES?
PRINCE RAJ?

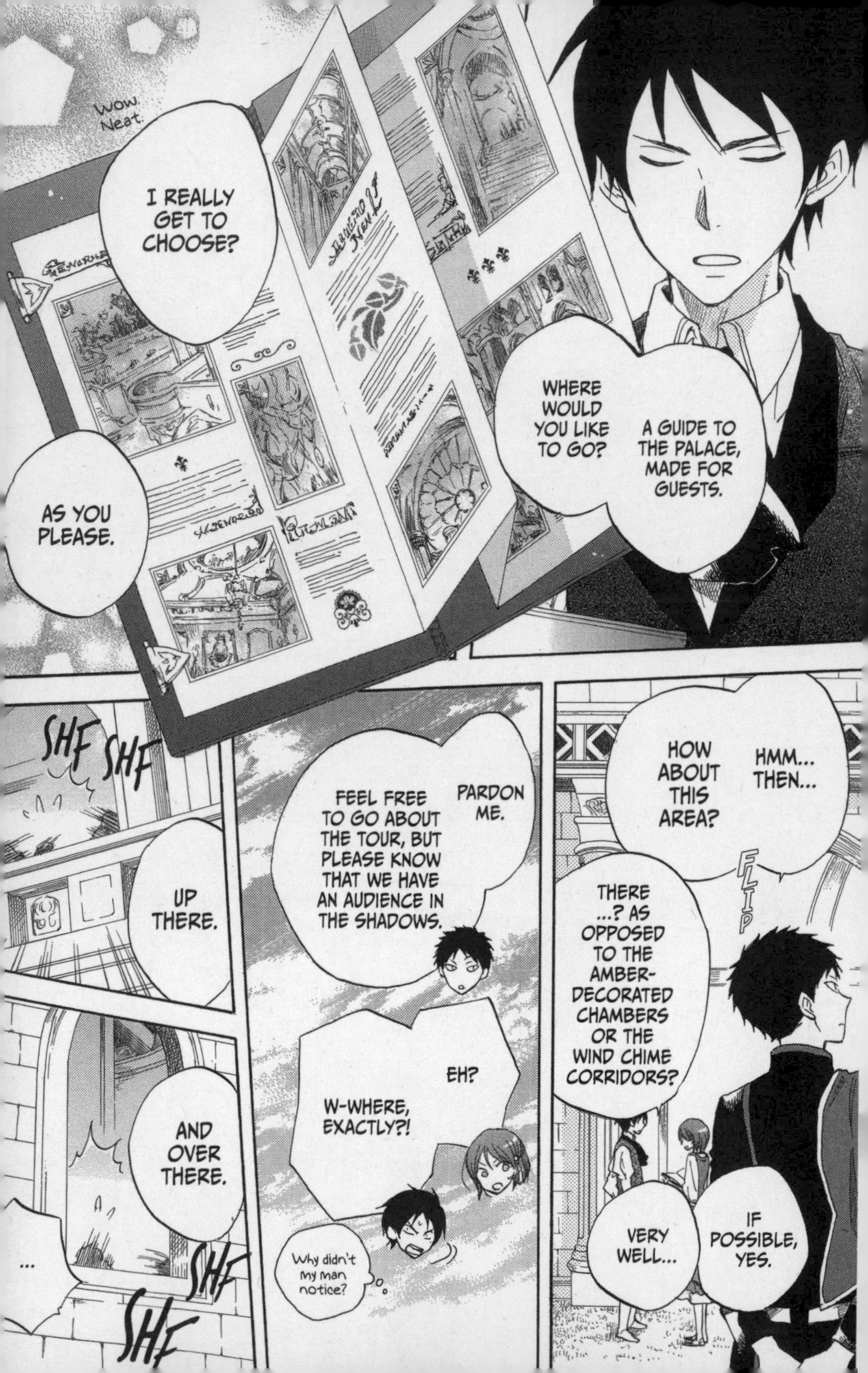
A GUIDE TO THE PALACE, MADE FOR GUESTS.
WHERE WOULD YOU LIKE TO GO?
I REALLY GET TO CHOOSE?
Wow. Neat.
AS YOU PLEASE.
HMM... THEN...
HOW ABOUT THIS AREA?
FLIP
THERE ...? AS OPPOSED TO THE AMBER-DECORATED CHAMBERS OR THE WIND CHIME CORRIDORS?
IF POSSIBLE, YES.
VERY WELL...
PARDON ME.
FEEL FREE TO GO ABOUT THE TOUR, BUT PLEASE KNOW THAT WE HAVE AN AUDIENCE IN THE SHADOWS.
EH?
W-WHERE, EXACTLY?!
Why didn't my man notice?
SHF SHF
UP THERE.
AND OVER THERE.
SHF SHF
...

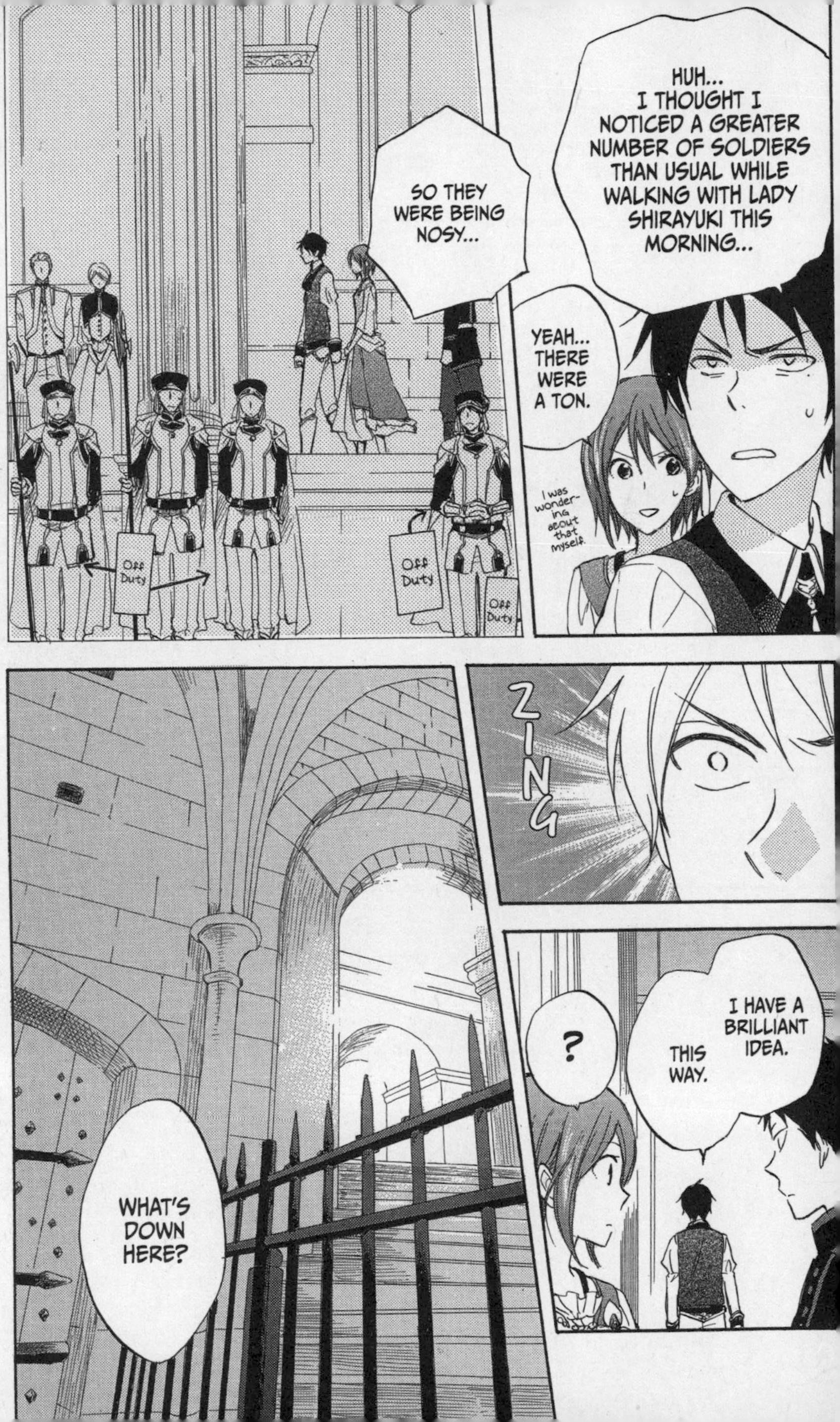
HUH... I THOUGHT I NOTICED A GREATER NUMBER OF SOLDIERS THAN USUAL WHILE WALKING WITH LADY SHIRAYUKI THIS MORNING...
YEAH... THERE WERE A TON.
I was wondering about that myself.
SO THEY WERE BEING NOSY...
Off Duty
Off Duty
Off Duty
ZING
I HAVE A BRILLIANT IDEA.
THIS WAY.
?
WHAT'S DOWN HERE?

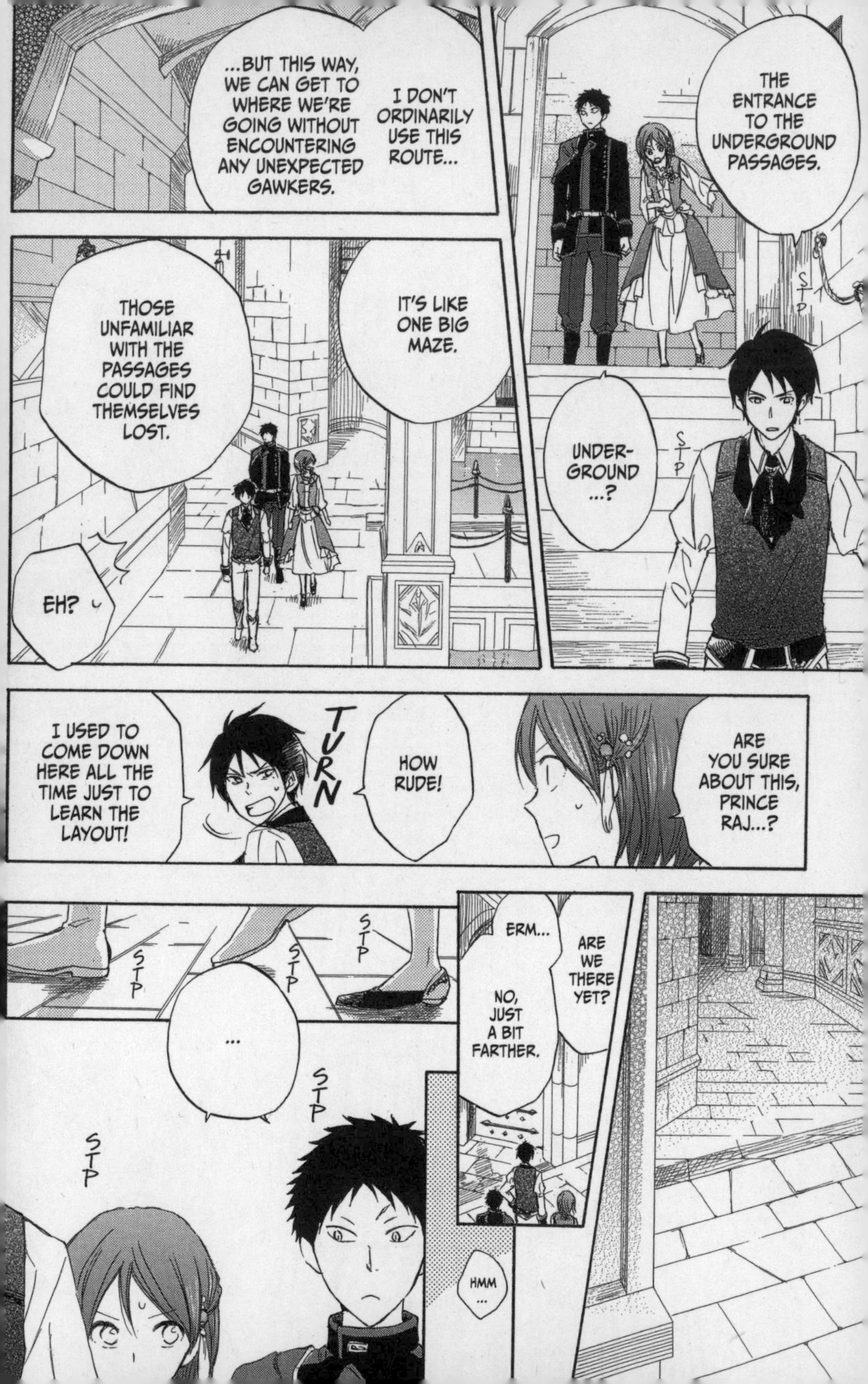
THE ENTRANCE TO THE UNDERGROUND PASSAGES.
STP
UNDER-GROUND ...?
STP
I DON'T ORDINARILY USE THIS ROUTE...
...BUT THIS WAY, WE CAN GET TO WHERE WE'RE GOING WITHOUT ENCOUNTERING ANY UNEXPECTED GAWKERS.
IT'S LIKE ONE BIG MAZE.
THOSE UNFAMILIAR WITH THE PASSAGES COULD FIND THEMSELVES LOST.
EH?
ARE YOU SURE ABOUT THIS, PRINCE RAJ...?
TURN
HOW RUDE!
I USED TO COME DOWN HERE ALL THE TIME JUST TO LEARN THE LAYOUT!
ERM...
ARE WE THERE YET?
NO, JUST A BIT FARTHER.
STP
STP
STP
...
STP
STP
HMM ...

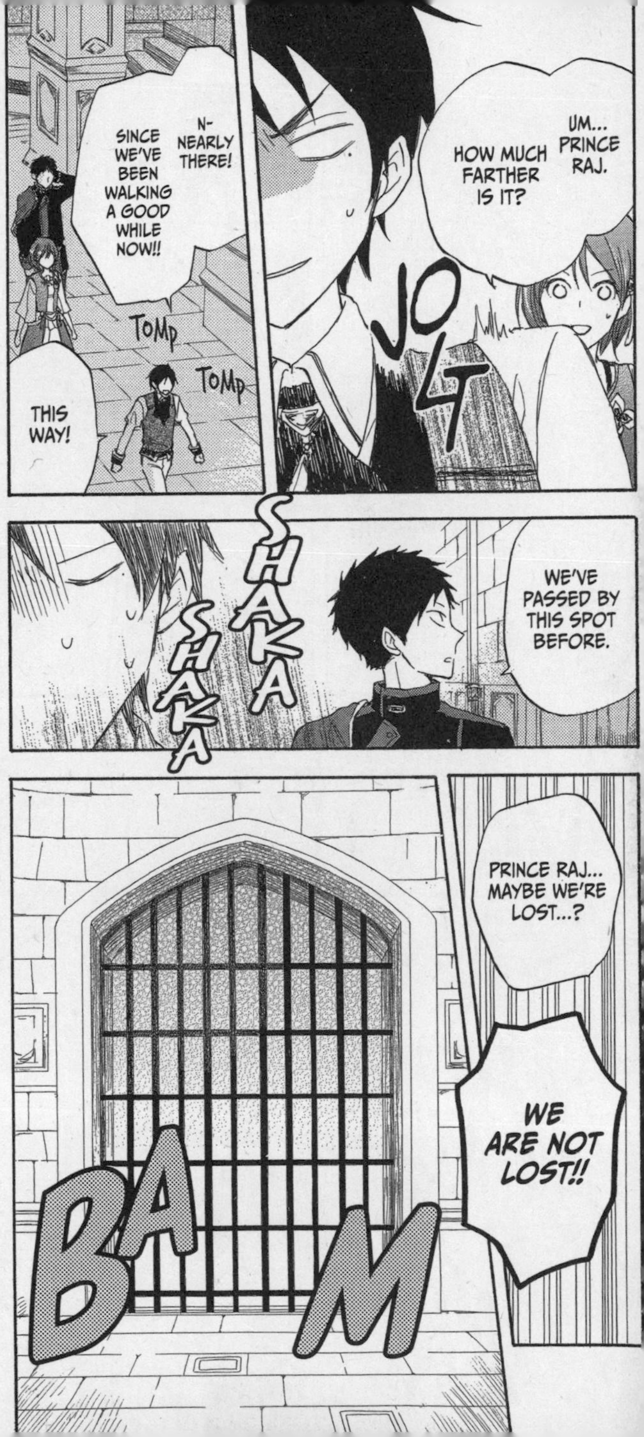
UM... PRINCE RAJ.
HOW MUCH FARTHER IS IT?
JOLT
N-NEARLY THERE!
SINCE WE'VE BEEN WALKING A GOOD WHILE NOW!!
TOMP
TOMP
THIS WAY!
WE'VE PASSED BY THIS SPOT BEFORE.
SHAKA
SHAKA
PRINCE RAJ... MAYBE WE'RE LOST...?
WE ARE NOT LOST!!
BAM

When chapter 19 ran in *LaLa DX*, I got to draw my first magazine cover.

That made me so happy!!

I wrote about this in my comment at the time, but they instructed me to make Zen look "especially princely." Hilarious.

Princely, they said... Princely!

When I turn off my brain, Zen can end up looking more like a scruffy background character from the city streets, but this time, I went all out to clean him up.

On the cover of that issue of *LaLa DX*, Shirayuki wears a dress with her hair tied back and her hands clasped behind her back.

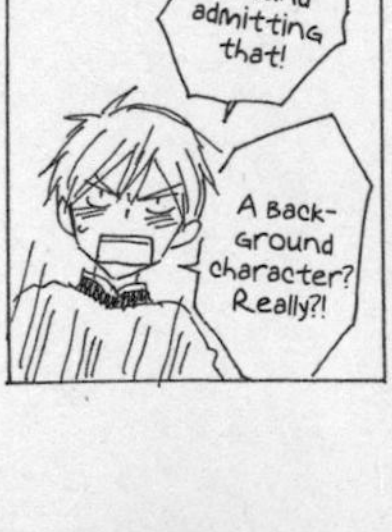
Don't go around admitting that!
A back-ground character? Really?!

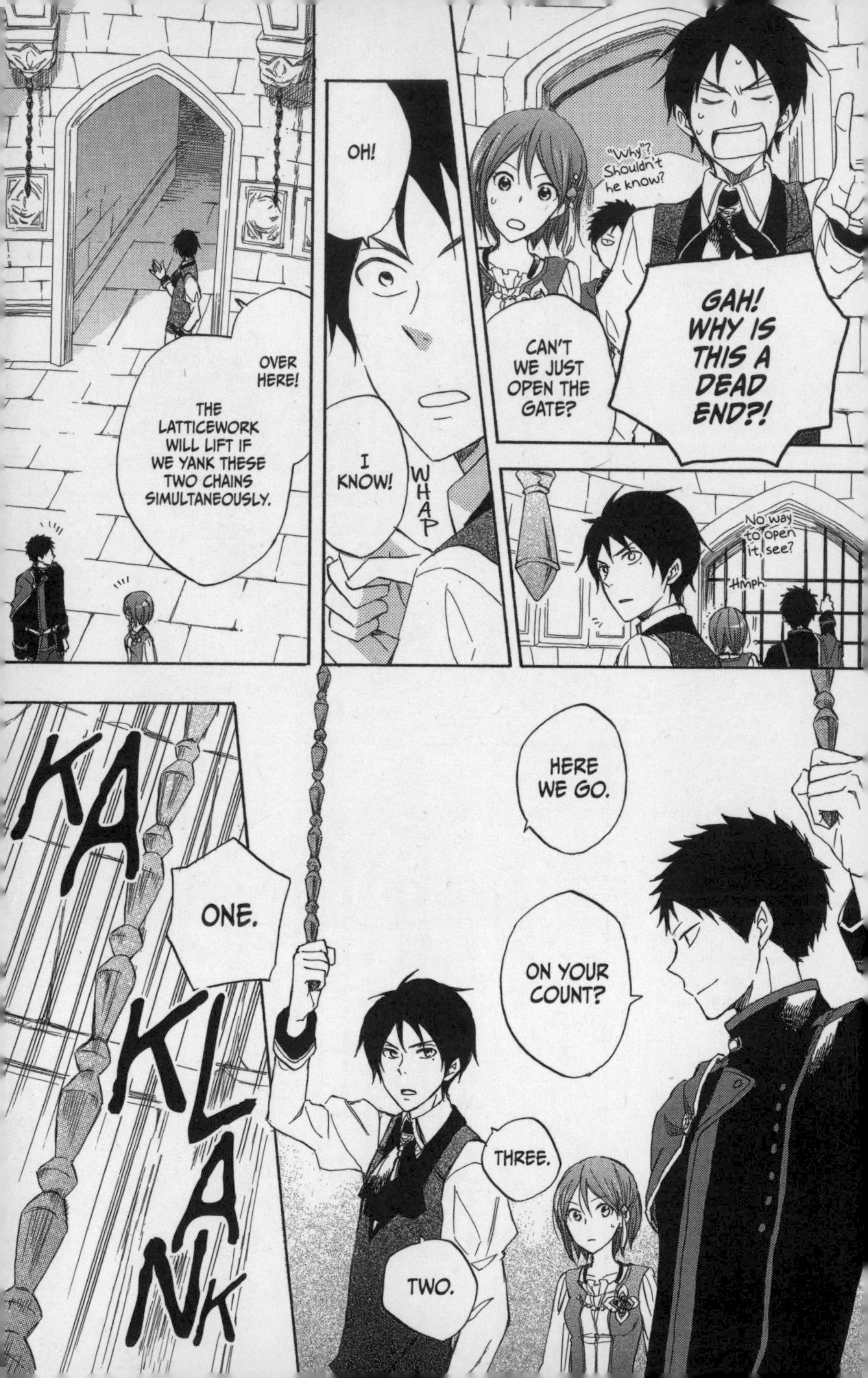
GAH! WHY IS THIS A DEAD END?!
"Why"? Shouldn't he know?
CAN'T WE JUST OPEN THE GATE?
No way to open it, see?
Hmph.
OH!
I KNOW!
WHAP
OVER HERE!
THE LATTICEWORK WILL LIFT IF WE YANK THESE TWO CHAINS SIMULTANEOUSLY.
HERE WE GO.
ON YOUR COUNT?
ONE.
TWO.
THREE.
KAKLANK

Chapter 21

It was fun portraying the butlers and maids when they're off the clock.

They maintain this elegant aura while on the job, but when they get a chance to unwind, they turn into squabbling boys and girls, make wagers and so on.

I think that's great.

You see it in movies a lot, where the masters will be having some outrageous conversation and the servants are just standing there, completely unflappable. I love that.

I always imagine them thinking, "This is no time to be waiting on these people!"

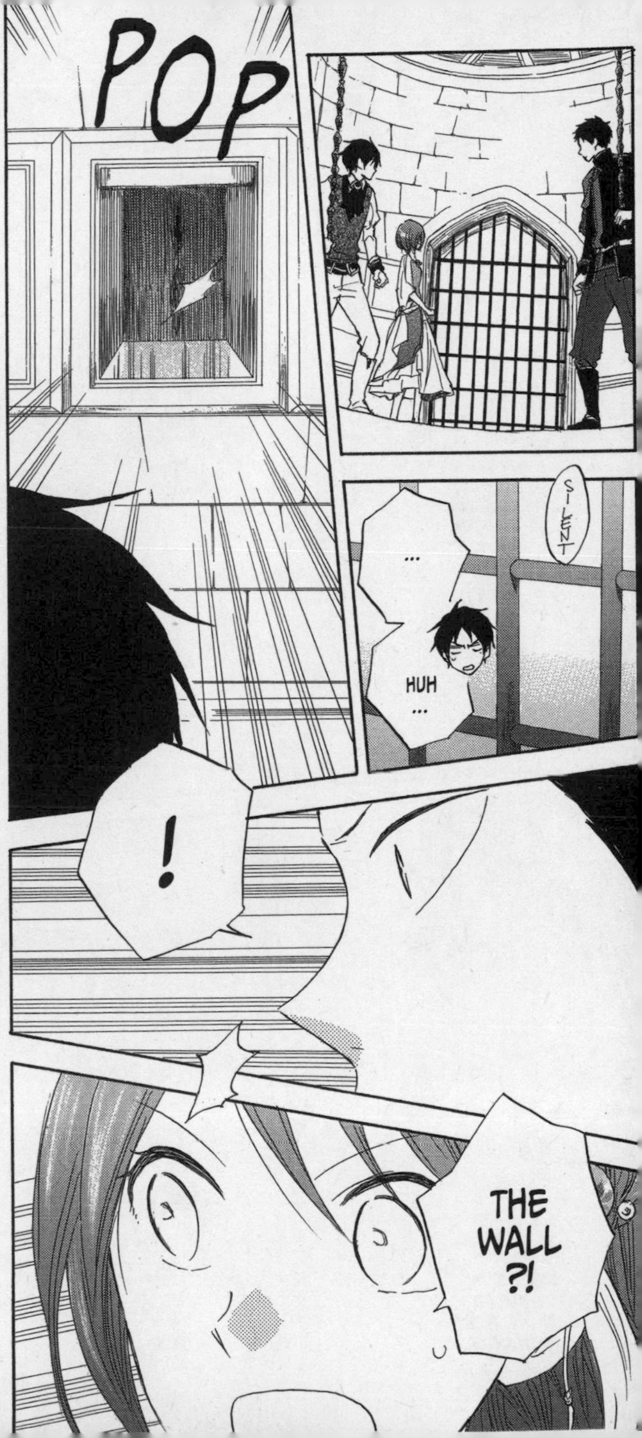
POP
SILENT
...
HUH ...
!
THE WALL ?!

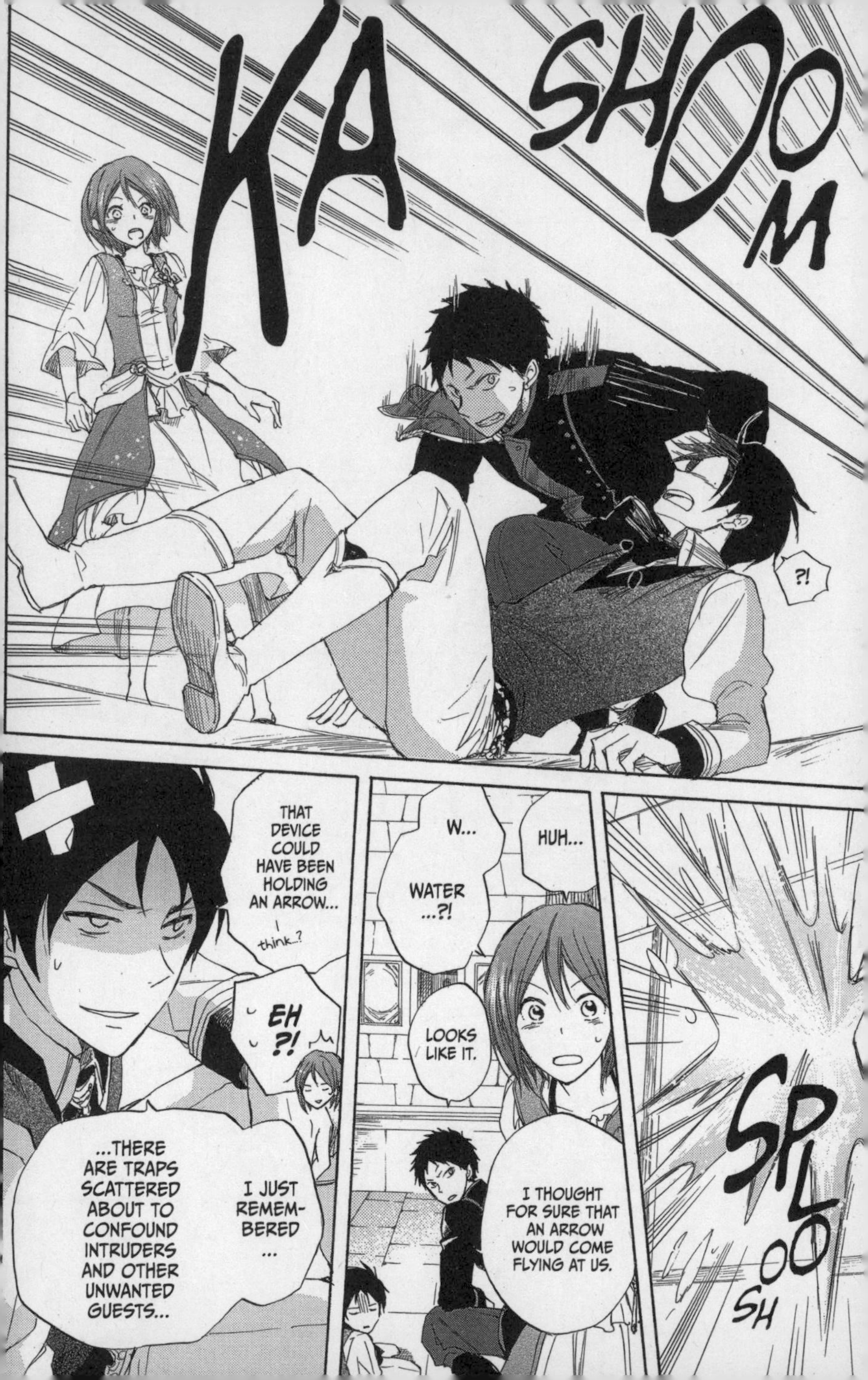
KA SHOOM
?!
SPLOOSH
HUH...
W... WATER ...?!
LOOKS LIKE IT.
I THOUGHT FOR SURE THAT AN ARROW WOULD COME FLYING AT US.
THAT DEVICE COULD HAVE BEEN HOLDING AN ARROW...
I think..?
EH ?!
I JUST REMEMBERED ...
...THERE ARE TRAPS SCATTERED ABOUT TO CONFOUND INTRUDERS AND OTHER UNWANTED GUESTS...

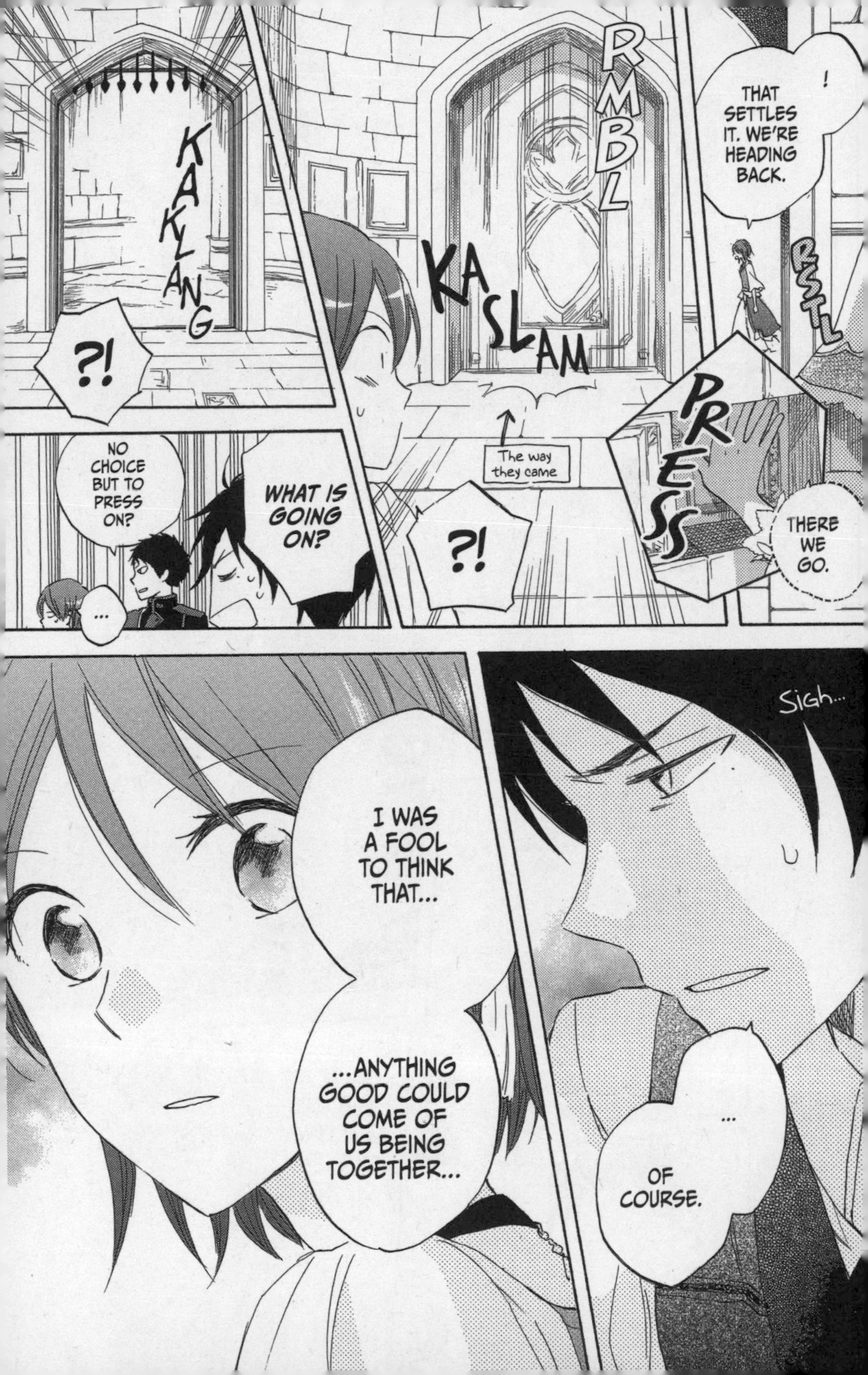
!
THAT SETTLES IT. WE'RE HEADING BACK.
RSTL
PRESS
THERE WE GO.
RMBL
KASLAM
The way they came
?!
KAKLANG
?!
WHAT IS GOING ON?
NO CHOICE BUT TO PRESS ON?
...
Sigh...
...
OF COURSE.
I WAS A FOOL TO THINK THAT...
...ANYTHING GOOD COULD COME OF US BEING TOGETHER...

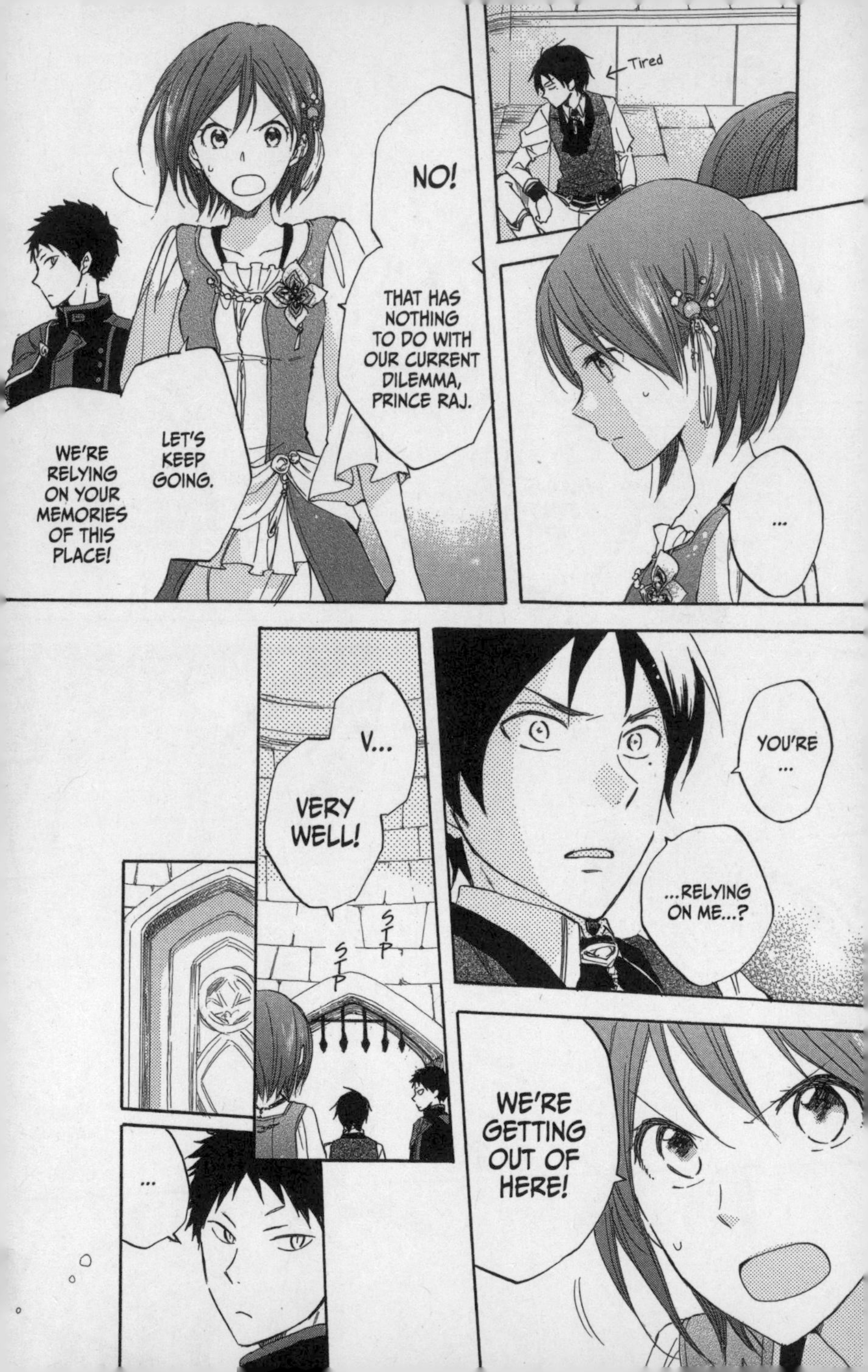
Tired
...
NO!
THAT HAS NOTHING TO DO WITH OUR CURRENT DILEMMA, PRINCE RAJ.
LET'S KEEP GOING.
WE'RE RELYING ON YOUR MEMORIES OF THIS PLACE!
YOU'RE ...
...RELYING ON ME...?
WE'RE GETTING OUT OF HERE!
V...
VERY WELL!
STP
STP
...

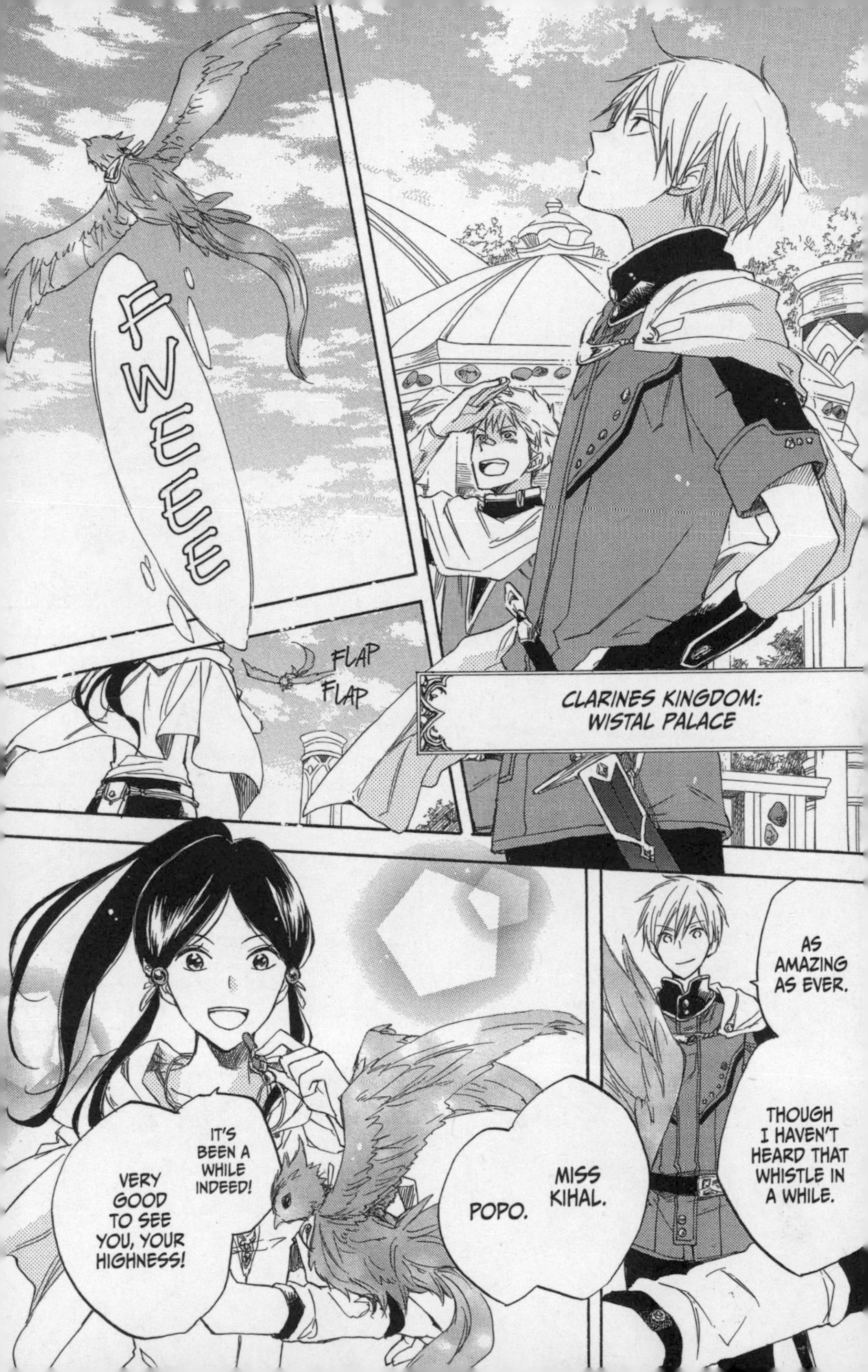
CLARINES KINGDOM: WISTAL PALACE
FWEEE
FLAP FLAP
AS AMAZING AS EVER.
THOUGH I HAVEN'T HEARD THAT WHISTLE IN A WHILE.
MISS KIHAL.
POPO.
IT'S BEEN A WHILE INDEED!
VERY GOOD TO SEE YOU, YOUR HIGHNESS!

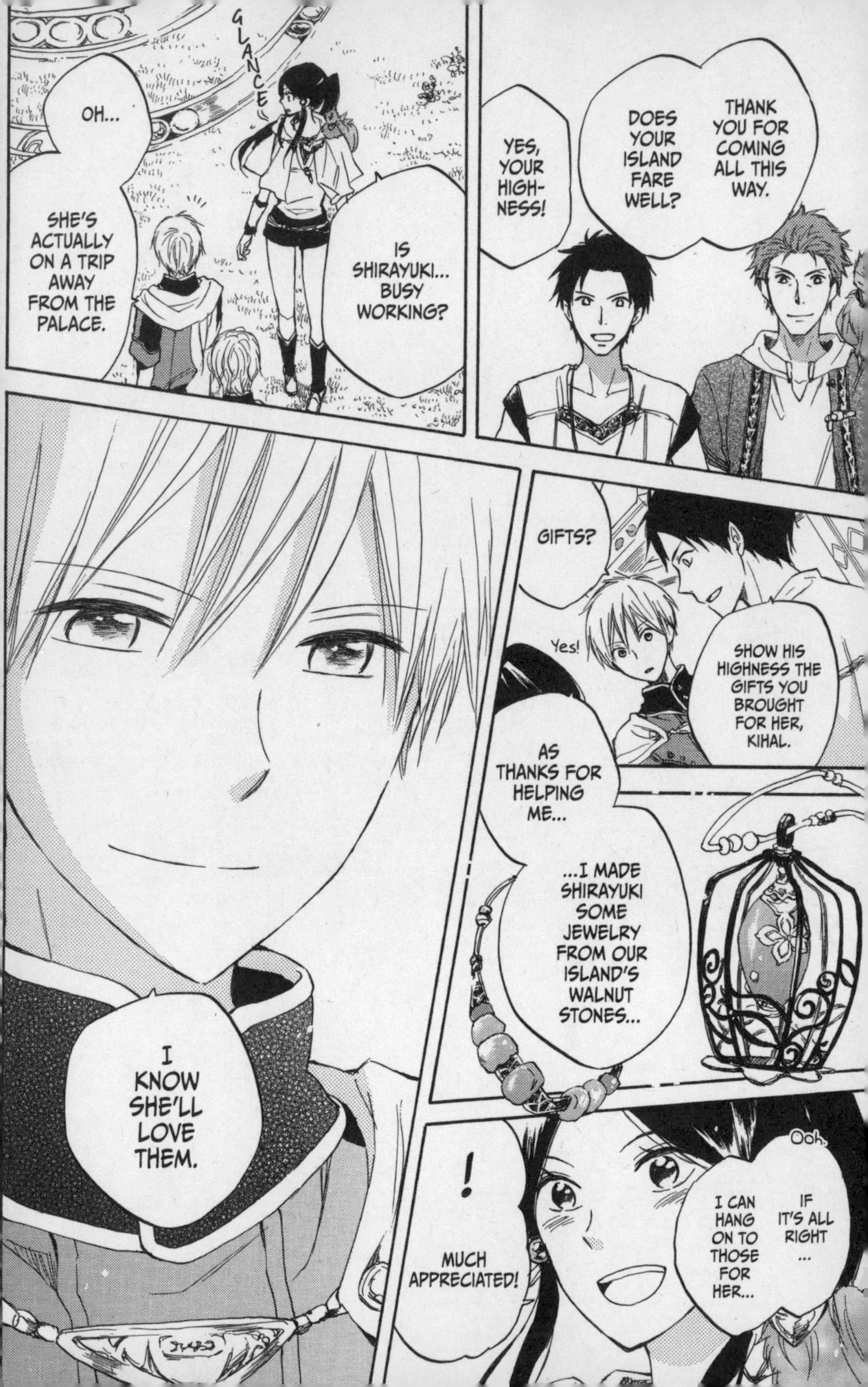
THANK YOU FOR COMING ALL THIS WAY.
DOES YOUR ISLAND FARE WELL?
YES, YOUR HIGHNESS!
GLANCE
IS SHIRAYUKI... BUSY WORKING?
OH...
SHE'S ACTUALLY ON A TRIP AWAY FROM THE PALACE.
GIFTS?
SHOW HIS HIGHNESS THE GIFTS YOU BROUGHT FOR HER, KIHAL.
Yes!
AS THANKS FOR HELPING ME...
...I MADE SHIRAYUKI SOME JEWELRY FROM OUR ISLAND'S WALNUT STONES...
Ooh.
IF IT'S ALL RIGHT...
I CAN HANG ON TO THOSE FOR HER...
!
MUCH APPRECIATED!
I KNOW SHE'LL LOVE THEM.

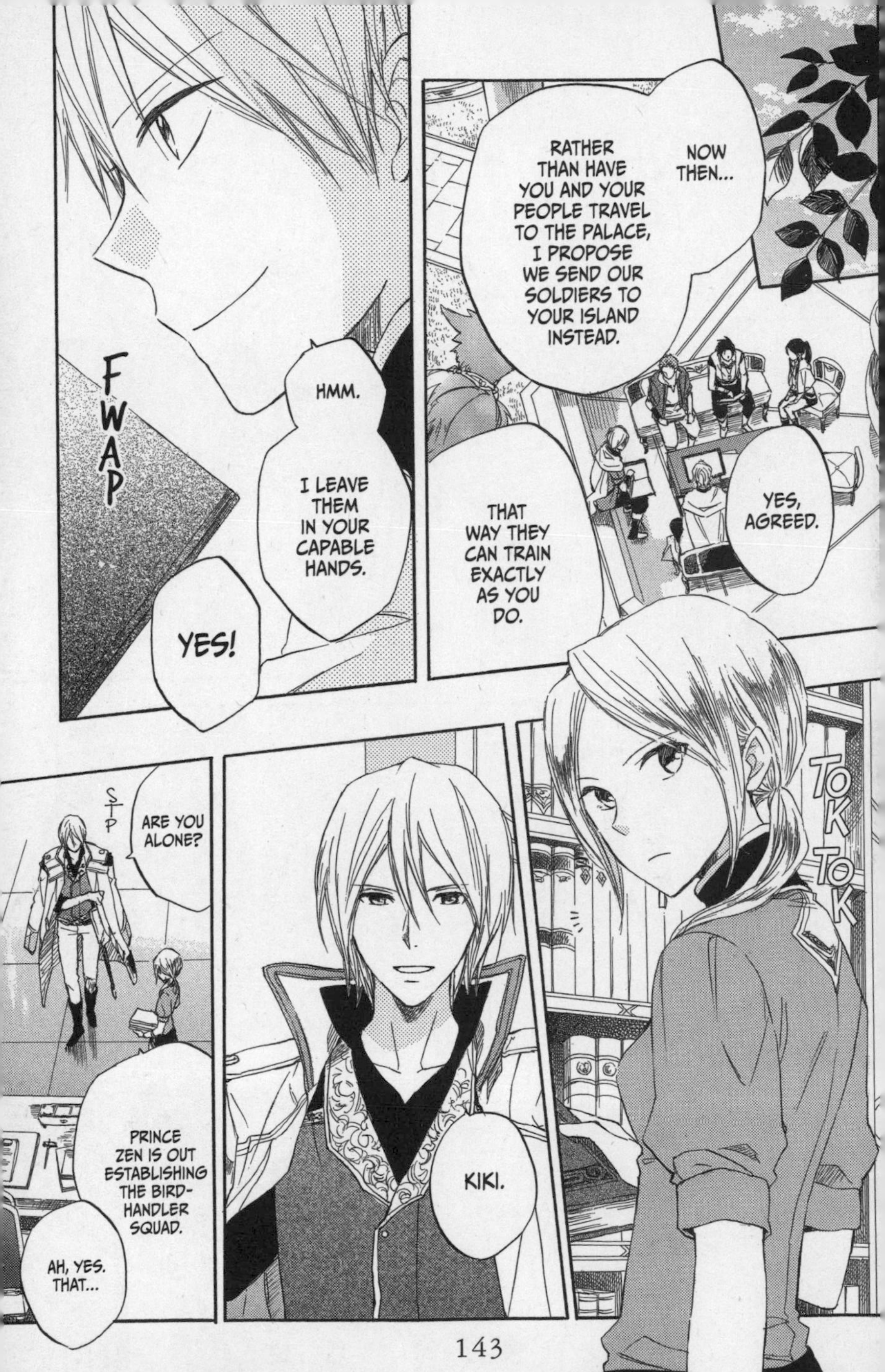
NOW THEN...
RATHER THAN HAVE YOU AND YOUR PEOPLE TRAVEL TO THE PALACE, I PROPOSE WE SEND OUR SOLDIERS TO YOUR ISLAND INSTEAD.
THAT WAY THEY CAN TRAIN EXACTLY AS YOU DO.
YES, AGREED.
HMM.
I LEAVE THEM IN YOUR CAPABLE HANDS.
FWAP
YES!
TOK TOK
KIKI.
STP
ARE YOU ALONE?
PRINCE ZEN IS OUT ESTABLISHING THE BIRD-HANDLER SQUAD.
AH, YES. THAT...

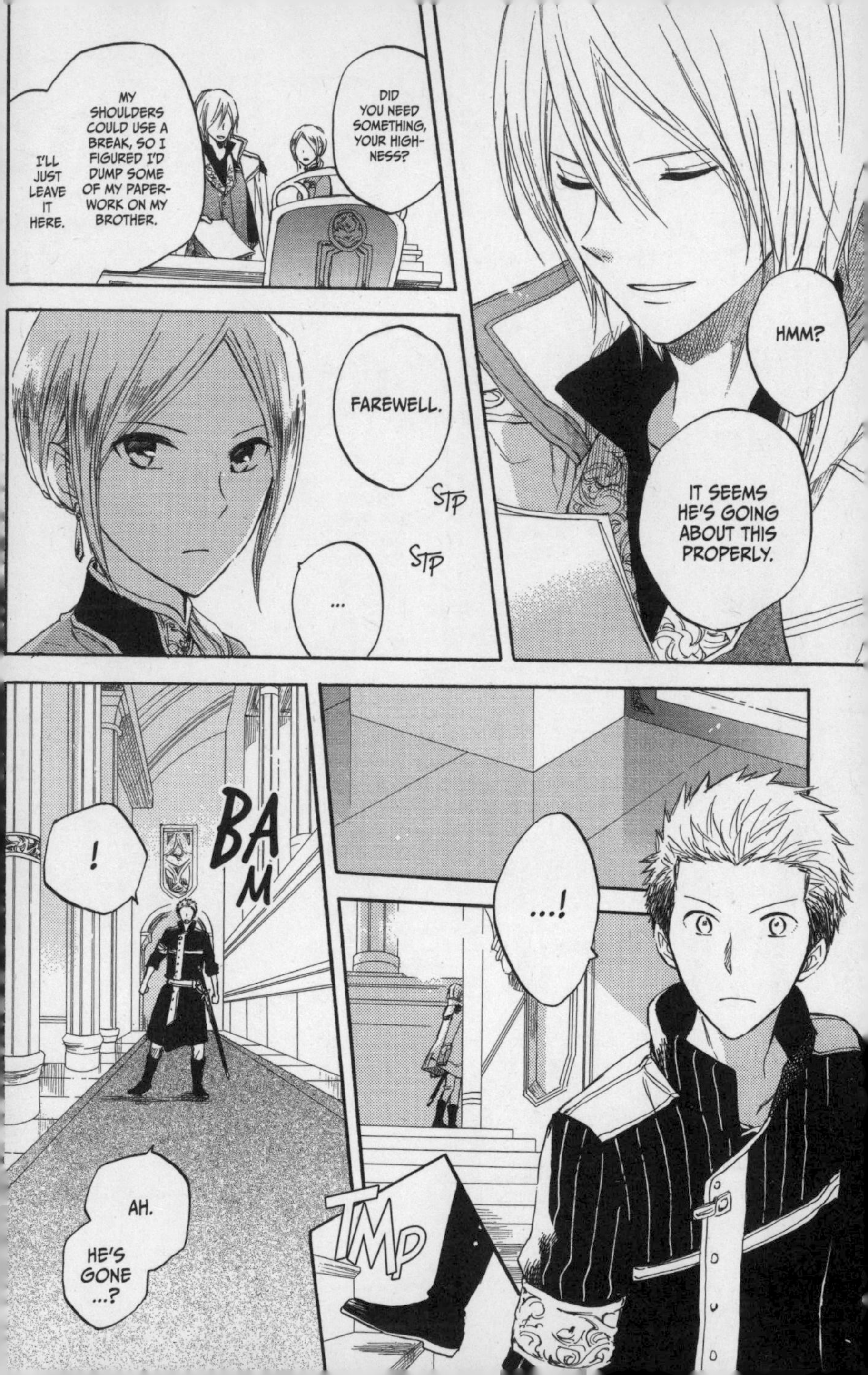
HMM?
IT SEEMS HE'S GOING ABOUT THIS PROPERLY.
DID YOU NEED SOMETHING, YOUR HIGHNESS?
MY SHOULDERS COULD USE A BREAK, SO I FIGURED I'D DUMP SOME OF MY PAPER-WORK ON MY BROTHER.
I'LL JUST LEAVE IT HERE.
FAREWELL.
STP
STP
...
...!
TMP
!
BAM
AH.
HE'S GONE ...?

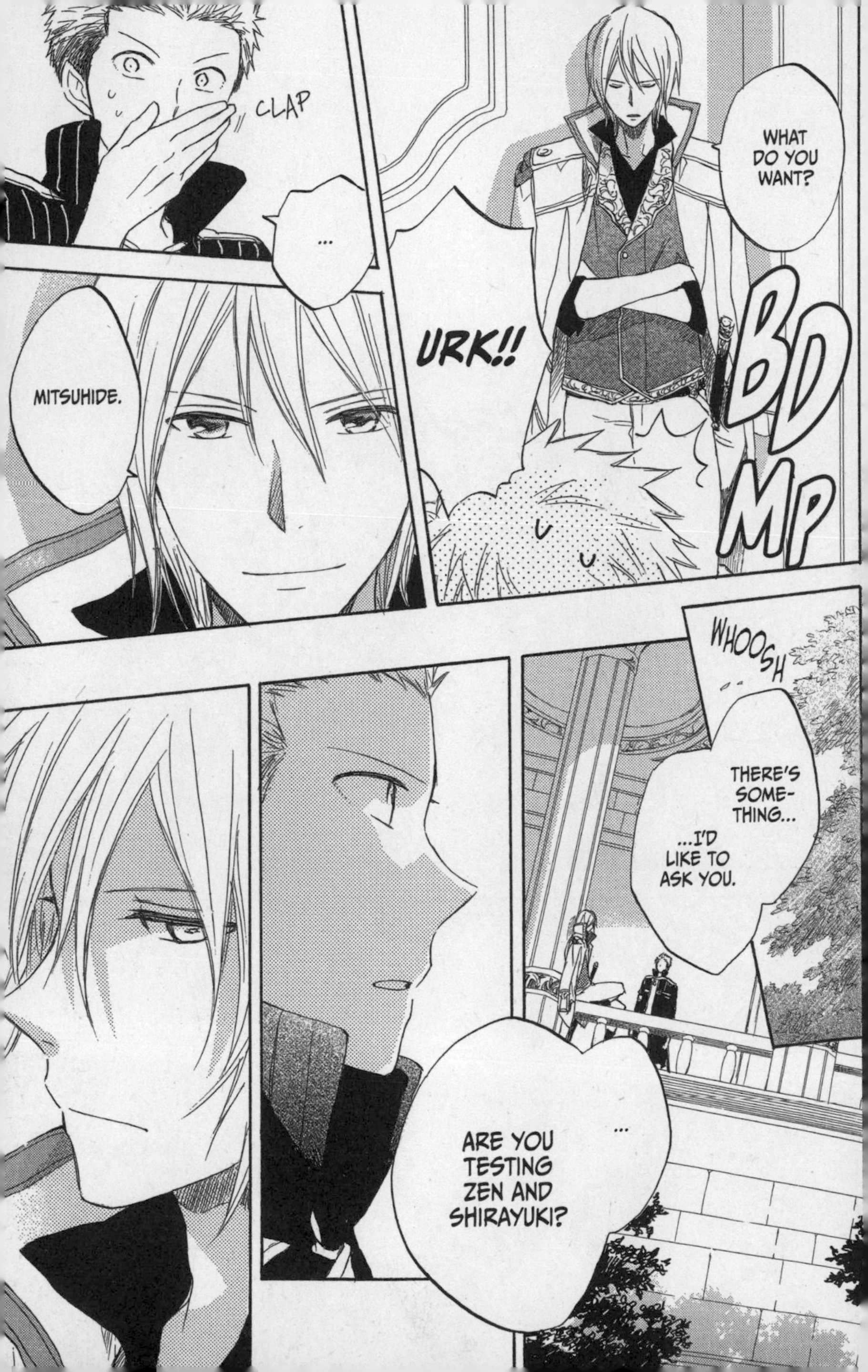

WHAT DO YOU WANT?
BDMP
URK!!
CLAP
...
MITSUHIDE.
WHOOSH
THERE'S SOMETHING...
...I'D LIKE TO ASK YOU.
...
ARE YOU TESTING ZEN AND SHIRAYUKI?

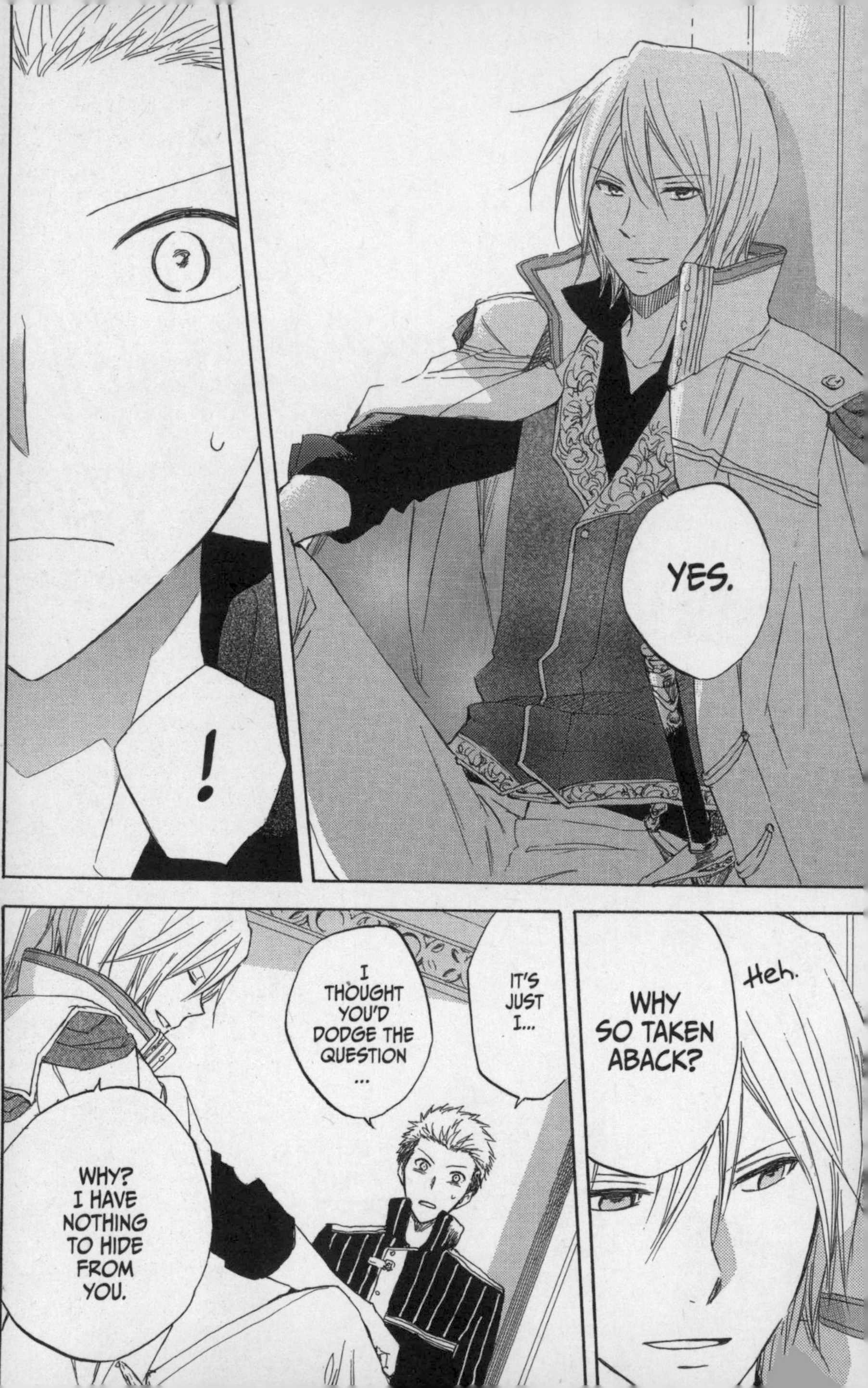
YES.
!
Heh.
WHY SO TAKEN ABACK?
IT'S JUST I...
I THOUGHT YOU'D DODGE THE QUESTION ...
WHY? I HAVE NOTHING TO HIDE FROM YOU.

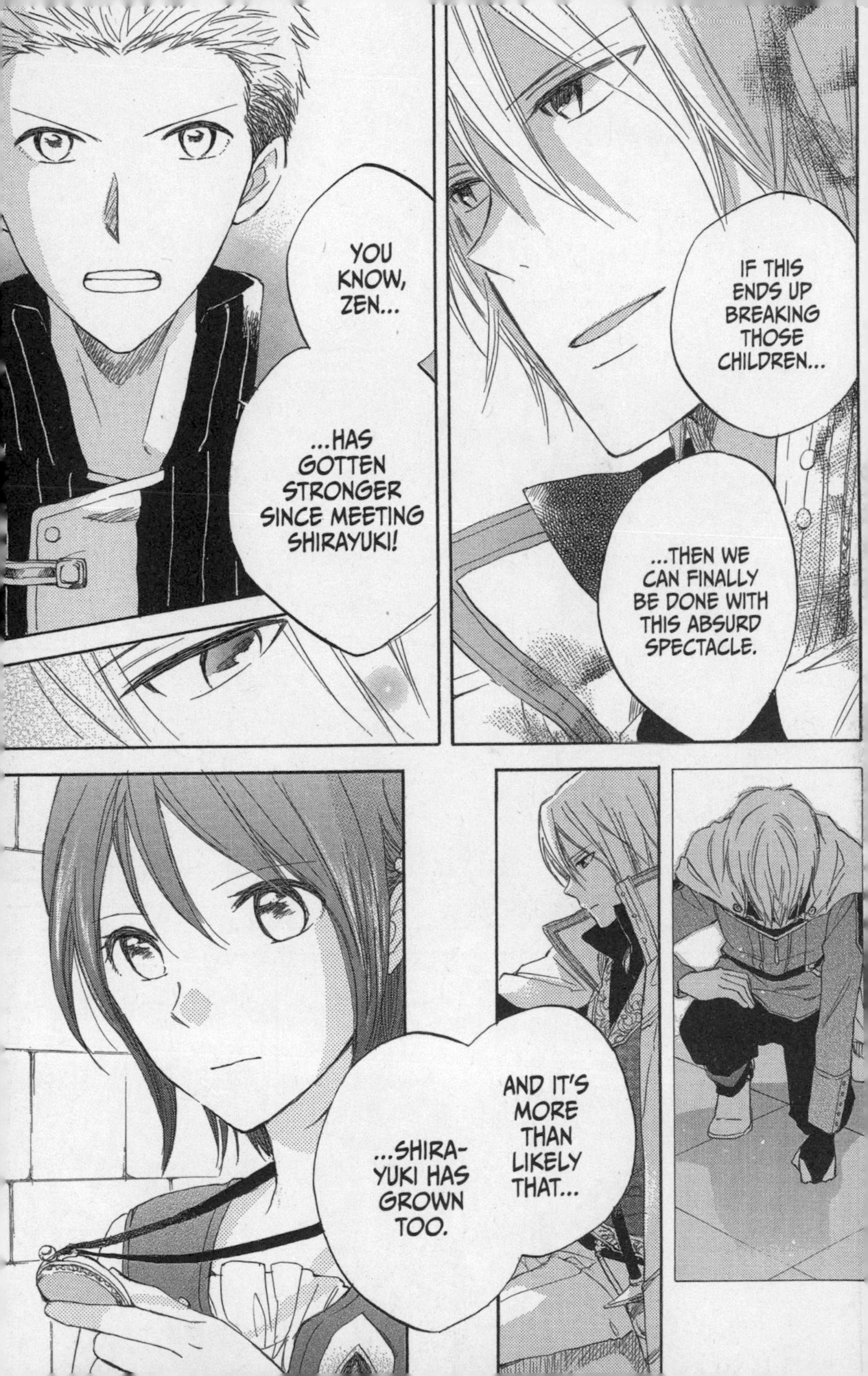
IF THIS ENDS UP BREAKING THOSE CHILDREN...
...THEN WE CAN FINALLY BE DONE WITH THIS ABSURD SPECTACLE.
YOU KNOW, ZEN...
...HAS GOTTEN STRONGER SINCE MEETING SHIRAYUKI!
AND IT'S MORE THAN LIKELY THAT...
...SHIRA-YUKI HAS GROWN TOO.

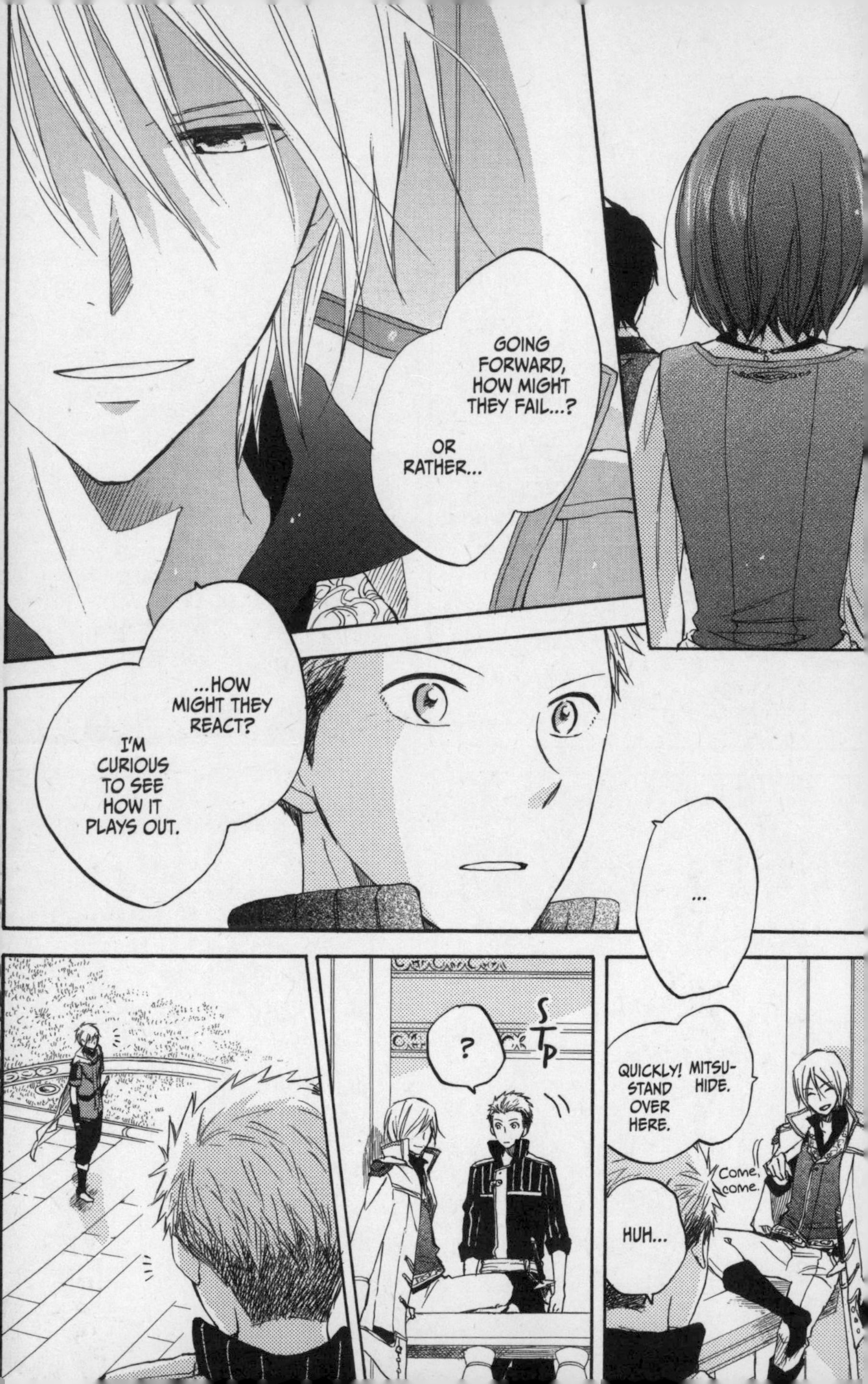
GOING FORWARD, HOW MIGHT THEY FAIL...?
OR RATHER...
...HOW MIGHT THEY REACT?
I'M CURIOUS TO SEE HOW IT PLAYS OUT.
...
MITSU-HIDE.
QUICKLY! STAND OVER HERE.
Come, come.
HUH...
?
STP

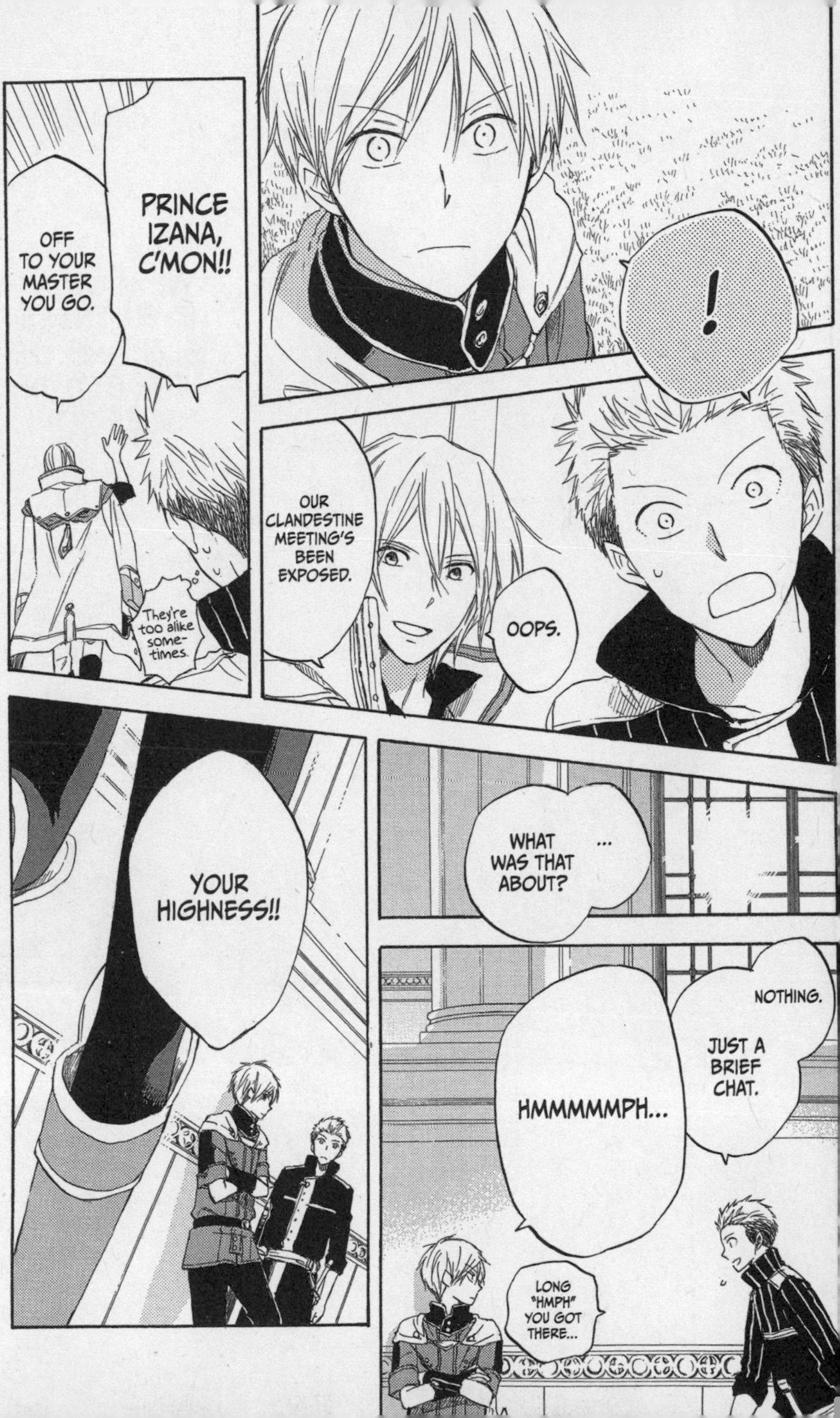
!
OUR CLANDESTINE MEETING'S BEEN EXPOSED.
OOPS.
PRINCE IZANA, C'MON!!
OFF TO YOUR MASTER YOU GO.
They're too alike sometimes.
...
WHAT WAS THAT ABOUT?
NOTHING.
JUST A BRIEF CHAT.
HMMMMMPH...
LONG "HMPH" YOU GOT THERE...
YOUR HIGHNESS!!

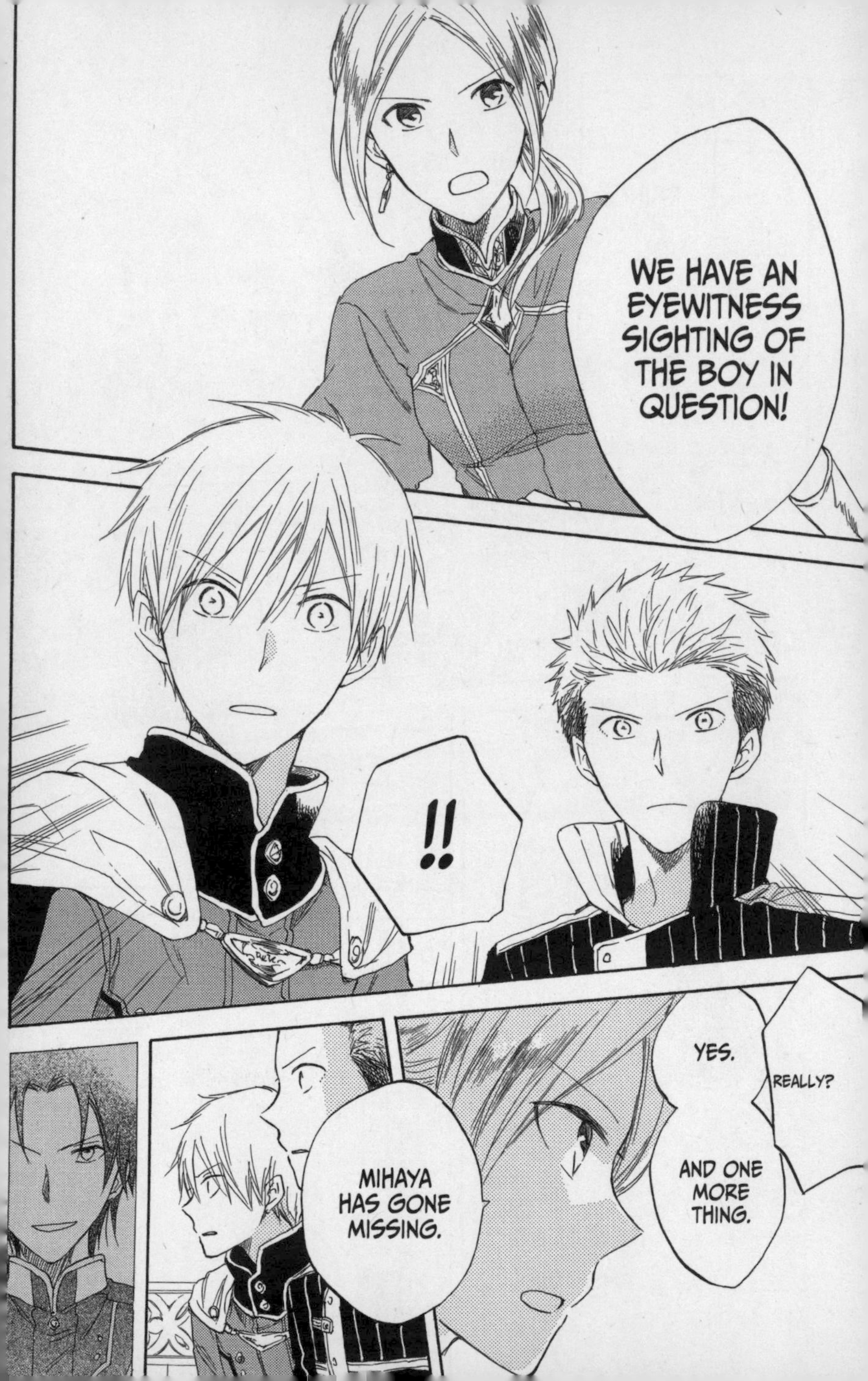
WE HAVE AN EYEWITNESS SIGHTING OF THE BOY IN QUESTION!
!!
REALLY?
YES.
AND ONE MORE THING.
MIHAYA HAS GONE MISSING.

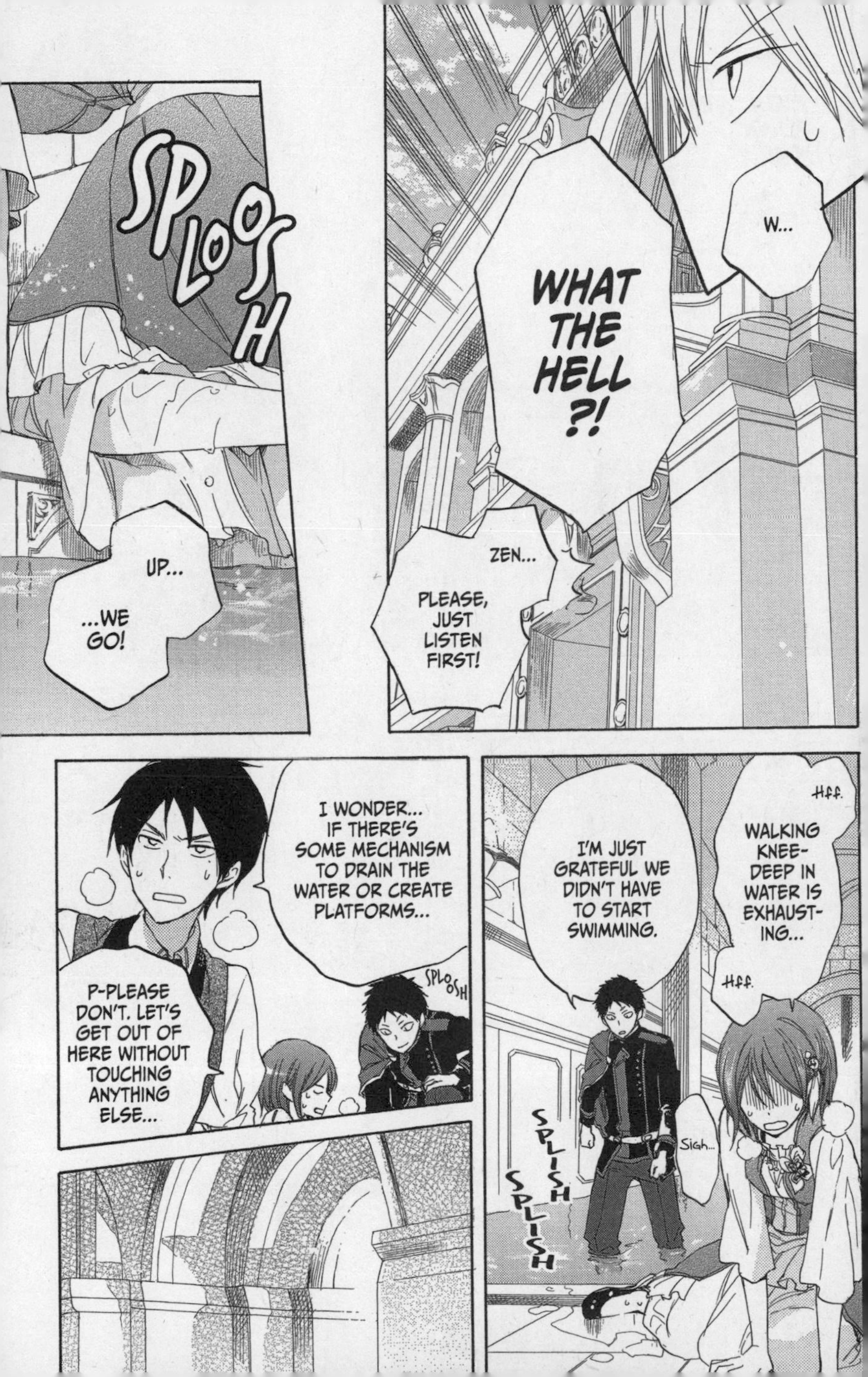
W...
WHAT THE HELL ?!
ZEN...
PLEASE, JUST LISTEN FIRST!
SPLOOSH
UP...
...WE GO!
Hff.
WALKING KNEE-DEEP IN WATER IS EXHAUSTING...
Hff.
I'M JUST GRATEFUL WE DIDN'T HAVE TO START SWIMMING.
SPLISH
SPLISH
Sigh...
I WONDER... IF THERE'S SOME MECHANISM TO DRAIN THE WATER OR CREATE PLATFORMS...
SPLOOSH
P-PLEASE DON'T. LET'S GET OUT OF HERE WITHOUT TOUCHING ANYTHING ELSE...

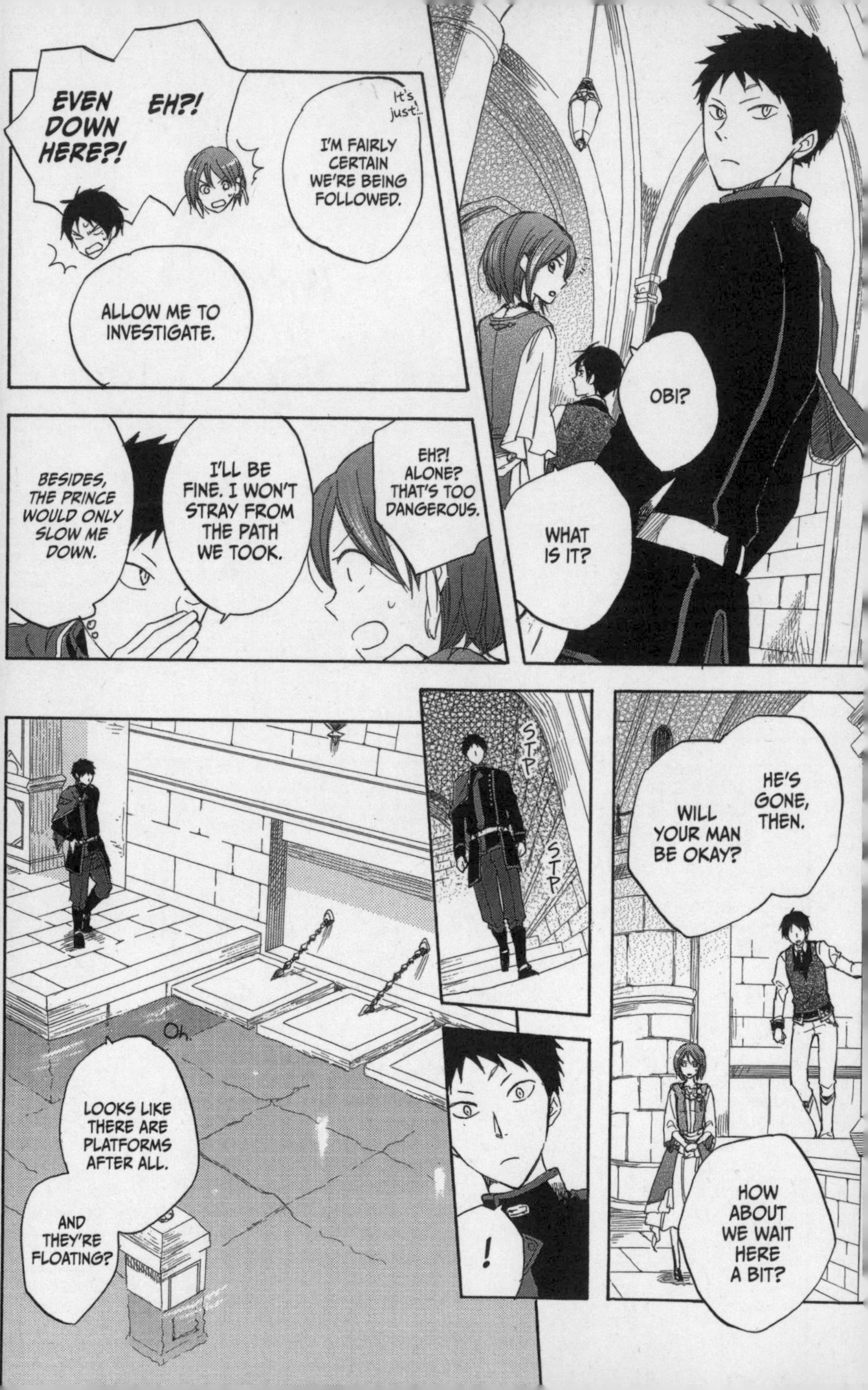
OBI?
WHAT IS IT?
It's just...
I'M FAIRLY CERTAIN WE'RE BEING FOLLOWED.
EH?!
EVEN DOWN HERE?!
ALLOW ME TO INVESTIGATE.
EH?! ALONE? THAT'S TOO DANGEROUS.
I'LL BE FINE. I WON'T STRAY FROM THE PATH WE TOOK.
BESIDES, THE PRINCE WOULD ONLY SLOW ME DOWN.
HE'S GONE, THEN.
WILL YOUR MAN BE OKAY?
HOW ABOUT WE WAIT HERE A BIT?
STP
STP
!
Oh.
LOOKS LIKE THERE ARE PLATFORMS AFTER ALL.
AND THEY'RE FLOATING?

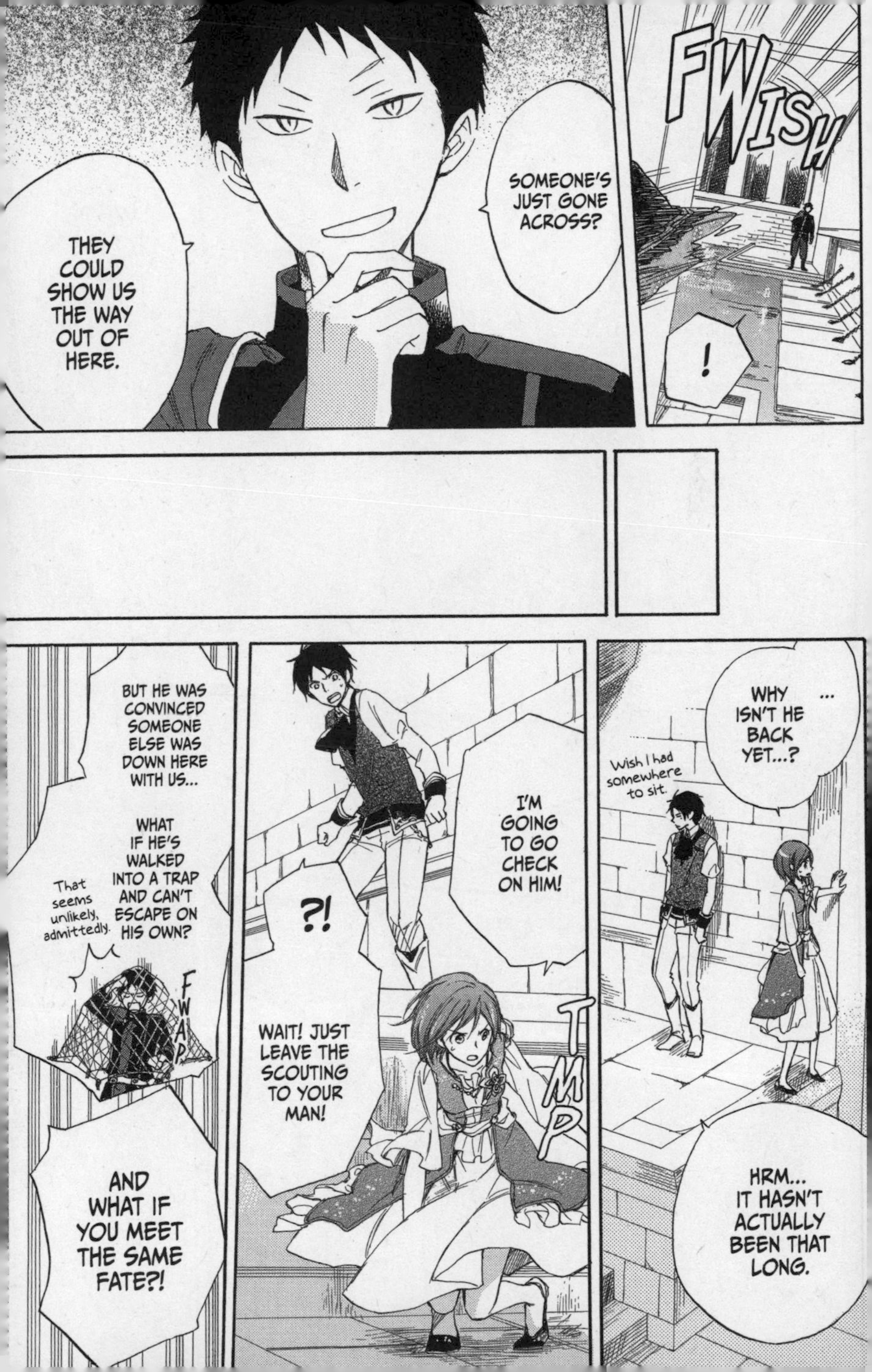
FWISH
!
SOMEONE'S JUST GONE ACROSS?
THEY COULD SHOW US THE WAY OUT OF HERE.
WHY ISN'T HE BACK YET...?
...
Wish I had somewhere to sit.
HRM... IT HASN'T ACTUALLY BEEN THAT LONG.
I'M GOING TO GO CHECK ON HIM!
?!
TMP
WAIT! JUST LEAVE THE SCOUTING TO YOUR MAN!
BUT HE WAS CONVINCED SOMEONE ELSE WAS DOWN HERE WITH US...
WHAT IF HE'S WALKED INTO A TRAP AND CAN'T ESCAPE ON HIS OWN?
That seems unlikely, admittedly.
FWAP
AND WHAT IF YOU MEET THE SAME FATE?!

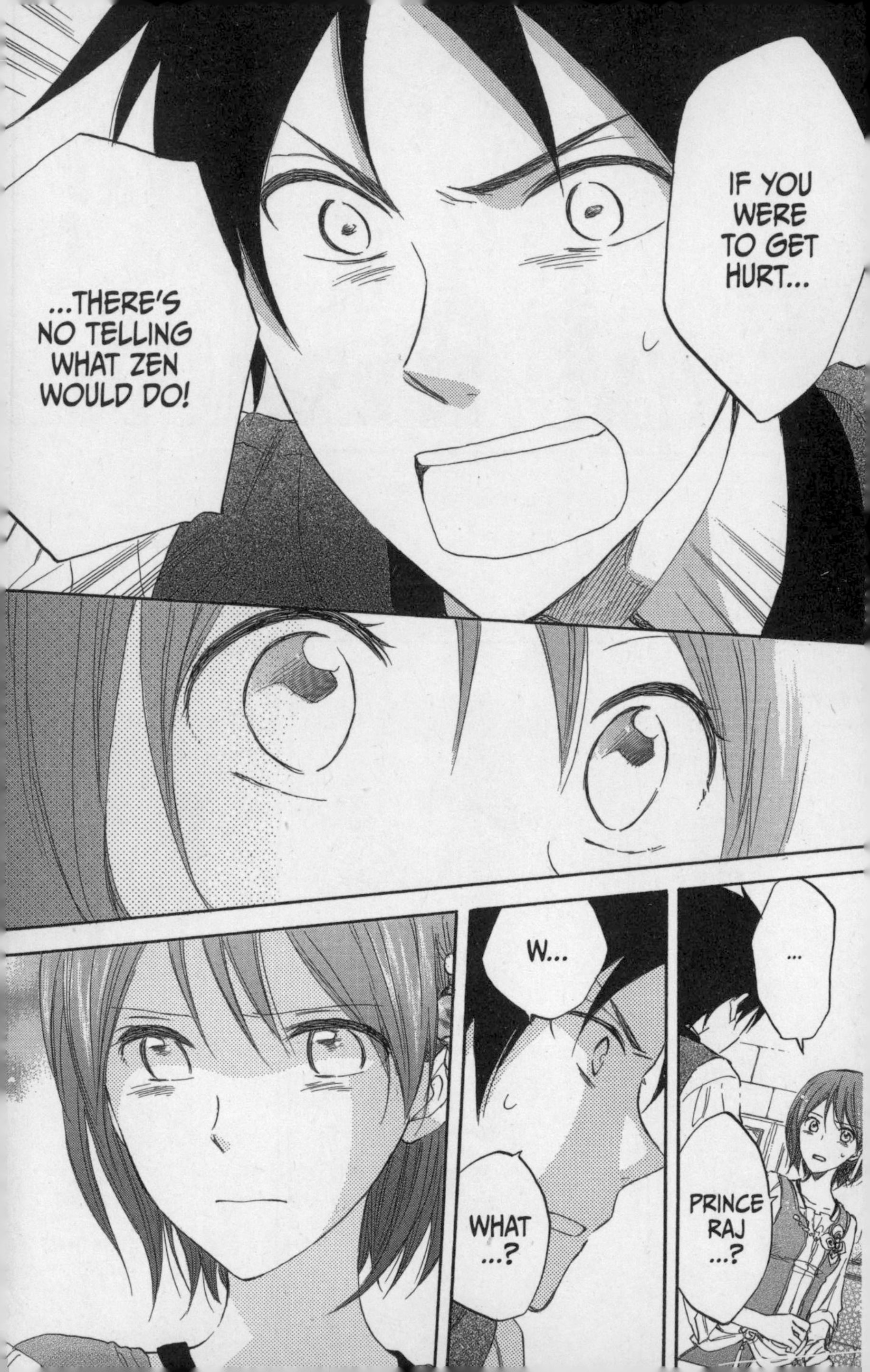
IF YOU WERE TO GET HURT...
...THERE'S NO TELLING WHAT ZEN WOULD DO!
...
PRINCE RAJ ...?
W...
WHAT ...?

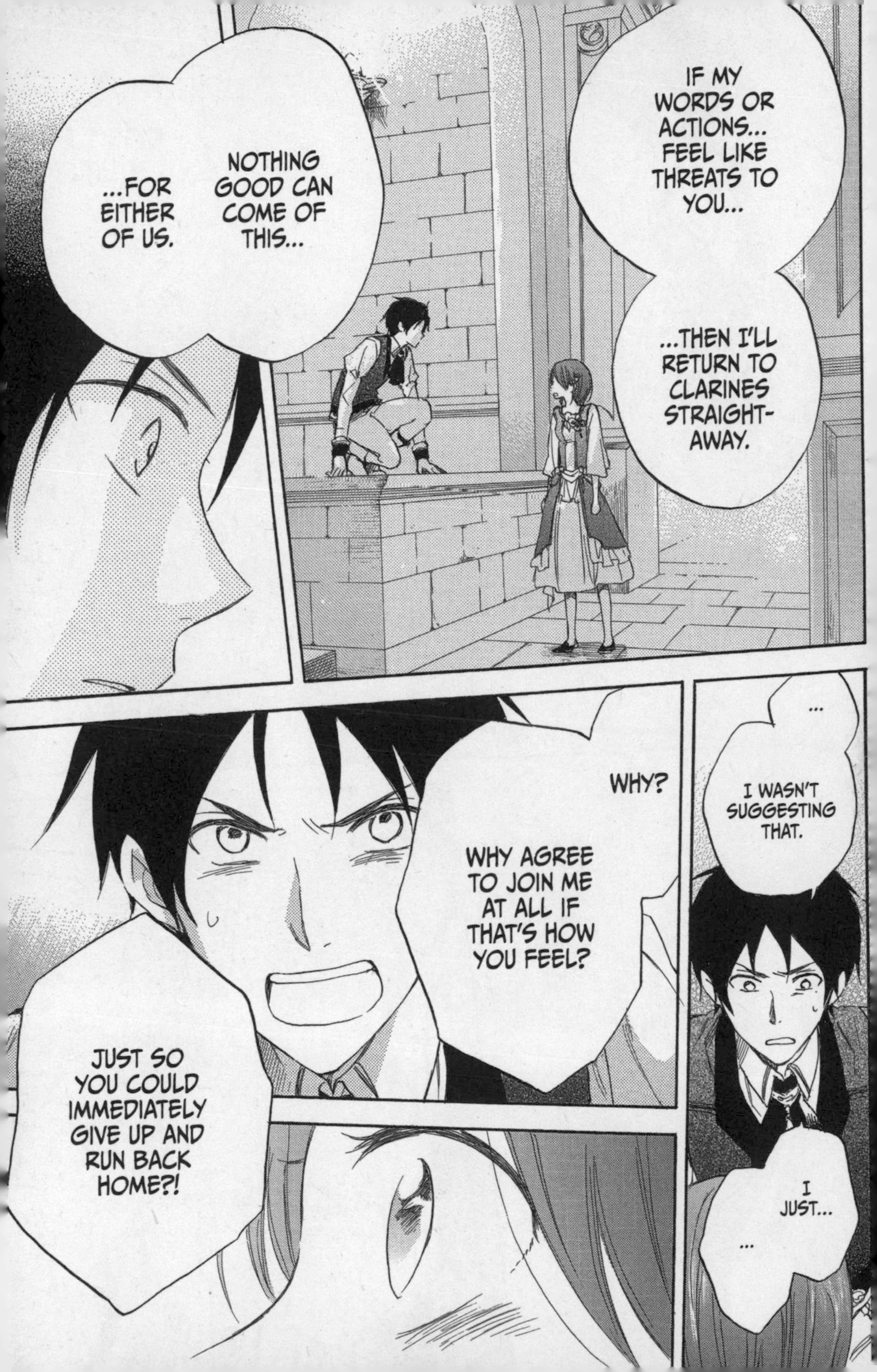
IF MY WORDS OR ACTIONS... FEEL LIKE THREATS TO YOU...
...THEN I'LL RETURN TO CLARINES STRAIGHT-AWAY.
NOTHING GOOD CAN COME OF THIS...
...FOR EITHER OF US.
...
I WASN'T SUGGESTING THAT.
I JUST...
...
WHY?
WHY AGREE TO JOIN ME AT ALL IF THAT'S HOW YOU FEEL?
JUST SO YOU COULD IMMEDIATELY GIVE UP AND RUN BACK HOME?!

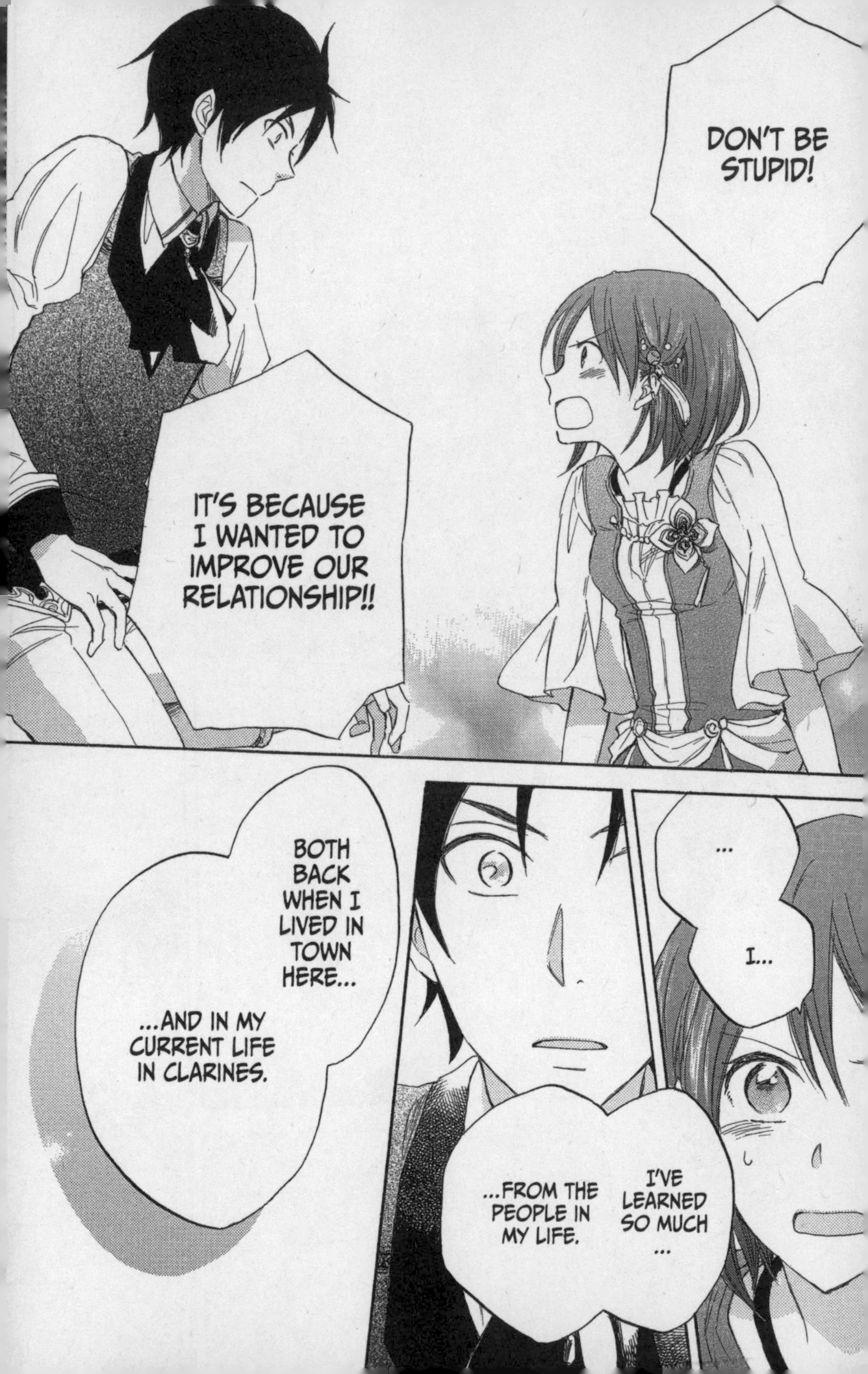
DON'T BE STUPID!
IT'S BECAUSE I WANTED TO IMPROVE OUR RELATIONSHIP!!
...
I...
I'VE LEARNED SO MUCH ...
...FROM THE PEOPLE IN MY LIFE.
BOTH BACK WHEN I LIVED IN TOWN HERE...
...AND IN MY CURRENT LIFE IN CLARINES.

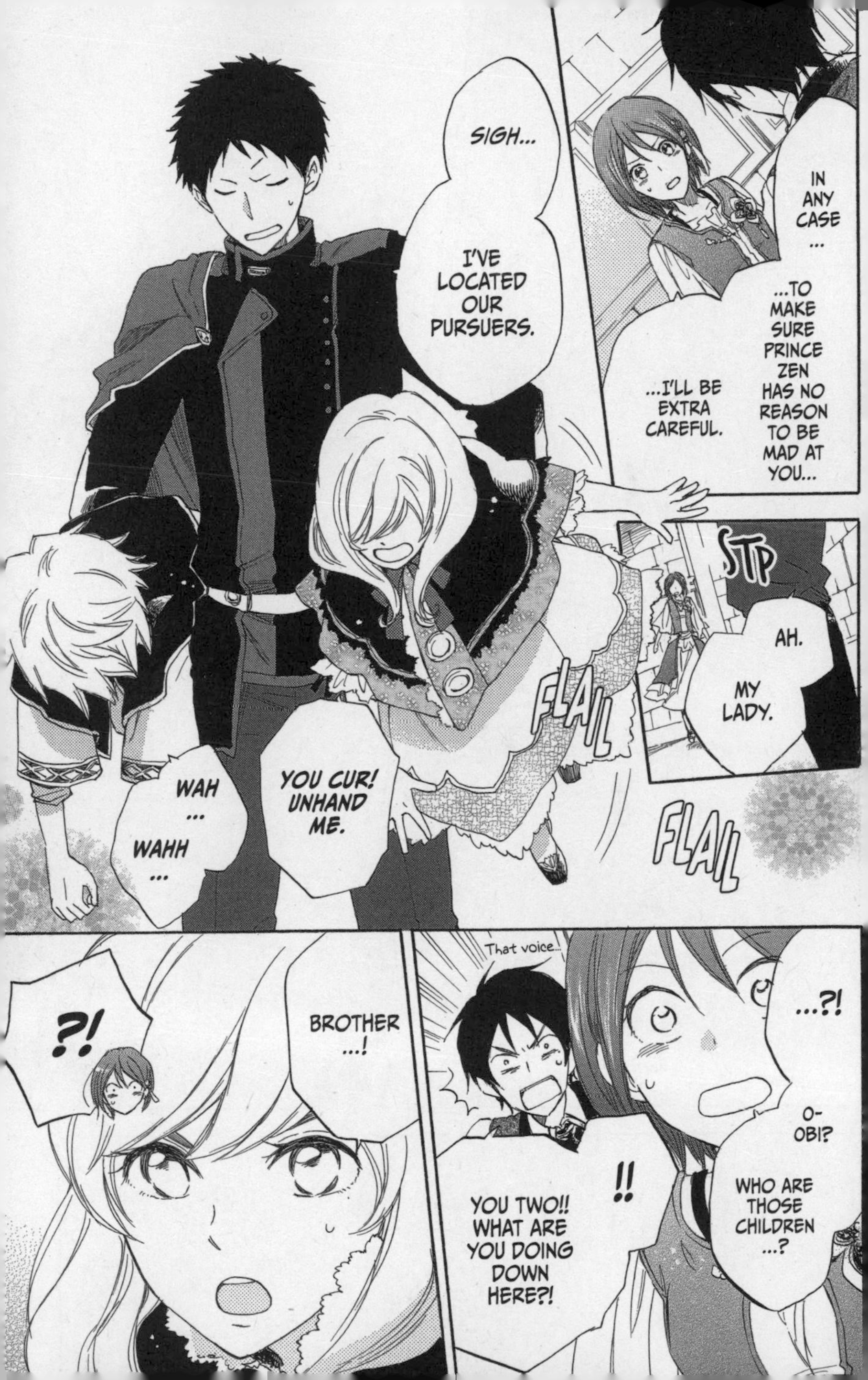
IN ANY CASE...
...TO MAKE SURE PRINCE ZEN HAS NO REASON TO BE MAD AT YOU...
...I'LL BE EXTRA CAREFUL.
STP
AH.
MY LADY.
SIGH...
I'VE LOCATED OUR PURSUERS.
FLAIL
YOU CUR! UNHAND ME.
WAH...
WAHH...
FLAIL
...?!
O-OBI?
WHO ARE THOSE CHILDREN...?
That voice...
!!
YOU TWO!! WHAT ARE YOU DOING DOWN HERE?!
BROTHER...!
?!

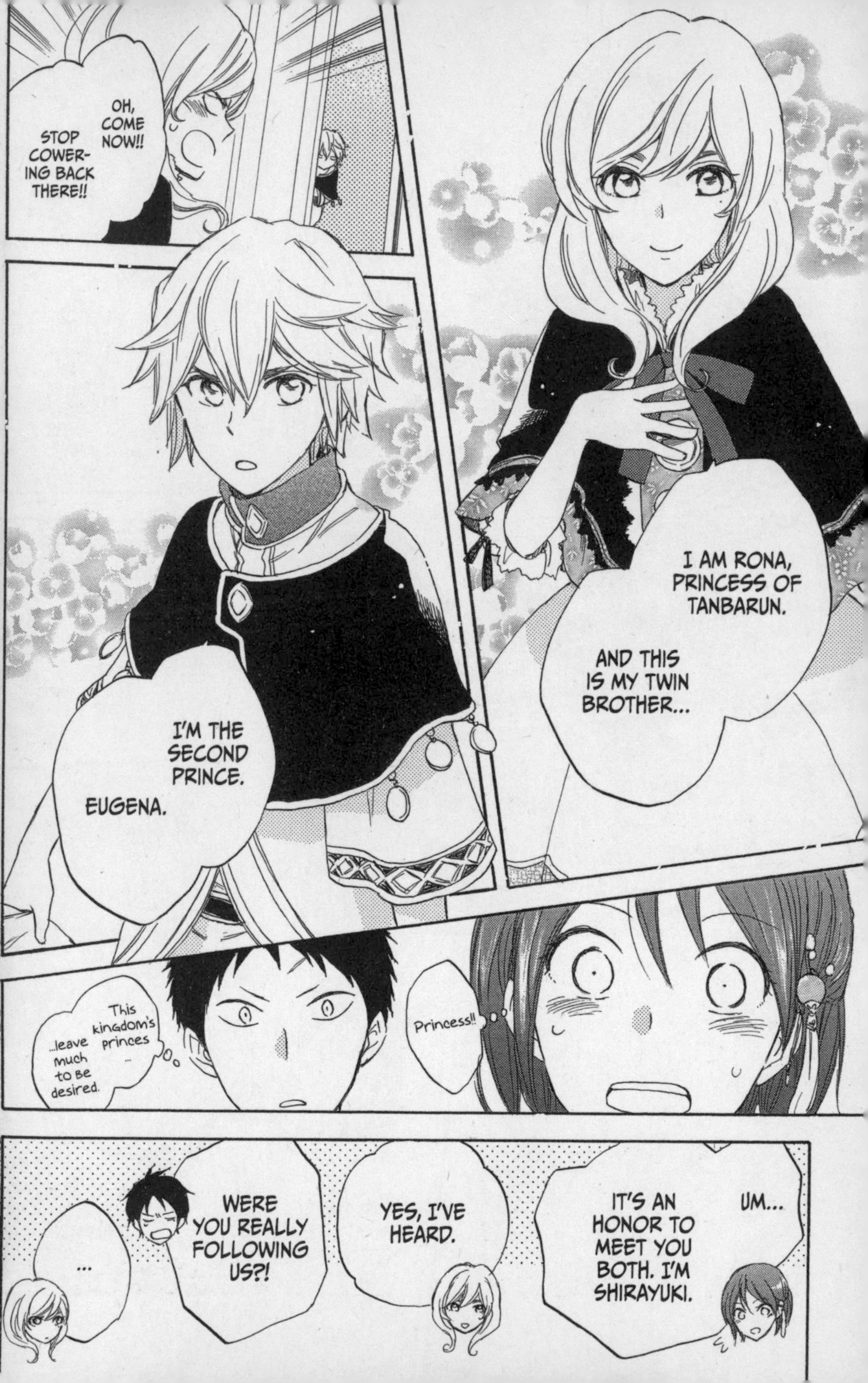
I AM RONA, PRINCESS OF TANBARUN.
AND THIS IS MY TWIN BROTHER...
OH, COME NOW!!
STOP COWERING BACK THERE!!
I'M THE SECOND PRINCE.
EUGENA.
Princess!!
This kingdom's princes ...
...leave much to be desired.
UM...
IT'S AN HONOR TO MEET YOU BOTH. I'M SHIRAYUKI.
YES, I'VE HEARD.
WERE YOU REALLY FOLLOWING US?!
...

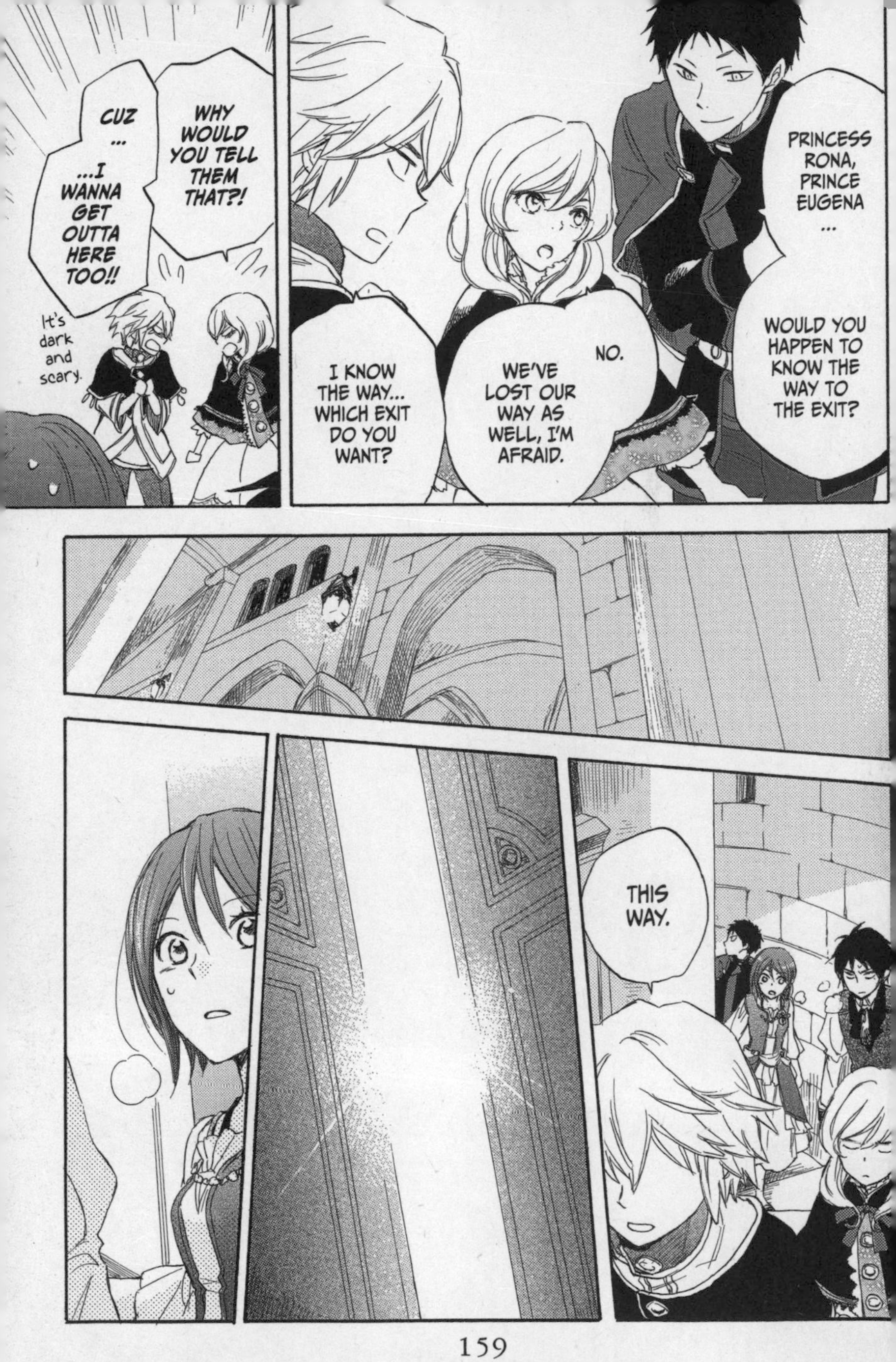
PRINCESS RONA, PRINCE EUGENA ...
WOULD YOU HAPPEN TO KNOW THE WAY TO THE EXIT?
NO.
WE'VE LOST OUR WAY AS WELL, I'M AFRAID.
I KNOW THE WAY... WHICH EXIT DO YOU WANT?
WHY WOULD YOU TELL THEM THAT?!
CUZ ... ...I WANNA GET OUTTA HERE TOO!!
It's dark and scary.
THIS WAY.

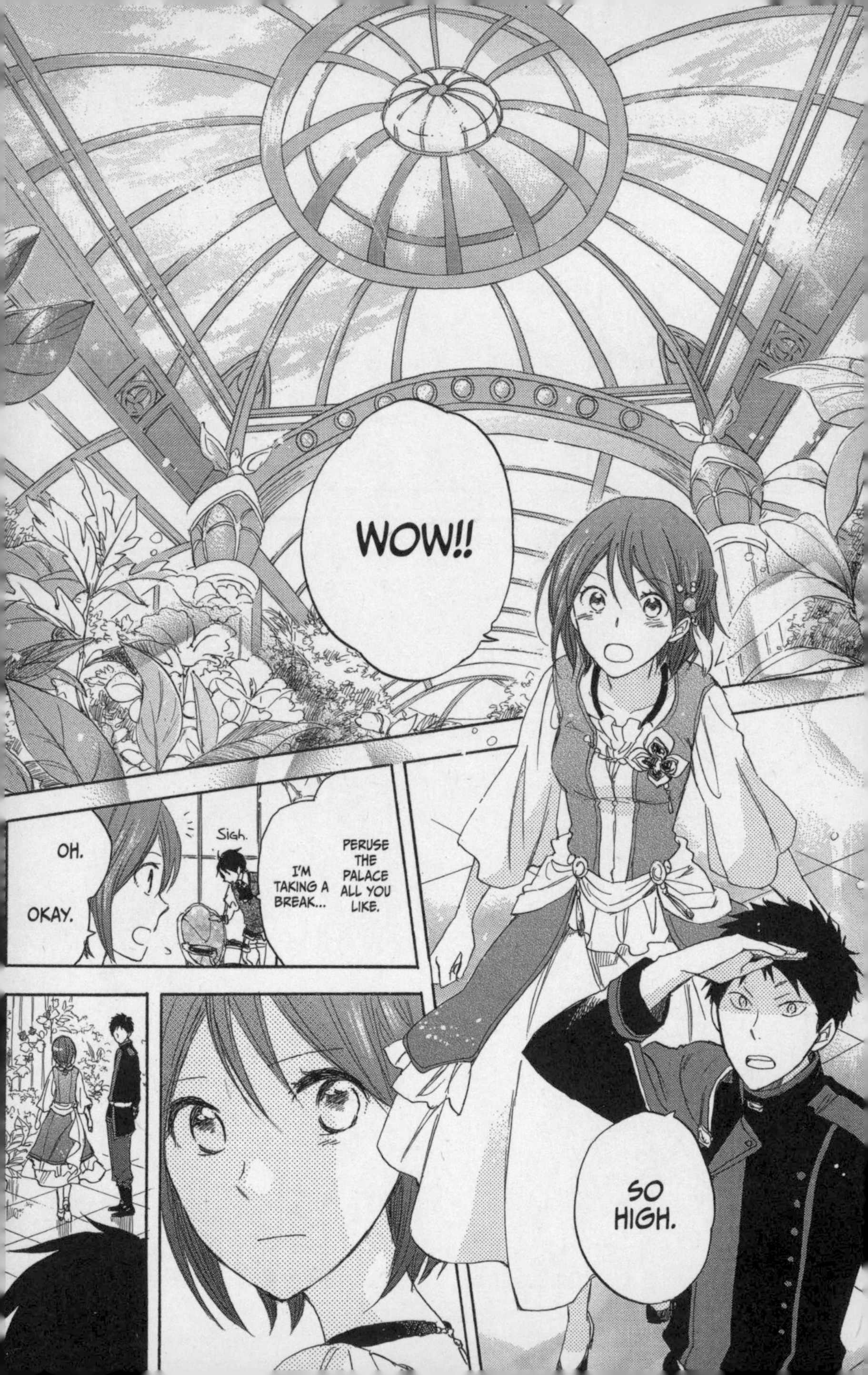
WOW!!
PERUSE THE PALACE ALL YOU LIKE.
I'M TAKING A BREAK...
Sigh.
OH.
OKAY.
SO HIGH.

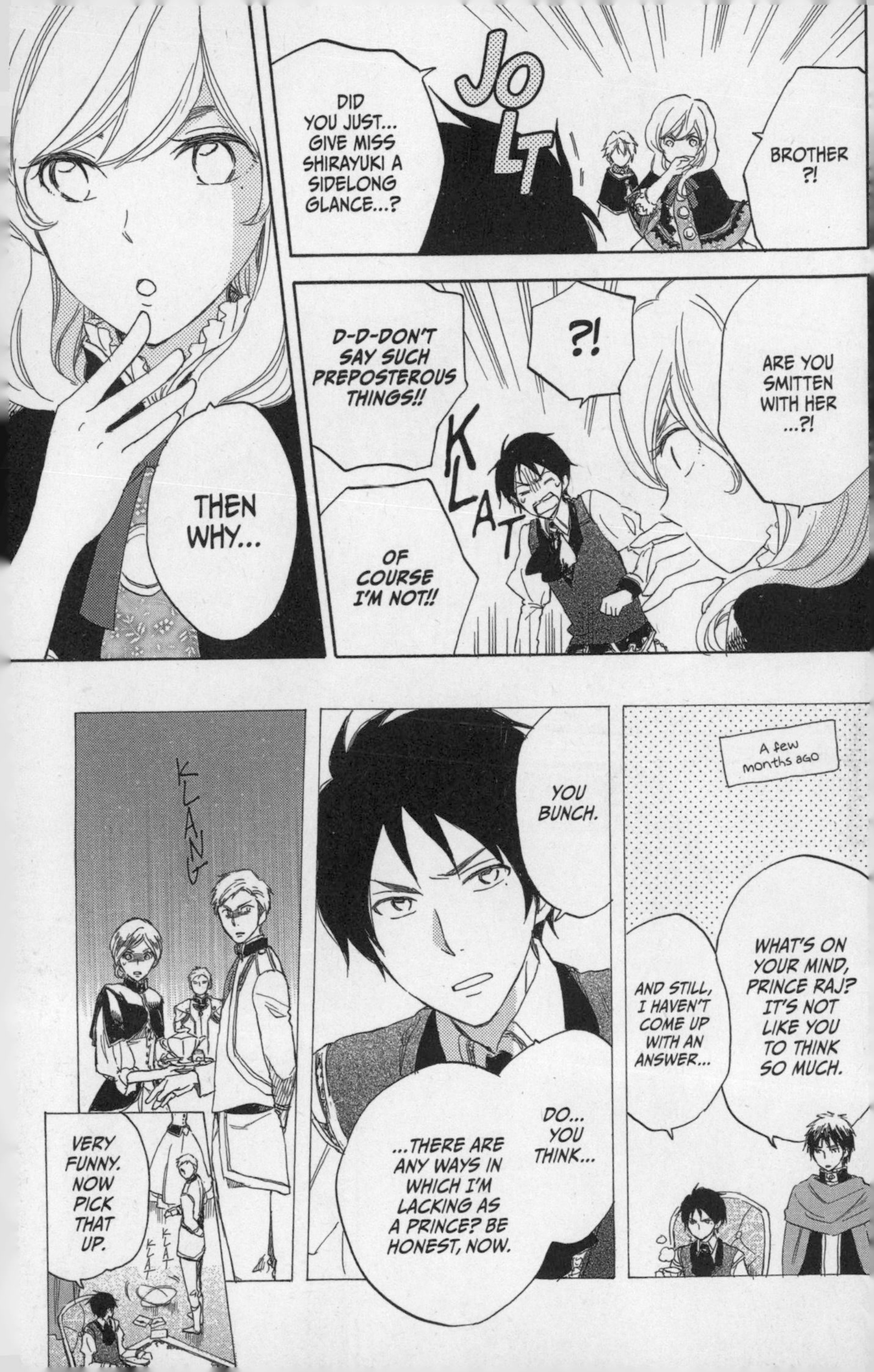

BROTHER?!
JOLT
DID YOU JUST... GIVE MISS SHIRAYUKI A SIDELONG GLANCE...?
ARE YOU SMITTEN WITH HER...?!
?!
D-D-DON'T SAY SUCH PREPOSTEROUS THINGS!!
KLAT
OF COURSE I'M NOT!!
THEN WHY...
A few months ago
WHAT'S ON YOUR MIND, PRINCE RAJ? IT'S NOT LIKE YOU TO THINK SO MUCH.
AND STILL, I HAVEN'T COME UP WITH AN ANSWER...
YOU BUNCH.
DO... YOU THINK...
...THERE ARE ANY WAYS IN WHICH I'M LACKING AS A PRINCE? BE HONEST, NOW.
KLANG
VERY FUNNY. NOW PICK THAT UP.
KLAT
KLAT

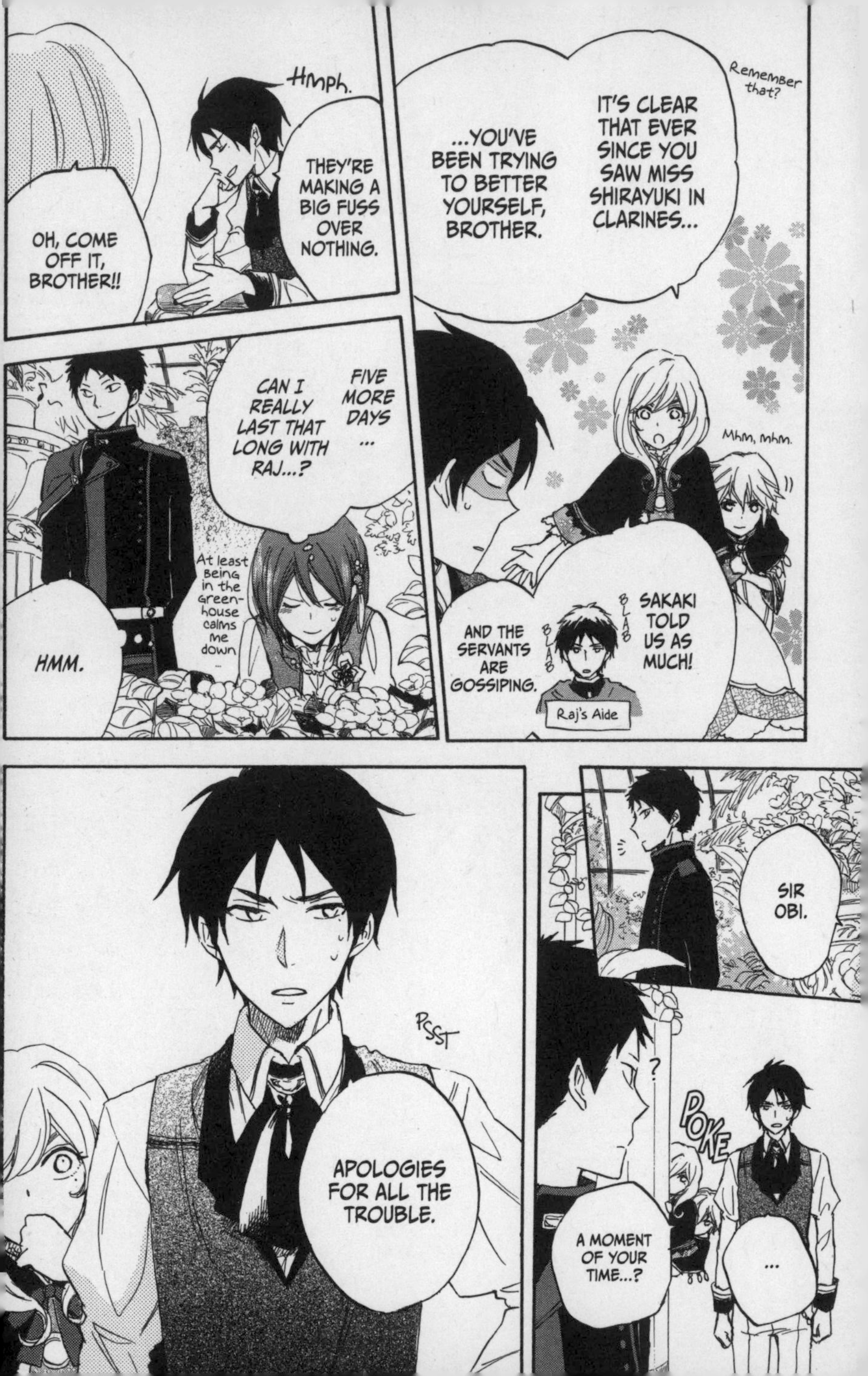
Remember that?
IT'S CLEAR THAT EVER SINCE YOU SAW MISS SHIRAYUKI IN CLARINES...
...YOU'VE BEEN TRYING TO BETTER YOURSELF, BROTHER.
Mhm, mhm.
SAKAKI TOLD US AS MUCH!
BLAB BLAB
AND THE SERVANTS ARE GOSSIPING.
Raj's Aide
Hmph.
THEY'RE MAKING A BIG FUSS OVER NOTHING.
OH, COME OFF IT, BROTHER!!
FIVE MORE DAYS...
CAN I REALLY LAST THAT LONG WITH RAJ...?
At least being in the green-house calms me down...
HMM.
SIR OBI.
POKE
?
A MOMENT OF YOUR TIME...?
...
PSST
APOLOGIES FOR ALL THE TROUBLE.

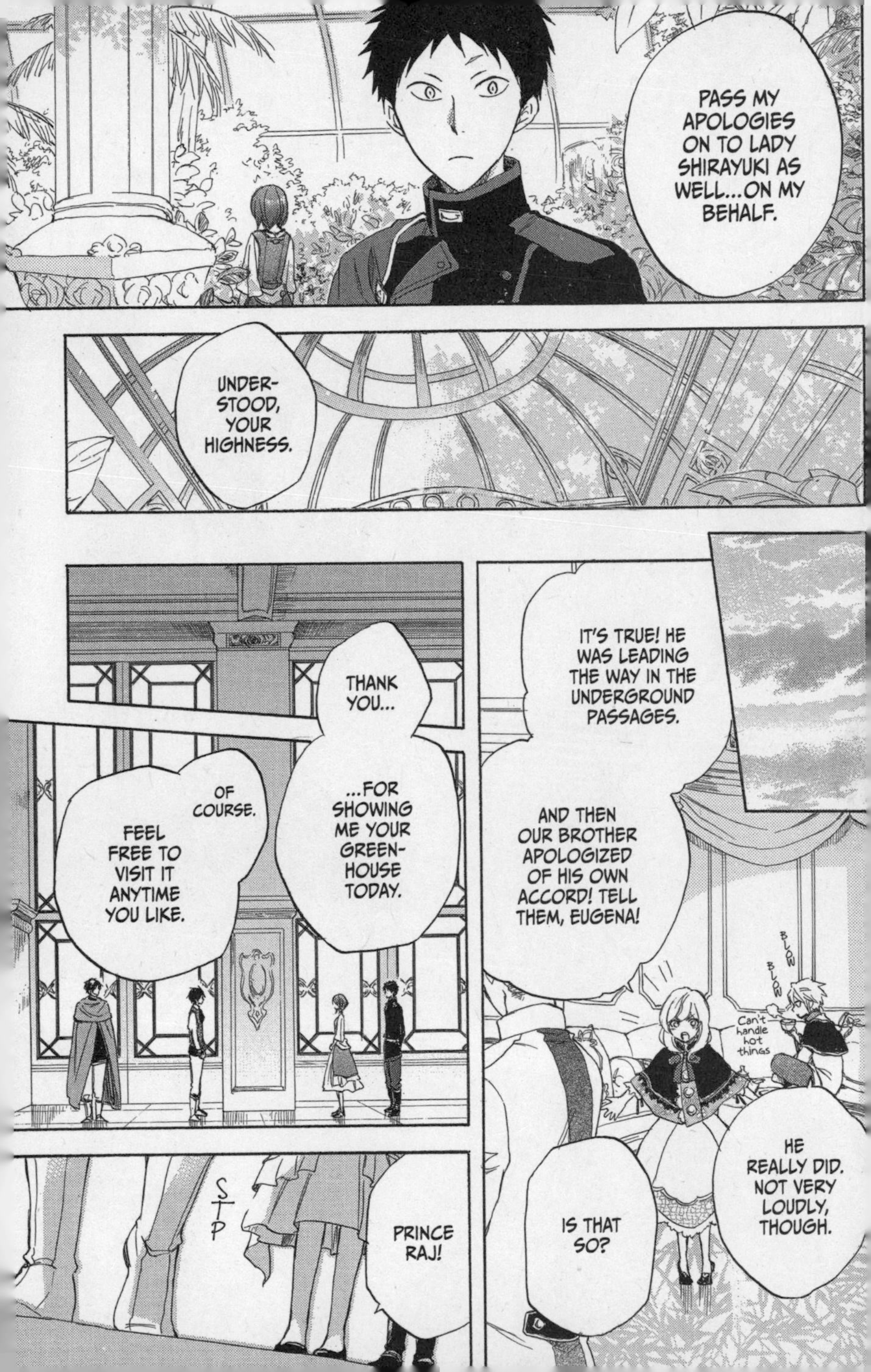
PASS MY APOLOGIES ON TO LADY SHIRAYUKI AS WELL...ON MY BEHALF.
UNDER-STOOD, YOUR HIGHNESS.
IT'S TRUE! HE WAS LEADING THE WAY IN THE UNDERGROUND PASSAGES.
AND THEN OUR BROTHER APOLOGIZED OF HIS OWN ACCORD! TELL THEM, EUGENA!
BLOW BLOW
Can't handle hot things
HE REALLY DID. NOT VERY LOUDLY, THOUGH.
IS THAT SO?
THANK YOU...
...FOR SHOWING ME YOUR GREEN-HOUSE TODAY.
OF COURSE.
FEEL FREE TO VISIT IT ANYTIME YOU LIKE.
STP
PRINCE RAJ!

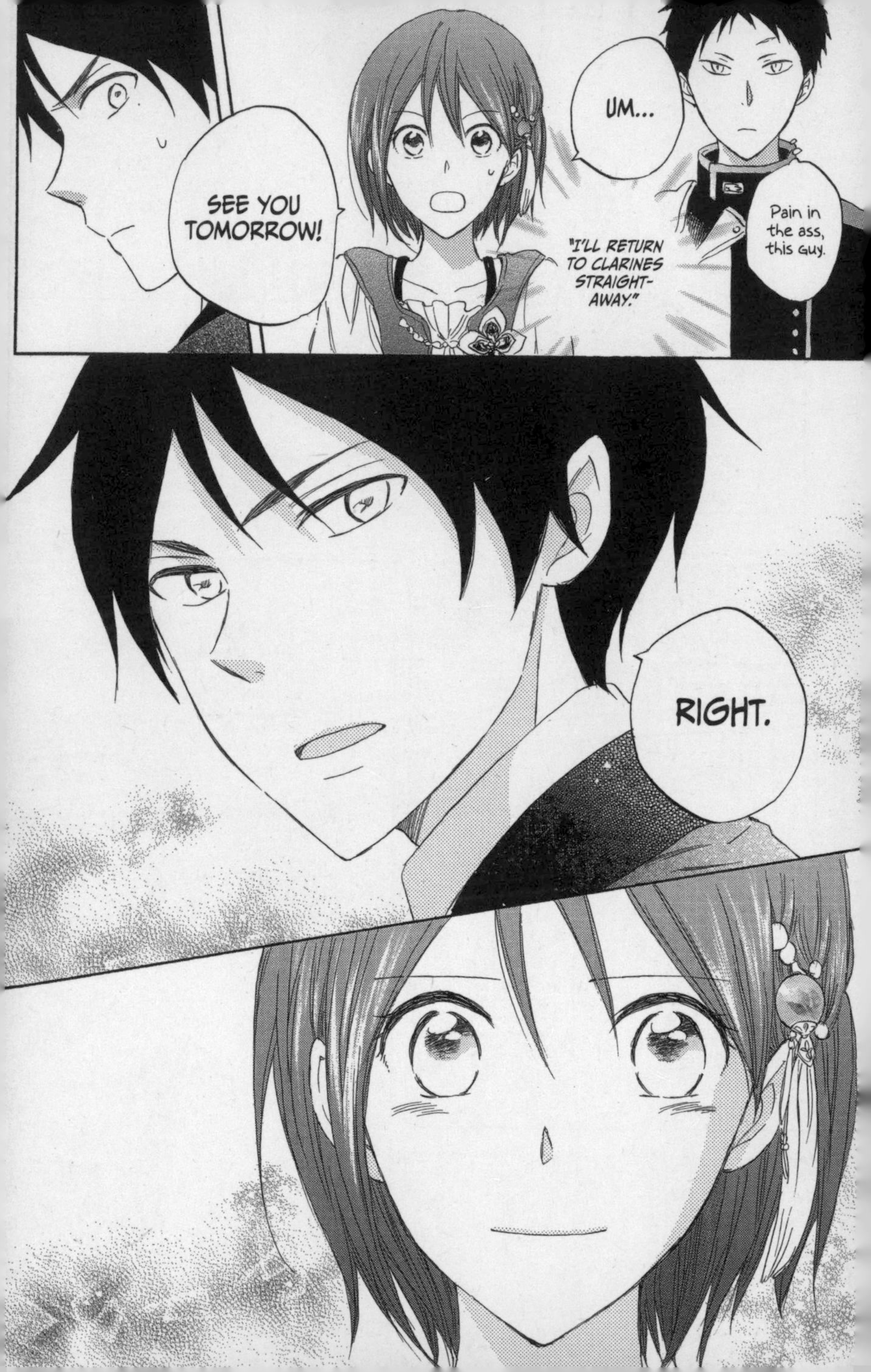
UM...
Pain in the ass, this guy.
"I'LL RETURN TO CLARINES STRAIGHT-AWAY."
SEE YOU TOMORROW!
RIGHT.

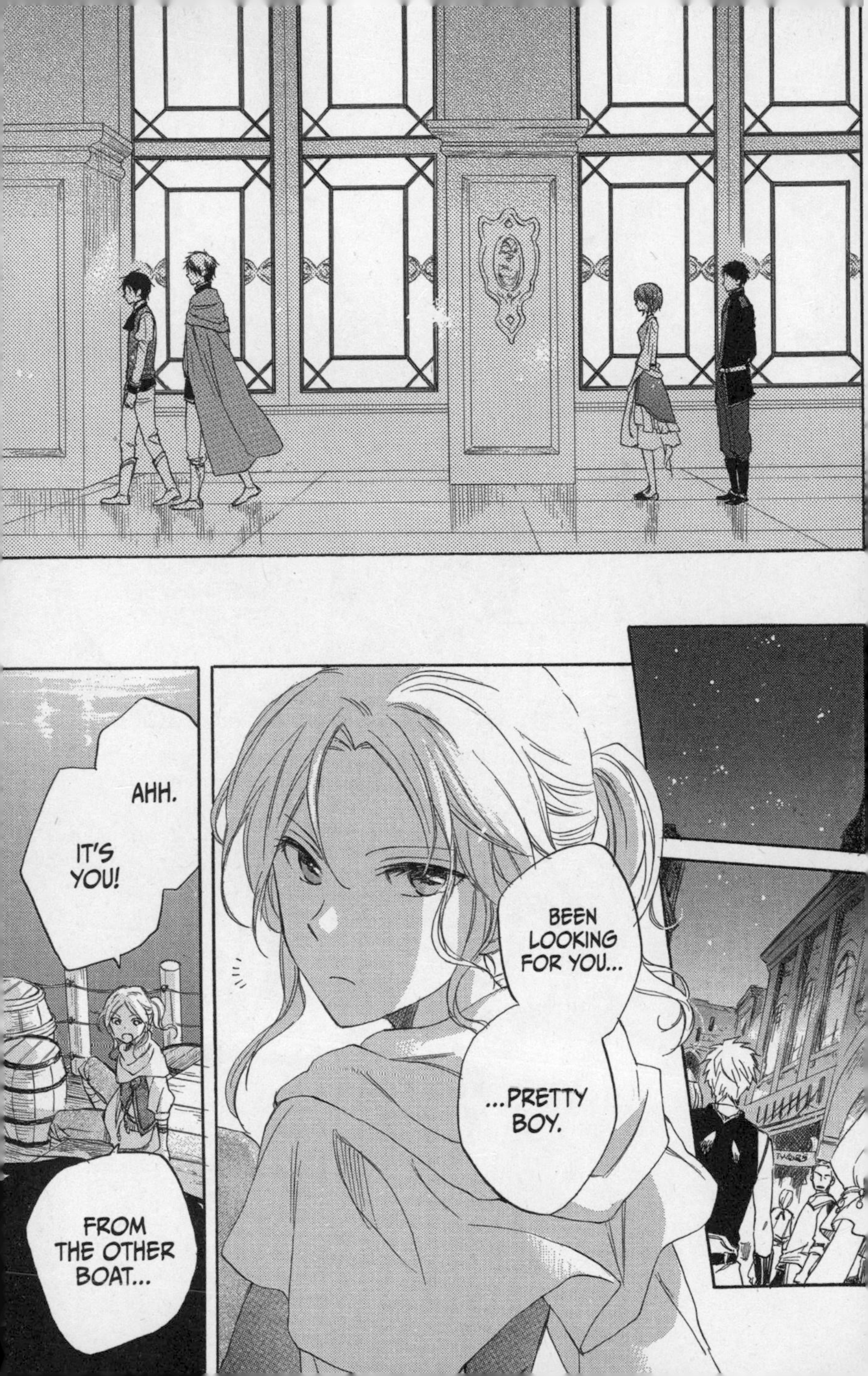
BEEN LOOKING FOR YOU...
...PRETTY BOY.
AHH.
IT'S YOU!
FROM THE OTHER BOAT...

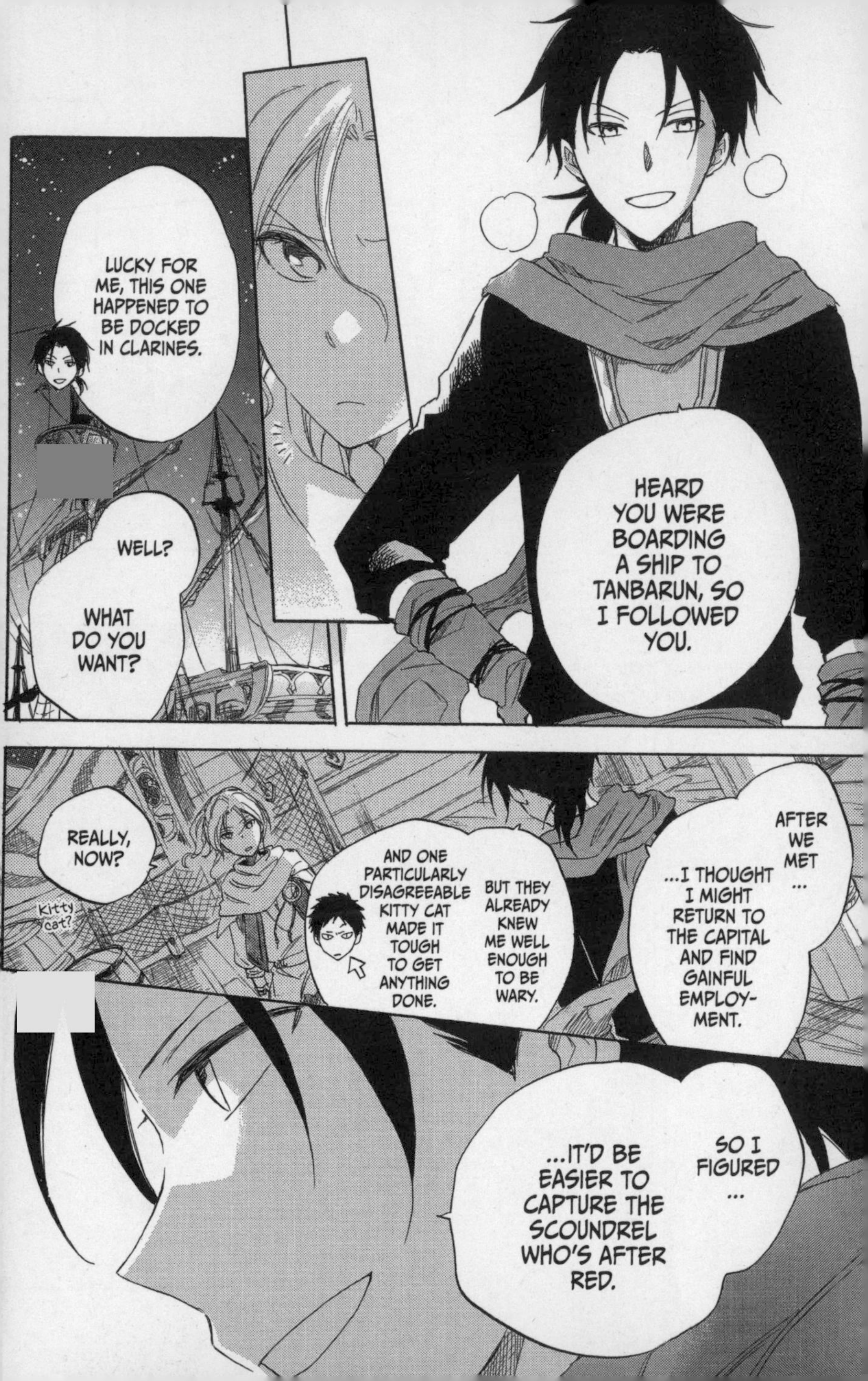
HEARD YOU WERE BOARDING A SHIP TO TANBARUN, SO I FOLLOWED YOU.
LUCKY FOR ME, THIS ONE HAPPENED TO BE DOCKED IN CLARINES.
WELL?
WHAT DO YOU WANT?
AFTER WE MET...
...I THOUGHT I MIGHT RETURN TO THE CAPITAL AND FIND GAINFUL EMPLOY-MENT.
BUT THEY ALREADY KNEW ME WELL ENOUGH TO BE WARY.
AND ONE PARTICULARLY DISAGREEABLE KITTY CAT MADE IT TOUGH TO GET ANYTHING DONE.
REALLY, NOW?
Kitty cat?
SO I FIGURED...
...IT'D BE EASIER TO CAPTURE THE SCOUNDREL WHO'S AFTER RED.

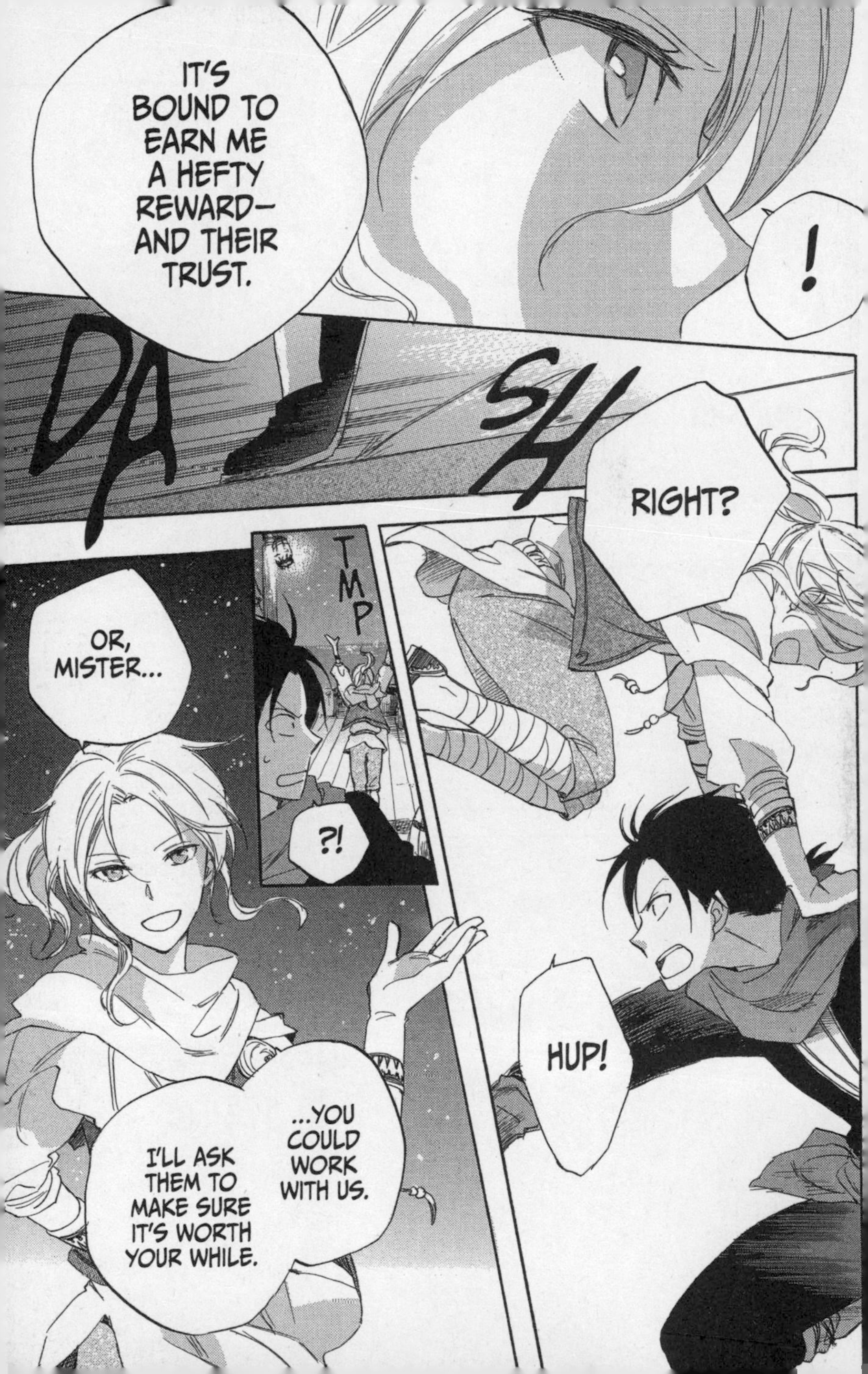
IT'S BOUND TO EARN ME A HEFTY REWARD—AND THEIR TRUST.
!
DASH
RIGHT?
HUP!
TMP
?!
OR, MISTER...
...YOU COULD WORK WITH US.
I'LL ASK THEM TO MAKE SURE IT'S WORTH YOUR WHILE.

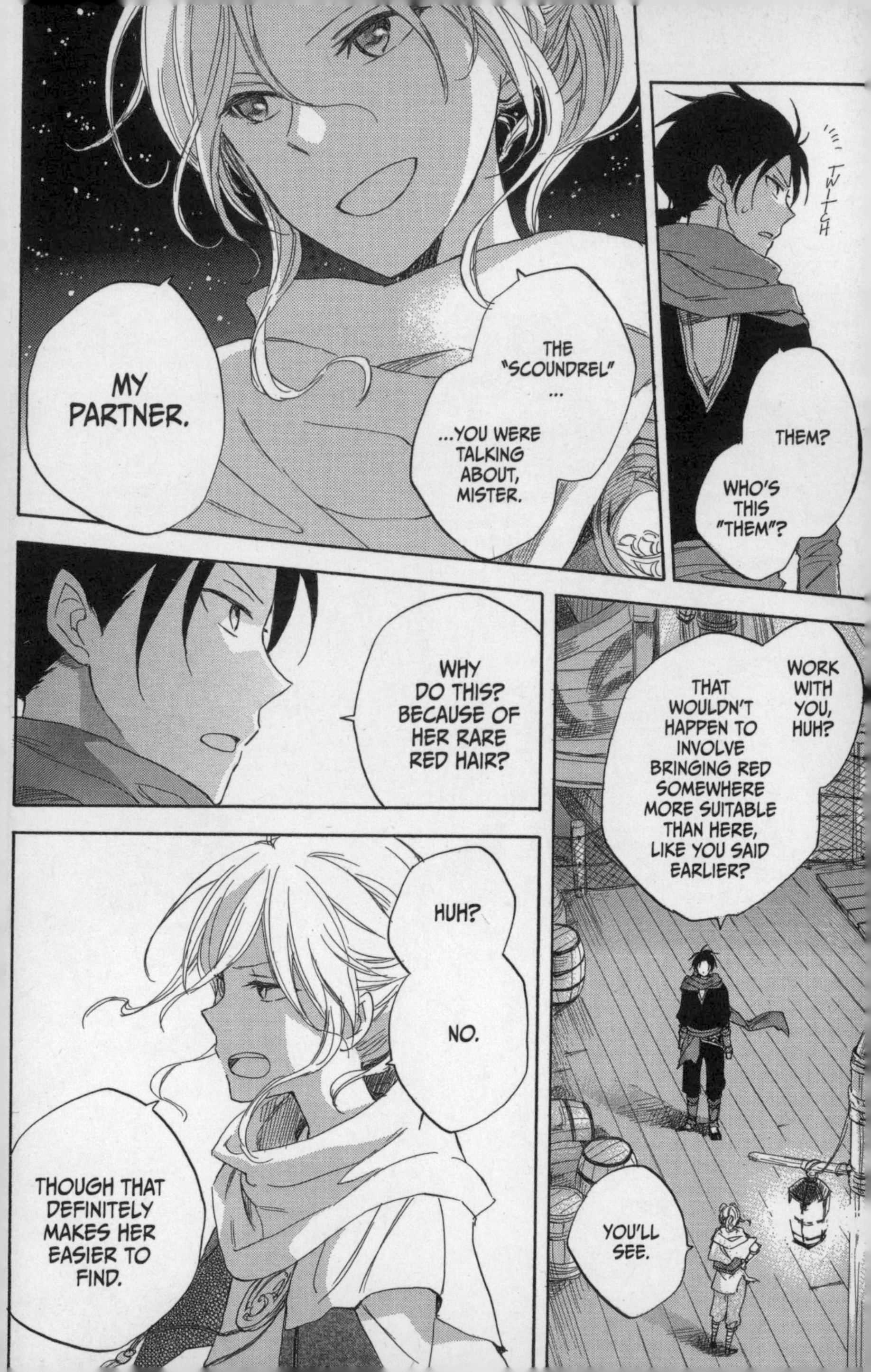
TWITCH
THEM?
WHO'S THIS "THEM"?
THE "SCOUNDREL" ...
...YOU WERE TALKING ABOUT, MISTER.
MY PARTNER.
WORK WITH YOU, HUH?
THAT WOULDN'T HAPPEN TO INVOLVE BRINGING RED SOMEWHERE MORE SUITABLE THAN HERE, LIKE YOU SAID EARLIER?
YOU'LL SEE.
WHY DO THIS? BECAUSE OF HER RARE RED HAIR?
HUH?
NO.
THOUGH THAT DEFINITELY MAKES HER EASIER TO FIND.

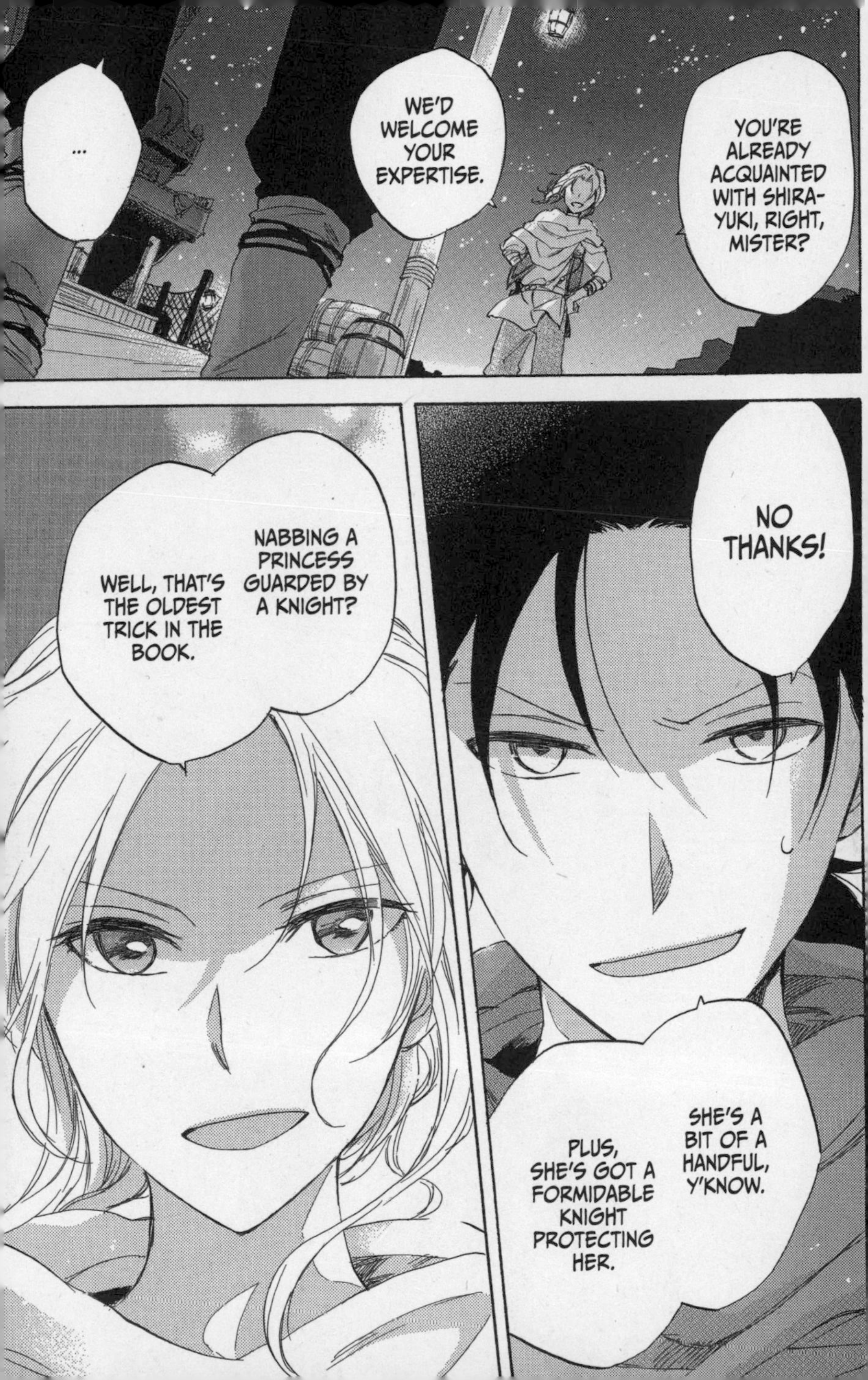
YOU'RE ALREADY ACQUAINTED WITH SHIRA-YUKI, RIGHT, MISTER?
WE'D WELCOME YOUR EXPERTISE.
...
NO THANKS!
SHE'S A BIT OF A HANDFUL, Y'KNOW.
PLUS, SHE'S GOT A FORMIDABLE KNIGHT PROTECTING HER.
NABBING A PRINCESS GUARDED BY A KNIGHT?
WELL, THAT'S THE OLDEST TRICK IN THE BOOK.

This bonus chapter
is called "Obi, Ryu and
the Flower Seeds."
I just came up with
that title!

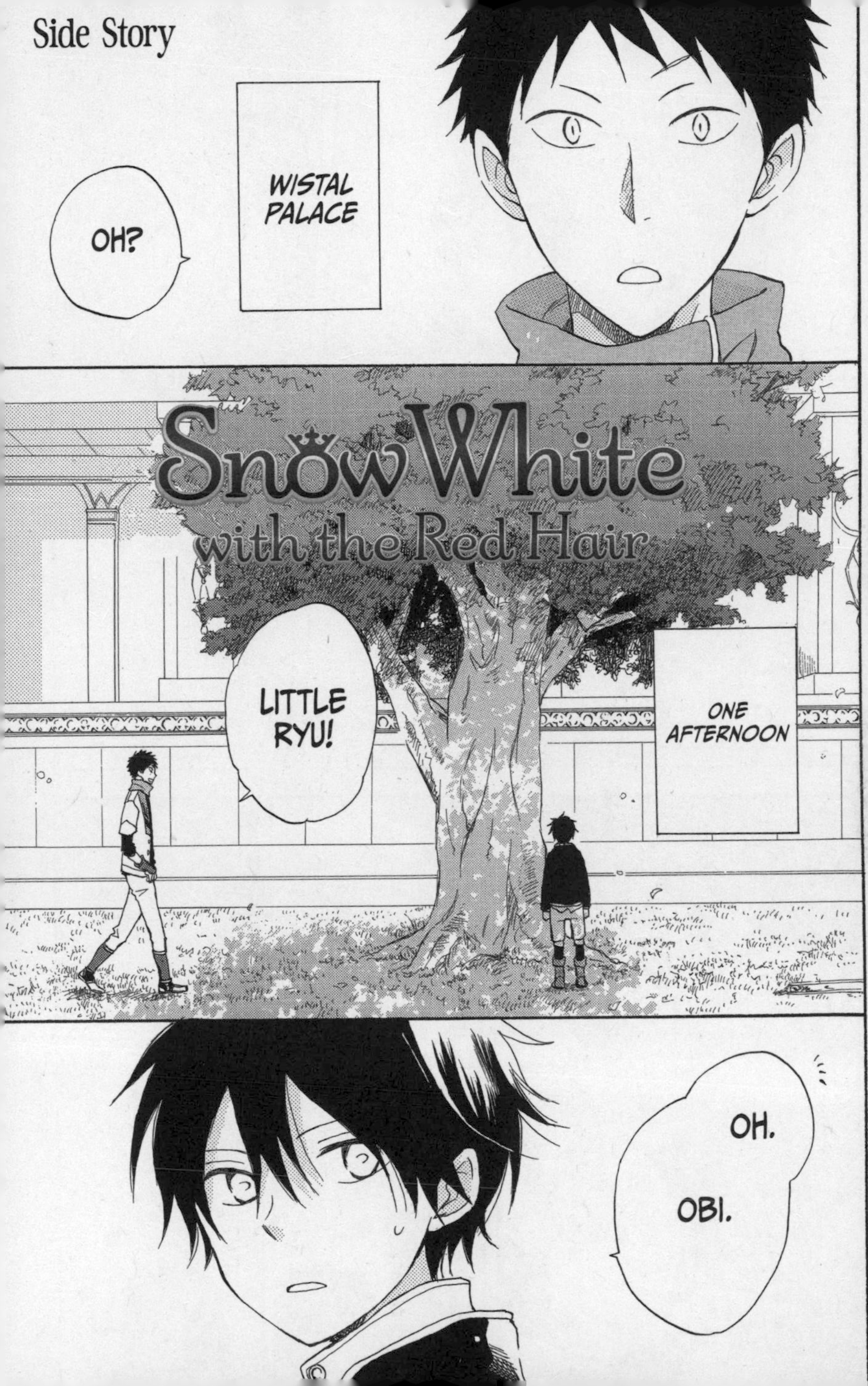
Side Story
WISTAL PALACE
OH?
Snow White with the Red Hair
ONE AFTERNOON
LITTLE RYU!
OH.
OBI.

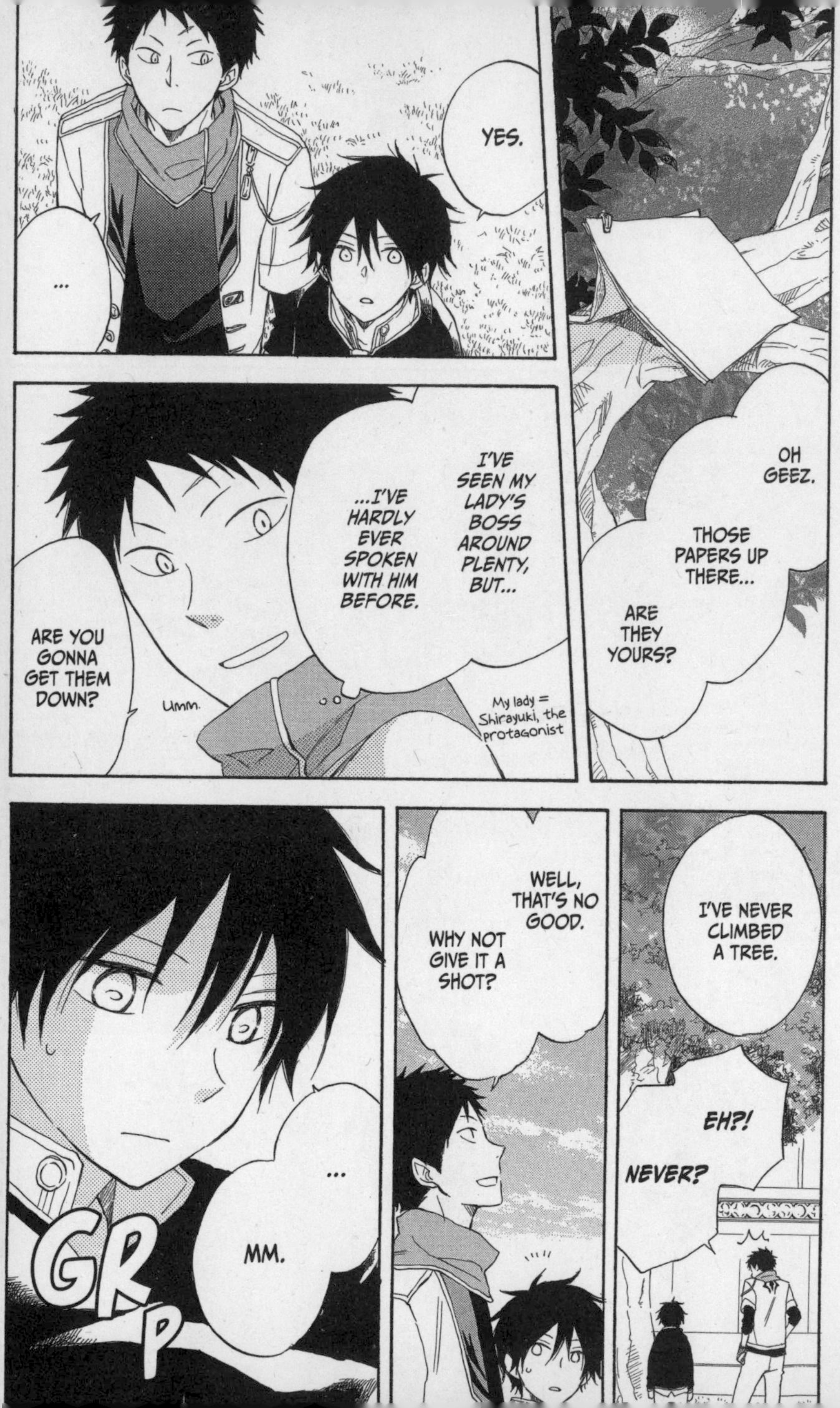
OH GEEZ.
THOSE PAPERS UP THERE...
ARE THEY YOURS?
YES.
...
I'VE SEEN MY LADY'S BOSS AROUND PLENTY, BUT...
...I'VE HARDLY EVER SPOKEN WITH HIM BEFORE.
My lady = Shirayuki, the protagonist
Umm.
ARE YOU GONNA GET THEM DOWN?
I'VE NEVER CLIMBED A TREE.
EH?!
NEVER?
WELL, THAT'S NO GOOD.
WHY NOT GIVE IT A SHOT?
...
MM.
GRP

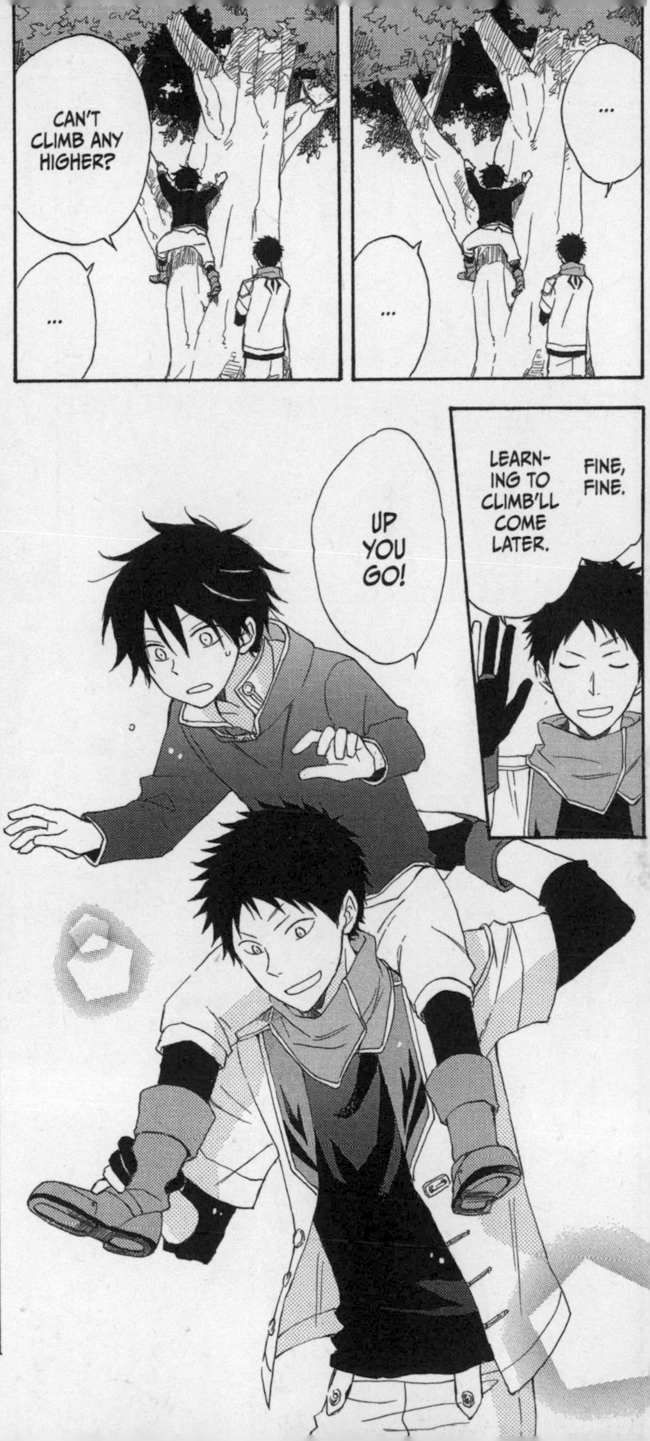
...
...
CAN'T CLIMB ANY HIGHER?
...
FINE, FINE.
LEARN-ING TO CLIMB'LL COME LATER.
UP YOU GO!

The Bonus Chapter

This story is told from Obi's perspective, but Ryu is kind of controlling the pace.

Since Obi is such a free spirit, he's more comfortable adjusting to other people's rhythms when he's around them.

Meanwhile, Ryu is always in his own world, no matter whom he's with. He asks indifferent questions and gives matter-of-fact answers, saying as little as possible.

What do these two have in common? Sometimes they both stop listening to what others are saying.

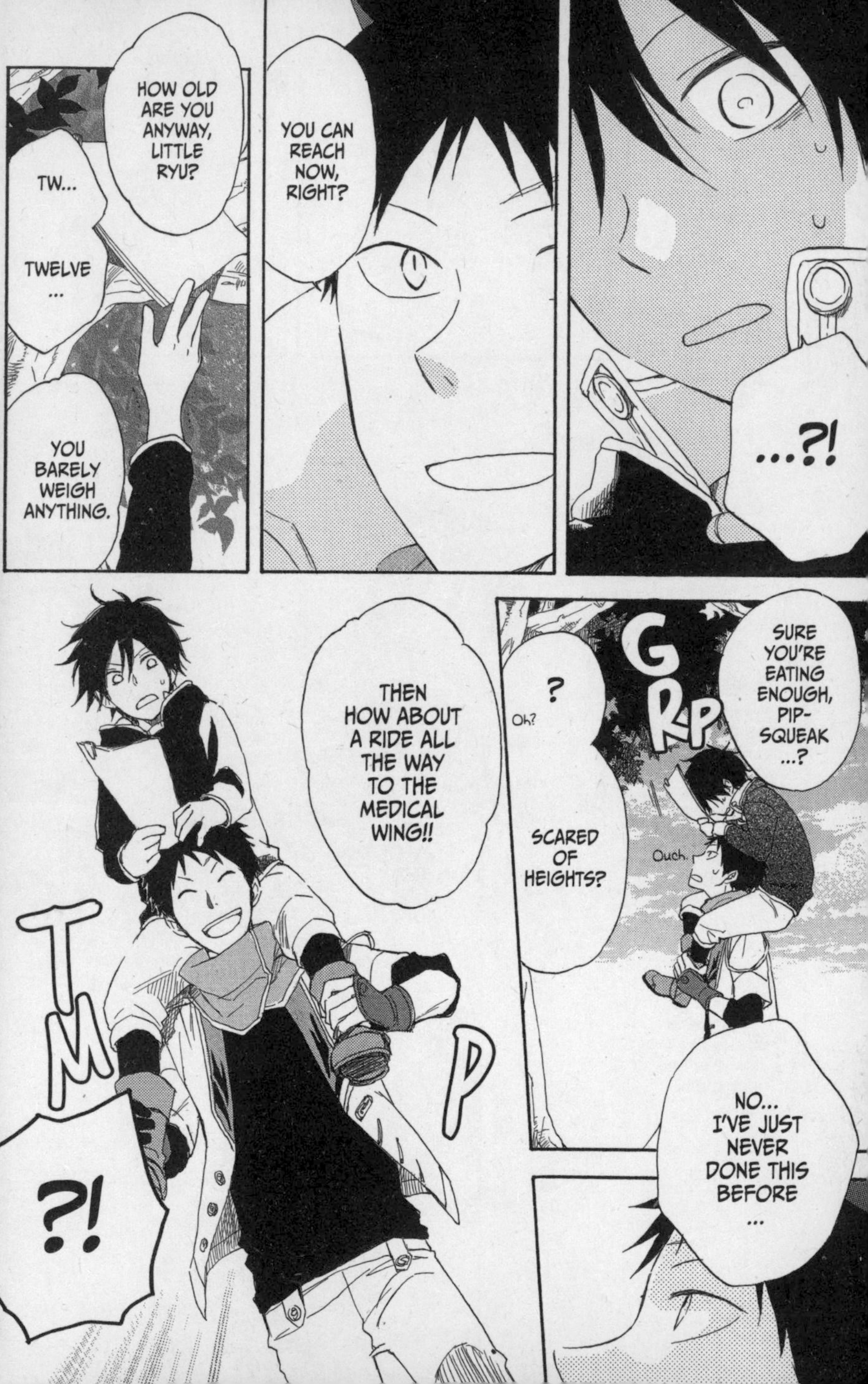
...?!
YOU CAN REACH NOW, RIGHT?
HOW OLD ARE YOU ANYWAY, LITTLE RYU?
TW...
TWELVE ...
YOU BARELY WEIGH ANYTHING.
SURE YOU'RE EATING ENOUGH, PIP-SQUEAK ...?
GRP
Ouch.
?
Oh?
SCARED OF HEIGHTS?
NO... I'VE JUST NEVER DONE THIS BEFORE ...
THEN HOW ABOUT A RIDE ALL THE WAY TO THE MEDICAL WING!!
TMP
?!

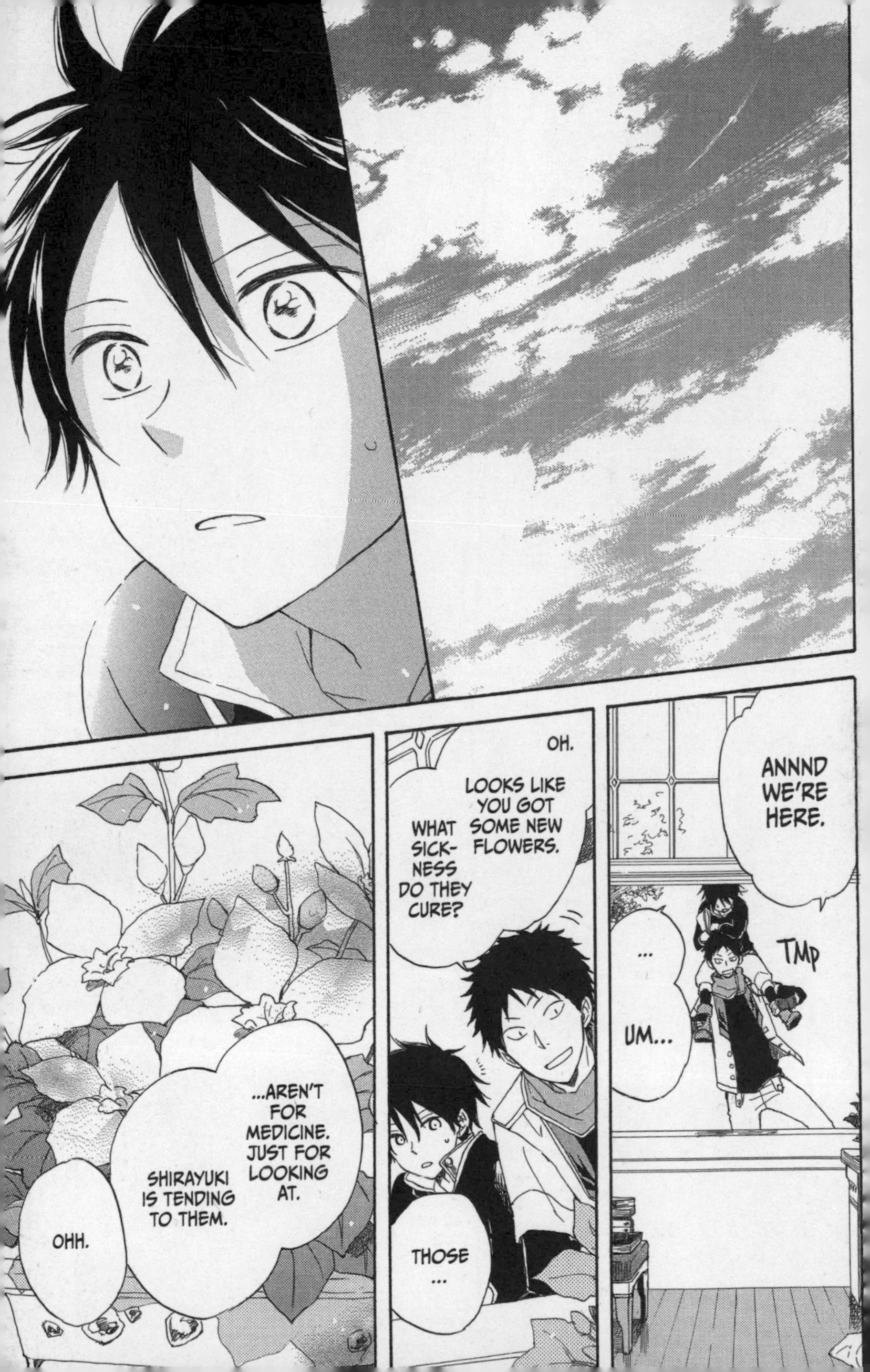
ANNND WE'RE HERE.
TMP
...
UM...
OH.
LOOKS LIKE YOU GOT SOME NEW FLOWERS.
WHAT SICKNESS DO THEY CURE?
THOSE ...
...AREN'T FOR MEDICINE. JUST FOR LOOKING AT.
SHIRAYUKI IS TENDING TO THEM.
OHH.

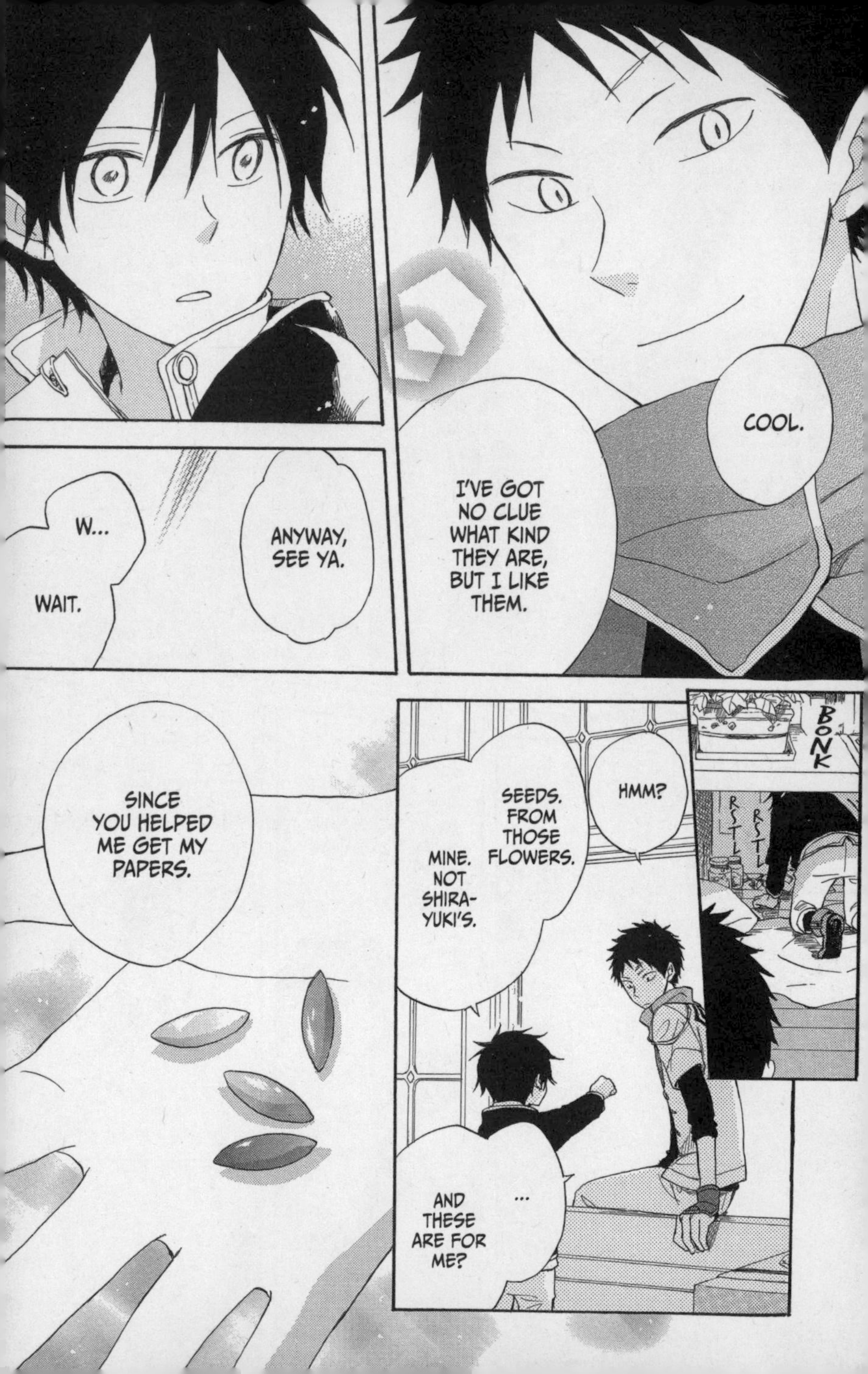
COOL.
I'VE GOT NO CLUE WHAT KIND THEY ARE, BUT I LIKE THEM.
ANYWAY, SEE YA.
W... WAIT.
BONK
RSTL RSTL
HMM?
SEEDS. FROM THOSE FLOWERS. MINE. NOT SHIRA-YUKI'S.
...
AND THESE ARE FOR ME?
SINCE YOU HELPED ME GET MY PAPERS.

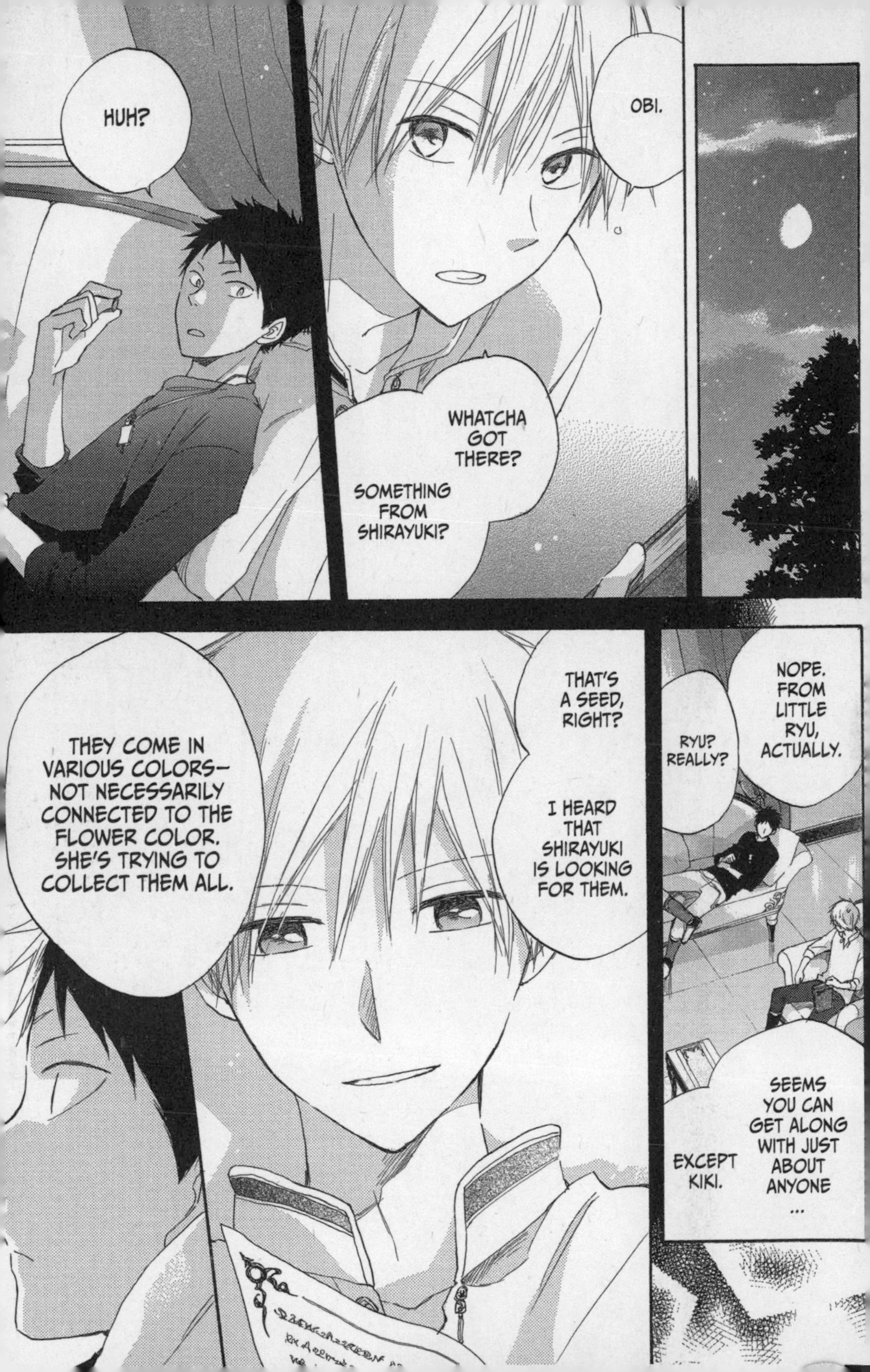
OBI.
WHATCHA GOT THERE?
SOMETHING FROM SHIRAYUKI?
HUH?
NOPE. FROM LITTLE RYU, ACTUALLY.
RYU? REALLY?
SEEMS YOU CAN GET ALONG WITH JUST ABOUT ANYONE ...
EXCEPT KIKI.
THAT'S A SEED, RIGHT?
I HEARD THAT SHIRAYUKI IS LOOKING FOR THEM.
THEY COME IN VARIOUS COLORS—NOT NECESSARILY CONNECTED TO THE FLOWER COLOR. SHE'S TRYING TO COLLECT THEM ALL.

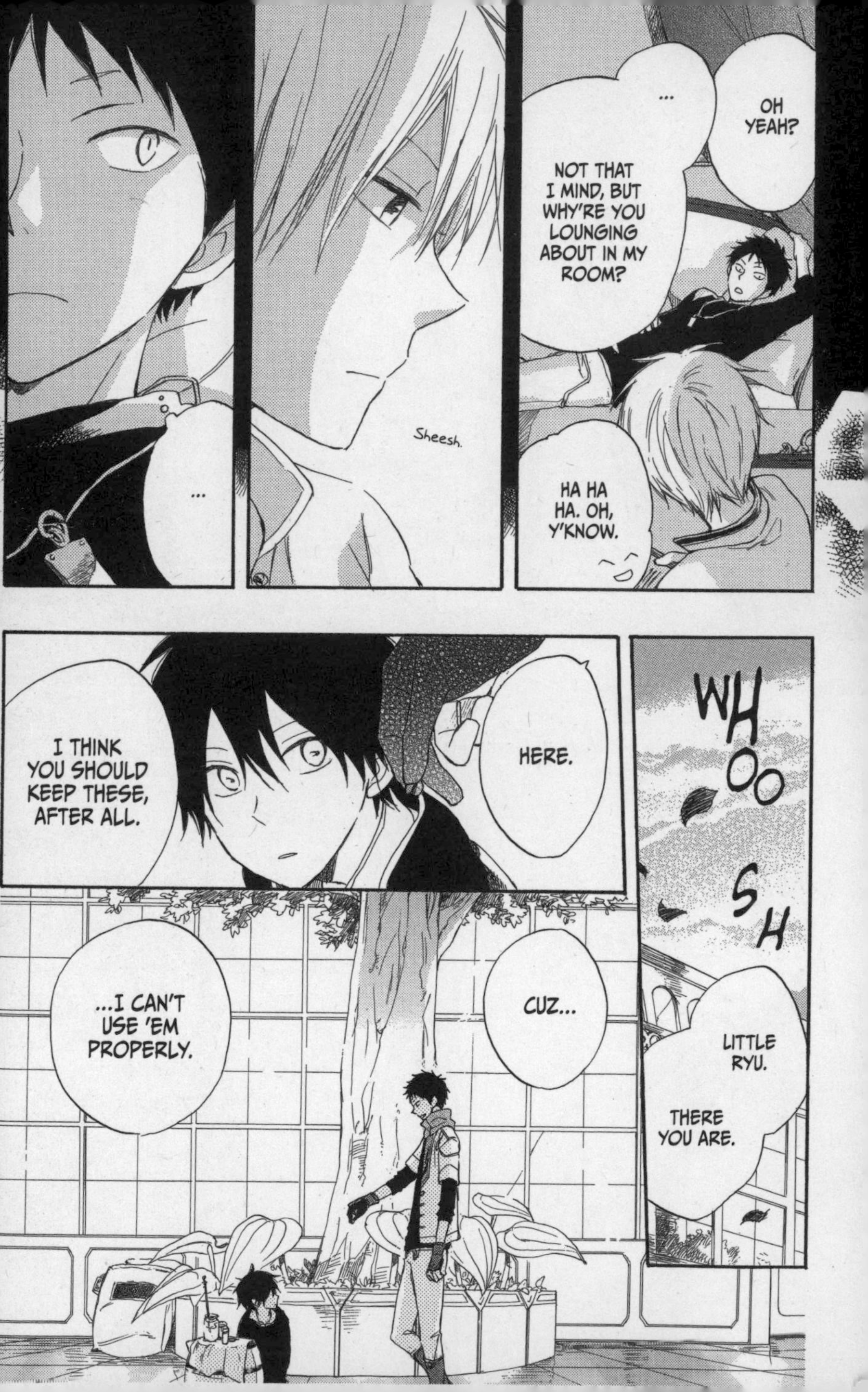
OH YEAH?
...
NOT THAT I MIND, BUT WHY'RE YOU LOUNGING ABOUT IN MY ROOM?
HA HA HA. OH, Y'KNOW.
Sheesh.
...
WHOOSH
LITTLE RYU.
THERE YOU ARE.
HERE.
I THINK YOU SHOULD KEEP THESE, AFTER ALL.
CUZ...
...I CAN'T USE 'EM PROPERLY.

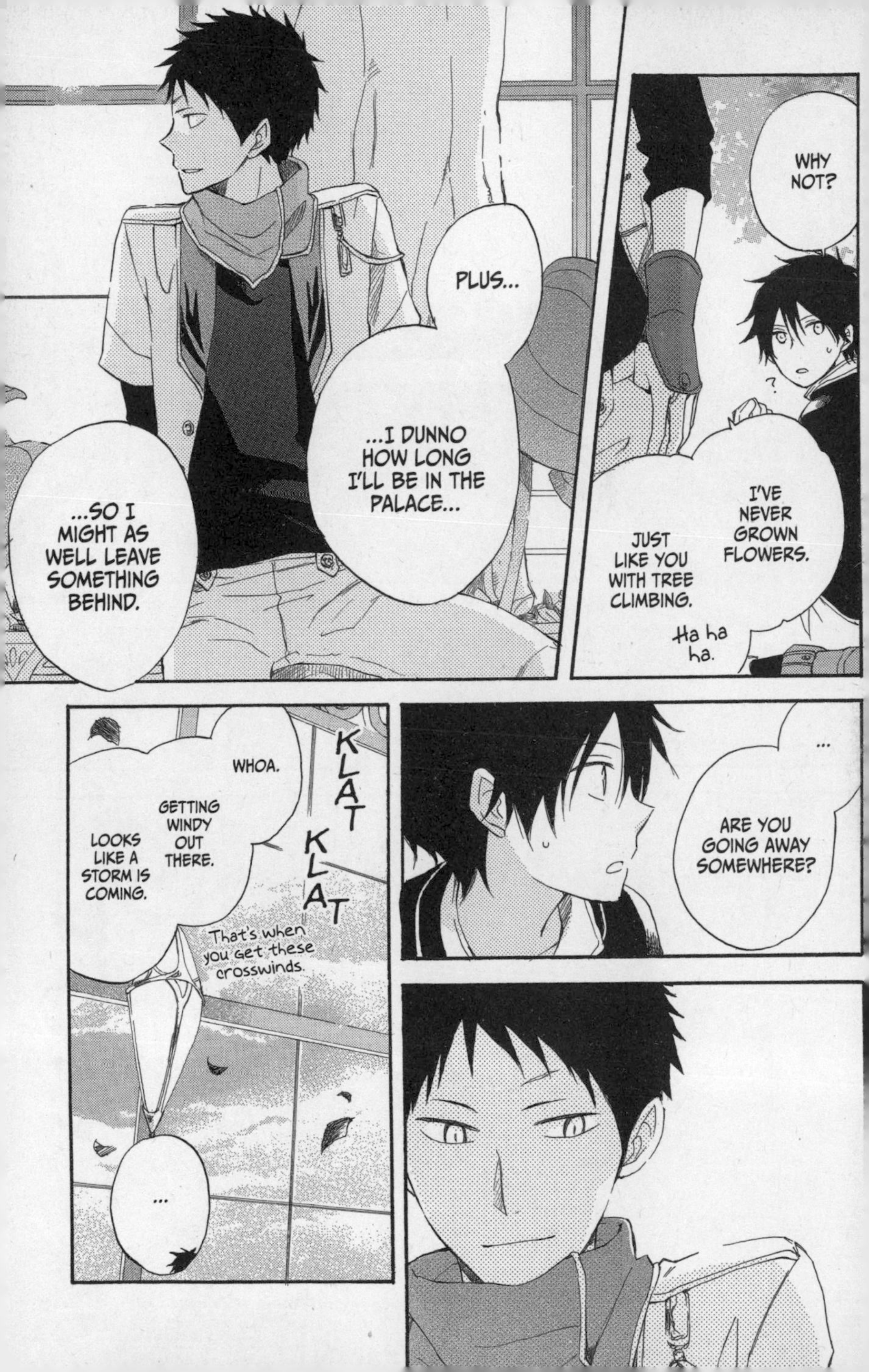
WHY NOT?
I'VE NEVER GROWN FLOWERS.
JUST LIKE YOU WITH TREE CLIMBING.
Ha ha ha.
PLUS...
...I DUNNO HOW LONG I'LL BE IN THE PALACE...
...SO I MIGHT AS WELL LEAVE SOMETHING BEHIND.
...
ARE YOU GOING AWAY SOMEWHERE?
KLAT KLAT
WHOA.
GETTING WINDY OUT THERE.
LOOKS LIKE A STORM IS COMING.
That's when you get these crosswinds.
...

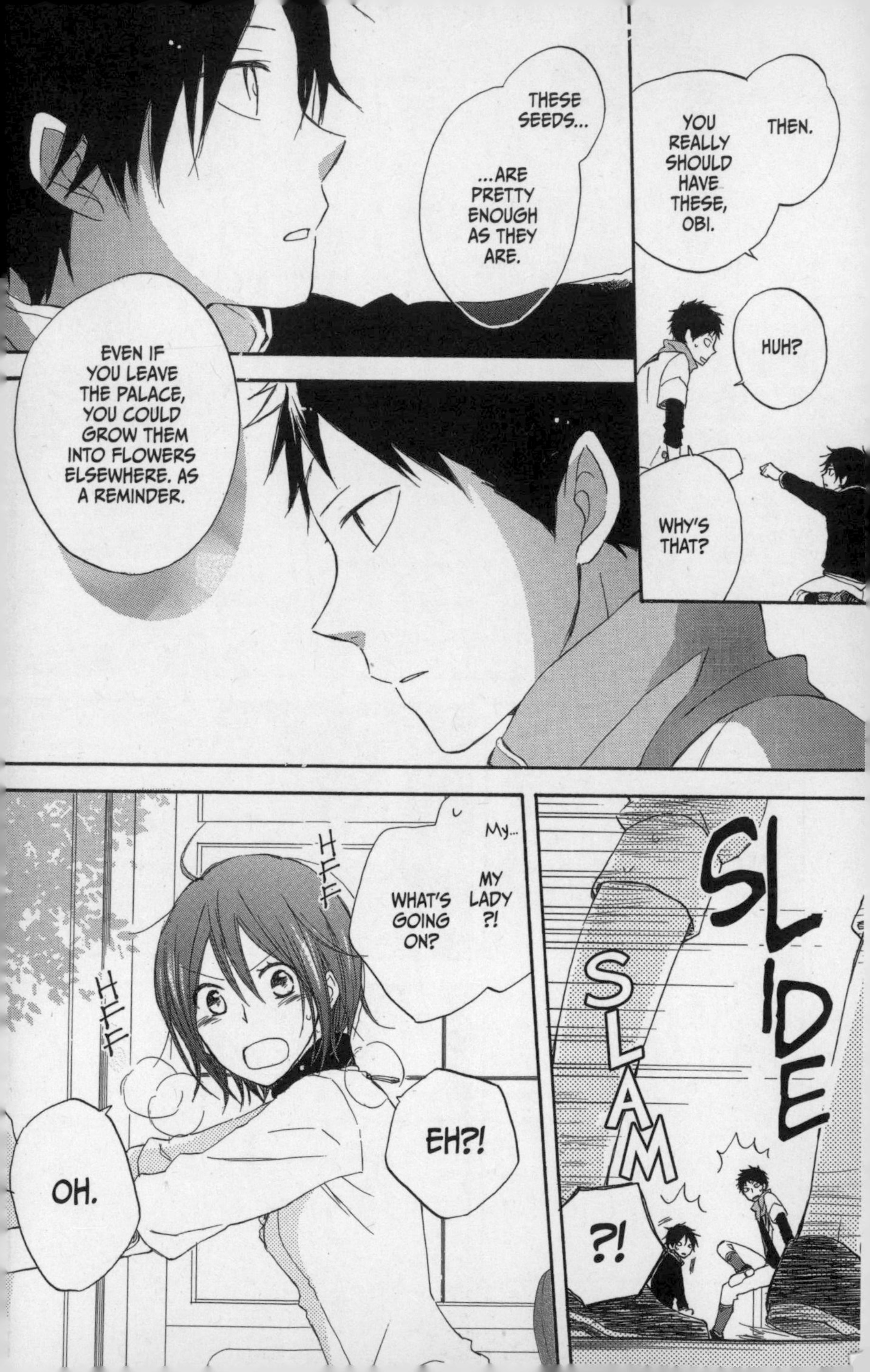

YOU REALLY SHOULD HAVE THESE, OBI.
THEN.
HUH?
WHY'S THAT?
THESE SEEDS...
...ARE PRETTY ENOUGH AS THEY ARE.
EVEN IF YOU LEAVE THE PALACE, YOU COULD GROW THEM INTO FLOWERS ELSEWHERE. AS A REMINDER.
SLIDE
SLAM
?!
My...
MY LADY ?!
WHAT'S GOING ON?
HFF
HFF
EH?!
OH.

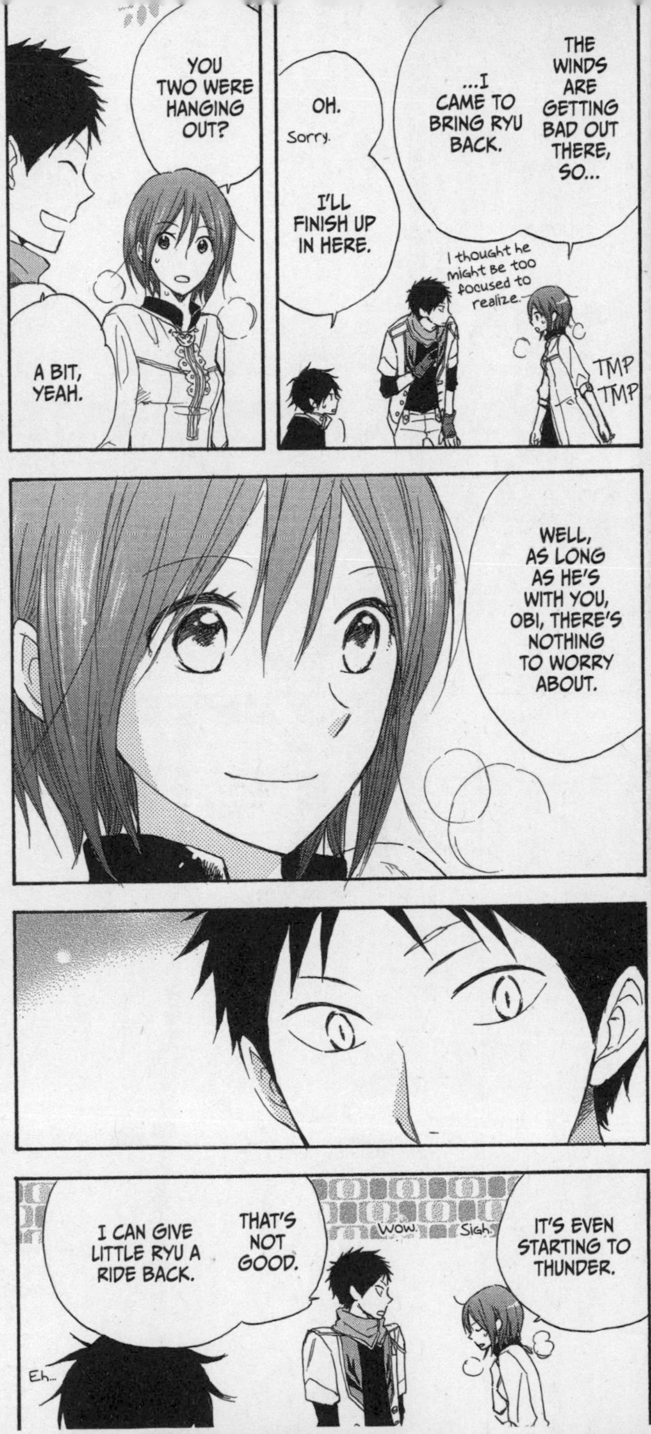
THE WINDS ARE GETTING BAD OUT THERE, SO...
...I CAME TO BRING RYU BACK.
I thought he might be too focused to realize.
OH.
Sorry.
I'LL FINISH UP IN HERE.
TMP TMP
YOU TWO WERE HANGING OUT?
A BIT, YEAH.
WELL, AS LONG AS HE'S WITH YOU, OBI, THERE'S NOTHING TO WORRY ABOUT.
IT'S EVEN STARTING TO THUNDER.
Sigh.
Wow.
THAT'S NOT GOOD.
I CAN GIVE LITTLE RYU A RIDE BACK.
Eh...

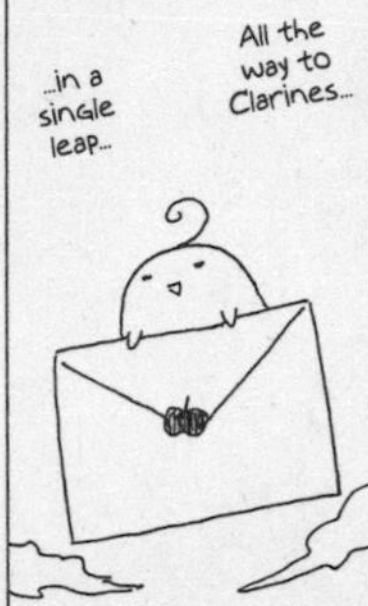
All the way to Clarines...
...in a single leap...

Thank you to everyone who sends me letters with your thoughts and feelings!

And fan art!!

I look at all of it and read every word!

It's a lot of fun reading what you have to say about the scenes, the dialogue, the characters, etc.

The most frequent topic lately is "What's up with Obi?" Oh ho ho!

I'm working hard to make volume 6 one that everyone will enjoy. Until next time!

空

—Sora

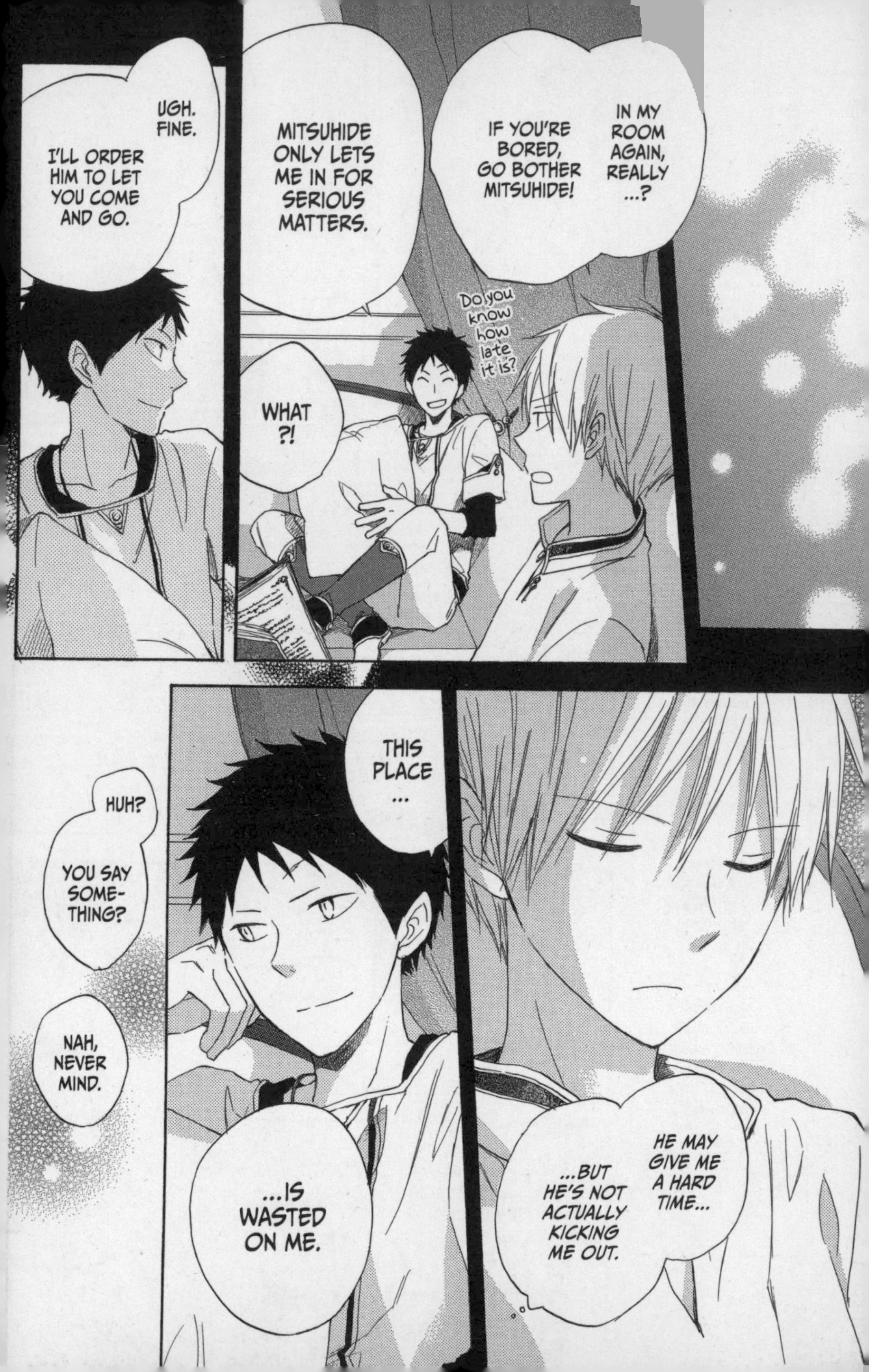
IN MY ROOM AGAIN, REALLY ...?
IF YOU'RE BORED, GO BOTHER MITSUHIDE!
Do you know how late it is?
MITSUHIDE ONLY LETS ME IN FOR SERIOUS MATTERS.
WHAT ?!
UGH. FINE.
I'LL ORDER HIM TO LET YOU COME AND GO.
HE MAY GIVE ME A HARD TIME...
...BUT HE'S NOT ACTUALLY KICKING ME OUT.
THIS PLACE ...
...IS WASTED ON ME.
HUH?
YOU SAY SOME-THING?
NAH, NEVER MIND.

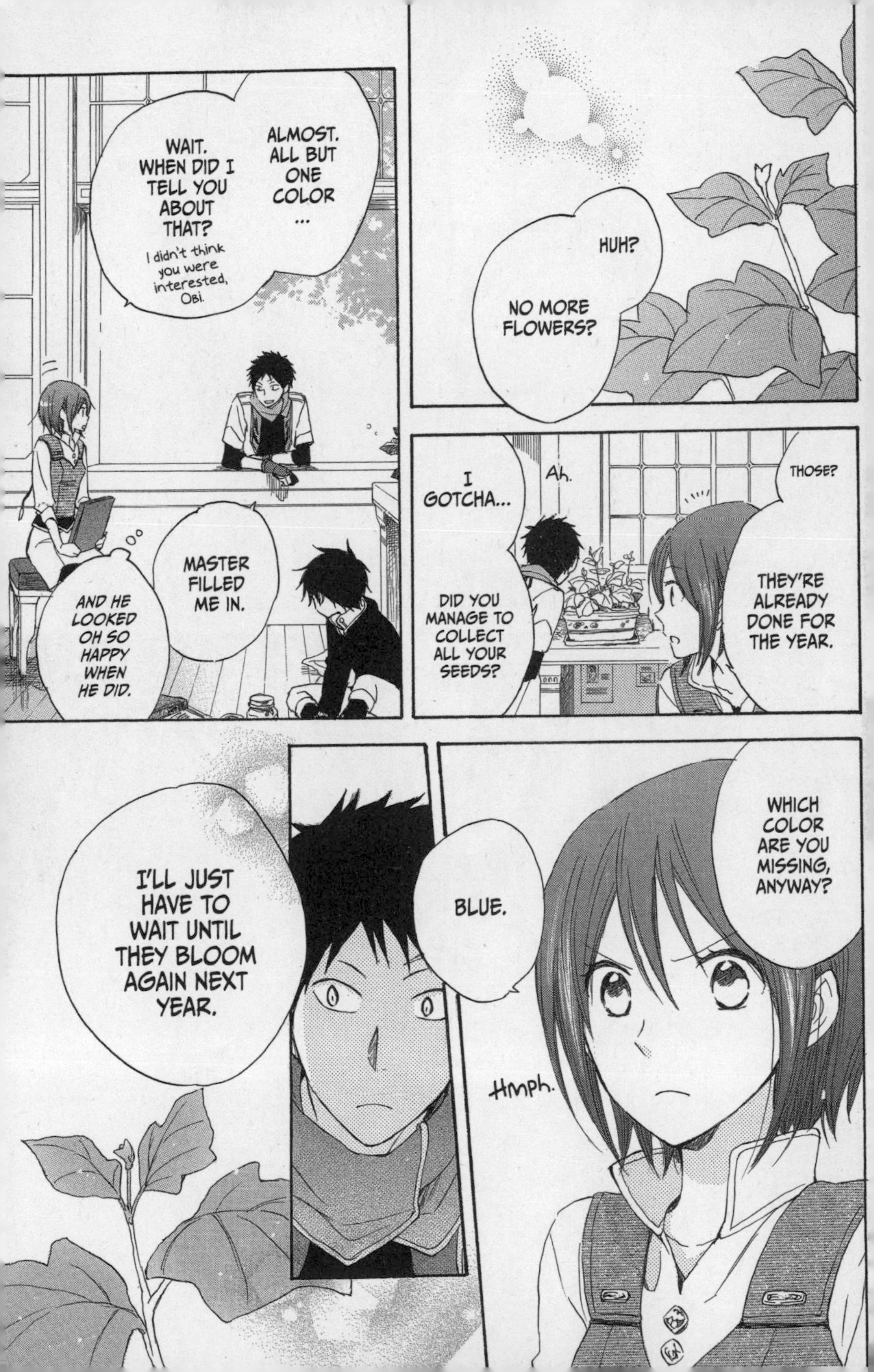
HUH?
NO MORE FLOWERS?
THOSE?
THEY'RE ALREADY DONE FOR THE YEAR.
Ah.
I GOTCHA...
DID YOU MANAGE TO COLLECT ALL YOUR SEEDS?
ALMOST. ALL BUT ONE COLOR...
WAIT. WHEN DID I TELL YOU ABOUT THAT?
I didn't think you were interested, Obi.
MASTER FILLED ME IN.
AND HE LOOKED OH SO HAPPY WHEN HE DID.
WHICH COLOR ARE YOU MISSING, ANYWAY?
Hmph.
BLUE.
I'LL JUST HAVE TO WAIT UNTIL THEY BLOOM AGAIN NEXT YEAR.

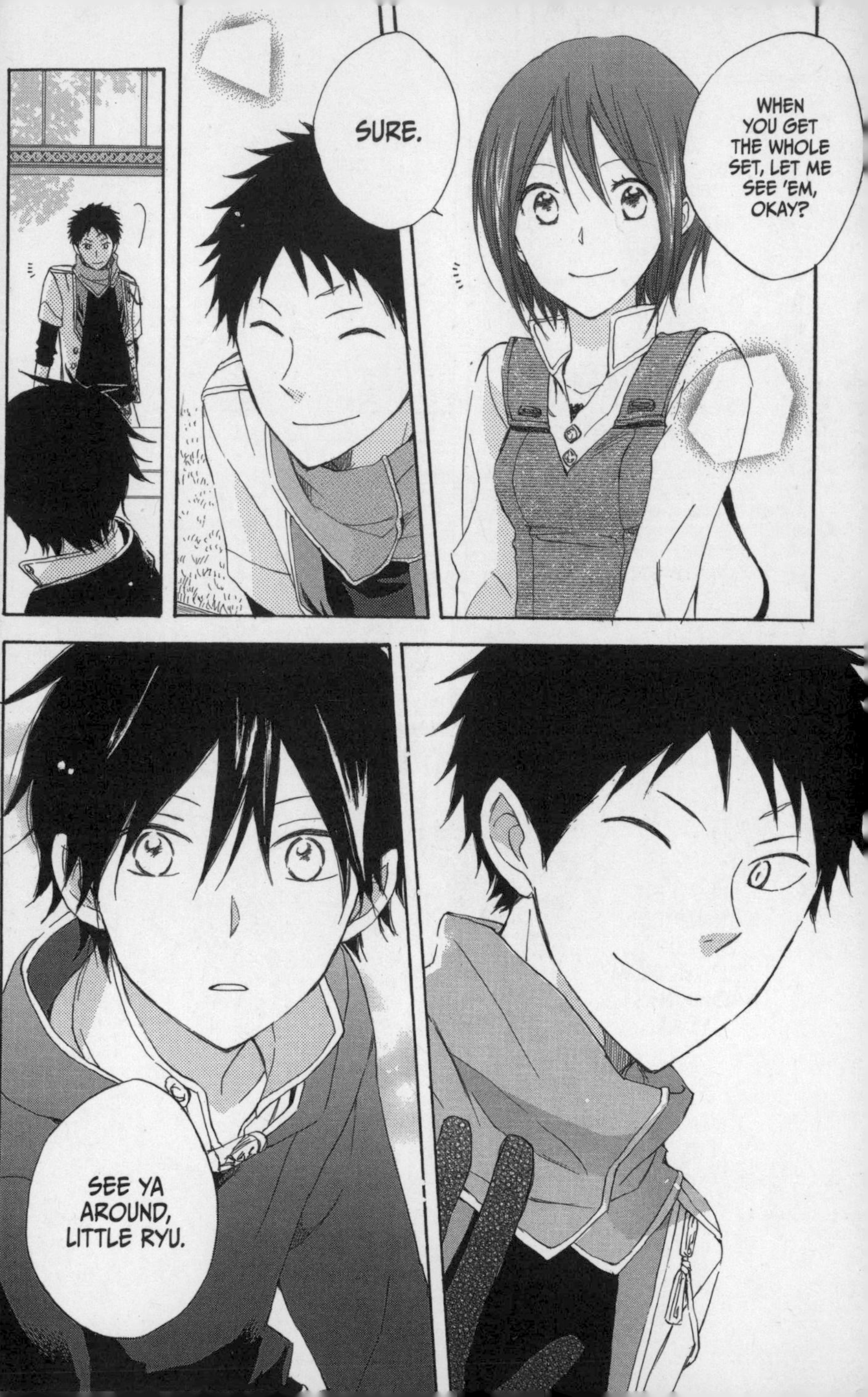
WHEN YOU GET THE WHOLE SET, LET ME SEE 'EM, OKAY?
SURE.
SEE YA AROUND, LITTLE RYU.

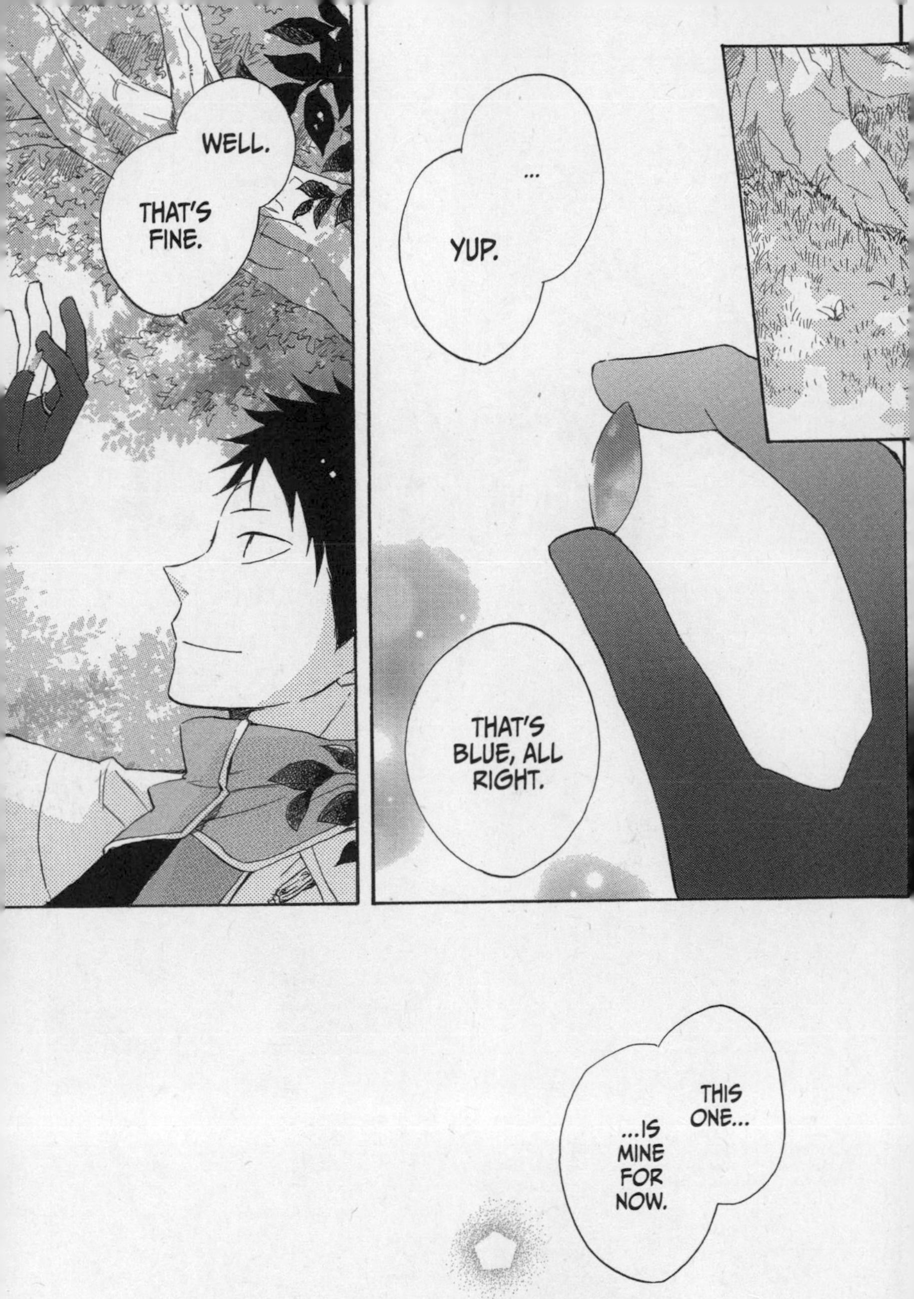
...
YUP.
THAT'S BLUE, ALL RIGHT.
WELL.
THAT'S FINE.
THIS ONE...
...IS MINE FOR NOW.

Snow White with the Red Hair
Vol. 5: End

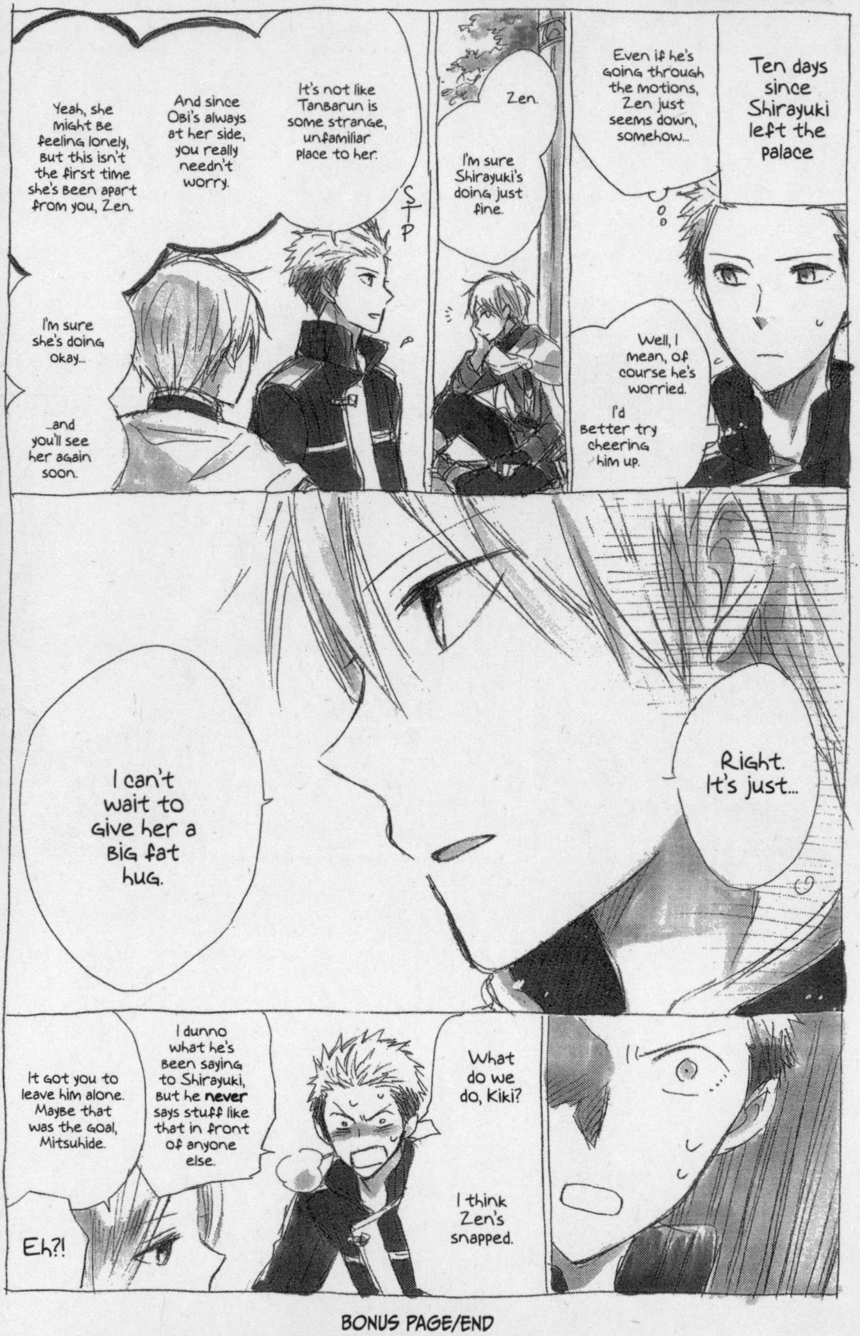
Ten days since Shirayuki left the palace
Even if he's going through the motions, Zen just seems down, somehow...
Well, I mean, of course he's worried.
I'd better try cheering him up.
Zen.
I'm sure Shirayuki's doing just fine.
It's not like Tanbarun is some strange, unfamiliar place to her.
STP
And since Obi's always at her side, you really needn't worry.
Yeah, she might be feeling lonely, but this isn't the first time she's been apart from you, Zen.
I'm sure she's doing okay...
...and you'll see her again soon.
Right. It's just...
I can't wait to give her a big fat hug.
What do we do, Kiki?
I think Zen's snapped.
I dunno what he's been saying to Shirayuki, but he **never** says stuff like that in front of anyone else.
It got you to leave him alone. Maybe that was the goal, Mitsuhide.
Eh?!

BONUS PAGE/END

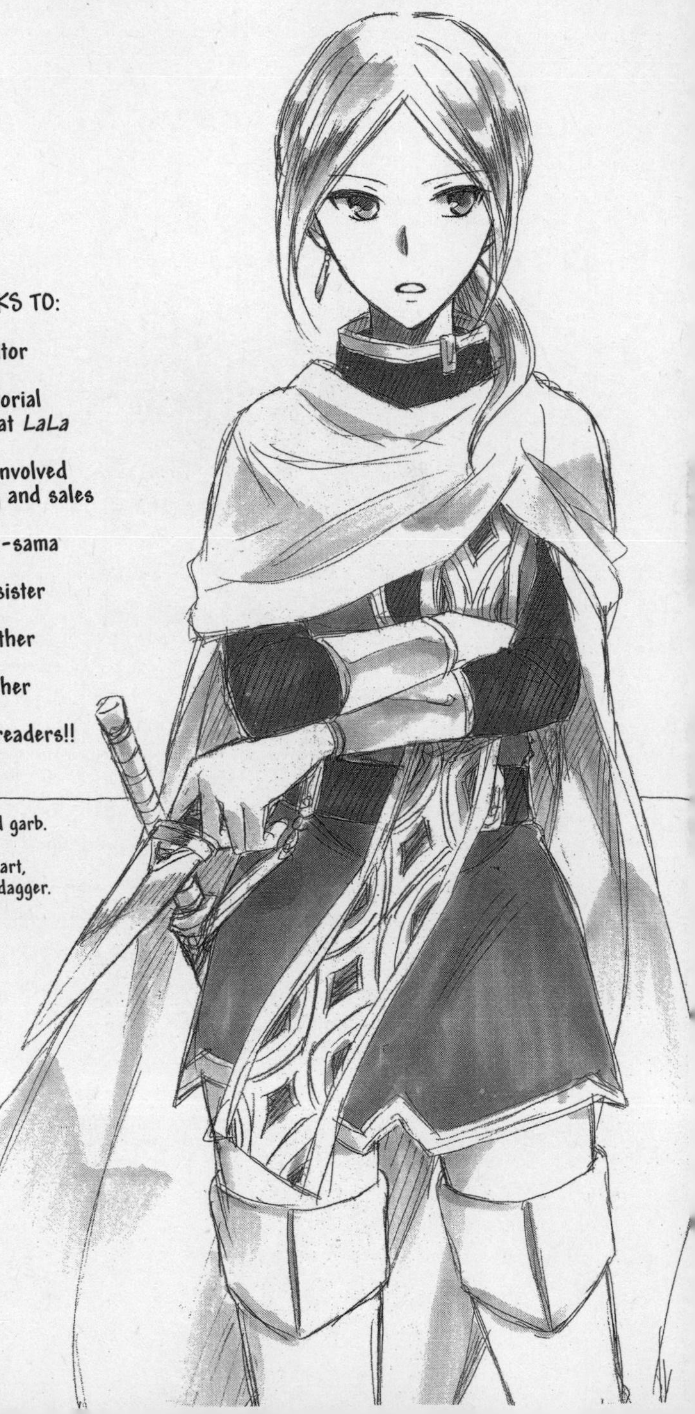

BIG THANKS TO:

-My editor

-The editorial department at *LaLa*

-Everyone involved with publishing and sales

-Yamashita-sama

-My big sister

-My mother

-My father

And all the readers!!

Kiki in palace guard garb.

In early concept art, Kiki was wielding a dagger.

—Sorata Akiduki
Winter 2010

Sorata Akiduki was born on March 21 and is an accomplished shojo manga author. She made her debut in January 2002 with a one-shot titled "Utopia." Her previous works include *Vahlia no Hanamuko* (Vahlia's Bridegroom), *Seishun Kouryakubon* (Youth Strategy Guide) and *Natsu Yasumi Zero Zero Nichime* (00 Days of Summer Vacation). *Snow White with the Red Hair* began serialization in August 2006 in *LaLa DX* in Japan and has since moved to *LaLa*.

Snow White
with the Red Hair

5

SHOJO BEAT EDITION

STORY AND ART BY
Sorata Akiduki

TRANSLATION **Caleb Cook**
TOUCH-UP ART & LETTERING **Brandon Bovia**
DESIGN **Alice Lewis**
EDITOR **Karla Clark**

Akagami no Shirayukihime by Sorata Akiduki
© Sorata Akiduki 2011
All rights reserved.
First published in Japan in 2011 by HAKUSENSHA, Inc., Tokyo.
English language translation rights arranged with HAKUSENSHA, Inc., Tokyo.

The stories, characters and incidents mentioned
in this publication are entirely fictional.

Printed in the U.S.A.

Published by VIZ Media, LLC
P.O. Box 77010
San Francisco, CA 94107

10 9 8 7 6 5 4 3 2 1
First printing, January 2020

viz.com   shojobeat.com

Takane & Hana

STORY AND ART BY
Yuki Shiwasu

After her older sister refuses to go to an arranged marriage meeting with Takane Saibara, the heir to a vast business fortune, high schooler Hana Nonomura agrees to be her stand–in to save face for the family. But when Takane and Hana pair up, get ready for some sparks to fly between these two utter opposites!

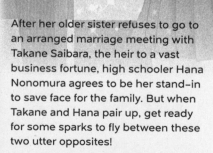

shojobeat.com

YOU'RE READING THE WRONG WAY!

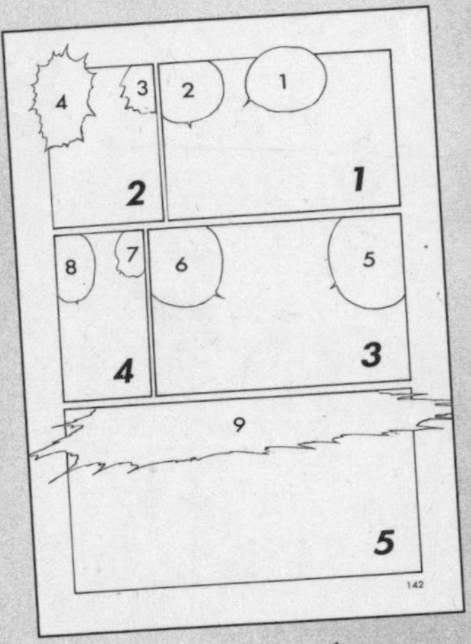
1
2
1
3
4
2
5
6
3
7
8
4
9
5
142

Snow White with the Red Hair reads from right to left, starting in the upper-right corner. Japanese is read from right to left, meaning that action, sound effects and word-balloon order are completely reversed from English order.

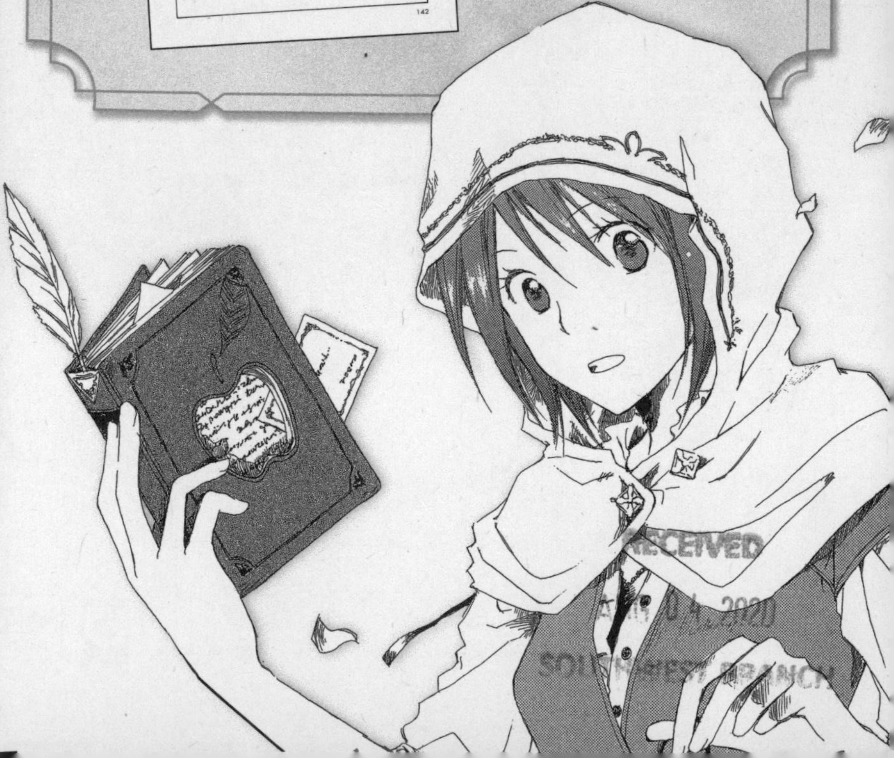